PRAISE FOR

KINGDOM OF GOD OR PAGAN EMPIRE?

Julien Stanford gets right to the point and managed to capture my attention right in the Preface! *Kingdom of God or Pagan Empire* is an eye-opening, comprehensive treatise on how we arrived "here," the point of insanity and mass chaos in America and makes it clear that unless we understand the past, we will never understand how to get back to a healthy, functional society. He charts disastrous ideas along our national journey, complete with their Red Sea, then parts it with fresh Godly insight.

Get ready for a jam-packed, factual, and well-researched book of truth with such rich prose and imagery that helps the 'medicine' go down much easier! This book is incredibly timely and needed! A must-read for all pastors, intercessors, and anyone concerned about the future of humanity, the church, and justice.

—**Theresa Griffith, President,**
Someone Believes in You
Camarillo, CA

Kingdom of God, or Pagan Empire?

JULIEN STANFORD

Kingdom of God or Pagan Empire?
© 2019 by Julien Stanford

Published by Deep River Books
Sisters, Oregon
www.deepriverbooks.com

Printed in the United States of America

Scripture verses quoted are from the King James Version. Public domain.

ISBN – 13: 9781632694997
Library of Congress: 2019941304

Printed in the USA

2019—First Edition

28 27 26 25 24 23 22 21 20 19   10 9 8 7 6 5 4 3 2 1

Cover design by Joe Bailen, Contajus Designs

For My Wife, Sylvia

TABLE OF CONTENTS

PREFACE

W hen I first set out to write a paper like this more than twenty-five years ago, I was of the naïve impression I'd be able to limit my scope to a rather narrow field. My intent was to make a simple comparison of religions; I had no desire to delve into areas that, no matter their respective merit, had little relevance to my thesis. However, as I began researching various sources for my paper, I found myself becoming increasingly frustrated. I sought desperately to draw parameters around my subject, but it was becoming clear that these were arbitrary. "Religion" would not obligingly confine itself to a neat little box. This forced me to increase the scope of my research, hoping that some reasonable cutoff lay just over the next hill.

Finally, I reached a point of hopelessness. Religion was everywhere, its effect touching every facet of human existence. The knowledge I would need to even attempt to do justice to this subject was far beyond my reach. For all practical purposes, I gave up on the project.

Nevertheless, the research I'd done had sparked a genuine curiosity. Though I could never imagine writing something intersecting so many diverse and complex fields, I became fascinated by the way in which these things were connected. Over the years I acquired many interesting books, and was exposed to numerous viewpoints. I took lots of notes, interjecting my own thoughts and conclusions as God gave me insight. As my notes reached critical mass, I consolidated them into brief papers dealing with some particular subject. Unexpectedly, the Lord showed me a way to finally bring all these years of study together into a single volume.

I will not pretend to offer much in the way of originality. Moreover, for those things that do suggest originality I can take no credit. It is not my intent to imply that I am but marginally more qualified than I was twenty-plus years ago. I have been privileged, as I believe Johannes Kepler first put it centuries ago, to "think God's thoughts after Him." There have been too many instances where my limited intellect was hopelessly out of its league, lost in a maze of dark corridors. With no idea of how or which way to proceed, the path would suddenly become illuminated and not merely dimly but brilliantly, pointing in a direction I could never have expected.

The subjects I intend to discuss have already been exhaustively treated and individually expounded. My modest contribution (but not-so-modest challenge) will be to connect these various subjects in a concise cause-and-effect chain without sacrificing coherence and meaningful content. It is my contention that ideas, even seemingly very radical, do not simply pop up out of nowhere. Some of today's most innovative views find their antecedent in antiquity.

Sadly, today for many, history begins at their birth. Because they have little or no knowledge of the events that precipitated current conditions, making sense of a cacophony of discordant notes is a hopeless quest. Rather than trying to sift through the noise, a sizeable number of people latch onto something that appeals to the emotional—which seems ennobling.

My mission is to provide context and perspective to the present conflict in our world, to put you in the best possible position to make an informed decision. If my objective succeeds, it will be evident this has been accomplished *despite* my considerable inadequacies and a nasty tendency to inject my own wisdom. This should leave little doubt as to the real source behind this and the One to Whom credit rightly belongs.

ACKNOWLEDGMENTS

No gesture can sufficiently express my undying gratitude to my wife, Sylvia; my soulmate in navigating the journey. Thanks to my children, Jay, Sam, Mykle Anne, Justin, and Eddie. I think I may have learned more from them than they have from me. Special thanks to Eddie for his research. Thanks to my brother, Don Stanford, for proofreading certain segments. Thanks to my daughter-in-law, Mallory Morgan Stanford, for setting up the web page. I am indebted to my editor, Carl Simmons. Thanks to my parents, Roland and Emma Stanford, for their endless sacrifices. Thanks to the three men who have been my most important spiritual mentors: Antoine Valdetero, Linden Keffer, and Stanford Broussard. I would also like to recognize the influence of these special people: Anne Hundley Dischler, Mike Campbell, Becky Lafleur, Don McGee, and Jack Harris. Above all, I thank my Savior, Jesus Christ, for rescuing a wretch like me.

INTRODUCTION

In the early 1960s the US Supreme Court made a bold decision to release the public square from the shackles of organized religion. This event emboldened "progressive" forces that had been restricted to nipping at the edges of a worldview set in place since the founding period. Thus unleashed, the way was cleared for the dawning of a new age of brotherhood. The new social experiment held so much promise—liberating the downtrodden from poverty, providing sex education for teens, dealing with the "root causes" of crime (instead of perpetuating injustice by seeking revenge against offenders), establishing a civil rights movement that might give redress to social grievances while setting free the historically disenfranchised from prejudice, and so on. Of course, this vision would have had no chance of being implemented were it not for one of the major political parties' enthusiastic endorsement of this view.

In less than two decades, the results were in. Despite aggressive legislating, often from the bench, of a new "compassionate" standard of morality, the number of persons below the official poverty level, teenage pregnancies, sexually communicable diseases, and the crime rate had all reached alarming proportions. Reining in the unintended consequences of "compassionate" programs would require still more programs to address new problems—which would, of course, unleash multitudes of more unintended consequences, on and on. Today, this vicious cycle has brought us to the brink of cultural and economic collapse—with one major political party showing only tepid interest in breaking the cycle, and the other incapable of acknowledging the disastrous results.

Perhaps nowhere has the failed vision of progressivism been more evident than with the aggrieved minorities it has championed (blacks in particular). Strangely, progressive solutions have never seemed to equate with its constituents breaking free from a culture defined by illiteracy, gang-sponsored genocide, free-flowing illegal drugs, single-parent households, and a general vacuum of morals. While patterns of destructive behavior have escalated, no acceptance of blame has been uttered nor tolerated. Nor has individual initiative been a permissible escape route—advancement must only occur within the acceptable confines of victimization and complete acqui-escence to progressivism as the *only* path to salvation. To illustrate, those who have managed to break out of this culture through personal initiative and self-sacrifice are never said to have *advanced* themselves. Instead of being held up as inspiring examples of courageous accomplishment in the face of great odds, they are bitterly denounced as traitors to the cause and accused of "acting white."

For progressives, simply removing barriers that have traditionally denied blacks equal access to opportunity is not enough. The new agenda demands equal *out-come*. As though advancement, success, and happiness were things simply *bestowed* instead of carefully nurtured, diligently pursued, and painstakingly *achieved*, any legislative action calling for less than transformation of the black population *en masse* is unacceptable. By exerting tremendous pressure within the black commu-nity to conform to a defeatist mentality, and demanding unattainable guarantees from outside this community, progressives effectively keep this crucial constituency beholden, trapped in its culture of misery. The weary refrain is that as bad as things are, they would just be so many times worse were it not for the courageous, untiring intervention of the "official voice" against minority oppression.

Yet those to whom this compassion is directed are robbed of any vision of hope. Stripped of that vision, without some reasonable expectation of escaping the cycle of violence and poverty, aspirations are cashed in for immediate gratification—the closest remaining approximation to meaning or purpose. First to be devoured by instant gratification's insatiable appetite are fundamental civilizing principles: per-sonal restraint, individual initiative, self-sacrifice, respect for the rights of others, and even for the very sanctity of life itself. To affirm this point, all such terms are described as code words for white racism. Such is the lofty plane to which the pres-ent progressive leadership has "lifted" the black community.

While fully acknowledging the gross miscarriage of justice blacks have suffered under institutional racism in the past—as well as isolated pockets of racism still lingering today—many Americans believe that the greatest obstacle *currently* fac-ing blacks is the modern progressive movement. The growing concern is that we are quickly coming to an impasse. A real danger exists that all common language will soon cease, ensuring America will be a nation hopelessly divided. Such polar-ization brings us to an important question: How did we get from Martin Luther King's "colorblind society" and the heady optimism of the Civil Rights Act of the mid-sixties to the bitter resentment and hopeless resignation that pervades much of the black community today, and a deep frustration of a white majority cast as the eternal scapegoat in a never-ending blame game?

The great social experiment of the sixties was also marked by a decision in pub-lic education to deliberately shift the emphasis away from traditional quantitative

skills toward much more subjective, self-esteem-promoting "life skills." Moral absolutes were cashed in for flighty ethics where each was encouraged to decide what
was personally right or wrong, irrespective of any negative effect upon those in
wider or even immediate orbit. Apart from the obvious dramatic rise in fractured
families, decline in personal responsibility, increased social apathy, and a drop in
technical skills, the preoccupation with *self* has coincided with a superficiality of
thought and uncritical acceptance of subjective experience and sensations—the
postmodern equivalent of logic and the alternative to healthy suspicion and substantive argument—once referred to as "the examined life."

The examined life has given way to the entitled life. Yet as government, in
accommodating the demands of its citizenry, seeks to fashion itself into the great
nanny, a growing sense of confusion and hopelessness pervades. History seems to be
moving toward a dramatic climax. The world is said to be on the verge of environmental collapse. The nation is being divided by internal progressive policies that,
instead of pursuing a course that minimizes and looks past differences of pigmentation in human beings, has consistently magnified, politicized, and finally codified
and *institutionalized* those differences. An invasion of illegal immigrants threatens
to Balkanize America, and so on.

If these things were not disconcerting enough, we currently find ourselves
under assault by fascists who operate under cover of one of the world's three
major religions. Though this element seeks nothing less than either the utter
destruction of the US or complete capitulation to the Islamic view, the world and
even a sizeable portion of our own citizenry insists we are primarily responsible
for this conflict. It is as though we are now living in an alternate universe where
those things that have always been axiomatic are now automatically disqualified.
Is there a way to understand how we got to this point? Is it possible to explain
what has happened and why? Is there a trustworthy source we may consult where
we may make informed choices in the midst of all this chaos, and *know* the
long-term consequences of those choices? To these questions, the answer is yes.
Unfortunately, because of a lack of historical knowledge coupled with revisionist
campaigns, revisiting this source, for many, is like asking one to take a second
look at the story of Santa Claus.

*   *   *

Of the several "great books of wisdom" in existence and the numerous religions
that have each made claim to represent *the* truth, why should the one book and
the one religion which excludes all other books or paths be deserving of either
special consideration *or* credibility? The question is fundamental to all objections
raised against the Bible's unique claim to be the inerrant, Holy Spirit-inspired Word

of God. Though the Bible has never been without its detractors, this present age has seen an open assault on its claims, unparalleled in history. Indeed, numbered among its present critics is the very formidable institution of "science" itself. [For the purposes of this book, unless otherwise indicated, "science" is a shorthand way of referring to that orthodox establishment which holds with a certain materialistic view, and with the political leanings that ordinarily follow.]

To the scientific community, religion has become an anachronism. It may be quaint and socially "useful" to honor one's religious traditions, but it is delusional and potentially destructive to base social policy on supposed historical truth claims that run counter to scientific orthodoxy. Science, it is said, has established a basis for rational systematic inquiry and logical conclusions. Thus, anything that does not fit into its box of rationality is necessarily *irrational* and, by implication, *false*. Within this framework, people coming back to life from the dead, seas being instantly parted, water being instantly turned into wine, great walls falling at the blowing of trumpets, and sight restored to the blind are all imaginary events that need not and should not be taken seriously.

Outside of the scientific establishment, religion is generally not treated with the same degree of hostility. In fact, polls seem to suggest a great majority of Americans recognize a supreme being, and many observe some formal religious worship. Though these surveys continue to be a source of frustration, embarrassment, and bewilderment to the scientific fraternity, it quickly becomes apparent under closer examination just how ready and willing the public is to take its cue from the authority of science. What polls seldom reflect is the degree of *seriousness* most "believers" attach to their religious observances. "Faith" is treated more often as a family heirloom passed on from generation to generation, taken off the shelf and dusted now and then to be prominently and proudly displayed as perhaps part of one's family crest. Such a faith is disconnected from any universal or eternal implications. Such faith has little if any relationship to a deep conviction that a sovereign, personal, eternal, intelligent, purposive, designing, loving Supreme Being exists—One Whom has revealed Himself both through the grandeur of the created universe and through real specific historic acts which are pregnant with all sorts of universal *and* eternal implications. Finally, this kind of "faith" has little power to reorder one's life, let alone contribute any meaningful dialogue to social issues.

Evidence abounds that the public has assuredly trimmed its religious leanings to the prescribed specifications of science. Many "mainline" Christian denominations no longer treat as important the historicity of certain events recorded in the Bible. Even the existence of the central figure of the Bible, Jesus Christ, is said to be unimportant in comparison with the *words* that have been passed down to mankind in His name—that is, when those words have been properly demythologized.

"Of *course* (assuming Jesus of Nazareth was an actual historic figure) He did not actually perform miracles, and of *course* He never actually rose from the dead. We all know as rational beings that science has *proven* such things do not happen. What *is* important, though, is the *symbolism* each of these events represent, all recognizable conflicts within the full spectrum of the human condition." Walking on water is a metaphor for facing fear head-on, restoring sight to the blind a metaphor for releasing our prejudices, rising from the dead representative of the eternal hope that mankind will continue to evolve with each passing generation to an eventual utopian state, and so on. Jesus, whether real or imaginary, is the personification of the great potential that lies in imperfect man—the exemplary life of love, courage, and tolerance in the face of the lowest, most unenlightened instincts in man, who is in turn personified, of course, by the evil entity Satan.

Formulated this way, the message of love and good will takes on a life of its own and becomes *the* source from which we may all draw strength and hope. To be sure, the reductionism does not end here. The concept of "God" must also be subject to redefinition. If God is not permitted to act significantly within science's box of "rationality," then He/it ceases to be of significance. If He exists, He is hopelessly unknowable and unapproachable. From the sovereign, transcendent, personal, immanent, omniscient, omnipotent, loving, purposive Supreme Being, He is reduced to little more than the original spark that set the universe in motion.

This line of reasoning prompts one at some point to seriously wonder if it may be possible to draw "strength and hope" from such a nebulous source. To the "Christian" whom streamlines his faith to the naturalistic/materialistic paradigm of modern science, can his *faith* be sustained by a liar, romantic ideals, or a fantasy about some imagined afterlife, when there is no God Who gives one whit about his plight, now or ever? Can this be the stuff of *hope*? Moreover, how is one's life substantially different for having submitted to this reductionist view of Christianity, as opposed to simply seeking to live the life of a benevolent atheist? Indeed, how are the two sets of beliefs substantially *different*? In short, what is the point of wearing a Christian label when the term has been stripped of all relevance?

Most "persons of faith" today obligingly concede the limitations of religion as tacitly imposed by science. Religion of a sort is okay, but almighty science establishes the rules of order; rules which if abandoned will lead to chaos and widespread disharmony. Science has positioned itself as the final authority. To those whom still desperately need a crutch, a little vague God-talk is permissible, and religion may comfort in a warm, fuzzy, harmless way, but it must not seek to *inform*. Therein lies the tyrannical, oppressive nature of religion taken too seriously, returning us all to the Dark Ages where superstition orders the day.

To be sure, scientific naturalism recognizes no significant difference in *kind* between Christianity and ancient pagan cults, merely *degree*. Christianity is simply a little more sophisticated version of the same old dangerous superstitions. From this assumption flow the two basic arguments thought to be devastating to Bible truth claims: 1) All religious views are subjective thus inherently inferior to and less authoritative than *objective* science; 2) given an array of subjective "beliefs," it is not possible that one set can definitively *prove* its view to be superior to any others.

The two arguments are loaded with intellectual dishonesty. The first argument assumes—or better, *pretends*—that religion can contain no objective component. In fact, the Bible predicates its subjective claims on *objective eyewitness testimony of specific historic events*. Further, argument one casts the two in an antagonistic and irreconcilable relationship; the obvious implication is that objectivity equals truth, and that subjectivity is necessarily false, or at best untrustworthy. This would tend to suggest that science occupies the high intellectual and moral ground because it binds itself to a strict code—accepting and proclaiming as "true" only those things that are measurable by the five human senses. It also suggests that science is no respecter of subjective belief systems, treating all such claims with equal cynicism and incredulity.

This former impression is easily dismissed. Certain basic assumptions are routinely made by science that clearly fall *outside* the realm of the five senses: There is underlying order in the universe and the governing laws can be counted on to *remain* constant; the pursuit and accumulation of knowledge is both possible and a worthy cause (though there is no reason to assume that the human brain, allegedly spawned by a random meaningless process, might ever yield sensory perceptions qualitatively superior to, say, hallucinations); human beings should be accountable for their actions based on some standard of proper versus improper conduct, etc. In a universe that is self-directed and purposeless, such assumptions and value distinctions are necessarily arbitrary and inconsistent. Yet it soon becomes apparent that without some set of underlying assumptions about reality, arrived at only by revelation or intuition (before the five senses ever come into play), human beings bog down into an incoherent state of paralysis.

Aside from preemptively eliminating the possibility of any objective standard, even before any facts are considered, argument two plays fast and loose with the term "prove." The existence of God, we are constantly reminded, cannot concretely be proven. This is a not-so-clever debating technique. The idea is to create a false category and then make the burden of proof entirely one-sided. Such things as God do not, strictly speaking, belong to the realm of "provability." A starting point, a framework for assessing reality, must be *assumed*. A theist is under no more obligation to prove God's existence than a materialist is to prove God does not exist.

What *can* be established concretely, however, is the pattern that attaches to each assumption. One bears profound evidence of order and integration; the other of disintegration in every facet of human experience. And, if one even allows for the *possibility* of God, a conspicuous body of evidence converges in a singularity in history. That singularity dares to portray one *specific* human being as a microcosm of *the* Supreme Being. And *that* portrayal is eminently subject to numerous tests—and has, in fact, endured these unceasingly.

Argument two conveys the impression that no single case can assert its superiority over any competing position unless it can produce an unbroken chain of hard physical evidence. Superiority of competing positions can only be achieved through strict employment of empirical tools. In fact, no such standard is adhered to either within our judicial system (where the stakes may literally be life or death) *or* the scientific method. Where hard physical evidence is scarce or impractical to obtain, which is often the case, there are any number of principles and methods routinely employed in lieu of such evidence: logical argument, cause-and-effect relationships, mathematical probability, the excluded middle, noncontradiction, extrapolation, circumstantial evidence, inference to the best explanation, and the like. As old as the rules of argument is the widely held concession that the more independent lines of verification a given position can demonstrate, the *stronger* that position becomes.

Hard physical evidence, though certainly desirable, is only one among many criteria, and only meaningful within the framework of working assumptions that *describe* one's reality. When these lines converge to establish a high degree of probability for a given premise, it may appropriately be conceded this position has achieved reigning eminence over all competing views. That is, it is said to have been *proven* by rigorous rules of investigation to be best able to *unify* all existing facts and phenomena within a consistent framework. This is not to say this position has been concretely established as *truth*; rather, the closest available approximation until hostile evidence and argument accumulates to the point of critical mass, overthrowing the reigning view for a new paradigm.

Many today are of the impression that it is this same rigorous method of investigation which deposed Judeo-Christianity some years ago as *the* credible authority from which ultimate reality may be defined, and subsequent value distinctions imposed. For this reason, those who attempt to argue for the reestablishment of Christianity's once-held authority are almost immediately branded unprogressive, unsophisticated, intolerant, superstitious, fear-mongering zealots so frightened by the future that they seek refuge in the past. In fact, Christianity as a dominant worldview has never been overthrown by the above rules of investigation. The Christian worldview was overthrown by enticing but never-proven *ideas*, which too often left unchallenged, fed off their own momentum. These ideas can be traced to specific events and movements in history: to a cultural secularist revival displacing transcendent authority in the Renaissance, to an idealism fostered by the period known as the Enlightenment, to a radical impulse that probably dates back to the French Revolution, to a romance with the material forces of change (Hegelianism, Marxism, and Darwinism), and finally to the deep convictions of an ivory-tower elite that has seen as its mission the aggressive implementation of its special, *superior* vision, bringing to fruition the utopian dream its forebears set in motion. Because Christianity has represented the main obstacle to realizing the vision, it has occupied "progressivism's" crosshairs for at least the last two-and-a-half centuries.

Most today are aware that a great political divide exists. Few, however, grasp the significance of that divide. Because it is very complex and carries such deep implications, explaining the nature of the divide is not possible without reaching far back into history to trace its development. Only such an informed (and sometimes challenging) context can give clarity to the conflict. To the Christian believer, this is an opportunity to discover the line of demarcation in this struggle. For the nonbeliever, this is an invitation to see the world in an entirely new light. The intent is to show that the Christian position is the only one that can squarely address the phenomena of the whole human experience without ever violating the principle of noncontradiction. More important than this, it will be evident that Christianity continues to be the only hope for individual *and* cultural redemption. But to truly appreciate and even begin to understand something as complex as Christianity, one must first be acquainted with the backdrop against which it emerged.

Section I

OUT OF THE WILDERNESS

CHAPTER 1

CLOSING THE GAP

To say the ancient world was shrouded in paganism is not to suggest that there was a homogeneity of religious belief at any one time. The wide range of diversity was given expression by definite common underlying assumptions about the nature of reality. When ancient man looked out into the surrounding cosmos, conflicting images stared back. On the one hand, he could see order of profound magnitude, great beauty in complex patterns suggesting other-worldliness, *transcendence*. On the other hand, he could see a marvelous creation that appeared to be broken and marching at all levels, inexplicably, to its inexorable death. For all the sublime beauty, he could not escape the reality that he was just an insignificant little pebble swallowed up in this vast immensity. To make his plight worse, he found himself subject to forces of nature that for no apparent reason poured out their fury on hapless beings. The sum of all these things produced a very confused and mixed message. How was he to reconcile order and beauty with waste, random cruelty, and death? What sort of coherent *truth* was he to derive from such a "standard"? Man was himself conflicted between a knowledge of truth that had seemingly been hardwired into him, though seriously dimmed by the fall (more on this later), and the merciless law of the jungle.

In that world, the law of the jungle is an impulsive reductionism where primal instincts and appetites are preeminent. Neither is the message of the jungle ambiguous—the mighty survive and rule at the expense of the weak. Nevertheless, individual tribes soon come to understand the simple expedient of strength in numbers. More complex city-states and then nation-states/empires were formed by those who recognized the value of preserving large diverse populations. Such populations offered maximum potential for exploiting the greatest possible range of skills and talents. For instance, those obviously deficient in military capacity could nevertheless demonstrate superior abilities in organization, farming, architecture, or any number of infrastructural needs, or perhaps might even engender that all-important sense of national unity and pride through inspiring works of art. Those who wished to scale the heights of power found themselves with a definite stake in promoting a general sense of security and welfare that encompassed potential contributors. This led, in turn, to the codification of ethics. Some of these codes, to be sure, were quite complex in structure. These emerging systems of government represented humanity's first attempts to close the gap between order and chaos.

All pagan governments shared this commonality: Whatever the outward appearance of a high moral code, human beings were expendable. Nowhere was this more evident than with the emphasis each of these governments placed upon the whole. There was no such thing in the world of antiquity as human intrinsic value. Everyone's value was entirely contingent, measured by one's usefulness to the group. The greatest morality, the one to which all others must bow, was enthusiastic support for whatever was deemed to promote the existence of the state.

Very early on, each tribe featured its own tribal deity. Eventually, each state patronized its distinct set of gods. Under these conditions, "religion" had nothing to do with any sort of "relationship" with the gods or even a chief god. Such an idea would have been an absurdity. Religion was essentially a matter of appeasing, of hitting upon enchantments that might soften the gods' wrath, and in the most ambitious (optimistic) exercises, of seeking to secure the favor of the gods by observing appropriate festivals and rituals and ultimately, offering (in some ancient societies) human sacrifices. Because the phenomena of nature are believed to result from some disposition of the gods, a dead cow, a rainbow, a violent storm, drought, military defeat, and natural disasters were all "signs" needing interpretation. A special priesthood was necessary to "divine" the will of the gods, a common theme in those times. Even with highly advanced pagan societies such as Greece, however, divining was a completely subjective process ranging from interpreting the movement of the planets to dissected human livers.

The desire for successful harvests, a matter of life or death in the ancient world, gave rise to the cult of the Great Mother—the giver and nourisher of life. This goddess was Isis in Egypt, Cybele in Asia Minor, Ashtoreth in Canaan, Hera in Greece, Artemis at Ephesus, Aphrodite in Cyprus, and so on. The Great Mother was universally associated with fertility cults. Not very surprisingly, these cults manifested worship through the open enthusiastic celebration of the basest sexual drives. It logically followed that if nature was the starting point, then no part of something so vital (and symbolically powerful) as the reproductive process could be ruled out of bounds. Indeed, since nature reflected the true, then rather than bestowing sanctity upon sexuality within a very narrow confinement, every unbridled urge in its most sensual form *must* be elevated to the sacred. Of course, saying all aspects of sexuality were sacred was just another way of saying that nothing about sexuality was sacred.

Pagan thought would probably achieve its highest form of organization under the Greeks. Aristotle reached beyond the gods to propose an essence existing as "uncaused first cause" removed from the cycle of change. As a backstop to infinite regression God was necessary, but just as necessarily detached and unknowable. Thus, it was the eternal universe and its phenomena that was primary. God was not Creator, a source of morality, nor an object of worship, merely the highest expression of divinity or actualization. Conceptualized this way, God could just as well be described as "the Great Nothing."

Despite great strides the Greeks would make in empiricism, their advancement of knowledge would be severely constricted by their immersion in the cycles of nature. The Greeks sought to establish an underlying uniformity but began with the flawed premise that a moral standard could be extracted from material patterns. This would lead to some ghastly assumptions about the human condition. For instance, Aristotle had these words to say in his treatise *Politics*:

> [T]hat some should rule and others be ruled is not only necessary, but expedient; from the hour of their birth, some are marked out for subjection, others for rule. . . . It is clear . . . that some men are by nature free, and others slaves, and that for these latter slavery is both expedient and right . . . against men who though intended by nature to be governed, will not submit . . . war is naturally just . . . we cannot consider all those to be citizens who are necessary to the existence of the state . . . no man can practice virtue who is living the life of a mechanic or laborer . . . the good of the state and not the individual is the proper subject of political thought and speculation. . . . The citizen should be molded to suit the form of government under which he lives. . . . Neither must we suppose that any of the citizens belongs to himself, for they all belong to the state.[1]

Aristotle's mentor, Plato, likewise believed in strict enforcement of practices that streamlined the efficient working of his idealized republic—abortion, infanticide, and eugenics, among others.

With the unmoved mover safely uncoupled from the universe but all the latter's components *imitating* the deity, certain assumptions could easily follow. The exercise of intellect (especially the more complex contemplative aspect), since it *most* closely imitated the deity was held by Aristotle to possess an element of divinity or something so similar as to make any significant distinction impossible. The further implication was that those most given to the contemplative life were repository to the highest degree of human divinity. Because no transcendent authority was permitted, it logically followed that "truth" should properly be interpreted by those that nature (and, by association, the gods) had favored with superior intellect, skill, and cunning—the philosophers ("philosopher-kings" for Plato). Yet to accept such a premise would then make it difficult to resist what would seem the logical extension, the deification (or something closely resembling) of the state.

If pagan thought found its highest expression in Greece, pagan *government* probably realized its crowning achievement in the Roman Empire. Rome, which borrowed many of its ideas from the Greeks (and virtually every other culture it contacted), was probably the most accommodating of all ancient regimes. The Roman aristocracy enthusiastically promoted religion as an opiate for the masses, with an important caveat: The government was the sole source of religious legitimacy. Without a license from the state, any religious establishment was transgressing supreme authority.

In the spirit of accommodation, Rome even extended to its citizens a kind of virtual freedom; virtual in that it did not actually entail the absence of state coercion, merely eligibility for the benevolence of state-sponsored goodies. Roman subjects were thus "free" to enjoy the good life that its gracious government had so generously provided. "Freedom," however, was not for everyone. Slaves (representing the oldest and most vigorously honored institution of the pagan world), unless they could acquire the necessary funds to purchase freedom, were forever deprived of the good life. Yet even those subjects who were not slaves were still divided into decidedly different classes, and "law" was applied relative to one's social standing.

For all the apparent religious freedom, there was a tacit understanding that *all* religions were acceptable only insofar as these various forms of worship did not interfere with worship of the state nor challenge the authority of the Supreme Benefactor, the Emperor. There were indeed many gods, but only Caesar was *Kyrios* (lord over the entire world). Moreover, for all the complexity of Roman law, one could nevertheless find no refuge. Caesar was the law speaking.

CHAPTER 2

SEPARATED TO
REVEAL A HOLY GOD

Somewhere near the beginning of the second millennium BC, a man by the name of Abram traveled with his wife Sarai from Ur of the Chaldees (Mesopotamia) into the land of Canaan. This man would not only be the progenitor of a new tribe, but of a race of men through which the world would receive an entirely new—indeed, in the strictest sense, the *only*—revelation of God. Unique in the ancient world, the descendants of Abraham (national Israel) would not give form to their concept of God through fanciful assertions or epic tales of larger-than-life national triumphs but through a specific covenant relationship. Not only did the details of the covenant reveal deep insights into whom this God was, but Israel's numerous failures to keep covenant would reveal the depths of this God's merciful character.

For the first time ever, man was not merely treated to empty *assertions* about God but was given an actual window (however limited) into His actual nature. The unfolding history of Israel would show that her God was a holy God, a God of perfect integrity. Unlike all the gods within the pagan structure, this God would not be given to arbitrariness and capriciousness, nor would He dissolve into universal elements or ideals; He would also deliberately lead His chosen people into hostile situations that would reveal something much more significant. Israel was to understand that her God was not just another tribal deity cast out of the old standard mold, but that He was the One true God—*the* Supreme Being. The God of Israel would throw down the gauntlet first to the "gods" of Egypt under the leadership of Moses, and in subsequent challenges to the Canaanite gods (for instance, Elijah's confrontation with the prophets of Baal on Mount Carmel, recorded in 1 Kings 18). In addition to all this, the God of Israel, in contrast to the normal, vague, abstract conceptualizations, would give insight into a *personal* God whose love for mankind was not limited to some detached imperceptible interest. This God was *intimately* vested in His creatures and especially, their heart-rending plight.

The thirty or so writers who would record the story of the Jews as a revelation of "the One True God" would come from all walks of life—from paupers to kings. In addition, the Writings were compiled over a thousand-year span by authors who in most cases not only lacked any knowledge of each other but were sometimes separated by hundreds of years. The seamless connection of differing genres—including histories, lessons, poetry, dramatic miracles, and a complex law code intimately tied into an even more complex atonement program—was attributed to the work of God's active agent, the Holy Spirit. That the overall message of all these diverse strands did not produce a mass of indecipherable babble, but instead far exceeded the sum of seemingly independent parts, would stand as some of the most compelling evidence that these men wrote under divine inspiration of that Holy Spirit.

To say that these writings were divinely inspired or "God-breathed" is not to say these men wrote in a robotic fashion while subject to some sort of heavenly spell. Rather, each man's own individual personality, writing style, intellect, etc., was a separate vehicle through which God's revelation was brought forth; the Holy Spirit provided additional details when knowledge was lacking, *ensuring* that no error of substance could emerge from any text. It is important to understand that all historic information and details were always secondary to the central purpose—revealing God and His plan. Only those details and events which were deemed necessary in accomplishing this specific purpose were recorded.

Writers of what we today refer to as the Old Testament, then, did not write from a strict historical perspective but from a *theological* one. This is not to suggest that these writers exempted themselves from a need for historical accuracy, or played fast and loose with real or imagined events when and where convenient. Much to the contrary; unlike other major religions whose teachings have very little if any connection with specific historic events, the Old Testament centered its truth claims in a specific people placed within the confines of a specific historic time span and geographic region. Its truth claims were hung on this single dramatic premise: The great God and Creator of all heaven and Earth had deliberately and with precision purpose "broken into history." It was this actual historic entrance into the normal course of human events that, by contrast, was intended to dramatically demonstrate the superiority of *this* God over all pretenders, establishing His power and faithfulness to sustain and bring His chosen people into possession of His promises, even in the face of overwhelming odds. It was equally intended to show the devastating ruin that awaited those who willfully turned away from His sustaining power, to point out the woeful inadequacy of men to achieve through their own efforts the holiness of God or effect in any degree their own salvation.

In view of these things, it is unrealistic to imagine Old Testament writers seeing the need for *historic* truth as anything less than crucial when relating the events upon which the foundation for *God's* truth was being laid. Indeed, the writers faithfully chronicled the failures (which far and away outstripped the triumphs) of their own people in stark, unflattering depictions, ranging from humiliating defeats at the hands of their enemies to heart-rending pronouncements of devastating future judgment for disobedience. This is not consistent with a self-serving agenda.

Even with the writers limiting their scope to a theological perspective, the OT has proven to be perhaps the single richest source of information for serious *secular* historians. That modern archeological digs have in a great many cases corroborated OT descriptions of otherwise little-known or unknown places and peoples has made it untenable for modern critics to dismiss these writers as little more than romantic idealists who conjured up fanciful self-serving allegories with little expectation of their writings ever being mistaken for literal history, as critics of old had been disposed.

Many are quick to point out strikingly similar concepts the OT writers share with their pagan counterparts, implying these ideas were either directly borrowed from or at least greatly influenced by Babylonian and Sumerian culture. While a possibility, it may also indicate a universal memory of very specific events which carried clear implications. The Sumerian flood tale and *The Epic of Gilgamesh* also speak of a great flood that far exceeded the normal scale.

All three accounts feature a man instructed to build an ark in the face of impending divine judgment. All three include this man's family plus some additional creatures boarding the ark. The similarities are noteworthy, but what about the differences? The duration of the flood is vague in the Mesopotamian stories but definite in Genesis. The judgment by the Mesopotamian gods is an act of capriciousness, or probably more accurately (as Kenneth Kitchen puts it), irritation. Judgment by the Supreme YHWH is directly connected to a moral failing in human beings. The description of the boats is vastly different. The detail given to dimensions and specific sealing measures in the Genesis account produces a much more feasible and seaworthy vessel (as well as meeting imposing logistical needs for the required time span) than the dubious box presented in the alternate accounts. The hero of the Mesopotamian plot emerges from his "ark" to offer sacrifices of appeasement to the gods; Noah offers a sacrifice of *thanksgiving* to YHWH, and so on.[1]

The Babylonian culture also featured a creation story in its epic tale *Enuma Elish*. Of all such myths of antiquity, this rendering is most frequently hailed for its "close parallels" to the Genesis narrative. Though OT critics regard *Enuma Elish* as antecedent to and heavily influencing the creation story in Genesis, the similarities are incidental. In *Enuma Elish* the gods are merely natural phenomena personified, impersonal forces changed into male and female deities who deny themselves no sensual pleasure. The Babylonian cosmogony, true to the chaotic state of pagan reality, springs from a *conflict* between the three primary gods. In the Genesis account, a sovereign, majestic, *monotheistic* God, rather than extending His essence, *speaks* the universe into existence out of nothing (*ex nihilo*).

Just as significant are the vastly different literary styles in which each cosmogony is cast. In *Enuma Elish*, the creation story is not meant (primarily) to explain the origin of the universe but to exalt Babylon's city-god, Marduk. This is done using dramatic techniques and fanciful embellishment in the epic style common to the ancient world. By contrast, the story in Genesis is a straightforward narrative that shows remarkable restraint and discipline—a simple reportage of facts without resorting to hyperbole.

Finally, each cosmogony carries a vastly different set of implications. In *Enuma Elish*, the starting point of creation is a chaotic state that only degenerates into more chaos—with human beings the final product of this process of degradation. As such, humans can never rise above being hapless pawns. The conditions of the universe ultimately reflect the *character* of the gods. In Genesis, the starting point is profound order supplied by a majestic all-powerful God Who is both fully immanent *and* transcendent. Because human beings are created in *His* image and likeness, they are endowed with a sense of purpose, dignity, and intrinsic value. This is nowhere else to be found in antiquity. This is an immediate effect evident to any whom seriously examine history—when God is elevated, man is elevated; when the concept of God is reduced, man is likewise.

Those who disparage the record of the OT maintain that monotheism is not unique to the Hebrew religion. Isolated instances of monotheism or close approximations are evident in ancient times. Egypt with its worship of the sun god Aten is such an example. Yet all such allusions, rare even as these are, pale in comparison to the strict formulation in the OT. To begin with, the observed pattern in antiquity is almost always *away* from a loose concept of monotheism *toward* polytheism. As evidence of this, pagan attempts to revive the former have relatively short shelf-lives. The OT concept of monotheism does not merely stand above its "parallels"; it inexplicably persists, despite a tidal wave in opposition, the natural flow of the old world.

The establishment of an intercessory priesthood offering sacrifices to YHWH finds its counterpart in pagan culture as well. Yet the pagan approach to intercessory sacrifice is 180 degrees out of phase with OT depictions. The Jewish priesthood does not engage in endless speculation and subjective interpretation of natural events. It has no need to "divine" the will of YHWH, for He has left them specific instructions as to what and how they are to sacrifice, down to the minutest detail. But the *why* is where Jewish and pagan forms of worship most sharply diverge. For the Jews, the reason for sacrifice is intrinsically linked to a past event that completely separated mortal man from the presence of God, an event known as the fall of man. While vague allusions to some sort of separating event are hinted at in some pagan myths, these invariably depict the fall as something that results from a cosmic accident or some grand unfortunate misunderstanding. How perfection could have fallen prey to a *mistake* is never made clear. In the OT, the fall is no mistake (by God) but the result of a deliberate act of rebellion against a holy God. This depiction is bursting with implications. It first means that there is an absolute standard to which man is privy and to which he has obviously been granted free will to resist. The sober reality is that man is separated from God. Yet the story, or the unfolding implications, does not end here.

Though YHWH delivered stirring victories into her hand, Israel did not forge her identity through military conquest but out of humiliating bondage in Egypt. The theme of deliverance was burned into the Hebrew psyche from inception. Yet YHWH did not merely want to *deliver* His chosen people; He desired to bring them into a land flowing with milk and honey. But inheriting the Promised Land, and continued residency, was predicated upon upholding God's standard. Because YHWH determined to distinguish Himself as a holy God, in contrast to the profane imaginary gods of the region, so too must His people be holy. Having already witnessed dramatic demonstrations of His power and the sheer impotence of the gods of Egypt to stay His mighty hand, the Hebrews agree to covenant conditions in exchange not just for YHWH's special protection but blessings of unprecedented proportions. Yet the words have scarcely left their lips when the murmuring begins. In their exodus out of Egypt, despite witnessing incredible miracles, each time trouble comes, the Jews yearn to return to the protection of the old familiar pagan gods. This constant looking-back will deny them the Promised Land for forty years.

The above is a theme that will play out throughout the Old Testament—a microcosm of the debilitating and enslaving effect of sin (literally falling short of God's mark) and God's desire to reconcile fallen man to Himself. Yet there is a wider resonance: Finally, there is a way to make sense of the mixed message of nature. There is beauty in the universe and echoes of transcendence because a perfect God created it. There is death and suffering because the curse of sin *marred* that original perfection. The obvious conflict is not a reflection of God's nature but of rebellious man. In this story, substitutionary sacrifice is dramatically different from the pagan concept. Here, sacrifice is not about appeasing but *atoning* for the rebellion that has caused this destructive rift. Atonement fully acknowledges the seriousness of this separation, as well as the holiness of a God who will not wink at sin, a God so holy that He cannot step outside of His perfect integrity to heal this condition and continue to reside in that same perfection. God is under no obligation to deliver helpless mankind from the consequences of its fallen state, but reveals that mercy is intrinsic to His nature by *choosing* to extend deliverance.

Yet there can be no shortcut in this process. If God is to rescue man it *must* be done within the framework of *justice*—and the demands of justice, as will soon become evident, are more exacting than any mortal can comprehend. Finally, atonement looks ahead to ultimate redemption, not just of fallen man but of the whole broken creation.

Upholding YHWH's standard proves to be an unbearable burden upon the Jews. The extensive law code the Jews are required to obey is unyielding in its impossible demands. Israel provides striking evidence of the pull to turn from the One True God to worshiping multiple gods. A recurring theme depicts the Jews *resisting* their God's specific command to separate from the religious practices and gods of the region. The Jewish national predisposition is to accommodate, imitate, and settle in with the practices of their neighbors. If Israel did indeed invent YHWH as a rallying point, a source of pride and special identity, we might wonder why she would choose to cast this myth in almost-constant national *failure*. Even hundreds of years after being settled in her Promised Land, Israel cannot seem to abandon her infatuation with regional patterns. Though she has uniquely enjoyed an unprecedented privilege—chosen subject of the King of all creation—she desperately desires an *earthly* king to lead her into battle. In times of distress, Israel is quick to repent and cry to her great God for deliverance. Again and again, such deliverance is granted. In times of prosperity, YHWH is a thorn in her side, a nuisance to be evaded. If YHWH *were* an invention, surely the Jews could have molded Him into a far more acceptable and self-serving image. Could YHWH have been a clever tool kings trotted out to maintain control? Unlikely. Israel's kings generally welcomed YHWH's imposing statutes far less than the common folk. In fact, the usual pattern was for kings to take the lead in idolatrous practices, building alternate "high places" of worship in violation of strict prohibitions.

What is perhaps most incredible in the history of the Jews is that, with every possible force of inertia to the contrary, YHWH does not fade away. Almost as amazing, neither do His chosen people. There is a powerful key here, the significance of which is often missed when studying the history of the Jews: the word "chosen." This reference is not incidental. The Jews did not and clearly *would not* have chosen YHWH. He is their God only because He specifically chose *them*. They frankly welcomed no part of the restraints and responsibilities, or the cost that came with identification with their God.

CHAPTER 3

THE JEWS ENTER CANAAN: A GENOCIDAL CAMPAIGN?

It is the intent of this book to consider a wide range of criticisms frequently leveled at the Bible. A considerable spectrum of critical sources will as well be addressed. We begin with the lower end of that spectrum, with a book by Timothy Freke and Peter Gandy that will be a source of discussion at various points throughout this book.

The subtitle of *The Laughing Jesus* (*TLJ* hereafter), *Religious Lies and Gnostic Wisdom,* gives away Freke and Gandy's premise: Christianity was originally based on lofty spiritual principles that, unfortunately, were corrupted by unscrupulous infiltrators who appropriated the Christ-message for their own selfish interests. The great corrupting factor of early Christianity can be traced to an odious approach called "literalism." Rather than accepting that words attributed to the Christ were mere figures, literalists placed an undue and unintended stress on the very words, worshiping words instead of seeing the symbols of liberation they heralded. The literalist approach to holding the Christ-message hostage to the material world would, in time, lead to religious authoritarianism.

"Luckily" for us, Freke and Gandy ride to the rescue with real solutions and offer to lead us back to the earlier pristine state. A return to gnosticism is the sure way to set the world free from literalism and the nasty, tension-inducing, war-fostering "fundamentalism" it has given rise to (the subject of gnosticism will be dealt with in a later section).

Our authors carefully set out important differences between gnosticism and literalism. "Literalism," we are informed, "keeps us asleep in an 'us versus them' world of division and conflict, inhabited by the 'chosen' and the 'damned'." One hates to intrude on Freke and Gandy's maudlin fantasy, but are they aware that "discriminating Gnosticism from Literalism"[1] already sets up an "us versus them" confrontation? Lest we get sidetracked, though, there's more brilliant exposition: "Gnosticism is about waking up from the illusion of separateness to oneness and love."[2] If we take these deep thinkers at their word, then the ignorance (of literalism) they seek to eradicate must be *part* of that oneness. In which case, it can neither be evil (or a mistake) nor possible to remove. In fact, isn't *the* solution a call for awakening by Freke and Gandy from the illusion that literalism can be *separated* from the grand oneness? But I trust that one last shimmering pearl will suffice to illuminate the superior thought processes at work: "Throughout history Gnostics have ceaselessly exposed Literalist religion as a pernicious source of ignorance, division and suffering."[3]

Expose ignorance, division, and suffering? Again, it seems criminal to point out the obvious, but doesn't this promote a *value* distinction—that one view is *preferable* to another? Yet isn't Freke and Gandy's whole point that it is the *inclusiveness* of gnosticism, a refusal to make those nasty distinctions, that establishes its superiority? How can this liberating view then proceed to *exclude* a position (literalism) and castigate an entire class of people just because they have a different view of reality? Consider this sampling of the intolerant and caustic tone set by the authors: "Fundamentalists hate the modern world"; "Religious Fundamentalism is an irrational pathology"; "But Fundamentalists aren't just monsters."[4] This all sounds very judgmental and, well, *divisive*. And incidentally, these less-than-charitable statements follow on the heels of the book's dedication "to all who love their enemies." A warning to those brave souls venturing to navigate Freke and Gandy's work: Incoherence does not take a holiday.

To be sure, addressing anything Freke and Gandy have to say is itself a formidable test of will. The overwhelming urge is to refuse any sort of reply that might dignify an approach that at best can be described as "tabloid journalism." Freke and Gandy find themselves the beneficiaries of an age that is particularly void of critical thinking. Today, unfortunately, *TLJ* is just the sort of sensationalist drivel that commands enthusiastic attention. For many, this mode of inquiry represents their primary source of information (disinformation, to be more accurate).

Of course, Freke and Gandy do not pretend to approach this as historians or theologians. Theirs is a philosophical position. They do maintain a thin pretense of scholarship, however. The historical/critical method is, as expected, given short shrift. Yet we would be remiss if we did not concede a point in the authors' favor: They are at least consistent in their assault on "literalism." They display a distinct and unflagging aversion to presenting and examining literal *facts*. Freke and Gandy employ the "aha" method of investigation—a method reminiscent of high-schoolers looking for any apparent surface inconsistencies, while refusing any acquaintance with that much bigger picture which would explain most, if not all, such seeming inconsistencies.

The preferred approach is to construct an artificial reality where serious obstacles and scholarly works that would otherwise intrude upon their most crucial premises are merely pretended away. For a display of their hapless arguments exposed to serious criticism, I recommend the masterful work *On the Reliability of the Old Testament*, by K. A. Kitchen. If Freke and Gandy really aspire to elevate their work beyond a tabloid hit piece, they might take on the arguments of serious scholarship seen in the works of, say, N. T. Wright, Ben Witherington, Gary Habermas, or Darrell Bock.

In place of substantive argument, the authors serve up, among other rhetorical devices, distorted anecdotes, baseless charges, gross oversimplifications, or self-contradictory claims. "The born-again Christian Timothy McVeigh belonged to this particularly nasty strand of Christian Literalism and until 9/11 held the record for the largest peacetime bombing of civilians in America."[5] The evidence suggests McVeigh was agnostic; he was quoted as saying that he did not believe in hell and that science was his religion.[6]

"Let's not forget that the Nazi SS who exterminated the Jews had emblazoned on their belt buckles the words 'God is with us.'"[7] But, Freke and Gandy might have bothered to ask, which "god" were these monsters invoking? It certainly was not the God of Christian tradition, as Hitler hated the church and saw it as an impediment to his designs. The God Hitler looked to was the mystical god(s) of nature (derived from pagan influences), that had ordained him for his special mission.

Nazism was *itself* a deeply religious movement that, of necessity, manipulated the masses through emotionally frenzied rallies. As approximately 90 percent of Germany was Christian; Hitler merely employed a Machiavellian strategy to incorporate Christian themes wherever possible to justify what was otherwise a brutal philosophy of militarism, informed not by Christ's teachings but by Darwinian and Nietzschean philosophy. Completely divorcing himself from any sort of Christianity that flowed from orthodox or traditional views, Hitler appropriated Christ as the ultimate Jew-hater. Nazis, it may be noted, continually persecuted Christian churches. Hitler's own personal secretary, Martin Bormann, wrote numerous notes quoting Hitler's contempt for Christianity because it artificially sustained the weak.

"Prior to the invention of books, in oral cultures traditions underwent subtle changes as they were transmitted, just as in the game of Chinese Whispers. Change was inevitable if only because of the imperfection of human memory."[8] Here the authors show their colossal ignorance of ancient preservation of oral records/tradition (to be dealt with in a later section). "A new genre called 'sacred scriptures' was created. Sacred scriptures are special and off-limits to the kind of criticism that might be applied to any other piece of literature."[9] There is no indication this is delivered tongue-in-cheek. I challenge the authors to point to *any other* piece of

literature that has been subjected to this same intense and sustained critical examination from every conceivable angle as the Bible.

The authors reject the idea that monotheism is a unique Jewish concept. "The
Tanakh [the Old Testament] was put together in the Hellenistic world when the
most important idea shaping men's perception of the divine was Greek monotheism."[10] Freke and Gandy apparently realize that this naked statement leaves their
backsides a bit too exposed, so they attempt a lame qualifier: "In the sixth century
BCE Heraclitus wrote about the one God who some call Zeus." Nice try, but laughable; Zeus was the chief god of a whole slew of gods. This is polytheism. "The One"
in Greek mythology is (as earlier stated) the unspeakable, unknowable, unfathom-
able—in other words, no more relevant than the Great Nothing. To their credit,
the authors realize this is too much of a stretch, even for their target audience, and
on the same page as their earlier outrageous statement contradict themselves *and*
toss in a little syncretism: "In a way, to call this Greek philosophy monotheism
is misleading, because it is actually more sophisticated than that. It is Monistic
Polytheism."[11] Good recovery. In a way, to call what Freke and Gandy engage in
tabloid journalism is misleading; it is less sophisticated than that. It is journalisti-
cally vacant.

"By definition only one of these religions (Judaism, Christianity, Islam) can be
the one true religion. But which one?"[12] If this were an honest question, the authors
would be well on their way to the answer. Resolutely, however, they refuse to veer
from the low road, and instead serve up the usual caricature of Judeo-Christian history. There is no effort to present a balanced treatment of *all* facts. Muslims, Jews,
and Christians are all lumped together, with no attempt to even see if there may be
substantive differences. It is of course axiomatic that Judeo-Christianity will share
superficial similarities with Islam, due to each making truth claims that carry eternal implications. Yet superficial similarities are magnified, while deep profound differences are ignored. No consideration is given to examining the *basis* for the claims
of each or the possibility that Islam is but a cheap imitation of Judeo-Christianity.
It is simply *assumed* that both must be equally incapable of making any sort of rational case, without ever consulting the mountain of available evidence. Everything
that follows ensures that no differences will emerge.

Freke and Gandy predicate their entire case against Judaism on a twilight-zone
scenario called the Hasmonean Theory (to be addressed later). For now, we will
content ourselves with certain criticisms of events surrounding the Jews in the OT.
The Bible does not mask the very violent aspect of the Jews incursion into Canaan,
their Promised Land. This, Freke and Gandy are certain, is a serious indictment of
the God of the Jews. "Do we really want to carry on worshiping a God who legiti-
mized the clearing of Canaan by the total extermination of every man, woman,

child and animal?"[13] This question is quite illustrative of the usual approach the authors take to very complicated subjects and events. There is a protracted context that identifies the special circumstances of this event, featuring a lengthy backdrop and all sorts of clues as to *what* is happening and *why.* In their usual ham-fisted way, Freke and Gandy jump to a convenient conclusion, without bothering to consider circumstances.

Let's look at some of those circumstances. Before the Jews take possession of the land, thirty-one kings and their people are marked for God's judgment/removal from the land. *Before* this decree is executed, we can clearly see a framework for examining the nature of YHWH's judgments. For instance, the global flood and the destruction of Sodom and Gomorrah both included warnings/preaching of coming catastrophe many years before the fact—the flood at least one hundred years in advance, and Sodom at least twenty-five years. It might be argued that these warnings were just formalities and that there never was any possibility of escaping impending doom. Hundreds of years beyond the Canaan invasion, however, in the book of Jonah, the city of Nineveh is marked for destruction because of excessive wickedness. God, nevertheless, commands Jonah to warn the people of coming judgment. After much kicking and screaming Jonah relents, warns Nineveh, and much to his dismay, Nineveh repents and is spared.

As with the judgment events mentioned above, warnings of judgment upon Canaan were put forth well in advance. Though the Jewish entrance into Canaan is often treated as a ruthless military invasion with a vision toward empire, there is nothing in the Bible to support this. Long before the Jews entered Canaan, the *reputation* of the Jewish God was well established in the land:

> And she [Rahab] said unto the men, I know that the LORD hath given you the land, and that your terror is fallen upon us, and that all the inhabitants of the land faint because of you. For we have heard how the LORD dried up the water of the Red Sea for you, when ye came out of Egypt; and what ye did unto the two kings of the Amorites, that were on the other side Jordan, Sihon and Og, whom ye utterly destroyed. And as soon as we heard these things, our hearts did melt, neither did there remain any more courage in any man, because of you: for the LORD God, he is God in heaven above, and in earth beneath. (Josh. 2:9–11)

This confession by Rahab is revealing. Dramatic and miraculous events that have taken place at least *forty years prior* are well-publicized throughout Canaan. The fear on the part of Canaanite inhabitants shows there is a clear expectation that all these events back in Egypt served as a precursor to an inevitable return to the land the Jews had earlier possessed. This presupposed knowledge and an admission that the Jews occupied this territory *before* its present inhabitants. The Canaanites (unlike Freke and Gandy) could add two and two. The God of the Jews served notice well in advance that anyone squatting on land He has set aside for His chosen was a usurper and would be dealt with harshly.

The Amorites' confrontation with the Jews just before entering Canaan was yet another indication that all these astounding events foreshadowed the fulfillment of prophecies that had been uttered hundreds of years before (Num. 21:21–25). The evidence continues to add up that the Canaanites had knowledge of YHWH's promise to Abraham, back in Genesis 15:7–8, of an *everlasting possession* to the Jews. One tribe in the region, Gibeon (obviously aware of this prophecy and of YHWH's intent) sought favorable relations with Israel in a face-to-face meeting, even going so far as to pretend to have traveled from far away for the meeting, appearing disheveled, dressed in badly worn clothing, and bearing moldy bread (Josh. 9); Israel would later learn of the ruse, but not until after she had entered a pact of peace with these people. Though this tribe was originally marked for judgment, because Israel had made this covenant (even under false pretenses), she was duty-bound to spare the Gibeonites, and did.

Bearing these things in mind, let us focus on the Amorites and their influence in Canaan. This group represented a malignant cancer (affecting the whole region) that not only was in for long overdue judgment, and illegally occupying land reserved by God, but whose presence would have wholly corrupted the mission God placed upon His chosen. Because this influence was so pervasive and intractable, there was no alternative but to annihilate. "But of the cities of these people, which the LORD thy God doth give thee for an inheritance, thou shalt save alive nothing that breatheth. . . . That they teach you not to do after all their abominations, which they have done unto their gods; so should ye sin against the LORD your God" (Deut. 20:16, 18). But notice whereas we move away from this epicenter of unrepressed wickedness, the Jews are *restricted* in their campaign (Deut. 20:10–15).

As for the fate of the children of parents completely given over to depravity, it is certain that God dealt with these far more mercifully than their own parents. The depths of cruelty to which these children were subjected ranged from being sold into prostitution to being offered up as sacrifices. In the eternal sense, we cannot speak definitively to their fate, but any judgment is likely to be far less severe, in comparison to a full lifetime of hardened rebellion. But in any case, children being victimized by the poor decisions of parents is neither unique nor new. As disturbing as this seems, we see this from a very limited and immediate perspective. God views it from a perspective of eternity which encompasses the whole picture within His unfolding plan.

We do, however, have a reference for understanding the difficulties that a huge chasm separating intellects can pose. What is a toddler, barely able to form simple words, to make of parents who take him to an emergency room to receive shots and stitches for a serious wound? Any parent who's ever been in a similar situation knows the heartache of his precious child looking up at him and wondering how a loving, trusted parent can now be "piling on" instead of making it better. We, of course, know that this *will* make things better. The child only knows what is imme- diate; this seems a cruel betrayal of sacred trust. Yet God's intellect is so many times greater in comparison to ours, than an adult's to a toddler's.

The Jewish entrance is not a genocidal campaign intending to destroy wan- tonly, but the clear intent is to *drive out* the evil influences whose continuing presence would fester among the Israelites. Nothing less than the vital mission of bringing the Savior *to the world* is precisely what is threatened by this extraordinary concentration of evil.

Notice also that when Israel finally fails in her mission hundreds of years later— and does in fact succumb to the pagan influences *because* she does not completely drive out as commanded—she *too* is driven from the land, her very *Promised Land*. And just as many Canaanites perished but no tribe was annihilated, so too many in Israel perish in her deportation but Israel herself is not destroyed.

Those who perished in Canaan *chose* to stay and challenge YHWH, despite ample examples of His power and numerous warnings. This was not some sudden, unexpected event that overtook them, forcing them to defend their homes. They *knew* they were poachers on land that was staked out and promised to the people of YHWH. As to the charge that this was a pretext to establish a Jewish empire, the original borders God set for the Jews back in Genesis *were never expanded*. What is perhaps most remarkable about those nations that chose to remain in Canaan is that they did so against common practice. As each city-state had its own chief god, gauging the relative strength of one's god in comparison to the god of a potential adversary was the first consideration when making that all-important decision of fight or flight. Having defeated the mighty god (and his pantheon) of the most powerful empire of the time (Egypt), there could be no doubt that the much weaker gods of Canaan would be no match for the God of the Hebrews. That they chose to stay and fight, in defiance of basic survival instinct, is some measure of the deprav- ity and utter contempt for the Jewish God that had been cultivated in them.[14]

Freke and Gandy continue to question YHWH's moral character: "[A]fter the miraculous birth of their much-longed-for child, God tells Abraham to build an altar of wood, tie up his son, lay him on the pyre and slit his throat. As if that wasn't sick enough, just as Abraham is about to carry out this dreadful instruction, God tells Abraham that it was all just a trick to test his fidelity! What kind of God is this?"[15] As with the judgments mentioned above, this does not represent business as usual but a dramatic departure. There is something very *poignant* in this portrayal. Two thousand years or so beyond this event, God the Father will sacrifice His only begotten son on the most unimaginably cruel altar of Calvary. Abraham is given a little preview of what that might be like for the Father. Though no doubt greatly distressed by the completely incongruous command, Abraham is convinced that if need be, God will *resurrect* Isaac. This expectation is completely at odds with any pagan take on child sacrifice. The sense of the violent breaking of trust with a child so precious to him, plunging a knife into his beloved, is unbearable. No doubt, Abraham would have much more easily plunged it into his own heart. But if God's promise of redemption *through* Isaac (as promised) was to find fulfillment, Abraham must trust God, no matter the severity of the test.

Isaac, as a type of Christ in this portrayal, carries the wood for his sacrifice on his back as the Savior will two thousand years hence. As the place of sacrifice is chosen and the wood placed on the altar, Isaac innocently asks, "but where is the lamb for a burnt offering?" Abraham replies, "My son, God will provide himself a lamb for a burnt offering" (Gen. 22:7–8). We can't begin to imagine the kind of heartache this father must have experienced as he is binding his precious son, knowing the awful deed he must do. Yet when God stays Abraham's hand and a ram is suddenly visible in a nearby thicket, he realizes the breathtaking prophetic power of the words he has just spoken. God has not merely substituted an animal in Isaac's place; He will provide *Himself* as a lamb. In this moment Abraham gained some small measure of insight into the heartache the Father will endure, the obedience *the* Son must manifest, and the unimaginable cost of salvation, because there will be no one to stay the hand of the Savior's executioners. Moreover, Isaac as the child of promise, would gain invaluable knowledge of the effect of perfect obedience:

> And the angel of the LORD called unto Abraham out of heaven the sec-
> ond time, and said, by myself have I sworn, saith the LORD , for because
> thou hast done this thing, and hast not withheld thy son, thine only
> son: that in blessing I will bless thee, and in multiplying I will multiply
> thy seed as the stars of the heaven, and as the sand which is upon the sea
> shore; and thy seed shall possess the gate of his enemies; and in thy seed
> shall all the nations of the earth be blessed; because thou hast obeyed
> my voice. (Gen. 22:15–18)

The biblical depiction of the Jewish sojourn into Egypt is another subject that frequently comes under criticism. There is no clear record of the Jews under bond-age in Egypt. As far as the exodus event is concerned, such a massive undertaking, so goes the argument, would surely have left behind discernable footprints. With no external source to corroborate, we may justifiably see this as entertaining fiction but still just one of those tribal legends.

Critics conveniently forget that records are made and kept for a reason. The idea is to chronicle the victorious campaigns of one's own nation. Any mention of other nation-states, tribes, or cultures, whatever the circumstances, will at the least be done with an eye toward presenting one's nation in the most favorable light. Ancient scribes were not aware of any responsibility for supplying succeeding generations (especially several thousand years into the future) with general information of surrounding regions which confirmed or refuted other ancient claims. They frankly did not write from what we would call a historian's perspective. This does not necessarily eliminate their writings from having historic value.

So, let's place this in perspective: The Egyptians have just suffered one of the most shocking and humiliating defeats in their history. Their gods have been *deliberately* singled out, mocked, and rendered irrelevant. Their mighty Pharaoh, his stubborn pride notwithstanding, has been forced to release a horde of defenseless slaves along with a considerable portion of the nation's livestock and wealth. As we recall, records in antiquity, whether crude renderings on cave walls or elaborate stories carved in stone, were almost always about promoting a sense of national pride. One can easily imagine ordinances immediately springing up that carried harsh penalties to anyone that even mentioned the Hebrews (or whatever name by which the Egyptians had known them). Not that the people would have had any *desire* to remember, but the state would have a considerable stake in purging any trace of Hebrew existence. Should we find it surprising, then, that no sort of record of this episode has been unearthed? In view of what is the clear observation of all historic cultures, would we not rather find the discovery of such a record shocking and extraordinary?

CHAPTER 4

JESUS: SAVIOR, OR JUST THE REVEALER OF HIDDEN KNOWLEDGE?

Today, there is a frequent failure to place Christianity within its wider Jewish context. The ministry of Jesus of Nazareth represented not some sectarian mutation but the logical conclusion of the Jewish atonement program. By no means had the dispensation of the Law (yoked to the Jews for 1,400 years) failed to achieve its objective. Though the story of the Jews had mostly been one of failure and then judgment, the settling of Israel at the epicenter of pagan depravity established a vital beachhead through which God's fuller revelation and blessings could flow to all tribes of the world.

Yet the Law did still more: It dramatically showed, through these 1,400 years, the utter incapability of humans to keep covenant with a holy God. No matter his striving, determination, or noble intentions, man could not elevate himself to God's level. His best efforts were doomed to fail miserably, even *with* God marking out a special people and supplying a detailed roadmap to success.

With the first advent of Christ, God now inaugurated the next phase in His unfolding plan: the dispensation of grace. The good news was that helpless men no longer needed to scale the sheer cliffs of Mt. Reconciliation. God had literally come down to walk among His creatures and experience firsthand every aspect of the human condition. Rather than demanding human sacrifice for His personal appeasement, God, in the person of Jesus the Christ, offered *Himself* on the altar for sinful humanity. Could there be any greater distinction separating paganism and Christianity?

The coming of the Messiah (literally "God's anointed") was the most eagerly awaited event in Judaism. What was most inexplicable to Jews was why God was delaying an event that held so much promise, when there was such a burning *need*. Yet the Hebrew Scriptures consistently revealed that God did not act according to the counsel of men. His unfolding plan was always accomplished within His predetermined, precise timing. Considering the range in which the Christ *could* have appeared, it strains credulity to suppose it coincidence that the coming of the Jewish Messiah would occur within the confines of the mighty Roman Empire, and at the height of its imperialistic reign. This time, Jesus the Christ would Himself throw down the gauntlet to the crowning jewel of the pagan world. Yet the gauntlet is not directed at the gods of the realm, for it is evident by now that they are themselves appendages of an idea. The challenge is directed at the Roman Empire itself and even more brazenly, at its human *kyrios,* the emperor.

There is a frequent misconception concerning the term "Christ" or Anointed One. Many erroneously assume that this title conveys perhaps some extraordinary measure of spiritual enlightenment. The normal tendency is to place Jesus the Christ in a broad context that makes Him roughly the equal and lineal descendant of "spiritual" characters like Krishna, Buddha, Zoroaster, and the like. "Christ" then becomes a designation of spiritual consciousness, a measure of one's self-realization. This requires either a gross ignorance or a deliberate denial of a two-thousand-year, carefully constructed specific context which leaves no doubt of the term's multilayered meaning.

In Jesus' day, any Jew who heard any reference to "Christ" immediately understood the implications. No other word could so deeply inflame the passion in Jews everywhere. It was *the* word that most succinctly summed up their hope—deliverance from sin and the grueling, heart-rending consequences it kept pulling them back into. Any suggestion that one might be *the* Christ fueled even deeper passions. Several were thought or *hoped* to be before Jesus' day; some, such as Bar Kochba, would make the claim after Jesus. Such an assertion, even if only vague, was an immediate invitation to immense scrutiny and controversy.

It is incredible that Jesus is so often removed from the immediate Jewish context, when it is this context which so easily explains why He was such a lightning rod for so many competing passions. To be sure, there is never any hint that Jesus viewed *Himself* or His *ministry* in any way distinct from this context. To the contrary, He went to fantastic lengths to identify Himself as the *fulfillment* of every facet of the Old Testament redemptive program. Everything He did established His unique qualifications to be *the* Anointed, from keeping the *Jewish* Law perfectly to dramatic demonstrations of His authority over the laws of nature.

Today, His message, though the most powerful and inspiring ever recorded, is invariably transformed into fuzzy consciousness-raising, and He a congenial spirit guide. While there is no question that He spoke sublime words of inspiration, these were often shocking, politically explosive, completely exclusive, and, buttressed by His deliberate miracles, served notice of Royal Authority: "The Spirit of the Lord is upon me, because he hath *anointed* me to preach the gospel to the poor; he hath sent me to heal the broken-hearted, to preach deliverance to the captives, and recovering of sight to the blind, to set at liberty them that are bruised: To preach the acceptable year of the Lord" (Luke 4:18–19, emphasis added). Jesus read these words directly from the sixty-first chapter of Isaiah as He stood in the synagogue. Upon finishing, He closed the book with these words, "This day is this scripture fulfilled in your ears" (Luke 4:21).

There is no doubt the Jews understood the audacious claims—that He was marking Himself as the Promised One of prophecy. Especially, there was no mistaking His deliberate use of the word "anointed," the literal meaning of Messiah. Incensed by His presumptuousness, they immediately ran Him out of the synagogue to a cliff, with the intention of throwing Him over the edge. At this point, but for a miracle that allowed Him to pass untouched through their midst, Jesus would have never made it to the cross. Yet for all the political hot water Jesus had so deliberately placed Himself in, He would not limit His claims to messiahship. He would deliver even more politically provocative and emotionally charged language that left no doubt that He considered Himself of the very essence of YHWH. A not-so-subtle implication hung in the air: A new *Kyrios* had come onto the scene. There obviously could not be two supreme lords of the world, especially represented by such diametric opposites. On many levels, this made Jesus of Nazareth the most dangerous man in existence.

If Jesus was a political opportunist, thinking to exploit a climate that was ripe for the taking, He would surely qualify as the worst tactician in history. He neither catered to the Jewish elite nor rubber-stamped self-seekers. Regarding the Roman Empire, He was public enemy number one. If He envisioned a revolutionary uprising, where did He suppose His constituency would come from, since He was constantly whittling His following down by increasing impositions? There was certainly nothing inherently appealing in His call for people to repent. He was stern and unyielding in His judgments against willful sinning and His pronouncements of the way to righteousness:

> Think not that I am come to send peace on earth: I come not to send peace, but a sword. For I am come to set a man at variance against his father, and the daughter against her mother, and the daughter in law against her mother in law. And a man's foes shall be they of his own household. He that loveth father or mother more than me is not worthy of me: and he that loveth son or daughter more than me is not worthy of me. And he that taketh not his cross [self-*denial*], and followeth after me, is not worthy of me. (Matt. 10:34–38)

This hardly seems to harmonize with any idea that Jesus was a nonjudgmental teddy bear. Neither does this square with "buffet religion," where ultimate truth may be cobbled together from the parts of any number of spiritual paths. Truth, as Jesus represents it, by its very exacting nature *divides*. Jesus' message is most at odds with today's popular notion that truth might lie in the direction of self-pursuit, the path of *least* resistance. Moreover, Jesus thoroughly rejected the concept of religious inclusiveness: "Enter ye in at the strait gate: for wide is the gate, and broad is the way that leadeth to destruction, and many there be which go thereat: Because strait is the gate, and narrow is the way, which leadeth unto life, and few there be that find it" (Matt. 7:13–14).

Though He displayed moments of great tenderness, Jesus was no silly sentimentalist. He was an immovable rock, encountering head-on the very forces of evil that wanted to thwart His mission: to overturn the curse of sin. Far from being embraced as a consciousness-raising avatar, Jesus was hated by religious leaders. He was scathingly critical of them, and made no effort to conceal nor soften His contempt. At one point, He denounced them as sons of "your father the devil" (John 8:44). But most revealing, none of His criticisms were directed at the *Law* that Moses had been given, and that these leaders now entrusted with. His anger was directed at the multitude of *new* laws cleverly circumventing and negating *God's* law while providing a pretense of piety. As much as they hated His bluntness, they absolutely despised His refusal to conform to their preconceived ideas of what the Messiah should look and act like—as a mighty conqueror dressed in royal garments and waited on by a heavenly host, and of *course*, full of praise for the religious elite and its magnanimous efforts to make the Law even holier. But *this* man standing before them in destitute poverty, presuming to correct them on matters of the Law, was contemptible! In their minds, His condemnation of their actions was all the evidence needed to prove He was an imposter.

Though it would signal the disintegration of the mightiest empire the world had ever known, there was nothing conventional in Christ's declaration of war. It consisted of no imposing weapon, nor mighty army. It bore not even a superficial resemblance to other Jewish would-be messiahs who had led military revolts (and would in the future), hoping to throw off the yoke of oppression. Nevertheless, it was of a character Rome could not have been more unprepared to resist. Christ would set up His kingdom in the midst of pagan supremacy, through complete submission to the Father's will, finally yielding Himself as a lamb before the slaughterers.

Though all humanity stands guilty before Him, the Savior of the world allowed himself to be placed on trial. But what "crimes" is He charged with? Three things, primarily: claiming to be the King of the Jews, and by wider implication, of the world (sedition against Rome); claiming to be the Christ of God (blasphemy); and making Himself equal with God (also blasphemy). If Jesus had been misunderstood and His actual message and claims badly distorted, His trial would have been His opportunity to set the record straight; He certainly had compelling incentive to do so. The horror of crucifixion is something so viscerally repulsive that the word was scarcely uttered by Jews. Aside from the indescribable agony (an entirely new word, "excruciating," would come into existence to try to impart some sense of the experience), the thought of being nailed to a cross was the worst kind of humiliation and shame a Jew could imagine. This was considered a cursed way to die.

We might have expected Jesus to take the occasion to say something like, "Listen, folks, there's been a huge misunderstanding. I've not been claiming to be *the* Christ. I've come to share with everyone Christ-*consciousness*! I have simply come to share techniques that were passed on to me that will enable each of you to get in touch with your true selves. As to my claim to be equal with God, it's true. But so are each of *you*! You've all been handed a bill of goods with all this elaborate law-keeping drudgery. Well, I'm here to abolish the shackles of 'religion' and offer you the liberation of *spirituality*! But if some of you want to continue in your traditions, that's fine, too. I'm not going to condemn anyone for following their true convictions."

Such a Jesus seems hardly threatening, even to this angry mob. Indeed, any *occasion* for such a mob would be thoroughly removed. If this was what He was about, what purpose would there be to His death—if He did not believe it could atone for anything? How would an innocent man dying the most brutal death conceived by the mind of man serve the cause of consciousness-raising?

Had He chosen to recant the claims attributed to Him, He would likely have been spared this horrible fate. Why did He choose instead to deliberately speak words that lent credence to these primary charges, words that would inflame His accusers even more, words that He *knew* would seal His fate? Is it rational to think a man could have done this if He were not convinced in His own mind, that He was indeed "guilty" of these three charges, and that His sacrifice was the only hope for humanity?

What about Pontius Pilate, who had presided over probably hundreds of these trials? What is it about the person of Jesus that elicits a measure of pity from even this old, hardened pagan? Though Jesus represents a greater threat, ultimately, to the empire than to the coveted position of this entrenched Jewish hierarchy, Pilate is most uneasy about sending such an obviously innocent and politically leveraged pawn to this merciless death. Yet there is probably more to his reticence. Pilate is no doubt struck by the aura of otherworldliness that surrounds this strange man. Though He is completely helpless, He still commands a certain majesty, even *power,* that belies the circumstances. Jesus' silence in the face of baseless charges is deaf-ening. Pilate has seen every kind of criminal and heard every imaginable defense. Christ's refusal to utter a word in His own defense only serves to illuminate His innocence.

Pilate struggles to fit this inexplicable set of inconsistencies into a framework that he might relate to. "Art thou the King of the Jews?" he asks. After acknowledg-ing in the affirmative, Jesus goes on to explain that He has come to bear witness to the truth. Pilate is struck by this apparent incongruity and reflexively asks, "What is truth?" (John 18:33, 38). The question is laced with irony. Pilate is no doubt taken aback by Christ's allusion to truth. The idea that some truth could exist, indepen-dent of raw power, is an absurdity. How can Jesus speak of "truth" as though it were some refuge when the *truth* of Roman might holds Him helpless at its mercy?

Pilate, already sensing the situation spiraling out of control, now hears, accord-ing to the Jewish leadership, that Jesus has claimed to be the Son of God. This sud-den revelation casts this mysterious man in a new and even more disturbing light. "Whence art thou?" he blurts out. Pilate is becoming desperate to extricate himself from what he senses is an untenable position. He is practically pleading with Christ to defend Himself, to make some small concession, *anything* that will enable him to let Him off the hook, for "knowest thou not that I have power to crucify thee, and have power to release thee?" Jesus' response leaves Pilate no refuge: "Thou could-est have no power at all against me, except it were given thee from above" (John 19:9–11). Pilate had come to preside over yet another of numerous routine trials. Unwitting and altogether unprepared, he has found himself sitting as judge over *the* pivotal trial of all history. For all he has done to try to dodge his responsibility and even try to pretend he can assume a neutral position, he must decide between empire and the Son of God.

The death of Jesus of Nazareth would leave His small inner band of disciples in a state of bewilderment and trembling fright. Huddled together behind locked doors, they could only try to imagine why this had all gone so terribly wrong. Yes, other purported liberators had come and just as quickly vanished, but they had been so certain it would be different this time, and they had compelling reason to believe so. Jesus had not merely claimed to be the Christ; He had come with power and author-ity to validate His assertions—not just ostentatious displays intended to make Him the object of attention, but real substantive authority always exercised in the most unpretentious humility. Never had a man represented such an easy coupling of power with lowliness so divested of contrivance. What seemed so obviously contradictory in any other looked so naturally and perfectly at home in this man. With an econ-omy of words Jesus revealed wisdom that confounded the most esteemed lawyers. In dramatic demonstrations that ran the gamut, He had revealed His mastery over all aspects of creation. Yet because no self-serving component could ever be exposed in any of this, there was never a doubt that *all* glory was being reflected to the Father.

There could be no doubt that God had finally come to deliver His people, which no power on Earth would be able to resist. Even after Jesus had been arrested, it was inconceivable that the Romans might even be able to keep Him incarcerated. As inexplicable as His apprehension had been, surely Christ must have *allowed* this, using this occasion somehow to further the implementation of His kingdom. Perhaps this was about giving the Master a greater and more dramatic platform from which to announce that the illegitimate empire's days had come to an end, and that the kingdom of God was now ready to take its rightful place. Now, however, with the Master's brutalized body lying disgracefully in the grave, there was no place left for hope, only swirling unanswered questions.

"Why had He not asserted His authority and power in that mockery of a trial? Surely had He desired, He could have summoned heavenly legions that would have set the entire Roman army to flight. Why then did He choose to remain silent?" Could they have been completely wrong about this man? Could everything He told them have been just a series of lies? But could a *false* messiah have done such mighty works as they themselves witnessed? "Still again, if He had truly been *the* long-promised Messiah, the King of the Jews, the great *Deliverer*, how could it have been possible that He should suffer such humiliating and total *defeat* at the hands of a pagan empire?" Their entire point of orientation lay in tatters. The only thing that seemed sure was that the authorities would now be looking for this "usurper's" close conspirators. Soon they would probably share the ignominious fate of their Master.

The first Sunday following Christ's crucifixion, something extraordinary happened—an event that had the power to completely translate a band of despondent, confused, and cowering souls into fearless, triumphant warriors. Of the clever explanations that have been advanced to explain that what the disciples clearly understood to be the resurrection of Jesus from the dead was instead "something *else*," all share a commonality: Not one is able to account for this dramatic about-face on the part of Christ's disciples. Whatever brought about this change was of a magnitude not merely sufficient to "put a positive face on things" with the passing of some time, but to radically *transform,* and within very close proximity to the crucifixion event—in fact, practically *overnight*. Moreover, the transforming event is independent of the disciples' state of mind, any possible predisposition to conspire or ability to manipulate, because it is wholly *unexpected*.

Though resurrection was a well-established concept within Jewish tradition, it was generally held as a one-time future event which would coincide with the Last Judgment. When one looks at the multitude of circumstances surrounding the death of Jesus of Nazareth, it is as though every possible future objection to the literal reality of Christ's resurrection were anticipated. The events converge to force a conclusion whether the investigator likes that conclusion or not. And though Second Temple Christians did not have the benefit of modern science's authoritative pronouncements, it seems reasonable to assume that they nevertheless understood that dead men typically did not come back to life. Nor can their understanding of the word "resurrection" within their own Jewish expectation be blurred into some pagan, disembodied existence. By far the most reasonable explanation is that from very early on, the inner circle and soon the wider following of Christ truly believed that He had bodily resurrected from the dead. The investigator is certainly free to disagree with the disciples' perception. He may think them foolish or unsophisticated in their reasoning, but he cannot deny, from any logical evidentiary standpoint, the *fact* of their belief. (Objections and alternate explanations to the resurrection will be addressed later.)

The New Testament record indicates that Christ was not merely resurrected, as astounding as this was. He was resurrected into a new body which combined elements of both the physical and the transcendent in a way never before manifested. This established not just reconciliation between heaven and Earth, but the compatibility that had existed before the fall. For Christ's disciples, not only is the resurrection something unexpected, but so are the multilayered resonances it generates. Like so many pieces coming together in a grand puzzle, so much of what the Master had said now seemed clear. Christ's words, now viewed against the backdrop of Old Testament prophecy, took on a breathtaking new meaning. The disciples remembered the words of Isaiah spoken several hundred years earlier: "For unto us a child is born, unto us a son is given, and the government shall be upon his shoulder: and his name shall be called Wonderful, Counselor, The mighty God, The everlasting Father, The Prince of Peace" (Isa. 9:6).

They recalled His chastisement for puzzling over such obvious connections. Now, however, the connections seem inescapable. Who but God controls the laws of nature? Who but God knows the very thoughts of men? Who but God can forgive sin? Who but God can raise the dead back to life? The words Jesus had earlier spoken now come into focus: "You *know* where I am going because everything I've done testifies to where I've come *from*. You *know* the way because *I Am* the way. I have lived truth perfectly because I am the *personification* of truth; truth exists because *I* exist—The Eternal Logos, the Divine Word of God, the foundation of all coherence and meaning. I *am* the life, the very Creator of the physical universe and the One with the power and credentials to regenerate fallen humanity" (see esp. John 14:5–14). Jesus had not merely come to deliver a sublime message; He had come to reveal that He *was* the message, the ordering principle of reality.

By having lived a perfect sinless life, by having kept every facet of the Law of Moses faithfully and perfectly, and by having given *Himself* as the perfect sacrifice, Jesus Christ had not only met the demands of justice but legally absorbed into His person separate and distinct Old Testament offices. As the Supreme King, Supreme Judge, Supreme Prophet, Supreme High Priest, and finally Supreme Sacrifice, Jesus Christ lacks no requisite qualification to intercede on behalf of sinners in the heavenly Holy of Holies (as opposed to the earthly type) and to save sinners to the uttermost. All His claims and demonstrations of power, now *validated* by His resurrection, equal an irresistible sum: This was not merely the authentic Messiah; this was and is God in the flesh. Only God possesses "sufficient coin" to meet such exacting demands.

Rather than some revolutionary sect to Jewish tradition, Christ's disciples see themselves as its logical and legal heir. Nothing Messiah has accomplished has come at the expense or the abolishing of the Law, but by His perfect *fulfillment.* "Think not that I am come to destroy the law, or the prophets: I am not come to destroy but to fulfill" (Matt. 5:17). Because He has kept the whole Law flawlessly, He has attained *righteousness* (the whole point of the Law), and His personal righteousness can now be *imparted* to believers. This will be the foundation of the new covenant. In their writings, the apostles and their close associates will draw out the far-reaching implications of this new covenant; all centered in this resurrection-transforming event. The Roman Empire will not mistake the most immediate of these staggering implications—Christians are claiming to worship a risen King whose authority exceeds even that of Caesar.

Very early, Christians come to understand some deeper meanings to the resurrection. Christ did not merely come to transform sinful man but to bring a *reordering* to the whole sin-marred creation. The Judeo-Christian cosmogony, fleshed out by the life, death, and resurrection of Jesus Christ, stands in bold relief against the pagan backdrop. Rather than borrowing upon pagan themes, it consciously, deliberately, and provocatively sets out to validate the material world but within a balanced perspective. Intrinsically tied into this radical departure is the idea that validation of the material is validation of God Himself—not just His existence, but His very character. Though evil is evident, this has been externally introduced into the universe (by humanity's rebellion) and is not sewn into its fabric. And though sin-marred, the material is no less real than the heavenly abode of God. Because evil need not be explained nor pretended away, it can be dealt with forthrightly. God's character, His holiness, His integrity, His omnipotence, and His justice are each inescapably tied into evil's remedy—reversing the curse of sin and restoring the original pristine state where evil can never again intrude. Christ's resurrection is the down payment on this ultimate reordering—not merely to snatch some partial victory out of death's jaws, to achieve a diplomatic compromise, but to totally *defeat* it in its every aspect.

Resurrection is a concept that could not have been extracted from the pagan world. It is essentially about "re-creation," and thus completely dependent upon the overarching concept of creation *ex nihilo*. Reincarnation, often forwarded as a close kin to resurrection, is fundamentally different in that it springs from the world-view of a self-contained, self-existent universe (pantheism) where, by definition, it is not possible to create, only to extend or spread the "life essence." Moreover, reincarnation is the antithesis of resurrection, in that death is never overcome but perpetuated. All forms of paganism deny resurrection because it is an affirmation of creation, which must in turn point to a separate *Creator.* The admission of a Creator implies the creation to be of a fundamentally different essence *from* and entirely subject *to* the Creator. Resurrection becomes, ultimately, the clearest affirmation of God's concrete existence, His absolute sovereignty, and His intimate *personal* involvement with His creation.

The rapid spread of Christianity coincided with the collapse of the Roman Empire. Yet it was not the initiative of Christians per se that set this event in motion nearly so much as Rome's response. The usual remedy to any threat was to answer with force. For some inexplicable reason, things did not follow the usual script. Persecution only emboldened Christians to become more vocal in their allegiance to Christ, to insist that He alone was *Kyrios*. Instead of bringing this little sect to a crashing halt, the shedding of martyrs' blood captured the imagination of much of the pagan world. "What could possibly possess a man or woman to willingly die for a religious belief? Was there really a transcendent truth, one not subject to the glory and might of the all-powerful Roman Empire?" Rome faced the unthinkable—a threat against which all its power was useless. Multitudes, inspired by Christians refusal to denounce their Lord even when it meant ruthless death, abandoned the empire for something even it could not offer—eternal life.

Yet this promise of new life *had* to be of a character that was understood to be radically different and qualitatively superior to any previous view—something that finally answered that most burning hunger in man. Would any have challenged the might of the Roman Empire for a new variation on the assortment of old pagan standard disembodied "afterlife" themes?

CHAPTER 5

POWER-HUNGRY MISOGYNISTS OR COURAGEOUS CHRISTIAN SOLDIERS?

In the first four centuries or so following the establishment of the church, important battles were fought that would solidify key doctrinal positions. In other words, the actual implications of Christ's life and teachings were drawn out, sometimes through passionate debate. This period, known as the era of the early Church Fathers, frequently comes under fire. The Church Fathers are themselves caricatured individually, and collectively forced into a monolithic template, as part of those rascally "literalists" Freke and Gandy love to disparage. With their usual low regard for logic, they size up the significance of the in-breaking kingdom of heaven: "Once martyrs were guaranteed a place in Heaven, Literalist Christianity became a mass-suicide cult, with adherents actively seeking death. It is interesting, however, that two of the most vocal exponents of martyrdom, Irenaeus and Tertullian, managed to avoid this fate themselves. Funny how it is always the foot soldiers of a movement from whom martyrdom is required, not the leaders who are urging others on to this glorious sacrifice."[1]

A "mass suicide cult"? Even for Freke and Gandy, this is crass. Salvation was never *contingent* upon martyrdom. Choosing to die where no threat of compulsion was present was clearly a violation of Christian principles. Heaven was already purchased by Christ's sacrifice, and no doctrine exists anywhere in the early church that dying for the Savior *per se* played any part in individual salvation. It is *because* life was so precious that the choice was so agonizing. Death was the hated enemy Christ had come to defeat. To reject the Savior, however, was understood to forfeit something much more precious than the present life. And it is for this reason that some Christians, faced with no other alternative, chose death. Martyrdom was never reduced to some perverse celebration of death but was the highest affirmation

of faith, not just in a new spiritual life in Christ but in His promise of victory ultimately over *physical death*.

But what of these Church Fathers who are so easily and often maligned? Is it
true they were power-seeking, self-serving opportunists perfectly willing to send
their congregations into martyrdom but unwilling themselves to make the supreme
sacrifice? Despite the usual assumption, the Church Fathers cannot be cast into a
standard mold. Their personalities turn out to be as widely diverse as the differing
circumstances each was born into, and the peculiar challenges that shaped the views
each of them stressed. A summary of the lives of those more influential in shaping
orthodoxy may be helpful.

Ignatius of Antioch, in his seven letters (written about AD 115) to the churches
around Asia Minor, put great emphasis on the grace that had come through Jesus
Christ. This was at a time when Jewish influences were seeking to transform Christianity into just another Jewish sect, where law-keeping was essential to any covenant relationship with God.[2] But Ignatius also resisted Greek influences with their
strong allegorical tendencies, which saw the Christ's divinity stressed at the expense
of His humanity. In the latter, Ignatius found himself opposing Docetism, probably
the earliest form of gnosticism. Docetism denied that Jesus had some in the flesh.
His physical appearance was a mysterious projection.

Born about AD 110, Justin Martyr's journey to Christianity by way of Greek
Stoicism and Platonism would become evident in the philosophical approach he
took to understanding the Scriptures. Without flinching, Justin challenged the
leading pagan intellectuals of his day, demonstrating that only Christianity, cast
within its Judaic context, could sufficiently explain the nagging riddles ancients
had wrestled with from time's opening curtain. Jesus as the divine *Logos* could alone
bridge the gap between man and the infinite, immanent (yet transcendent) God.
Justin's premise was that the Greeks had dimly grasped some elements of truth, but
that only Christianity could close the loop.[3]

Irenaeus of Lyons (b. AD 130) emphasized the unbroken chain the orthodox
position could trace back to the apostles, and thus to the direct teachings of Christ
Himself. Exotic stories of Jesus, no matter how appealing, lacked this fundamental
connection. Under men like Irenaeus, orthodoxy largely took shape as a way of
distinguishing the legitimate from the fanciful. Through the force of his writings,
persistently and painstakingly pointing out the inconsistencies, self-serving handling of Scripture, and internal incoherence, gnosticism (the primary challenge to
the apostolic tradition in his day) was largely relegated to the margins, never to seriously compete again.[4] Irenaeus also emphasized the centrality of Christ in the Old
and New Testaments. His main thrust—Christ was no incidental character, but the
sum of the whole Bible story.

Tertullian (b. AD 160), the son of a Roman centurion, put the conflict between orthodoxy and heretics in terms of ownership. Without apostolic authority, late-comers preaching a new gospel had no legal right even to participate in discussions concerning doctrinal truth. Tertullian was as tenacious in his criticism as he was incisive in his arguments. He was also the first to describe God as a "Trinity."[5]

Origen of Alexandria (b. AD 186) was one of the most prolific writers of the early Christian era. Among his works is an eight-book set thoroughly and master-fully refuting the fallacious arguments of Celsus, probably the most famous pagan intellectual of the second century.

Athanasius (b. AD 300) brought the full weight of his scholarship to bear against Arius and the doctrine that Jesus (though divine) was a created being and thus inferior to the *eternal essence* of God the Father. Though this was a new view of Christ that had never been held within the Church, it is a position that was now gaining a sizable amount of support within orthodoxy, especially in Alexandria. For Athanasius, it came down to this: If either Christ's full humanity *or* full divinity were denied, then He lacked requisite qualification to effect salvation.

When the Council of Nicaea convened in AD 325 to consider a question that virtually all had assumed was long settled (the nature of the Savior) the position of Athanasius and his mentor, Alexander, easily prevailed. This by no means, however, marked the end of Arianism. Arius curried favor with the Emperor Constantine, and through political intrigue gained a plurality of bishops supporting his view. Arianism, through a sort of end-run, became the new orthodoxy. Constantius, who assumed the throne after Constantine's death, threw his full support behind the new position and made life hellacious for Athanasius, banishing him to exile several times and generally terrorizing his congregation. In the face of constant impe-rial intimidation, Athanasius wrote one polemic after another against this heresy. Though Athanasius was certainly not alone in this stand against Arianism, had he faltered as point man for the opposition, the momentum of this view might have been too formidable to overcome.[6]

John Chrysostom (b. AD 350) came from a wealthy home. John lived at a time when the two great theological schools of thought were engaged in serious debate about the proper approach to interpreting Scripture. The Alexandria school favored the allegorical approach, heavily influenced by the Greek treatment of mythology—a methodology that would come to be summed up as "spiritualizing the text." The Antiochene school stressed the historical literal approach as founda-tional to preserving the absolute truth of God's Word. Not that the latter eschewed the spiritual content of Scripture, but spiritual meanings, it was held, must flow naturally and unambiguously from the literal meaning which, in turn, was depen-dent upon specific historic events.

Though John was born into wealth, as a young man he turned his back on worldly comfort to pursue a life of asceticism in the mountains surrounding Antioch. Asceticism was the natural choice for many who, no longer sobered by the constant threat of persecution (the 313 Edict of Milan now in force), nevertheless desired that intense environment which brought Jesus Christ into sharp and intimate focus. The pursuit of ascetic life is something that flies directly in the face of claims that the "literalists" were all about an aggressive and ruthless power grab. At the heart of asceticism was self-surrender, self-*denial*, retreat from the material to more fully embrace the spiritual. Ascetics not only had few worldly possessions but, due to the extreme conditions to which they were exposed, often suffered from poor health. As this was in a day when no cameras, press agents, nor press corps were available to craft some useful image, there was nothing in this rigorous life that lent itself to political ambitions.

So it was that John Chrysostom, health failing after several years of this unforgiving grind, reluctantly left the monastic life to find himself eventually embroiled in one of the great confrontations of his day, the two great schools of theology locked in bitter struggle. The discipline and dedication nurtured in his mountaintop years would serve him well. As with his predecessor, Athanasius, he refused to waver on an issue that held such far-reaching implications. John's skillful oratory and unchallenged command of Scriptures (from the years spent in constant contemplative study) would eventually bring him to the position of bishop of Constantinople, a position he never sought. Like Athanasius, John also found himself having to dodge the fiery darts of political enemies bent on unhealthy compromise. Though finally banished to live out his last days in the mountains of his youth, his unending fight to preserve the historic foundation of the faith would prove successful.[7]

Augustine of Hippo (b. 354) emerges as perhaps the least likely of all church fathers. Though raised in a Christian home, Augustine became contemptuous of this religion while still in his youth. By his own admission, he gave himself to every sexual satiation that appealed to his lusts. A gnawing emptiness would propel him into philosophy. Yet substantive answers continued to elude him. Gifted in oratory, Augustine doggedly ascended the social ladder in hopes of finding that elusive sense of fulfillment. It was during his social climb that he again exposed himself to the Scriptures, this time through the dynamic preaching of Ambrose. Certain that his intellectual pursuit had already placed him far beyond any attraction to the Christian message *per se*, Augustine nevertheless admired Ambrose's skillful handling of the Scriptures and thought it useful to study his techniques.

After attending several services, Augustine found a strange thing happening. The original attraction to style was being replaced with an attraction to content. Augustine was coming to see that his youthful dismissal of Christianity had resulted from seriously flawed presumptions. It had not been Christianity failing to hold up under serious scrutiny, but a failure on the part of Augustine to appreciate the multiple levels of meaning packed into each Bible passage. Moreover, in his youth, he had looked at Christianity very narrowly, unaware of the far larger context in which it lay. Augustine was coming to see that the quest for answers which had driven him to a profligate lifestyle, philosophy, and a craving for social acceptance, had come full circle in the least expected solution of all. To his utter amazement, *only* Christianity could answer the hard questions and satisfy the deep hunger.

Augustine's special call would be to confront the two extreme views seeking inroads in his day. Pelagianism was based on the premise that men could choose to live righteously thus making Christ's sacrifice superfluous. Salvation was thus something that could be achieved through human effort alone. Donatism also took a dangerous position. Though recognizing Christ's essentiality, those of this persuasion believed salvation was afforded only to those most conspicuous in personal righteousness—a piety strictly enforced by an unyielding legalism. Augustine argued these were essentially two sides of the same coin—elevating self-righteousness to an undeserved status while seriously diminishing the central element of the gospel, God's grace. Where were either of these extremes consistent with the liberty to which Christ had called His people?[8]

In concluding this summary, there are a few important points worth emphasizing. If the early Church Fathers had sought to invent a self-serving religion that gave them political leverage, they would not have introduced serious confrontations over the nature of their supposed founder. They would not have invented a founder whose essential nature was so enigmatic as to resist simple explanation or definition. This complexity would result in heated debates and sometimes deep division. Yet in each of these key battles that threatened to split the apostolic church, Providence always supplied that specially qualified person, usually out of the most unpredictable circumstances, to steady or right the ship. In numerous cases, this special person was in the position of having to *oppose* the power structure, including the imperial throne itself.

It is also clear that a considerable divergence of opinion existed *within* the community of orthodoxy (the literalists or traditionalists). Settled positions, especially those most complex in nature, came about through a balancing of divergent views. But even such arguments, for all the friction and passion they engendered, still took place within confines that were distinctly orthodox. It was this very fact that allowed eventual compromise.

Thus, we see two important things happening during this approximate four-hundred-year period. Heated disagreements among competing factions either filtered out and refined or eventually gave way to agreeable doctrinal positions. In the latter case, though some compromise was necessary, neither side was forced to surrender that which was considered non-negotiable if Scripture was to retain supremacy. The other thing was heated disputes against factions with which no one within the considerable umbrella of orthodoxy could compromise without doing irreparable harm to Scripture and, especially, the person and mission of Christ.

Though there is much for which to commend the Church Fathers, it would be dishonest to deny those black marks that are part of the record. Because Christianity was under constant assault, first through physical persecution and then through any number of sources seeking to discredit it, and because in these early stages new converts were most susceptible to the deliberate confusion fostered by radical groups appropriating the name of Jesus, Christian leaders tended toward the reactionary side. No matter how well-intentioned or otherwise devoted to the cause of Christ, these were all flawed men, some more so than others. For instance, Tertullian became very legalistic in later life, prescribing in detail outward appearances that constituted proper worship. John Chrysostom would play a prominent role in Christian anti-Semitism. Origen finally wandered out into the tall weeds and effectively lost contact with historic grounding, pursuing views that tended increasingly toward the speculative—a sad tarnishing of an otherwise impeccable legacy of selfless service. The flaws of the Church Fathers loom so conspicuously because they are so loudly contrasted against what are otherwise lives of inspiring courage and untiring devotion to God and their congregations under relentless opposition.

As to the claim of the Church Fathers' willingness to throw the rank-and-file into the martyrdom-threshing machine while exempting themselves, here are the facts: Ignatius was martyred. Justin Martyr was beheaded. Though it is uncertain, there is a tradition Irenaeus was martyred. It is certain his predecessor Pothinus (as bishop of Lyons) was, as well as Irenaeus' spiritual mentor, Polycarp. Origen finally died from protracted tortures to which he was subjected in prison; his father was martyred while Origen was in his teens. John Chrysostom eventually succumbed to the grueling conditions of an imperially forced march.

Though they had their moments of what we today are quick to label intolerance, on balance the Church Fathers—rather than the ruthless tyrants *or* spiritual simpletons often portrayed by critics—were thoughtful, deliberate, and self-sacrificial. And though some of the extremes are deplorable, their contributions would far outweigh the debits.

*   *   *

Amidst the fuller revelation Christ's coming brought was a new insight into the nature of God. Though Christ had done or said nothing to challenge the monotheistic concept of the God of the Jews, a deeper unexpected meaning had arisen *within* monotheism. There was indeed the one God but within this Godhead were three distinct persons. Yet these three persons were each God—God the Father, God the Word (come in the flesh as Jesus Christ), and God the Holy Spirit. On the face of it, this looked like another pagan formulation of polytheism. Yet there were definite implications that set this at odds with any pagan view. To begin with, these three persons existed from eternity in perfect equality and perfect agreement, as evidenced by Christ's complete obedience to the Father's will, even unto death. If any possibility of dissension existed between these divine persons, surely this would have been pushed to the breaking point by the horror of crucifixion.

Even though this mysterious relationship defied any simple explanation, the early Christian community, because of the profound unity of purpose and perfect integrity evident, never sought to cast this relationship outside of Jewish monotheism. Indeed, YHWH had provided some insight into the complex nature of multiplicity existing within unity as far back as the book of Genesis. "Therefore shall a man leave his father and his mother, and shall cleave unto his wife: and they shall be one flesh" (Gen. 2:24). When a man and a woman enter into the institution of marriage, they assume a unity so intricate and intimate that it carries the potential to actually bring a new life into existence. Though marriage (especially in its idealized form) obviously represents a special kind of bond where two hearts (and individual goals) are understood to mesh into one, there remain two distinct individuals even within the most inspiring examples. And though both husband and wife are each "married," it is understood there is but one "marriage." If we allow that the concept of marriage of mere human beings has the potential to defy ordinary mathematical logic, then is it incomprehensible that a *perfect* unity could exist among three divine persons whom are utterly indivisible in terms of essence, eternality, purpose, and agreement?

In any case, the existence of three persons in one God will give a new clarity to reality. Specifically, the problem of "the one and the many" is finally addressed. That is, up to this point humanity has had to make a choice between two *apparent* contradictions. As far as the eye can see, there is clear division of objects, ranging from stars to people. But it also seems intuitive (indeed, undeniable when considering, for instance, the concept of language) that there is an underlying unity, a sense of connectedness that holds all things together. If there really is a universal oneness, however, then the appearance of multiplicity must ultimately be false. On the other hand, if the appearance of division is real, if human beings are truly distinct personalities whose individuality is not eventually merged into some amorphous ether, then the idea of ultimate oneness/connectedness must be abandoned. The internal incoherence of either position makes it impossible to sustain intrinsic human value.

With Christianity's deeper insight into the nature of God—that is, multiplicity existing *within* perfect union—both the one *and* the many were now validated and without contradiction. There *appeared* to be division and there *seemed* to be an underlying unity, because this was intrinsic to reality's Author. No longer would the world need to be regarded as a hopelessly unknowable and frightening set of conflicting realities. Because it was the purposeful creation of an immutable God who had revealed Himself through the progressive stages of His unfolding plan and now most vividly *in the flesh*, certain reasonable assumptions could be made. Because God had never demonstrated any arbitrary characteristics in His dealings with mankind, the physical laws He had created to govern the material universe must likewise be predictable. With the emergence of this new worldview, the "cosmos" is no longer divine—and by extension, neither physical phenomenon nor mortal man is to be worshipped. Pantheism gives way to transcendent monotheism, and with the concept of *creation*, suddenly the universe becomes ordered, uniform, coherent, and intelligible. The mysteries of the universe no longer need be "divined" but are now open to *discovery*. This new understanding will provide the basis for the modern scientific method.

CHAPTER 6

THE GOD-MAN WHO
REVOLUTIONIZED THE WORLD

If the horrific assassination of President Kennedy, abruptly ending that short mythical romance known as "Camelot," is seen by the Left as the great American tragedy of modern times, then the disintegration of the Roman Empire, for secular historians, may be the universal tragedy of the ages. The period following is often and pejoratively referred to as the "Dark Ages." This appellation conveys very powerful symbolism of something that far exceeds the simple passing of one historic period into another. "Dark Ages" portrays a stark reality, a vacuum of civilizing principles in the wake of a collapsing universe. It was unarguably a dark time for the forces of paganism insofar as they had lost their hegemony and were pushed back to the margins of civilization. But was it truly a dark time for *humanity*? Is it possible that under the dark veil modern historians have superimposed over this period, there might lie remarkable evidence not of a collapsing but a *reordered* universe?

If Jesus of Nazareth truly were the unique Son of God, and His life, death, and resurrection faithfully represented in the four gospels, then some of the most compelling evidence for this should be seen in the effect it would have on the civilized world. We should expect to see a radical world transformation, separating the new order from the old. In fact, this is what we do see. To begin with, no longer enslaved by primal instincts, man (not just an elite class of philosophers) was now able to reach for a higher, ennobling, examined life. This, combined with the new idea that man had intrinsic value wholly apart from any assigned rank, would profoundly revolutionize government, economics, education, the arts, and science, as well as introduce entirely new concepts to the world such as hospitals and charitable giving.

As an outward effect, the first impact Christianity would manifest was as a braking force on institutions that had been regular features of the pagan world—abortion, infanticide, and euthanasia. Under Christianity, no human life was considered expendable. Christians gave themselves to the care of the impoverished and downtrodden, regardless of religious affinities. The long-held tendency to reduce sexuality to hedonistic eroticism (incest, prostitution, homosexuality, marital infidelity, bestiality, etc.) had no place in the new, valued view of mankind. Following on the teachings of Jesus Christ, the status of women would begin to dramatically change. With the advent of Christianity, womanhood became something to be honored and cherished. From this commitment to affirming the sanctity of life would evolve the concept of human rights.

Freedom from the enslaving effect of sin would translate to a hunger for civil liberties as well. Yet this new optimistic view of man, made in the very image of the Creator, set on an odyssey of discovery and reunification with his Maker, would be counterbalanced by the doctrine of original sin. Yes, within man was the potential to reflect the brilliance of God's glory, leading to expressions of beauty never known. On the other hand, left to his own devices and divorced from Christ's regenerating influence, man was capable of the most depraved and ruthless behavior. The dual optimistic and suspicious view of man recognized a need for a structure that offered optimum creative human expression, coupled with well-delineated restraints on *all* forms of power. None of this is to suggest that this structure materialized overnight, but even in embryonic stages, this represented an astounding break with the past.

The concept of covenant, dating all the way back to YHWH's original pact with Abraham but restricted to the Jews, now took on a new significance. God had now inaugurated a new covenant with all mankind, activated by faith in the death and resurrection of Christ. This sacred enjoining of two parties would soon become the centerpiece of legal safeguards. The violation of this agreement by either party rendered the covenant void. Thus were sown the first seeds of "social contract." Yes, other lengthy documents had been drawn up in antiquity for legal redress. But while there was a show of law, the common folk understood that they lived and breathed at the pleasure of the king. The elaborate concoction of statutes notwithstanding, they were living under a system not of inclusive law but of exclusive will.

Social contract, however, would be a bold departure from all previous thought. Because all men were created in God's image, all were, regardless of pedigree, ultimately equal in value. No one individual should be entitled to greater or fewer protections. So long as the king was permitted to be the final judge of what was lawful, no subject truly enjoyed any such thing as "rights" and "law," was but another tool by which governments exercised tyranny over the masses. In addition, Christians had a working model to consult in their lineal predecessors, the Jews. Though Israel had been under monarchies for much of her history, she had nevertheless demonstrated a remarkable division of powers in the administration of her affairs. Though subject to king, the Jewish priesthood was entrusted with the Law with which kings were bound to comply. Prophets, though subject to both, often sternly rebuked king *and* priesthood when so commanded by YHWH.

With the breakup of the Roman Empire, central government gave way to smaller enclaves of authority in the eighth century, in a social system known as feudalism. From the usual post-enlightenment perspective, feudalism is a term that carries a very negative undertone. The typical imagery is of the robber baron and his band of armed retainers exploiting peasant farmers who worked the land for bare subsistence. While there were negative features within this social arrangement, the larger picture is frequently ignored. For centuries, the outlying lands of the old empire had been subject to various groups of marauders. With no longer any imperial army of consequence to fend off these attacks, individual defense systems were devised. Wealthy lords recognized that the sensible thing was to sacrifice a portion of their wealth (usually in the form of land or land usage) to vassals in exchange for protection. With each party equally vested, complex contracts detailing specific rights and duties between lord and vassal were drawn up. These contracts would grow exceedingly complex, eventually incorporating such features as consent to taxation and definite checks on potential abuses.[1]

As will always be the case with any social system, there existed clear examples of corruption. Most notorious perhaps were the sordid deals that involved the Catholic Church. Secular lords would use their influence to secure ecclesiastical offices for abbots and bishops. These "men of faith" would in turn supply services that included military support. While it is true that the Catholic Church did adopt some perverse practices over time, there was a transcendent and *internal* mechanism operating whose pressure would finally end such practices; eventually manifesting in the Protestant Reformation. If it is fair to indict the Catholic Church for its abuses, then it is proper to give due credit for its central role in promoting representative institutions.

The feudal system, with the powerful backing of the Catholic Church, established a dispersion or decentralization of power—resulting in a promotion of individual rights, leading eventually to the Magna Carta of 1215. Returning home from a failed military campaign, King John of England sought to recoup his losses through massive taxes and inheritance duties imposed on feudal barons. John's campaign had already been largely conducted under public protest, due to a callous disregard for common law. John's punitive measures, piled on top of his military blunders, represented the highest contempt for any standard of justice. Several barons would meet with John at Runnymede, presenting the king with a document known as the Articles of the Barons. The king, faced with the potential of a massive uprising by those upon whom he was most dependent, agreed to its terms. This document would provide the direct basis for the Magna Carta. The Catholic Church would take the lead in posting this document and frequently reading it to the faithful. *Lex Regia* (the king is the law speaking), undisputed canon in centuries past, had now been fully repudiated.

Though thoroughly saturated in feudal law and custom, the Magna Carta is unmistakably the lineal predecessor of and a kindred spirit with the Declaration of Independence and the US Constitution. Consider: included in the Magna Carta were guarantees for all freemen against arbitrary disregard of common law (those accepted traditions and customs built up through centuries of medieval experience), the right to be judged by a jury of one's peers, tax by consent, and guarantees of religious freedom. The overriding theme of the document: men should be under law instead of under will.

The reign of Edward I, near the end of the thirteenth century, would further the cause of representative government. It was becoming clear the king's best interests could only be served insofar as justice was dispensed with equity. To this end, the king called together assemblies of knights, burgesses, and representatives of lower clergy to negotiate with the "community of the realm" (as the concept of inclusiveness was coming to be known) over, among other issues, consent to taxation. These assemblies served as a prototype Parliament. Any fair assessment of history must concede that modern constitutionalism's roots are firmly set in that period which (according to standard progressive indoctrination) is supposed to be a blight on the road to civil liberties. Moreover, constitutionalism is not some deliberate *reaction* to, nor even an unrelated parallel development, but it is the natural outworking of religious assumptions that we are today told are the most enslaving in all history. There is nothing anywhere to be found in the universe of pagan assumptions that could have nurtured ideas of intrinsic human value, sanctity of life, nor individual human freedom. To the contrary, all these ideas were (and remain) anathema within the pagan worldview.

The freedom revolution of the Middle Ages was centered on one specific concept: private property. The concept had, of course, existed loosely in the Greek world and in a more advanced form under Roman rule. We recall, however, that under all pagan forms of statecraft, all men were assuredly not created equal. Approximately half of the population of the empire was made up of slaves. A slave had no rights and was completely at the mercy of his master.

In Rome, as with virtually all ancient regimes, a social tier system was a given. To the extent "rights" existed at all, these were relative to one's social class. Property rights to individuals could only be granted by the state, where one did not so much own as possess by conditional permission. The lesson medieval constitutionalists could take from this was self-evident. Without individual private ownership (a sacred zone free from state intrusion), freedom was a chimera. Beyond this, protection of property rights had to apply to all equally. The rights of the holder of a very small tract of land had to be as secure as the rights of the holder of thousands of acres. Anything less, and the avenue to prosperity (for all) was subject to rescission by the state. Thus, the most esteemed landowner had a definite stake in preserving property rights of the most modestly endowed of his fellows, and vice versa.

During the feudal period, courts that were convened to decide property disputes were second in importance only to criminal cases. Constitutionalism, social contract, and common law were all converging in the direction of ownership rights.[2] The emerging strength of common law was its own emergence over time—a steady accretion of lessons learned from actual judicial decisions. Common law was further strengthened by its respect for precedent balanced nevertheless against a willingness to allow for measured adjustments as new facets within complex cases were uncovered. In contrast to the previous ingenious divination of law, law was becoming a process of *discovery*.[3] Personal human dignity (personhood) was most coming to the fore in common law, and the essence which most set it apart from Roman property rights.

Where in the ancient world might medieval constitutionalists have derived the notion that possession of individual property was not just a conferred privilege of the few but a *sacred right* of all, no matter how grand or modest their treasure? Again, the answer was to be found only within the pages of the Bible. The Commandments specifically forbade the theft of property. Since it is not possible to steal what is communally shared, these commandments tacitly recognized and *sanctioned* private ownership. Many of Christ's parables had featured private property (often money) as a main theme.

Private property, as freedom proponents were coming to see, was the most powerful check on state encroachment. The ability of private citizens to enter into mutual agreements, buying and selling not according to the interest of the state but their own, would unleash the power of the free-market. The free market, composed of ever-branching spontaneous non-coerced interactions spurred fierce competition to provide an ever-expanding range of better and more affordable goods and services. This represented the antithesis of the state's normal planning impulse and would turn the usual situation topsy-turvy. The state's resources (gained from taxation) would be directly dependent upon the success of its citizens. This was a win-win situation, where both citizen and state stood to profit. In the pagan world, prosperity for either had usually come at the expense of the other. A new state-to-citizen relationship had developed. The state was responsible to provide its citizens a zone of protection and relative safety, in exchange for its cut on all profits.

Law was sacred and just only to the extent that rights of private ownership were secure. *This* was the guarantee that one was truly free to pursue and to attain the rewards his own God-given abilities and work ethic were capable of yielding. This is the kind of freedom that spoke directly to the human spirit, that put the ordinary citizen in the best possible position of imitating the Creator—of engaging in individual *creativity*—constantly looking for novel ways to express the myriad texture of life. The ripple effect could scarcely be measured. Among the expanding ramifications, private ownership meant one had a real stake in the consequences of his choices. Their effect could no longer be diffused among limitless communal holders, where it was effectively impossible to reward virtue or single out blame. The seeds of personal responsibility within the wider community had been sown.

Yet another unforeseen benefit of private ownership was the generation of wealth. Old assumptions were giving way to a new understanding. Wealth was not a static but a dynamic quantity. It was something that could both be expanded and contracted in strict proportion to *productivity*. This, the spirit of innovation, let loose by the freedom revolution, was ever seeking out new and better ways of fine tuning. The generation of wealth would lead to something that only the most privileged classes in antiquity had enjoyed—leisure. Leisure would have much more value than mere respite from one's labors. Without this crucial ingredient, the explosion of discovery, the quest to probe the deepest pathways of the human condition, and the desire to capture in art the glory of God would have been far less likely. Blocks of time (open to an expanding class) for quiet introspection, for indulging curiosity, for *communing* with the Spirit of God, were as foreign to the ancient world as intrinsic human value. And even if not often directly producing key innovators, this new class would now sponsor the best and the brightest from the less privileged, whose special contributions would otherwise have never been brought to the world.

In its classical definition, art has been represented as that which inspires to reach for something higher, greater, something that provokes thought, causing one to look past the mundane, whether straining to see beyond the horizon or looking deep within in reflective examination. Perhaps the truest test of art could be summed up in its timelessness—its ability to reach across any age and communicate a life-affirming grace and beauty.

During the Middle Ages, artists, inspired by the life and indescribable sacrifice of Jesus Christ, devoted themselves to expressing God's magnanimity on canvas or, in the case of Michelangelo, on the ceiling and walls of the Sistine Chapel. Rembrandt, Raphael, and da Vinci not only gave glory to the God of heaven but sought to expose the depths and complexity of the human soul, a little-explored concept within paganism. Yet great works in stone and glass were constructed as well, in the form of majestic cathedrals reaching heavenward to touch the splendor of God. In literature, Shakespeare's great tragedies (*Hamlet*, *Othello*, *King Lear*, and *Macbeth*) employed psychological subtlety to explore the resonances of human flaws, woven in and around exceedingly complex plots, themselves composed of various intricate subplots. The hues on his canvas were comprised of a rich poetic and emotional language that achieved a depth of expression possibly never rivaled outside of the Bible. The tension that animated Shakespeare's tragedies would not have existed if not for the backdrop of Christian morality. Other great writers unashamedly influenced by Christian themes were John Milton, John Bunyan, and Charles Dickens, with a frequent and recurring thread—self-sacrifice and an appeal to Christian conscience.

In the world of music, the church's influence was even more direct. A Benedictine monk, Guido of Arezzo, was the originator of modern musical notation. D. James Kennedy, in writing of Guido, "underscore[s] three main developments: 1) With the notation of music it became possible to compose, and music could exist in itself outside of the performance! It could be written down and taught from a score. 2) Order, rules and logic—i.e., music theory—followed from notations. 3) Polyphony (more than one melody playing at the same time) developed. So also did harmony."[4] Bach, an orthodox Lutheran, is almost universally considered the father of classical music. An enthusiastic promoter of Christianity who frequently and publicly affirmed Christ as his source, Bach would influence great musical artists such as Beethoven, Mendelssohn, Mozart, Brahms, and others. Today, sadly, that influence is waning.

Perhaps most to benefit from leisure would be the noble enterprise of science. Science, under Christendom, went hand in hand with theology. Where theology sought to uncover a more perfect knowledge of the Creator in His written word, science explored a deeper insight into God through His created order. The lineup of famous scientists who made this their starting point puts the lie to the seldom-questioned adage that "science" and "theology" were always separate spheres in violent conflict. Consider just a few of these names (*founders*, by the way, of the listed branches): Louis Pasteur (bacteriology), Gregor Mendel (genetics), Johannes Kepler (celestial mechanics), Isaac Newton (calculus, dynamics), Carolus Linnaeus (taxonomy), Joseph Lister (antiseptic surgery), Georges Cuvier (comparative anatomy), and Michael Faraday (electromagnetics).

By releasing humanity from the bondage of sin—at least those considerable segments yielding to His regenerating power—Christ had reanimated the God-breathed human spirit, tethered now to a changeless standard, free to explore the unknown possibilities and facets of creation as far as an inspired imagination could take it.

CHAPTER 7

RACISM AND SLAVERY

Today, rather than acknowledging the tremendous contributions of that distinctive culture which directly descended from the Christian worldview, Western thought is singled out as the source of slavery, racism, and practically every evil that currently exists in the world. Admittedly, the charge of racism does bear some validity. Few realize, however, that the term "racism," as it originated and evolved in Western Europe, had little relationship to vitriolic connotations now associated with the word. As Dinesh D'Souza shows in his book *The End of Racism*, racism emerged about the fifteenth century and sprang naturally from the remarkable advances the Western world exhibited in government, economics, philosophy, religion, and technology. Due to unprecedented levels of world exploration, all these advances coincided with an emerging body of knowledge of cultures from all over the world. To the typical informed Westerner, it was impossible to overlook the huge chasm that separated Western culture from all others. Racism was simply a way of trying to account in scientific terms for these apparent disparities. Since all cultures did not appear to be equal, it logically followed that all *races* could not be. Biology, so it seemed, had predestined some races for greatness, some for mediocrity, and some for perpetual cultural stagnation. Formulated as a theory of biological *superiority*, racism contained no component of fear and thus no requisite stimulus for promoting hatred of those whom were thought to be incapable of posing a serious threat.

These were not ideas that grew out of isolated enclaves of the superstitious and irrational; these were ideas that were advanced in the universities and higher institutions, representing the state of the art in progressive thinking. In fact, few serious liberals today would have trouble recognizing the names of such revered icons of the Enlightenment period as Hume, Voltaire, Kant, and Hegel, all esteemed apologists for the emerging racist thought of their day. In D'Souza's words, racism did not originate "in ignorance and fear but as part of an enlightened enterprise of intellectual discovery."[1]

Unfortunately, the true underpinnings and nature of racism have become so distorted that it has become nearly impossible to separate the institution of racism from the institution of slavery. For most today, the two are essentially one and the same. Yet, the two actually have no necessary relationship. Slavery, unlike racism, did *not* originate with Western civilization and does not have a relatively recent beginning. From all available evidence, slavery has existed from time immemorial in every age, geographic region, and culture except about the last 200 years, where it was *first* recognized as an immoral institution *by* Western culture, and *then* eradicated. Slavery was not only practiced by all cultures but was almost universally regarded as the unquestioned *right* of victor over vanquished. Moreover, nowhere can it be shown that slavery in the ancient world divided up over questions of race.

On the relatively rare occasions where the institution of slavery was philosophically in dispute, the question was far more likely over *who* fit subjects for slavery were than whether the *institution* was in and of itself proper. Slavery was understood to be such a natural consequence of war that in many cases battles were preempted if "underdog" nations could achieve favorable terms of surrender. Such nations, dubious of battle, would customarily send out envoys instructed to sue for peace, seeking to negotiate the best possible conditions of servitude. Not all slavery was coerced. Some voluntarily sold *themselves* into slavery to pay off debts; biblical references to slavery generally featured this type of indentured servitude.

Nevertheless, today's standard revisionist treatment of history leaves the impression that slavery is, for all practical purposes, the invention of Western civilization. Common in all such revisionist history is an open antipathy toward nearly all ideals peculiarly Western. From Columbus' first "invasion" of the Americas to the African slave trade, white Europeans have been the despoilers of pristine nature and a scourge of violence and racial oppression. Yet the America that Columbus encountered was far removed from the Edenic setting that has largely been promulgated. Though some groups were friendly and hospitable, other native tribes exhibited features of brutality that were beyond anything the European visitors had ever before seen or imagined. Common among these practices were cannibalism and human sacrifice, carried out in vivid grotesque horror. "Cannibalism was prevalent among the Guarani, Iroquois, Caribs, and several other tribes. Moreover, the Aztecs of Mexico and the Incas of South America performed elaborate rites of human sacrifice, in which thousands of captive Indians were ritually murdered, so that their altars were drenched in blood, bones were strewn everywhere. . . . The law of the Incas provided for punishment for parents and others who displayed grief during human sacrifices. When men of noble birth died, wives and concubines were often strangled and buried with their husbands and masters."[2]

The revisionist history lesson largely ignores such disturbing facts and proceeds to place Columbus in a class with Adolf Hitler, as kindred spirits across the centuries in racial and ethnic "cleansing." The vast decline in the American Indian population in the approximate 150 years following Columbus' arrival is said to be hard evidence of the white man's campaign of genocide against peoples of different color. However, while perhaps some exceptions can be cited, D'Souza points out that "the vast majority of Indian casualties occurred not as a result of hard labor or deliberate destruction but because of contagious diseases that the Europeans [inadvertently] transmitted to the Indians."[3] To put this in perspective, D'Souza reminds us of the deadly bubonic plague that swept through Europe in the fourteenth century, and the 25 million European lives lost in its wake. Those who hold present-day America guilty of crimes against humanity have yet to accuse the Mongols of Central Asia— the likely transmitters of the bubonic plague—with "genocide." Finally, though predictably omitted from the progressive view of history, there is another side to the "cultural exchange" that took place between white Europeans and American Indians. "From the Indians the Europeans probably contracted syphilis. The Indians also taught the white man about tobacco and cocaine, which would extract an incalculable toll over the next several centuries."[4]

Because a relatively small European contingent conquered armies of far superior numbers and, within a relatively short period, relegated all other cultures to near obsolescence, this arrival is characterized as an "invasion." This again looks past important facts. It is true that much of the territory gained by Westerners was achieved on the battlefield. However, establishing one specific group's legitimate, historic, exclusive claim to *any* bit of land is virtually impossible since, up until the recent Western invention of basic human rights, all land was understood to be the property of whoever could take it by force. In other words, historically, all inhabitants of some territory became so by conquering the *previous* inhabitants. In this regard, white Europeans were certainly no setters of historic precedent.

Moreover, in America, raiding parties of natives attacking white settlements were at least as common as the reverse. Further raiding parties of natives also attacked *each other* both before and after the arrival of white settlers. True Western precedent lay in its singular conquest of *irrationality*. From a historic perspective, long-term goal-oriented concepts were virtually non-existent outside of Western culture. The American tribes Columbus encountered shared a common theme with all other non-Western cultures—immediate survival and instant gratification. In marked contrast, the culture Europeans introduced to the Americas was uniquely geared to structured progress and long-term development. "However small their numbers, however crude their representatives, Europeans came to the Americas with a Civilizational ideology that was unquestionably modern, even if embryonically so. Among the ingredients . . . were a rational understanding of the universe, as well as a new understanding of individual initiative. By contrast, the Indians still lived in the world of the spirits—the enchanted world."[5]

Western ideas did not coalesce into the new dominant culture because they were imposed externally but because, of all competing alternatives, they simply worked best. In short, Western culture was demonstrably *superior* to all others. Even those today who protest the violation of property rights and human rights in the white man's dealings with the Indians must appeal purely and exclusively to *Western* ideals. Absent these ideals, informed by a Christian worldview, the issue of individual or group justice does not even arise.

As provocative as is the issue of white Europeans' legal or moral claim to occupation of the Americas, this pales when set alongside the subject of the African slave trade. Again, white Europeans are indicted with sole responsibility for this deplorable practice. Moreover, it is this practice and the resultant exploitative economic system built on the backs of African slaves that are directly fingered as the cause of all present black pathologies in America. Literally no present crisis within the black community can in any sense escape this all-encompassing antecedent—at least according to progressivism. If young black males tend to engage in more criminal activity than any other demographic, it is not because they have had their culture systematically stripped of any moral restrains by manipulative politicians but because of a never-ending "legacy of slavery." If young black males are murdered by young black males more than by any other demographic, it is still attributed to the omnipresent legacy of slavery.

The predominant image of the evolution of black slavery in America follows this scenario: Greedy European traders carried out raids along the west coast of Africa, seeking to nab unsuspecting natives for chattel on the slave market. Thus began the trans-Atlantic slave trade that would result in the brutal deaths of many Africans before ever reaching the shores of America. Those who were "fortunate" enough to survive the crossing were soon introduced to the barbarism intrinsic to Western "civilization." So consumed were whites with hatred for blacks that they left no stone undisturbed in their determination to degrade and humiliate. From separating families and savage whippings to mutilations and the routine practice of raping slave women, there was very little in the way of brutality that Western law did not openly sanction. Because of the torturous nature of slavery in America and the psychologically debilitating effect it has passed down to slavery's descendants, this shameful episode in history can rightly be regarded as "America's holocaust."

The portrait the above paints is deeply disturbing and altogether revolting. It is not hard to understand how those who have had this story continuously pounded into them would view all white America with grave suspicion, and indeed feel powerless to escape the legacy of slavery. But what are the facts regarding all this? It is true that European merchants were enticed by their own personal greed to engage in the shameful practice of buying and selling human beings. It is true that Africans lost their lives in the perilous Atlantic crossings. It is undeniably true that black slavery existed as an institution in America, and that instances of severe oppression did in fact occur. Yet there is much more to the story that is seldom mentioned.

To begin with, long before greedy Europeans got involved in the African slave trade, Africans were *already* engaged in the widespread use of slave labor. As with most ancient regimes, employing captured tribes in the practice of forced labor was commonplace and unquestioned. Turning the long-existing institution of local slavery into the lucrative wealth-generating global enterprise it would eventually become required no major African philosophical shift. On the contrary, this was a logical expectation, when faced with the enticing promise of unprecedented profits. All that was required was a demand, a commitment to supply that demand, a geographically well-suited logistics facilitator/middleman, and old-fashioned human greed on the part of all "business associates." Europeans created the demand, African chiefs created the supply, and Arabs acted as go-betweens. All profited richly. So prosperous, in fact, was this business arrangement that anti-slavery legislation sweeping through Europe in the mid-1800s was received with less than enthusiasm by African suppliers. "In a bizarre development, tribal leaders in Gambia, the Congo, Dahomey, and other African nations that had prospered under the slave trade sent delegations to London and Paris to vigorously protest the abolition of slavery. . . . Perhaps the fairest generalization is that no Africans opposed slavery in principle, they merely opposed their own enslavement."[6]

What is inexplicably so often overlooked about the slave trade is the most obvious: Slavery was, above all else, an *economic* system. Those who engaged in this venture had a vested interest in both preserving the lives of their property and getting them to market in as good a shape as possible to command top dollar. Terrible Atlantic storms were common, and the possibility of losing an entire ship in a particularly violent storm quite real. At the mercy of the fluctuations of the prevailing market, slave merchants could not arbitrarily adjust their prices to compensate for losses. This placed a premium on not just getting slaves to market but getting them there in the best health and physical appearance reasonably possible.

The combination of these three above factors—serious physical risk, the need to achieve a reasonable profit margin, and an uncertain market—created the highest possible incentive to pursue the only avenue over which slave merchants could (barring the unforeseen) consistently exercise any control, preservation of the product. Crew members of slave ships were thus, ironically, more expendable than the slaves they oversaw.

None of this, however, is to suggest that slaves were treated like royalty. To be sure, Atlantic crossings were drudgery for slaves *at best*, but they were not the genocidal cruises led routinely by out-of-control pathological criminals popularized in Hollywood. History consistently records that as powerful an emotion as hatred may be, it is no match for greed. Even if *all* slave ships had been manned by nothing but the most hate-filled racists, the lesson of history prevails—profits trump personal feelings.

Even in its most *favorable* forms, coerced slavery is a gross violation of human dignity. It is this Christian conviction that would finally bring an end to paganism's last remaining institution, wherever Christianity's influence reached. Orthodox Christians, led by William Wilberforce, spearheaded the abolition of slavery in Europe—an irresistible movement that would eventually wind through the whole Western world. But let us pause to consider the magnitude of slavery's overthrow. Nowhere in history had an oppressed group ever found relief from its oppressors without taking the initiative, rising and throwing off the yoke of bondage through violent upheaval. Yet the struggle that had ended slavery in the Western world was entirely *internal*—initiated, debated, and decided within and at considerable expenditure of human capital *from* the "empowered class." Those who despise Western culture can indeed point to atrocities in the unfolding of this nation. Most of these events are portrayed far out of proportion to facts. Nevertheless, these unquestionably shameful episodes in history cannot be defended. Yet whether the Salem witch trials, incidents involving American Indians, or black slavery, there is a mechanism which, again, shows up nowhere else under any other worldview of history—the injustice is eventually ended from within. There is a collective moral *conscience* that will not permit the oppression to continue.

When considering the overall contribution of Western culture, it is fair to factor in the debits with its credits. It is important to remember, however, that not all living under that vast canopy called Christendom were in fact *Christians*. The worst of Western injustices were committed either in gross distortion or direct *repudiation* of Christian principles. Furthermore, to suggest that Christianity exhibited powerful positive influences wherever it went is by no means to imply the *ideal* was always upheld. Men, even sincere committed Christians, were still subject to the sin-principle inherent in all from birth. Corrupting influences and carnal temptations were still prevalent, and it was inevitable that some in high positions of authority would succumb, with the resultant devastating effect. Even those who did not succumb were not suddenly endowed with flawless judgment. Western culture is not remarkable for its glimpse of human failings. What *is* most remarkable, however, is that despite the multitude of sinful characteristics inherent in man, an influence was introduced to the world which both sufficiently restrained these impulses *and* appealed to man's "better angels." An unprecedented system of freedom and innovation was unleashed, a culture demonstrably and dramatically superior to all others in innumerable ways.

CHAPTER 8

THE US CONSTITUTION AND THE PHILOSOPHY THAT INSPIRED OUR FOUNDING

Perhaps the noblest experiment in human history would take place shortly after the American Revolution. A new system of government would be put in place that would bring the freedom revolution to its highest plateau. It requires considerable ingenuity for modern progressives to imagine that the US Constitution that would emerge from months of careful though sometimes passionate deliberation was an unapologetic effort to hand government an open-ended grant for the acquisition of power. Moreover, according to the revised edition of our nation's founding, the Constitution's framers were driven by a unifying expedient—severing as much as possible all ties with archaic theories that placed religious assumptions in a central role. In other words, government could only be as effective and impartial in dispensing justice as was its commitment to religious neutrality. Thus, we are led to believe, the rallying cry of the Constitutional Convention was "separation of church and state."

Of course, there must be some explanation as to why the Founders thought it in their interest to devise a strong central government. As with nearly every issue, progressives explain this through the lens of economic determinism, a Marxist lens to be sure (and to be discussed later). Accordingly, the signers of the Declaration of Independence were motivated not by altruism but by their own selfish property interests which they now saw imperiled by England. To accept such a notion, we must believe those who pledged their "lives, fortunes, and sacred honor" were inviting a war with the mightiest military in the world, knowing they would be hanged for treason should they lose—an outcome that, considering the odds, was guaranteed absent divine intervention. While property rights were indeed an issue, this was merely one of many grievances stated or implied in the Declaration. Moreover, all classes stood to profit from a government that emphasized the rule of law over will and that guaranteed property rights.[1]

The usual recasting of the intent behind the US Constitution begins with a blurring of two major events that take place in close historic proximity—the American Revolution for Independence in 1776 and the French Revolution of 1789. Both uprisings, we are told, were radical experiments that sought to free the common folk from the yoke of an oppressive ruling class (at least, that is apparently the bill of goods America's common folk bought from their own wealthy elite). Both revolutions were necessarily iconoclastic, tearing down sacred traditions that had only served to protect the entrenched class at the never-ending expense of commoners. In fact, not only were these uprisings kindred spirits, but the French Revolution, again we are told, was inspired by and borrowed many of its ideas from the previous revolution in America. Some suggest the French version was the *continuation* of the American.

To the contrary, however, any similarities between the two are superficial. It is undeniable the French Revolution was authentically radical. Among its lofty goals was the complete dismantling of existing institutions, severing any continuity with the past, and setting society on a new, never-before-charted course. Its ideals were contemptuous of experience as a basis for law. Moreover, it envisioned a utopian society which centered all authority in its legislative body, with but a minimum of restraints on that body's ability to acquire power.[2] In short, the bloodbath in France was a little veiled *repudiation* of the rule of law.

The American Revolution, by comparison, was spurred by a desire to honor and enforce the rule of law that had specifically been established in its various original charters with the English king. In the 1760s, the British crown had introduced three new onerous tax bills in the Colonies, implemented measures for trial without benefit of jury, imposed severe restraints on trade, and suspended colonial legislatures. This last act was especially egregious. In their entire 150 or so years of the American experience, the colonists had only recognized the authority of their own colonial legislative bodies to impose taxation. Thus, the driving intent behind our founding was not to reinvent but to resist tyranny and to *conserve* the rule of law.

What's more, in complete disharmony with any radical impulse, our Founding Fathers were reluctant to separate from the motherland. To this end, they exhausted every conceivable avenue over at least a *ten-year period*, until only the one alternative remained. When finally forced to sever ties with the mother country, the Founders wanted there to be no doubt why this was happening and who was the offending party—the true violator of the rule of law. The Declaration of Independence, addressed to the "candid world," was an indictment of the king for breaking faith with his subjects in America. In the end, by having allowed Parliament to enact punitive measures against the Colonies, King George III had perpetrated a breach of contract.

The far-too-seldom-asked question today is *where* did Thomas Jefferson get the idea that all men are created equal, and that this was such a fundamental truth as to lie beyond dispute? In all of history, this Jeffersonian view is truly novel and a contribution that causes considerable discomfort to the approved interpretation. Jefferson, we are often reminded, was a student of John Locke (1632–1704), the recognized source of "enlightenment thought." As with his predecessor, Jefferson was a "philosopher"—one well-grounded in the rational world of objective facts, eschewing emotional appeals that were beyond material tools of investigation. As such, Jefferson, according to this view, would become the chief restraining force on any efforts to infiltrate "religious" views into our Constitution. It is a source of embarrassment, then, that the great guardian against dangerous religious intrusion should so nakedly invoke a Supreme Being as the *source* of freedom and rights. To add insult, his concept of God, specifically his allusion to a Creator, could only have arisen within a distinct Christian worldview. In fact, if one merely accepts the obvious, there is no mysterious explanation to be divined. Jefferson was merely reflecting an assumption that his forebears had brought to the New World when they had left England in the early 1600s.[3]

After attempting to fuse the American and French Revolutions into essentially a single event, modern secularists then portray social contract as an "Enlightenment" innovation that, once again, was largely due to the influence of John Locke. Because Locke wrote the Treatises of Civil Government, and because Jefferson and James Madison looked to these writings as their primary source, we are told, there can be no doubt of the secular nature of the American experiment. Yet in 1620, twelve years before Locke was *born*, forty-one male passengers of the *Mayflower,* still *en route* to the New World, signed the Mayflower Compact, a document based entirely on governance by social contract. This document, clearly rooted in Christian covenant, would form the basis for a system of government which would become considerably complex in a very short time. "[I]n an amazingly brief interval, the founders of New England had created most of the features of representative, balanced government: a theory of constitutionalism, power wielded by consent, annual elections with an expansive franchise, a bicameral legislature, local autonomies, and a Bill of Rights . . . [all] in the span of a single decade."[4]

Any objective look at history reveals that Locke, Jefferson, Madison, and virtually all Founding Fathers were inheritors of constitutional ideas that unmistakably followed a linear progression. There is substantive continuity from the US Constitution to the Revolutionary War to Blackstone, Montesquieu, and Locke; to the Pilgrims, to English law, to the feudal period, and to the church. The imagined radical departure with the Christian past is nowhere to be seen *except* and explicitly within the French Revolution. This latter revolution was indeed influenced by Enlightenment ideas and, before this, the Renaissance. So, what was the Renaissance, what is meant by the so-called Enlightenment period, and how or why did each come about?

CHAPTER 9

THE RENAISSANCE
AND THE ENLIGHTENMENT

The Renaissance roughly took place from the fifteenth to seventeenth centuries. To the extent this shift and then the Enlightenment occurred, humankind (at least the West) was experiencing something akin to a "second fall" of humanity. Centuries of unchecked corruption and excesses by the Catholic Church finally all but extinguished the divine light and cleared the field for the resurgence of pagan influences—and with it, the seeds of the satanic counter to Christ's magnanimous invitation. The Renaissance was, at least in part, an attempt by humanist scholars to return to models preceding the advent of Christianity, emphasizing classical Greco-Roman ideals. Renaissance humanism reflected a transition from a God-centered to a man-centered interpretation of all reality. This movement coincided with much emerging progress in diverse fields. Discounting a millennium of deep and far-reaching Christian influence that informed all their working axioms, humanists attributed disproportionate credit to the new primacy of intellect.

With the church, as a political entity, being considerably weakened by questionable practices and assailed by the Protestant Reformation, forces within the Renaissance saw this as an opportunity to wrest authority from ecclesiastical sources and reassert the old pagan dictum *Lex Regia* (the king is the law speaking). This was, of course, enthusiastically endorsed by European monarchies. Even England, where constitutionalism, common law, and property rights had steadily melded in a new order, would not be exempt. In the early 1600s, a bitter struggle between King James I and Parliament would take place over ultimate authority. The king insisted final authority rested in the royal line and took measures to enforce authoritarian policies. The Parliament, in resisting, repeatedly invoked the Magna Carta. This struggle, along with secular (pagan) inroads the Renaissance had made throughout

Europe, would factor into the Pilgrims' determination to forge a new truly free-in-Christ society in America.

The tension between throne and Parliament would not find final resolution until "the Glorious Revolution" (also known as the Bloodless Revolution) of 1688, which deposed King James II in favor of William and Mary. This would approximately coincide with the beginning of what is now referred to as "the Age of Enlightenment." As with the label "Dark Ages," there is a deliberate intent behind this latter description, especially when these two terms are set side by side. Just the verbalizing of these terms practically preempts an entire 1,700-or-so-year period from ever making it into the arena of serious debate. If one uncritically accepts the premise of this artificial juxtaposition, the discussion is ended before it ever begins—"Why would anyone want to give superstition an equal footing with science?" In any case, the Enlightenment would carry on and amplify the Renaissance's diminishing suspicious view of human nature, increasingly giving way to a suspicious view of religion, and Christianity in particular.

The Enlightenment also suffered from a nostalgic fallacy that the "golden age of man" lay in the classical Greco-Roman world. Most notably, Enlightenment intellectuals were enamored of the Greek philosophers, believing these had long ago uncovered a system which yielded proper modes of conduct and interpretation through unaided human reason. Enlightenment "philosophes" saw as their duty the restoration of ideals that had been buried by "religious intolerance." Where Renaissance humanism may have made some effort to separate Christian *precepts* from religious authoritarianism (Erasmus, in particular), the Enlightenment would throw the baby out with the bathwater.

This little "second fall" would be far less dramatic and noticeable than the original in its immediate effect, but would prove to be, in some ways, nearly as devastating in its eventual impact. As with its antecedent, *pride* would again prove the fatal ingredient. The Enlightenment reflected a philosophical position that highly revered rationality as a basis for uncovering reality. It can be thought of as a mutation that grew out of the order provided by Christian theism. Its departure from (and eventual competition with) Christianity would result from two main causes. First, it was concluded, if stressing objectivity in relating to the world around had produced such marvelous progress in so many differing fields, then exorcizing all (or most) subjective beliefs could only lead to even greater and unimagined progress. Second, an emerging elite intellectual class, rather than giving God the glory for such unprecedented progress, chose instead to give the glory to man. Turning a blind eye to the evident causes of the freedom revolution, this self-appointed class decided that progress must reflect something inherent in nature and perhaps more so in humanity.

Deliberately ignoring painful lessons of history, a new conclusion was reached about the nature of human beings that could not be justified by any experience from the past. In its fully developed form, Enlightenment thinking rejected the concept of original sin, deciding man was inherently *good* and would manifest this if placed within the "right environment." But in the years to come—for the multitudes who would find themselves subject to the good intentions of an elite class determined to implement the "right environment"—this prospect would be especially frightful. The "right environment" invariably would always seem to break down into something that strangely resembled that period in history which preceded Christianity—widespread enslavement. Moreover, it evidently never occurred to the "enlightened" intellectual class that the eradication of any subjective component would be a self-defeating proposition. This would eventually result in an unintended and most unwelcome consequence—the disintegration of ultimate truth. To be sure, what might the laws of physics have to say about the rightness or wrongness of murder, rape, theft, etc.?

Ironically, it was probably the church's accommodation of Greek thought that first opened Pandora's box. Rather than addressing foundational premises and exposing its destructive reductionism, the church conscripted Greek philosophy, integrating it into systematic education. In the thirteenth century, Thomas Aquinas sought to make Aristotelian philosophy the framework of Christian apologetics, even borrowing Aristotle's "natural ethics." Aquinas believed he could use Aristotle's methodology to show a high probability for the existence of the Christian God. In time, this compromise with essential paganism would prove the church's undoing.

In adopting Aristotle's epistemology, Aquinas sharply departed from early church father Augustine. Rather than predicated on divine revelation, truth and a virtuous life were attainable through unaided human reasoning, although these needed to be *supplemented* by revelation to effect salvation. Instead of contained *within* God, truth was a kind of neutral essence, powerless to resist human reason; revealing its secrets to persistent probing. Yet to accept this Aristotelian premise, Aquinas had to ignore revelation's stark indictment of natural man: "Who changed the truth of God into a lie, and worshipped and served the creature more than the Creator" (Rom. 1:25). Moreover, if, as Aquinas implied, reasoning equaled "channeling" God (rather than the means commonly employed by natural man to rationalize *rejection* of revealed truth), then God was Himself forced to bow before absolute reason and truth.

Of course, Aquinas differed with Aristotle in many significant areas, but it was the areas of agreement that would prove fatal. The phenomenal world was again primary, and the rational mind had become the absolute in place of God. Because he reversed Augustine's formula and made faith an appendage to reason, Aquinas had unwittingly made the two antagonists. This would signal not just the unraveling of faith but (in time) of reason as well. Even the most basic utilitarian truths derived from survival experience had first to borrow the theistic principle that survival was preferable to extinction.

Roman Catholic accommodation followed by certain Renaissance/Enlightenment strains (infatuated with Greek philosophy's emphasis on human autonomy) would yield a new concept called deism. This view, which reduced God to a sort of mechanical hands-off designer (absolutely forbidding Him any miraculous intervention), would provide an acceptable haven for those who were comforted by the idea of God (especially the civilizing influence) but offended by the negative aspersions Christianity had cast upon man's basic nature.

The Enlightenment would turn the tables on Christianity and make man ultimate judge, including of God Himself. As far as humanists were concerned, God—at least the God of the Bible—was found wanting. Those of the intellectual class decided the Bible, and especially Christianity's emphasis on original sin, was an impediment to achieving *authentic* communion with God who, increasingly, was something to be experienced on man's own terms. God was well on His way, once again, to becoming "unknowable" and irrelevant.

With revelation now cast *against* reason, the implication was inescapable: Revelation had been reduced to the refuge of the irrational. Yet again, it was the church that had unwittingly set the table for this new antagonistic relationship. It was Aquinas (and those of his accommodating mindset) who had gambled that it would be possible to defeat pagan incursions using paganism's own rules. The gulf that now seemed so unbridgeable between revelation and reason had simply not existed before this fatal miscalculation. Reams of evidence loudly testified that human reason was *animated* by the divine revelation of Christ—the very unifying principle of all existence.

It would only be a matter of time before deism would give way to atheism (or its slightly watered-down cousin, agnosticism), where reality must entirely confine itself to the materialistic sphere. If God really had no useful role to play, then why not simply dispense with any such pretense and let man, finally set free from inhibiting religion, assume his rightful destiny?

Perhaps the most significant of early atheists (if not an atheist in the strictest sense, at least in practical terms) would be David Hume. Hume turned his brand of skepticism into an impregnable fortress defended by frightful guns, savaging quaint forms of convention. While it's true that Hume's relentless surgical knife excised key religious premises (i.e., miracles), it by no means stopped there. Once set in motion, Hume's cold empiricism left *all* approaches to epistemology (the basis for accumulating knowledge) bleeding badly. Hume argued that neither the inductive (the uniformity of past experiences in relation to future expectations) nor the deductive (based on an acceptance of self-evident truths) method could sufficiently shed assumptions to be of value in acquiring objective truth.[1] There was no way to *know* concretely that just because certain "physical laws" had displayed a consistency in the past, they necessarily *would* in the future. Likewise, to allow that a truth was "self-evident" was to deny it a basis in provable fact.

Hume's unsympathetic skepticism threatened to empty the whole Enlightenment enterprise of meaning. The concept of metaphysics (that which seeks to establish the nature of reality—underlying structure, principles, purpose, etc.) was now on the verge of collapse. It was disillusioning now to see how many propositions (including basic to scientific investigation, i.e., constancy of physical law), now divorced from a divine transcendent authority, had been reduced to group hunches that could no more be placed on empirical scales than bold supernatural claims, and thus of no more value according to the rules of skepticism.

For Hume's dismayed fellow travelers, too much time and energy had been invested to now be forever constrained to issuing only concrete statements of what is. There simply *had* to be a way to extract purpose and meaning from the reasoning process and to discover what *ought* to be. Try as they might, Hume's peers could find no fault with the logical progression of his conclusions. Frustratingly, it could not be shown that he had faltered in his fidelity to the "rational rules of logic." What did soon become apparent, however, was that Hume's rigorous adherence to logic was self-refuting. Underlying Hume's position was a subtle assumption of his own—that being a skeptic was preferable to, wiser, or somehow nobler than being a non-skeptic. Yet by what objective standard was this concluded?

If one truly took skepticism to its logical conclusions, the acceptance that the five senses were relaying reliable information was also based on an unprovable assumption. Still further, using *rules* of logic to mark out a position (even that no set of rules was reliable) was either a tacit admission that underlying truth did exist, or that Hume's skepticism was an exercise in absurdity. Either way, skepticism was an acid that disintegrated its own container. For all the determination Enlightenment humanists had committed to constructing a "rational" reality that was free of any enslaving faith dimension, they found that something very similar would be necessary if any vector of progress were to be charted. If the body of Enlightenment work were to be salvaged, a new ultimate interpretive principle would need to be worked out.

It would fall to Immanuel Kant to rescue the intellectual enterprise from Hume's extreme empiricism (knowledge derived from the five senses) as well as from the forces of extreme rationalism (knowledge acquired from the reasoning process) and achieve a synthesis through his "transcendental method." Kant argued that sensory experiences could not in any practical sense yield knowledge without synthetic *a priori* judgments. In effect, Kant was claiming to have discovered a new faculty in *man* (independent of some transcendent source) that employed special concepts ("categories") which, rather than correlating certain experiences to a known order (in the true empirical sense), ascribed to the human mind an ability to construct a general form to which the very understanding of order must conform. Having identified this new faculty, Kant would go on to address the remaining problem, "How are synthetic *a priori* judgments possible?" Though presuming to have preserved epistemology *and* God's place in the universe, by making *man* the source of knowledge, Kant had made God superfluous and effectively forfeited any possibility of knowing ultimate reality. To whatever extent God may have been "salvaged," He was now utterly unknowable.

A century after this great contribution to philosophy, Friedrich Nietzsche would skewer Kant's "Table of Categories," revisiting Kant's vital question, "How are synthetic judgments *a priori* possible?" Giving due reverence to Kant's formidable rhetorical capability, Nietzsche summed up Kant's convoluted answer: "*By means of a means . . .* but is that—an answer? An explanation? Or is it not rather merely a repetition of the question?" Nietzsche pointed to the proper question, "Why is belief in such judgments *necessary?*" The simple answer, as he would observe, was that human beings could not possibly function without them, even if *false*. Nietzsche would also mock the young German (Tubingen institution) theologians enamored with Kant who "went immediately into the groves—all seeking for 'faculties' . . . when one could not yet distinguish between 'finding' and 'inventing.'"[2] Kant, at any rate, would serve as an important bridge between the Enlightenment and its successor, the Romantic period (beginning approximately the late eighteenth/early nineteenth century).

It is fascinating that the Romantic period would reject most of the rigid rationalism and extreme empiricism of its predecessor taking it on faith that things were indeed moving by an irresistible force toward a bright future—man's human potential just barely tapped. It is noteworthy that the Romantic period *would* retain, in particular, the Enlightenment's autonomous and optimistic view of man's nature. Scientific advancement, it was now appreciated, could not really be value-neutral. Yet humanists were confident that this new brand of metaphysics, because it had a powerful resistance to the supernatural, would be far superior. Because it would limit itself to the material universe, it would be the new anti-religion, a belief system that would erode the stringent boundaries of intolerant religions, revealing the common thread underlying all such belief systems and thereby paving the way for a new dawning age—the brotherhood of all men.

CHAPTER 10

PROVIDENCE AND LIBERTY

As in so many instances in the unfolding story of the Bible, just when it seemed all was lost, hope would suddenly appear in the most unexpected form. As Divine Providence had supplied Joseph in Egypt, Moses also in Egypt (many years later), Esther in Persia, and (with the incipient church) the early Church Fathers, Providence again intervened to preserve a strain of the precious liberating light Christ had purchased. Just when it seemed the light was fading all over Europe, Martin Luther nailed his ninety-five theses to the church door at Wittenberg. Only a hundred years later, a thin ray of that restorative light, refusing compromise with corrupting influences, accompanied a ship full of brave passengers embarking for the New World, intent on modeling Christ's shining city on a hill.

It is incredible the Enlightenment should be linked with the US Constitution, since it is the former which nearly *derailed* the freedom revolution. The extent to which American Founders even cited Enlightenment sources is miniscule once we move past the earliest stage of that period. This earlier stage features men such as Locke, Montesquieu, and Pufendorf, all thinkers whose political philosophies were largely based upon Judeo-Christian theistic principles. Of all sources consulted by the Founders, by far the most frequently cited was the Bible.[1] The fully developed Enlightenment thought of the founding period was decidedly hostile to Christian theism.

It is true that much of Enlightenment thought was sweeping through Europe, with the concept of private property suddenly finding itself in peril once again. Fortunately, in America, Enlightenment ideas found practically an institutionalized resistance. This is no accident. Of all nations that have existed, there is only one that came into being out of a specific Christian vision and was thereafter nurtured on Christian principles—a nation which saw itself as a *model* for Christian society. Although the modern take on our founding period casts the framers as inheritors of Enlightenment thought who saw as their mission the deliberate secularization of all government institutions, this fails to square with any of the working assumptions that factored into the Constitution.

In a clear break with Enlightenment sentiment, the framers were very mistrustful of human nature. They were heavily influenced by the concept of original sin and reflected this in the multitude of restraints on power. Perhaps above all they were serious students of history, carefully gleaning hard-won knowledge through the centuries of experience. They were well acquainted with the depths of depravity to which human beings could sink. They recognized that the natural tendency was to consolidate and centralize power, and that all power tended toward corruption. The Founders agreed that the key to freedom lay in the implementation of a *system* which could withstand the various onslaughts of human depravity in whatever form it should manifest. The question was never *if* corrupting elements might enter, but *how* to effectively check their eventuality.

The framers were not opposed to change but understood that it had to be done with the soberest deliberations; it must not be placed under the control of radical impulses. History showed that the noblest motives, when hastily put in motion, had produced some of the most miserable tyranny. Change must have numerous braking forces to ensure that when it did come, it reflected a serious appreciation for unintended consequences. In other words, would the proposed change result in a net gain or loss to society?

Moreover, the framers did not lock themselves into any one specific approach to government but sought to bring the best elements from each system that could demonstrate from the historic record that it had genuine *long-term* merit. Yet they were always careful to weigh against negative features inherent to each. Nor did they slavishly align themselves with any single figure of history. For instance, though they had great respect for Locke where he defended social contract, they rejected his endorsement of unchecked authority in a single legislative body, recognizing its inherent threat to freedom.[2]

The framers believed that the Constitution had to be beyond the power of legislative bodies to tamper with. In fact, all forms of power had to be subject to the Constitution, or they would soon have no relevance. The framers' use of the term "the people" would be quite distinct from the idea that would follow in France. In the American version, "the people" were defined within a concept that recognized the right of all citizens to call for a special Constitutional convention, to elect representatives to draft a system of laws whose authority superseded any legislatures, to then be submitted to the ratification process, setting in place (if ratified) a Constitution that would be a *fixed* standard. Fixity, in fact, was the overriding theme of the framers' intent.

Fixity, it was understood, was the only assurance of continuing liberty. It is thus mind-numbing that we are now led to believe that the framers viewed the

Constitution as an ingenious consolidation of federal power. When one views the multitude of restraints on all forms of power, it is impossible to miss that the dominant concern was for *limiting* government authority. How else might we explain the numerous obstacles to action; the separation of powers through the three branches of government, the electoral college, the executive veto, the ability of Congress to override executive veto through a super-majority, the various principles of representation, a bicameral legislature, and multiple assorted checks and balances within exceedingly complex arrangements?

Beyond all this was the delicate balance of power between the states and the federal government. All this combined *ensured* that the wheels of change would grind agonizingly slowly. In fact, the French would be contemptuous of the American Constitution with its impediments to reflexive action. As far as the French were concerned, a constitution should be malleable to the ever-changing needs of the people. In France, "the people" translated to an unchecked democracy where, theoretically, 51 percent could vote to enslave the other 49 percent. Immediately following on the heels of the grand experiment in France to place supreme power in the hands of "the people" would emerge the dictatorship of Napoleon.

That the US Constitution did not impose a government-mandated belief system upon the people is not evidence of an indifference toward or mistrust of religious principles on the part of the Founders. That they recognized such principles as vital to the survival of the nation is clear from the record. Putting the state (federal government) in the business of inculcating religious beliefs would have accomplished far more harm in the long run than good. Modern progressives, however, have reinterpreted this to suggest that government has a vested interest in *opposing* religious expression in any form within the civil sphere.

This emphatic position rests on a single clause in the First Amendment: "Congress shall make no law respecting an establishment of religion or prohibiting the free exercise thereof." Putting any consideration for context aside, if one simply takes the wording at face value, there appears to be no possibility of confusion. *Congress* (the federal government) is not to give special consideration to one religion over any other. Nothing is said nor even implied that exercising religious principles in the public forum is a *danger* to government function or individual freedom. To preclude any doubt as to the specific intent of the first part of this statement, Congress is expressly *prohibited* from interfering with individual expression.

Again, as though to preempt any possible misunderstanding that there are implied zones where individual religious conviction may not intrude, the words "free exercise" are inserted. How, then, have we arrived at an understanding that places "religion" in such a tight confinement? The answer lies, purportedly, in a certain letter to a religious group.

The phrase "wall of separation between Church and State" has been invoked so many times that many today are of the impression these words occur in the Constitution. Even among those who know this metaphor is taken from a personal letter from Thomas Jefferson to the Danbury Baptist Association of Connecticut (written in 1802), there is still a widely held belief, through an apparent process of ingenious divination, that this letter provides the *intent* behind the First Amendment (written thirteen years *earlier*). This has been taken by progressives as a mandate to eradicate any religious connotations from the public arena. First applied to a court ruling in 1947, this has quickly metamorphosed from a cautious suspicion of religious absolutism to open contempt and all-out war on Christian principles.

It strains credulity to suppose a proper understanding of the First Amendment could not be reached by our own courts for nearly two hundred years. Surely it seems reasonable to concede that if anyone would have understood the original intent, it would have been the framers themselves. If the modern court did indeed properly discern the intent, then we must conclude that both Congress *and* George Washington deliberately and almost immediately violated the law. Just one day after passage of this amendment through the House, the same House of Representatives passed a resolution calling for a day of prayer and thanksgiving. Shortly after this, Washington issued a proclamation that set aside a National Day of Prayer and Thanksgiving. His words are illuminating: "It is the duty of all nations to acknowledge the providence of Almighty God, to obey his will, to be grateful for His benefits and humbly to implore His protection and favor. . . . That great and glorious Being who is the beneficent author of all the good that was, that is, or that ever will be, that we may then unite in rendering unto Him our sincere and humble thanks for His care and protection of the people."[3]

Beyond these militating circumstances, there is a *context* in which Jefferson's comments take place, a context that is available to anyone interested in a simple, logical, straightforward explanation without recourse to arcane incantations. It can readily be admitted that Jefferson was highly skeptical of federal and generally any sort of government intrusion into religious matters. This was not, however, because Jefferson was hostile to the exercise of religion but because history had already demonstrated (most evidently with the Church of England) that *national* establishmentarianism had considerably weakened freedom of personal conviction. If one examines the broader context of establishment issues as well as Jefferson's specific reference to "wall of separation," the natural inference is to the prohibition of a *nationally* endorsed religion. No prohibitions were placed upon local or even individual *state* governments. Consider this statement Jefferson penned to Samuel Miller in 1808: "Certainly, no power to prescribe any religious exercise or to assume authority in religious discipline, has been delegated to the General Government. It must then rest with the States, as far as it can be in any human authority."[4]

Though during his presidency, Jefferson refused to issue religious proclamations, he frequently uttered public statements recognizing the social need for nurturing religious morality. In his first message to Congress, Jefferson stated, "While we devoutly return thanks to the beneficent Being who has been pleased to breathe into them the spirit of conciliation and forgiveness, we are bound with peculiar gratitude to be thankful to him that our own peace has been preserved through so perilous a season, and ourselves permitted quietly to cultivate the earth and to practice and improve those arts which tend to increase our comforts."[5] Among the several instances of Jefferson's support of religious proclamations prior to his presidency, while governor of Virginia, he issued a proclamation calling for "a day of publick and solemn thanksgiving and prayer to Almighty God."[6]

Maintaining even the flimsiest connection to context, the simple intent behind the First Amendment was to preempt federal encroachment into individual state authority over religious liberties. There is simply no contextual justification for extending this "wall" to *all* civil government. If *the people* decided that their tax dollars should support some local or state religious promotion, there was nothing which constitutionally precluded this. Furthermore, this was the common understanding until the middle of the twentieth century. The Bill of Rights was specifically concocted to *preserve the rights of individual states* from federal usurpation. This was done to allay fears that states would eventually become little more than appendages of a multitentacled federal monster. This was perhaps the great and final sticking point in the Constitution's final ratification. How then could it be argued, as it has been for several decades, that the Fourteenth Amendment (ratified in 1868) applied the Bill of Rights *against* the states, effectively holding them hostage to a vast federal bureaucracy? This takes us beyond mere esoteric divination, descending into a form of polemical schizophrenia.

CHAPTER 11

FOUR WHITE MEN AND THE MOST BRUTAL CENTURY OF HUMAN DESTRUCTION

Early nineteenth-century intellectualism had a quasi-religious character. It reasserted the emotional, speculative, and spiritual dimensions the Enlightenment had so consciously sought to expunge. One Romantic philosopher in particular, G. W. F. Hegel, sought to undo the damage Kant had done and put God back into the human experience. To do this, the God-concept, insisted Hegel, had first to be freed from authoritarian dogmatic religion and "unveiled" as the rationalistic essence of the universe. This essence was the "absolute spirit (or mind)" embedded in the universe and was most conspicuously manifest in the efficiency of the modern state. Reason was the conduit to spirit, and thus the means to self-actualization. Much of this totalitarian formulation found its antecedent in Greek thought. Where Aristotle had perhaps only hinted at it, Hegel's idealistic pantheism now boldly proclaimed man the crowning achievement of an unfolding natural progression.

Hegel would shift the concept of meaning to the historical plane, from being to becoming. Though he clearly embraced a monistic system, Hegel sought to infuse his universe with differentiation—a cyclical process of competing ideas working through history, thesis challenged by antithesis, finally leading to synthesis.[1] This was a "dialectical process," echoing but reformulating Plato's dialectic method to proclaim a philosophic breakthrough. The history of man had thus been a struggle to achieve spiritual progress for mankind and self-knowledge for the individual. Man had a duty to recognize and then assume his divinity and take responsibility for a higher harmonizing humanistic morality. Yet to all practical purposes, the spiritual was no longer the distinct transcendent plane of Christianity, and God was now experienced as a subservient force. Moreover, linking human reason to divinity still further reduced God and now effectively eliminated any remaining relevance.

The Enlightenment, and Hegel perhaps in particular, would lay the ground-work for many who would in turn shape the thinking of modern times. Four nineteenth-century gentlemen, in particular, would exert a profound influence over twentieth-century currents, unwittingly ushering in the most brutal century in recorded history. The unintended consequences of Karl Marx, Charles Darwin, Friedrich Nietzsche, and Sigmund Freud would see the return of civilization to the wilderness from which Christ had rescued it.

The body of work represented by this group was filled with untried, unproven speculations. Yet because their ideas were promoted under the pretense of cutting-edge science, they were accorded an almost unquestioned credibility. Darwin and Freud, specifically identified with scientific disciplines, displayed none of the tradi-tional predictive element in their work. It is remarkable that in a more critical age, these gentlemen (Marx, Darwin, and Freud especially) might have easily been cast aside as frauds.

Marx was influenced by Hegel's dialectical process but centered the conflict in matter (more specifically, conflict between social classes). In 1849, Marx pub-lished his *Communist Manifesto*, a preliminary to his expanded version *Das Capital*, which would appear in about 1863. Marx would closely tie his views to Darwin-ian materialism, believing his own "dialectical materialism" to have uncovered the same inexorable forces in nature at work in a historic human struggle. For Marx, the chief cause of class division was economic inequality. He centered his theory on economic determinism—the idea that money and property (capital) was the ulti-mate animator of all institutions, including religion. "Religion" was simply a con-venient invention used by the ruling class (the bourgeoisie) to exploit and control the working class (the proletariat). Marx believed this historical struggle between classes was quickly coming to its final stage, with the proletariat, in a dramatic cli-max, throwing off the yoke of its long-time oppressor. The result would be a new classless society where antagonistic forces were dissolved in a single utopian vision. No longer would the many be deprived by the few. All would reap an equal bounty from the storehouse of nature. The common man's chains falling away, the world would see a time of prosperity and brotherhood never known.

Implicit within Darwinism, morality was just another component of the his-toric process. Religions were but another reflection of the unfolding evolution-ary scheme, with Christianity simply the culmination of a movement that sought to give expression to a natural civilizing impulse. In his primitive state, man had originally been restricted to representing this drive in awkward, mysterious ways. Natural selection, however, would continue to eliminate features that were damag-ing to the whole, until primal animism would give way, after thousands of years, to the higher civilizing principles of Christianity. This same natural selection was now pressuring those supernatural elements of Christianity, useful in a more primitive time, to fall away as well. Enlightened man no longer had any need for superstitious fluff, and it was assumed that the evolutionary process that had yielded the higher morality of Christianity would continue its march toward a higher, nobler civilization.

Nietzsche, writing near the end of the nineteenth century, believed the time had come to dispense with sentimental religious pretenses. Since the effect of Enlightenment thought had been to eliminate the concept of moral absolutes, it was a denial of reality to continue to hold on to the old religious superstructure. Religion, though perhaps once an institution that boasted of some ennobling elements, was now reduced to a comforter that artificially equalized the masses. Religion was now the last refuge of the weak who could not hope to compete with the noble, defiant, self-determined "superman" in the real world. Nietzsche simply took Darwinism to its logical conclusion and pronounced the effective "death of God." He further reduced the meaning of life to a "will to power." Darwin's demolition of the only remaining vestige of a fixed source of morality would produce a void of absolute value and purpose that "men of vision" would recognize as their duty to fill.

If Sigmund Freud is generally referred to as the father of psychoanalysis, he is no less the father of the modern "sexual revolution." Freud's major contribution would lie in the scientific respectability with which he would cloak sexual perversions. If Marx had uncovered class division as the great social evil plaguing humanity, then it would fall to Freud to divine the malignant condition that beset the individual. To that end, he would conjure up an entirely new "science" out of whole cloth, a method which treated for the source of neuroses—repressed sexuality. The historic spiritual tension in everyone, the struggle between good and evil, was now reduced to unrequited erotic impulses. Conveniently for Freud, his modern enchantments did not actually have to "cure" anyone. The science of psychoanalysis was so obscure, so shrouded in mystical rhetoric, that it was impossible to define what might constitute a cure. The schools of psychology that would arise from Freud's research would feature an underlying theme—the most complex and abstract elements of human beings could now be placed in a test tube and dissected into identifiable subcomponents much like any other system. The bottom line: human nature could be restructured through aggressive education and training, especially if indoctrination began in the earliest stages of development.

The practical effect of these four men combined was that all essential elements of ancient paganism were effectively restored: state empowerment again the source of human salvation; the restoration of nature to divine status; militarism the final determiner of truth; and an intercessory priesthood (psychology) which enthusiastically celebrated primal sexual urges. The cumulative effect was to reduce man to a natural phenomenon, a creature essentially locked into nature, thus incapable of ever transcending its bounds. Man was not only a slave to his urges but headed for a conflicted, emotional state of paralysis if he tried to suppress them (thus the priority for plugging his urges into the proper social network as early as possible).

The devastating effect of Marx, Nietzsche, and Freud have long since been evident, their ideas thoroughly discredited before the close of the twentieth century (though the genies they released can't seem to be stuffed back into their bottles). Yet the most pernicious Enlightenment child, Darwinism, continues to receive vigorous defense. This is peculiar considering its close kindred spirit with its repudiated brethren. Darwinism has been nothing less than an acid that has eaten through all civilizing principles, leading us into a relativistic worldview where right and wrong are no longer defined by anything but political expediency. This being so, perhaps Darwin's story deserves a closer look.

CHAPTER 12

THE DARWINIAN TRIUMPH

What were the circumstances surrounding "the most important scientific discovery in history"? Was the theory of evolution the triumph of dispassionate logic over emotion-driven superstition (otherwise known as "religion")? Was it accepted almost immediately by the scientific establishment because the supporting evidence overwhelmed any opposition? The conventional wisdom, of course, answers to the above with a resounding yes. But what do the *facts* say? Do they attribute this victory to empirics or to the prevailing zeitgeist? They point to the latter.

The world that Charles Darwin was born into was a world of convulsion. The French Revolution had just sent shock waves through Europe, its implications still settling out. Though many were repulsed by the barbarity of this conflagration, many others seemed to see it as something of a watershed—an unfortunate but necessary cleansing and historic partitioning, a definitive separating of the old repressive order from the new Age of Enlightenment. The Western world was now, for better or worse, involved in a passionate romance with *progress*. Stability—achieved through nearly two millennia of painfully accumulated knowledge about the nature of man, the state, and reality, and painstakingly gained through the didactic approach that had given birth to the modern scientific method—suddenly found itself the *enemy* of progress.

The French Revolution having opened the first major rift in stability, numerous smaller fissures were now carving up the face of the old order. "Change," it was now understood, was the engine of progress. Yet this was a concept of change that conformed to no previous understanding—the gradual surrendering of cherished but faulty assumptions to the unsympathetic verdict of history. This new change was spontaneous, radical—innovation almost for the very *sake* of innovation. The ethos of innovation, as the French Revolution had shown, contained no element or patience for looking back, only forward to the "brave new world" that surely awaited.

The nineteenth century was ushered in by a sense that reality itself could be mystically subdued, perhaps even *transformed*, through force of will. Human will, after all, with men like Hobbes, Descartes, Rousseau, and the aforementioned Hume, Kant, and Hegel, had been hemming reality in since the seventeenth century. Reason, the means through which reality was apprehended and once axiomatically viewed as child to underlying transcendent assumptions (specifically Christian theism), suddenly found itself cast more often in an *antagonistic* relationship with its withering parent. Though it would have been inexplicable to men like Galileo, Copernicus, Newton, Kepler, and Linnaeus (not to mention a certain monk named Mendel), a divine hand was increasingly seen as a hindrance to intellectual discovery.

With change elevated to a sacrament, progress almost universally equated with the common good, and *resisting* progress very nearly reduced to the evil counterpart, a theory of evolution—*any* theory of evolution—could not have hoped for a more thoroughly tilled nor fertile soil. And so it was. Before a very young Charles Darwin boarded the *Beagle* on his famous five-year voyage of discovery, various theories of descent from a common ancestor were already in the pipeline. Darwin's own grandfather, Erasmus (who died before Charles was born) advanced his own concept of evolution in his scientific treatise *Zoonomia*. But it was the more sophisticated work of French biologist Jean-Baptiste Lamarck that dominated the field. Lamarck developed his theory around subtle adaptations to environmental pressures. Lamarck envisioned each organism in a state of internal flux, countless fluid impulses always ready to respond to changing environmental urges. The problem with his theory, as with all theories submitted, was the lack of a credible *vertical* evolution-inducing mechanism. It was becoming evident that nature exhibited considerable variation *within* kinds, but what evidence was there to indicate that a continuous progression *connecting* kinds was occurring, or had occurred? Such dramatic changes would obviously require dramatic and powerful pressures, far exceeding any fanciful conjectures currently described. A legitimate theory of evolution would require more than evidence of lateral change, wishful thinking, and imaginative speculation—or so one might have thought.

The voyage of the *Beagle* round the coast of South America is often cast, for twenty-two-year-old Charles Darwin, as anything from a crisis of faith to a soul-stirring epiphany. A dramatic conversion from a deep personal Christian conviction to atheistic naturalism has obvious literary appeal. But it is Darwin's own consistent personality that makes this a high improbability. No doubt, Darwin's voyage was a dramatic rite of passage that did indeed entail a very real loss of innocence. Well before his exposure to the exotic strains and geologic wonders of South America, certain crew members of the *Beagle* had already shocked young Darwin's sensibilities by assailing his Christian faith, probing the reliability of certain Bible passages. But what exactly was the nature of this faith?

Regarding what appears the supreme irony (a man of deep faith mysteriously transformed into a champion of unbelief), there is little to indicate that Darwin's Christianity ever represented much more than a high order of social etiquette. After this, what remained of Darwin's religion was a combination of sweet naivete and casual indifference. Yet it was not indifference toward religion itself. Religion was a cherished family heirloom (even paid respectful homage by Darwin's atheist father), but he had never had any compelling reason to regard it as an overarching canopy, informing every aspect of reality and fitting the entire array of experience into a coherent whole. Even in his training for the ministry, there is little to suggest he was ever seriously challenged to probe the depths of his beliefs. As it was, within aristocratic society, God was already being watered down, depersonalized, and permitted less active a role in the ongoing affairs of His creation. Indeed, it was becoming increasingly difficult to distinguish the Christian God from the altogether amorphous "God" of Eastern monism.

Finally, that Darwin's Christian beliefs never approached anything resembling a well-thought-out exegesis would be evident by the mature Darwin's later reflections on his loss of faith, in particular, swipes at certain "barbaric doctrines." The very nature of his protests would demonstrate a glaring ignorance of complex doctrinal points (especially the plan of redemption through the outworking of history, culminating in Christ's incarnation and resurrection). His facile remonstrations lacked the sophistication of any schoolboy philosopher. Christianity was no less a superstition, or any more objectively grounded than African voodoo rituals.

An imagination that would become ever so sensitive to gradations in nature could allow no such gradations among competing religions, even when separated by huge chasms. No assigning degrees of credibility, no assessment of the authenticity of manuscripts employing the same rules of scholarship any other ancient *secular* document might undergo. In the end, the man who was ever-vigilant for signs of sentiment creeping into the scientific method would pronounce a sweeping rejection of Christianity because, if true, its claims would have eternally doomed his own father, brother, and most of his best friends. This made Christianity, in Darwin's words, a "damnable doctrine."[1] So much for the triumph of cool logic.

That his fateful voyage drastically altered the course of Darwin's life there can be little doubt. That Darwin suffered a loss of Christian faith and subsequently converted from immutability to mutability of species aboard the *Beagle* is debatable. Christianity, for Darwin, was never able to offer but the mildest objection to any assaults on his provincial world. Yet even the staggering diversity of tropical life he encountered would not likely have so quickly elicited such a radical conversion.

Such an act, after all, would have been nearly akin to throwing one's *manners* overboard—a vulgar display of the worst barbarism. No doubt, Darwin's fantastic encounters kindled a powerful passion and a frantic need to process this explosion of discovery. Any number of possibilities may have teased his imagination.

Rather than this representing a foreshadowing of his theory of evolution, it seems more likely this represented the early stages of Darwin's uncanny ability to compartmentalize—to simultaneously house competing worlds without allowing any one to intrude upon any other. Thus disposed, Darwin would be free to entertain the most radical possibilities while preserving a retreat of quaint convention. This ability would be indispensable in the years ahead when the theory would first begin to suggest itself. But compartmentalizing would also allow him the luxury of infusing one world with passion while letting another quietly wither away, without the untidy business of confrontation. In a more candid moment perhaps, the mature Darwin might have had the grace to admit that the substance of his "loss of faith" was mostly a process of gradual recognition that such faith had never truly existed.

Perhaps the greatest oddity surrounding the theory of evolution is that Charles Darwin should have been the one to bring such a convention-shattering premise to the world. Darwin displayed none of the radical spirit and philosophical drive of his grandfather. It is inconceivable he might have ever considered himself a visionary crusader for a new world order. The only thing he loathed more than the spotlight was personal controversy. And yet, a new world order would be the result of his life's work. Was Darwin motivated by a desire to win his father's approval and prove he was not the hopeless failure projected in his youth? Was he driven to slay the imposing God of Christianity and thus extricate his own father and friends from a horrible eternal fate? No doubt these would become very powerful motivators, but one suspects not fully cemented until after the tragic death of his ten-year-old daughter. He could not reconcile the cruel, prolonged, torturous wasting away of his little precious Anne with any kind of a loving God.

The end of Darwin's five-year voyage found him in possession of an impressive collection of exotic specimens and numerous notes taken aboard the *Beagle*. In these five years, Darwin had gone from near obscurity to a well-respected authority on the workings of nature—a member of the elite scientific society. Darwin had already surpassed all expectations by light years. But a chord had been touched that would not allow him to rest on his laurels. What did all this new information mean? If Darwin was not easily given to the popular notions of his day, neither was he ignorant of nor immune from such notions.

As the most important scientific discussion of the day was over the question of mutability, it seems unlikely Darwin could have contented himself with merely cataloging his great array of specimens. Could he have allowed this new wealth of information to sit on the sidelines while perhaps the most important question in history was being debated? Since no amount of facts, specimens, or other bits of evidence, no matter how impressive, can ever interpret themselves, Darwin was limited in what he could do until he committed to a framework. Because immutability offered no (immediate) opportunity for scientific advancement, perhaps the solution suggested itself. He would simply see how far he could take the evidence within a framework of mutability. If he came to an impasse, then it would become obvious that mutability was a nonviable concept. What could be fairer or more *scientific*? Yet what impasse could resist a vigorously exercised imagination encased in a finely honed mind of multiple compartments, especially as a philosophical commitment began to coalesce?

Natural theology was a popular religious philosophy of the day. The unfortunate descendant of Aquinas' scholasticism, this took the view that the God of the Bible could be discovered through human reason, without recourse to the Bible. Adherents of natural theology such as Adam Sedgwick needlessly put themselves in the position of trying to defend an idea they *assumed* was the biblical position. The book of Genesis, however, though it did imply fixity of basic *kinds* (cats, dogs, fish, birds, horses, elephants, etc.), did not preclude considerable latitude for modifications *within* each kind. As has now become apparent, within each basic type (biblical "kind") exists the genetic code containing all the potential varieties of that type. In cases where varieties are isolated from the main population, new species can occur, where two varieties of the same kind lose the ability to interbreed due to the *loss* of genetic information. This last point is key, because this means the introduction of new species has no relationship to *higher* complexity, thus irrelevant to any *evolutionary* process.

Emergent species, unfortunately for zealous natural theologians, were mistakenly thought to be synonymous with the "kinds" referred to in Genesis, thus were ascribed to special acts of creation. Where Darwin undermined stability of species, blurring the line between these and varieties (referring to the latter in some cases as "incipient species"), it was feared the biblical principle of immutability of basic types had been overthrown. As this happened at a time when the science of genetics was not available to show that change is limited to a fixed range dictated by the genetic code, it was assumed that the undermining of fixity of species (not fixity of kind) meant change was theoretically limitless. This had the effect of simultaneously weakening biblical authority and raising the credibility of science to a level that, for many, overshadowed the Bible.

The Origin of the Species would be the result of twenty years' sorting and consolidating of Darwin's own collection and notations, experimentation, and interrogation of the best available information. It would not be an easy twenty years. Almost as soon as he began this long process, he was stricken with severe physical ailments (headaches, stomach pains, etc.) that would often limit his work to no more than a few hours a day, sometimes no more than a few hours a week. Nevertheless, Darwin pressed on. Driven by a fear, perhaps, that the end of so massive an investment of time and effort might not be taken seriously (or even expose him as a fraud), he sought desperately to anticipate every conceivable objection. Where he could produce no workable solutions, he simply banished objections to oblivion. Yet for all his foresight in considering potential obstacles, only occasionally was he to demonstrate any vision for *philosophical* implications, specifically possible long-term devastating consequences. His overriding commitment was to methodology (assaulting the restrictive canons of legitimate science). If there were long-term consequences to consider, that would be for others to ponder, not for one of such delicate sensibilities.

The near-universal romance with "change" and "progress" palpable, Darwin's dogged determination accomplished far more than an innovative treatise brilliantly executed. He had served up the perfect metaphor for the age. Yet Darwin's brilliance was not so much a reflection of his *scientific* knowledge, formidable though it was, as his deft application of rhetoric, perhaps never equaled. Darwin subtly blended scientific reasoning, teleology, imaginative and near unbounded argument, manipulating pivotal terms such that they might support *either* side of an argument as expediency ordained, and managed even to conscript ignorance of his proposed processes in the service of his theory. All this, of course, was carefully seasoned with just enough scientific fact to create the impression of a seamless hypothesis—the impressive sum of which made the dissection of its components, much weaker in isolation, almost impossible.

This served to deter all but the most resourcefully diligent from negotiating the semantic labyrinths to see that solid evidence had been replaced with marvelously imaginative conjecture. In Darwin's own words, his treatise was "one long argument." After soldiering through Darwin's monumental work, one had not perhaps been so much convinced as charmed or *mesmerized* into acknowledging plausibility. As a salute to his persuasiveness, some of the greatest intellects of the day were so smitten by his clever handling of thorny problems that any will to objectivity was all but extinguished. And if this will was greatly subdued, the will to rationalize now admitted precious few obstacles. In short, Darwin may have been the first to raise the thoroughly modern concept of "style over substance" to an art form.

Darwin's primary evolution-inducing mechanism was "natural selection"—the idea that nature chose and perpetuated, from an almost endless array of variations at her disposal, those specific characteristics that best suited organisms for survival in their environments. By contrast, those groups that could not adapt quickly enough to successfully compete fell by the wayside—giving rise to the famous phrase "survival of the fittest" (coined by Herbert Spencer). The *analogy* upon which Darwin formulated natural selection was *artificial* selection—the deliberate methods breeders employed in producing desired strains from existing species. Yet it was in this analogy, the very heart of his argument, that Darwin set the table for the unconventional and *uncritical* nature of his investigative methodology that was to dominate throughout his treatise.

Darwin reasoned that the impressive examples of human-engineered "evolution" was but a microcosm of the efficacy of nature which, by comparison, could boast of such superior resources as a far grander laboratory, practically limitless time, and the formidable pressures of competition, in accomplishment of her fantastic evolutionary scheme. Neglected in this key analogy, however, were several crucial points. It was common knowledge among breeders that the quest for exotic specimens was almost, if not always, accomplished at the *expense* of survivability. In other words, exotic strains could exist only in the most carefully *controlled* environments!

A second important point was that natural selection evinced no sign of innovation but *conservation*. Natural selection, when it acted at all, acted to keep kinds from becoming extinct, not to produce higher complexity of species.

The most important point dismissed in all this though, was the *intelligent design* factor of artificial selection. Without a preexisting specified plan, nature's "selection," subject to prevailing forms (including regressive), could not have hoped to compete with the careful planning and deliberate manipulation of artificial selection. Upon close inspection, it's hard to imagine any more powerful argument *against* transmutation of kinds than artificial selection. On these three above points, Darwin's analogy should have fallen.

Of Darwin's pivotal terms, none were perhaps so important (or malleable) as the word "advantage." *Advantage* accounted for the long neck of the giraffe, though it was by no means evident why from an evolutionary scale it *should* have, since it could also account for the *short* neck of the hippopotamus. To critics who protested, the response amounted to classic circular reasoning. Where apparent inconsistencies existed, it could be assumed that if whatever conditions nature had evolved were *not* advantageous, they would not have persisted. Likewise, the "fittest" in evolutionary terms were those organisms that left the most offspring; and *why* were these deemed the fittest? Of course, *because* they left the most offspring! This is the equivalent of asking why a runner is consistently faster than his fellow competitors. Answer: because he consistently reaches the finish line first. Formulated this way, "advantage" and "fittest" are each reduced to mere tautologies. "Advantage" thus was merely a label placed on an outcome after the fact without any objective explanation as to how this outcome was arrived at or why *it*, among all possibilities, should have logically been anticipated.

Darwin seemed remarkably unperturbed that his great hypothesis was itself supported by numerous hypotheses. Logically, this should have weakened his overall position. When all was said and done, Darwin had pointed to no clear evidence in nature that a progression from one basic type to another *had* taken place; only considerable circumstantial evidence (if one's imagination permitted) and a "mechanism" where if just the right staggering number of events were fortuitously aligned for it to then *act* upon (out of limitless competing alternatives), evolution *might* be possible. This of course would set the stage for the Darwinism that was to follow. Never would it be an enterprise dealing with precise predictions but always and only an *explanation after the fact*. Thus unfettered, there could never be a limit to its application even (or especially) when hard facts proved intransigent. It must surely be a tribute to Darwin's powers of persuasion or to the then-existing fertile soil (probably both) that his theory achieved exemption from the all-important falsifiability criterion, and that *ignorance* of his thesis—transmutation of kinds—was somehow converted into the *probability* that his theory was true.

Perhaps his chapter "Difficulties on Theory" most effectively captured the essence of Darwin's methodology of imagining and gift for oversimplification, especially his effort to address the staggering complexities of the eye:

> To suppose the eye, with all its inimitable contrivances for adjusting the focus to different distances . . . could have been formed by natural selection, seems . . . absurd in the highest possible degree. Yet reason tells me that if numerous gradations from a perfect and complex eye to one very imperfect and simple, each grade being useful to its possessor, can be shown to exist . . .then the difficulty of believing that a perfect and complex eye could be formed by natural selection, though insuperable by our imagination, can hardly be considered real. How a nerve comes to be sensitive to light, hardly concerns us . . . but I may remark that several facts make me suspect that any sensitive nerve may be rendered sensitive to light, and likewise to those coarser vibrations of the air which produce sound.[2]

Yet the gradations of eyes to which he referred did not spring from a single ancestral line, meaning all these various designs had to evolve *independently*. Darwin's ignorance of DNA overlooked the radical differences in genetic information separating these "gradations." Moreover, the new unimaginably complex machinery necessary to convert Darwin's sensitive nerve into a light receptor would have already been of a magnitude sufficient to make this a prodigious leap of faith. Yet for this primitive light receptor to be "selected" it would have needed even far more complex computational machinery to interpret the meaning of light signals and convert into a survival response.

Competition, of course, was the centerpiece of Darwin's theory. But it was the *brand* of competition that set his contribution apart from all previous Lamarckian themes. In the unlikely combination of factors that gave birth to Darwinism, perhaps no other part of the story conveys such irony. In 1798, Thomas Malthus published *On Population*, a principle concerning all populations in general. His premise was that there were but two basics checks on population—vice and misery (i.e., famine, war, disease). Malthus' theory (still often misunderstood) was not a doom-and-gloom forecast of some impending catastrophe, sounding a clarion call for immediate corrective action. He merely observed that populations will always expand or contract according to *food supply*. His principle proposition stated that, if all things are equal, those less affected by disease, war, or famine will tend to proliferate at a higher rate than the reverse. In other words, just as populations could not for long exceed the food supply, neither would they remain, for very long, *smaller* than available food permitted. Thus, his theory was a polemic *against* unrestrained progress, hardly conducive to a theory of evolution.

Nevertheless, from Malthus' principle of population, Darwin gleaned that elusive law of universal pressure, the natural imperative constantly pressing upon stability of kinds—the drive to survive in an arena of *ruthless* and *relentless* competition for available food. Malthus would become so closely associated with the proposition of natural selection that the reference would often be to the "Malthus-Darwin theory." Had he lived to see it, Malthus would have been mortified. Compounding the irony, in his latter (1803) edition, Malthus allowed for another check on population—personal restraint. This was a tacit admission that his earlier premise (as a universal biological principle) was seriously flawed. The growing data were demonstrating the reverse to be the rule among humans. The affluent tended to proliferate at a far *lower* rate than the poverty-stricken.[3] This also represented a dramatic and qualitative difference between humans and all other types, surely eliminating man from any evolutionary process if one existed at all. Yet Darwin, in his typical tunnel vision, did not even allow this later correction to factor into his theory.

Darwin, wisely, did not deal directly with the subject of man's place in his theory. Yet he did leave strong clues that man was not exempt from the process. Any doubt of his intent was laid to rest twelve years after the *Origin* was published with his *Descent of Man* in 1871. Darwin utterly detested any effort to separate humans from the *universal* evolutionary impulse. If natural selection, the epitome of ruthless competition, *excluded* man, then in Darwin's own mind, his theory was an abject failure. This, of course, called for an all-out assault on the *miraculous*. The miraculous, so went the thought, was a renegade causal agent that laid waste the uniformity of science. Though on occasion he flirted with the idea of a higher good, he understood this was perilously close to allowing a divine foot (of some sort) in the door. The only avenue left for Darwin was to assign causal agency to the completely neutral element of *chance*. Chance, it was reasoned, would supply natural selection with a generous horde of candidates if only sufficient *time* were placed at its disposal.

Chance, it was decided, represented a far higher fidelity to the scientific method than "miracle." Yet "chance" was merely the anointed placeholder for *ignorance*. Darwin would himself admit this is what he meant by his use of the former. But who could describe the substance of ignorance? How, for instance, might one distinguish it from a vacuum? How was the cause of science advanced by transforming *ignorance* into a credible explanation? Was an entirely new paradigm to set its foundation on ignorance? If the prospect of invoking "miracle" to shore up recalcitrant gaps was too tempting and thus stifling to scientific inquisitiveness, could the invocation of "ignorance" be any less tempting? And could *anything* be more antithetical to the advancement of knowledge than conferring scientific prestige and limitless efficacy on "We haven't a clue"?

Moreover, if critics suspected this zealous concern over the disruptiveness of miracles was a pretext to remove God from the equation altogether, they had some justification. Why, for instance, should it have been assumed that miracles conveyed arbitrariness when their occurrence had *always* been to accomplish some *specific purpose*? *Where* could it be shown (apart from creation and *the* resurrection testifying to authorship of physical law) that the miraculous had ever represented anything but a *temporary* suspension of physical laws and only in isolated cases? In fact, the incidence of miracles was so infinitesimal that their statistical probability could not possibly have represented a threat to scientific discovery. The great irony was, only the preservation of so improbable a framework as evolution *would* have required such a high incidence of miracles! Thus, the ubiquitous threat of miracles was every bit as much a mental contrivance as the system it "endangered."

Though Darwin had managed to completely misunderstand Malthus, this should not be taken to mean he never gained an appreciation for serious discrepancies within his formulation of natural selection. At the time of the publication of the *Origin*, Darwin had every confidence that natural selection was the primary mechanism of evolutionary change. Doubt began to creep in relatively soon, however. By the time of *Descent of Man*, Darwin had assigned a considerably greater role to "sexual selection" than to natural selection. What might have brought about such a drastic change of heart?

To begin with, Darwin was aware of the inherent limitations of natural selection—that it could only act upon those variations already present but had no power to *bring* these into existence. In addition, if natural selection was unrelentingly and mercilessly moving toward a state of perfection, why (as Gertrude Himmelfarb muses) did it allow gradations of *imperfection* to persist?[4] If it had already pronounced obsolescence upon those supposed earlier forms, then why was the world still teeming with them and, in many cases, *coexisting* near their advantaged counterparts? Wasn't the compelling feature of natural selection (and its main selling point) that ruthless competition *eliminated* weaker organisms?

If these questions (and many other "exceptions" to what should have been the rule) represented serious obstacles, the problem was no better *within* species. Every example of social organization stood *against* the free-for-all individualism of Darwinism. One could hardly point to a more serious drag on personal survivability than taking on a parental role.[5] Nature, as it turned out, appeared to be *most* selective in its application of ruthlessness.

Though Gregor Mendel had begun experiments in genetics at about the time the *Origin* appeared, these findings would not be widely published until well after Darwin's death. Darwin, of course, knew nothing about the science of genetics, but Mendel's results would be devastating to the idea that segregation and recombination of genes could engineer gradations of increasing complexity sufficient to produce new kinds. It would be left to de Vries, following Mendel's lead, to discover that only abrupt and complex disruptions within subunits of reproductive cells (later identified as DNA), either through copying errors or external invasive agents, could bring about the sort of novel *and* transmittable changes (called mutations) required to even admit the *possibility* of new kinds. Yet by the very violent nature of a mutation, it was understood that the prospect of extracting even a few "good" mutations was extremely low. A mutation produced a smearing, no increase, and usually a net *loss* of information. Of course, this would be a problem for succeeding generations of Darwinists to work out, long after the theory was well entrenched. Neither would these latter disciples be any less adept in the art of circular reasoning. If genetics had placed near-insuperable hurdles in evolution's path, then natural selection, it would be assumed, must be far more formidable than previously imagined.

Darwin's own growing disenchantment with natural selection coupled with an increasing reliance on inheritance of acquired characteristics meant, for all practical purposes, that he had come full circle in his evolution odyssey, *back* to the old Lamarckian theory. A skeptic might have taken the occasion to point out the obvious—the evolution theory was back to square one, lacking once again, a credible mechanism. Why then was such a significant development practically unnoticed? Why was the whole Darwinist approach not scrapped *altogether*? The short answer is: the spirit of the age would not permit it to fail.

Within a period of hardly more than ten years, the Darwinian tidal wave had left in its wake a new reigning scientific paradigm. Critics found themselves in the unenviable position of having to attack the motives of a man whose character was beyond reproach. Darwin's closest allies, Joseph Hooker and T. H. Huxley, were likewise men of unquestioned principle. Apart from the *Origin's* clever argument, it enjoyed significant public popularity. To oppose such a powerful, brilliantly conceived and articulated theory *altogether* was to court political suicide. One faced the very real possibility of becoming, relatively quickly, scientifically *and* socially irrelevant. This not-so-mild form of extortion did indeed, in a remarkably short time, swing the balance in Darwin's favor. By the time Darwin had largely abandoned his own primary mechanism (natural selection), too many had given up too much to even try to return to a pre-Darwinian position. Besides, with so many among the esteemed describing his fine garments in such vivid detail, the emperor could not possibly be as naked as he sometimes *appeared*.

That the *Origin* reflected a philosophic position more than a fidelity to the scientific method (a fact pointed out by several scientists at the time) would not be allowed to detract from its supporters' enthusiasm. It seemed to answer all the important questions, therefore it *must* be true—or at least the closest approximation to the truth! Only the hardest-hearted philistine could resist its charming explanatory power. But what if appearances that looked like such a sure thing turned out, on closer inspection and with more information, to be *misleading*? What if it was not some evolutionary process that had brought man out of the jungle? This haunting prospect was not completely lost on Darwinists, especially those painfully aware that, though compelling, the theory was a deductive argument that failed to prove its central thesis.

As a point of interest, after detecting a certain stench in the wind, Huxley himself would glimpse some of the forces that had unwittingly been unleashed. The odor emanated from something called ethical Darwinism—the view that the weak or "unfit" should not be artificially sustained by government welfare. From this would emerge the philosophical concept of "social Darwinism." More benign strains existed in the eugenics movement, advocating the sterilization of certain "undesirable" elements of society. Its more malignant forms would manifest in hypernationalism, most insidiously in militaristic racism. Huxley vigorously protested that evolution was never meant to be—indeed, could not be—a guide for morality. Morality, he rightly observed, was always in conflict with nature, and men were duty-bound to resist its pull.[6] It is inconceivable a man of Huxley's intellect would not have immediately recognized the paradox he had exposed. How could it ever be possible to combat what, according to Darwinism, man was part and parcel to?

Thoughtful Darwinists like Huxley did indeed appreciate their peculiar position as pivotal subjects of history. If the tremendous gaps of Darwinism yet to be filled in could be by yet-unearthed evidence, then they would be judged courageous forerunners and enlightened standard-bearers of the single most important scientific discovery in history—in which case, their considerable gamble would have been justified. On the other hand, had they gambled wrongly, the judgment of history would be harsh and unforgiving. Not only would they bear responsibility for the architecture of a false science but for the promulgation of a false religion as well. Absent any real falsifiability principle, commitment to Darwinism was understood to mean that all lines of retreat were cut off. There could be no turning back. In a more ominous sense, commitment under these terms was intuitively understood to mean that any disconfirming evidence (especially a pattern) would necessarily *ensure* that "scientific naturalism" must become less scientific and *more* philosophic. In short, it must become *doctrine*—the emerging outline of a new pervasive religion where reality, pounded by wave after relentless wave of dogmatic decree, finally capsizes.

CHAPTER 13

MARXISM

Since Marxism features the ideas of Darwin, Nietzsche, and Freud, it may be instructive to see Marx' dream of socialism implemented on a grand scale and in its most ostentatious form. Marx, in close identification with the currents of his time, took his cue from nature. Communism (Marx' particular brand of socialism) was essentially an extrapolation of the patterns evident in the natural world. There was no question that the most efficient models of social organization and production were on display in beehives, ant colonies, prairie-dog communities, and the like. Though in all such communal examples the individual had a specific role, each assignment was nevertheless carried out in perfect concert with fellow workers to the extent that individual identity was lost to a collective consciousness. It was evident that in each observable example, only that which advanced the whole had value. Since Darwinism had reduced human beings to just another organism within an impersonal evolutionary process (albeit a highly evolved and complex organism) there was no reason to suppose social models that worked extraordinarily well on the small scale would not work equally well on the larger.

Though itself a product of nature, human identity, Marx reasoned, would achieve its highest state of consciousness through its struggle (labor) to survive against the imposing impediments of nature. Consciousness was only possible within the framework of struggle, but struggle only assumed significance within terms of a *social* structure. Capitalism (Marx' description for free-market economies) had alienated men with its emphasis on competition, set against man's inner yearning for a cooperative spirit. Christianity, and the drive toward private ownership it had given rise to, was responsible for fostering the most serious threat to collectivism—the individual. If man were to achieve his workers' paradise, his glorious destiny through immersion in the whole, religion (especially Christianity) and private property had to be abolished.

Marx predicted that the capitalist system was headed for an inevitable crisis. Eventually its two primary sources, available workers and available fertile land, would reach a point of exhaustion. The demand for new and better machinery to produce more and cheaper goods to remain competitive would force capitalists to do with less profit. This would result in reduced wages and fewer jobs. The ruthless competition of capitalism would bring this pattern to its logical conclusion. With too few workers left to generate the vital "surplus value," profits would cease, and capitalism would grind to a halt.[1] Governments, largely subsidized by capitalist exploitation, would no longer possess any means for exerting authority over the masses. Workers, set free from their historic chains, would rise to assume the reins of control, finally taking responsibility for their own destiny. All business, under this system, would be owned and managed by the state (a new kind of state, to be sure, representing the interests of the people).

No longer would any able-bodied man find himself agonizing over the uncertainty of the job market, held hostage to faceless manipulative forces. The state would not only guarantee the worker a job but a house, food, clothing, medical care, and all the "necessities" of life. Yes, the existence of the state (even in this imagined nebulous form) would initially represent a necessary evil, but as workers became accustomed to their assigned responsibilities (determined according to the skills and abilities of each) and began to experience the unprecedented rewards from this massive liberation of the human spirit, the state would become superfluous and eventually wither away. The generation of wealth and leisure (not just for an elite class but for all) resulting from this unshackling would make it unthinkable to even consider some other way. Anyone refusing to accept his assigned role in the economy of the hive would automatically and instantly find himself ostracized by his own fellow workers. "The people," recognizing their shared ownership in all factories, land, institutions, goods, etc., would *become* the state, to the extent it remained at all.

It all sounded too good to be true. Unfortunately, this would prove the case. When finally implemented, it was not the state that finally withered away but any vestige of respect for, or intrinsic value associated with, human life.

Communism, though it portended exciting social change, remained problematic for its enthusiastic supporters, who were skeptical as to how such radical change might be implemented. Even Germany's labor movement that quickly embraced Marxist principles, though revolution remained the currency of official rhetoric, gravitated toward policies of reform of the capitalist system through parliamentary pressure. Over time, it was felt, the superiority of Communism would be so evident that governments would be forced to adopt most of its features, resulting eventually in a complete transformation in responding to the will of the people. The hard-liners, on the other hand, those who intuitively understood the revolutionary nature of Communism, realized that reinventing society was something that would be resisted by many, especially the profiteers of the old order. For the hard-liners, the French Revolution was the model for radical change.

The Russian Revolution of 1905, though a failure, had weakened the ruling structure and exerted internal pressures leading to reforms. By 1917, the monarchy of Tsar Nicholas II was yet considerably more weakened by, among other things, poor management of the military during World War I, draconian responses to public criticism, and abysmal economic conditions. After several failed attempts at negotiating an acceptable solution between the throne and the Russian Parliament, the tsar abdicated. A provisional government filled the void, but the instability that had been growing for some time was scarcely stemmed. One dedicated Communist, Vladimir Lenin, recognized the opportunity that had presented itself. Lenin took advantage of the confusion and anger to capture the popular sentiment, giving the people a scapegoat against which they could vent—the affluent. Meanwhile, his Bolshevik Party tapped into the populist yearning for an all-nurturing state, promising the masses "peace, land, and bread." Just a few months following the abdication of Tsar Nicholas, Lenin's party was sufficiently emboldened to stage the Bolshevik Revolution, overthrowing the provisional government and taking control of the nation. Private property was outlawed; public utilities and institutions were placed under the direct control of the state; state debts were declared void; banks were nationalized; inheritance rights were abolished; and so on.

"The people" were represented by a single political party. There was no need for an alternative to the Communist Party, since by definition this party was the consummation of every worker's dream. Despite its grandiose claims, Communism quickly had the look and feel of any other absolutist dictatorship. Any dissension was immediately suppressed.

A fixed standard clearly spelling out what constituted "dissension" would have been frightening enough. Dissension under the Soviet Union, however, was constantly being redefined in the direction of expanding intolerance. One scarcely knew when he might suddenly find himself branded "enemy of the state." Without benefit of trial, as many as 100,000 citizens were executed within the first two to three years. Upward of two million (mostly of the educated middle and upper classes) fled the workers' paradise for their lives.[2] They understood that no matter how faithfully they toed the partly line, because they were distinguishable from the ordinary peasantry they would be viewed with growing suspicion. It would only be a matter of time before something as innocuous as reading *any* pre-revolution literature would fall under the heading of "subversive."

Directives from Central Planning were to be carried out with an iron hand. There was no place within Communism for following the spirit of the law. Any deviation and the guilty party faced the full weight of an unforgiving regime. This would lead to gross inefficiencies, ensuring the eventual implosion of the system.

Perhaps the most serious miscalculation was in assuming an idealized static set of conditions, upon which the state could weigh needs in relation to real value. The problem was that "static" conditions had a nasty habit of never remaining static. State planning could not hope to compete with the spontaneity and self-correcting machinery of the free market, which could not only readjust to changing conditions rather quickly but could much more easily chart new trends reflecting market forces.[3] Planners, on the other hand, were essentially flying blind. To anticipate and then stave off unintended and harmful consequences, planners would have needed to possess the knowledge, foresight, and wisdom of an all-knowing, all-seeing, and almighty God. As the world would find out near the close of the twentieth century, nowhere would the Communist miscalculation be more evident, its arrogant pretensions more deficient.

Section II

THE ENLIGHTENMENT ONSLAUGHT

CHAPTER 14

HIGHER CRITICISM, AND THE WELLHAUSEN DOCUMENTARY HYPOTHESIS

T he Enlightenment would not be content to fashion itself into an alternate worldview that merely competed with Christianity for the right to describe reality. It would, instead, deliberately reach its tentacles deep into the very heart of Christian basics. The nineteenth century would give rise to a new form of critical examination called "higher criticism" (in contradistinction to "lower criticism," which had concerned itself with the process of transmission of original documents; i.e., whether original writings had been faithfully preserved, and their integrity maintained).

Until this shift, sound Bible scholarship (and any other sort) had been based on the harmonistic method.[1] While resisting exotic explanations, this method assumed the reliability of ancient sources, so long as basic consistencies and harmonies were evident. This approach allowed the facts to lead wherever they would, not reflexively rejecting certain conclusions simply because they seemed to support the orthodox view. There existed a tacit understanding that speculative subjective theories must not drive the scholarship, but facts based on tangible, external data. Reliable research must proceed from the known to the unknown (the inductive method). Likewise, attempting to judge an ancient culture by casting the examiners' own cultural assumptions into the past would have, by consensus, rendered the examiners' findings highly dubious. In a deliberate break with past methodologies, the new form of scholarship reached for a hypercriticism that saw, as its duty, the dismantling of orthodoxy. It was simply assumed, without proof, that the orthodox version must be contrived.

The most insidious strain to emerge from higher criticism would be the subdiscipline "literary criticism" (or source criticism). Literary criticism set out with a single specific mission—to uncover evidence that the Pentateuch (first five books of the OT) could not be the work of a single author. As is so often the case, when one sets out to find evidence of a specific nature, seldom does he return instead with evidence refuting the thrust of his work. This approach would owe much to Hegel's dialectics, the idea of "being" replaced with the idea of "becoming." All religion was placed within the evolutionary paradigm, religious development the outworking of superstitious folklore of an unsophisticated time and people. All religion was thus man-centered, with divine intervention disproved not by rigorous rules of investigation but by placing it out of court.

Because cutting-edge science had lent its weight to a simple-to-complex progression within history, those writings that featured religious concepts deemed too sophisticated to have been developed within purported timeframes (as the writings themselves claimed) were automatically suspect. In other words, detailed eyewitness accounts were dismissed—not because external evidence exposed fraudulent claims, but because the evolutionary scheme would not permit levels of sophistication to exist at certain times that were not consistent with acceptable assumptions. Too much sophistication at the "wrong time" meant, of course, that someone *had* to have monkeyed with the original writings.

Literary criticism would be the tireless methodology by which scholars would cull from ancient texts multiple independent sources that had been intermingled by conspiratorial redactors (editors), weaving these various strands together perhaps as much as a thousand years later than the time the original documents were supposedly written.[2] No literary work would find itself a more fit candidate for this esteemed "scholarly" approach than the Bible—especially its foundation which rested on the first five books of the Old Testament (called the Pentateuch, the Torah, or simply The Law), purportedly written by Moses himself.

As stated previously, the Bible told a very dramatic story which, if contrived, would have made it difficult to explain the continuity of thought, key events unfolding against the historical backdrop, and geographical descriptions consonant with chronological settings. What follows is a brief summation of that story.

About the twentieth century BC Abraham journeyed to the land of Canaan to become the father of what would become the chosen nation of God. Through this nation would emerge a savior who would reconcile fallen mankind to its Creator. Abraham, his son Isaac, and grandson Jacob were collectively known as "the Patriarchs." Jacob fathered twelve sons who formed the twelve tribes, which in time collectively made up the nation of Israel. Jacob's favorite son, Joseph, was sold into Egyptian slavery by jealous brothers. In Egypt, Joseph rose from lowly slave to second ruler in the land. A terrible famine throughout the region lured the house of Jacob down into Egypt for the only available grain. Joseph, in charge of selling and dispensing Egyptian grain, finally revealed himself to his brothers in a heart-rending confrontation.

Joseph's exalted position in Egypt secured a choice stretch of land for Jacob's family in the land of Goshen. Here the Hebrews enjoyed the hospitality of the Egyptian ruler for many years, until long after the death of Joseph. Sometime later, a pharaoh assumed the throne "who knew not Joseph" (Ex. 1:8) and thrust the now-considerable Hebrew population into slave labor. Years passed, until a deliverer was sent by God to take His people (the Jews) out of Egypt and into their Promised Land in Canaan—essentially the same land their forefathers had occupied centuries earlier, before circumstances ordained the relocation to Egypt. This great deliverer arrived in the person of Moses, who ironically had been raised in the Egyptian court as the adopted son and legal heir of the Pharaoh. At one point in his adulthood, Moses became aware of his actual Hebrew ancestry and consciously set aside the royal trappings to embrace his blood kin. Following a frightful flight into the desert, Moses was confronted by God and then prepared for his mission—a return to the Egyptian court to demand the unconditional release of his people.

Following a series of miraculous signs, Pharaoh finally conceded, and the Jews began their long trek out of Egypt under Moses' leading. Murmuring and open rebellion denied the Jews their Promised Land for forty years. While in route, however, a complex law code was given (now known as the Deuteronomic code), the Tabernacle (the portable prototype of the coming Temple) was constructed as the center of worship, and the Levitical priesthood was instituted as a special intercessory class between God and the people. This marked the beginning of a special covenant the people entered with YHWH. About 1400 BC the Jews, led by Moses' appointed successor, Joshua, entered the Promised Land.

The Jews were ruled and guided during the next few hundred years by judges and prophets. The period of judges ended when the prophet Samuel, responding to the demands of the people, anointed the first king of Israel, Saul. Saul, though initially a faithful executor of God's commands, fell into ever-increasing apostasy and was replaced by David (approx. 1000 BC). Under David's leadership, Israel enjoyed many stirring victories and probably the most celebrated period in her history. David's son Solomon built the first temple (approx. 950 BC).

Following the death of Solomon, about 900 BC, the kingdom suffered a split. The southern half, remaining loyal to the house of David, consisted of the tribes of Judah and Benjamin as well as the Levitical priesthood, and was collectively known as Judah. The northern half, comprised of the remaining ten tribes, carried the collective name Israel (sometimes Ephraim) and established its own separate places of worship, priesthood, and kingdom. For its approximate two hundred years of existence, the northern kingdom descended into greater demonstrations of apostasy.

Israel's sinking depravity was finally met with judgment, in the form of the destruction of her capital Samaria accompanied by Assyrian captivity in 722 BC.

The southern kingdom, Judah, though hardly a model of righteous and obedient living, maintained at least a semblance of a conscience before, and contact with, YHWH. In the two hundred-plus years of the northern kingdom, not a single king was ever said to have done "that which was right in the sight of God." Some, such as Ahab, went to breathtaking lengths to explore the depths of evil. By contrast, Judah, in her 330 or so years of separate existence, featured eight kings out of twenty total who were worthy of praise. These eight represented those times of reform when the Jews, heeding the warnings of their prophets, purged the land of pagan altars of worship and repented of national sin, recommitting to the Law Moses had delivered centuries before. Yet these times of repentance are short-lived. Bit by bit, Judah followed her northern sister into eventual total severance from the very God who brought her out of captivity into her Promised Land. Judah's imitation of Israel probably reached its zenith with the kingship of Manasseh, who not only embraced witchcraft and astrology but sacrificed his own children to pagan gods.

Two years after the reign of Manasseh, God raised up the last of the good kings in the person of Josiah. Josiah waged perhaps the most aggressive campaign against idolatry of all reforming kings, destroying all prohibited "high places" of worship, purging the land of all idols, and leading the nation in a period of heartfelt mourning for grievous sin. A refurbishment project of the temple (which had fallen into a deplorable state from years of neglect) resulted in a key discovery (622 BC) by the high priest—the Book of the Law. Apparently for many years God's ordinances had become so ignored that the sacred Law of Moses (the Deuteronomic code) had gone missing without even raising a whimper of concern among those entrusted with its oversight and execution.

Although Josiah's efforts were successful in turning the people back to the Lord, the die had already been cast. The best that Josiah's reforms do is to temporarily stay the judgment that God had decreed through the prophets Isaiah, Micah, Hosea, and Zephaniah. Manasseh, sadly, had already brought the people beyond a point of return. The fate that Israel (the northern kingdom) had suffered would soon be shared by Judah. Following the short life of Josiah, as though to show the relative shallowness of this "turning back to God," the people immediately returned to their idolatrous ways—and if possible, to an even deeper state of depravity prior to Josiah's reign. A series of invasions by the Babylonians beginning about 605 BC resulted in the end of the southern kingdom. For several years after, the people were taken away in waves into Babylonian captivity, culminating finally with the city of Jerusalem and its sacred temple lying in ruins by 586 BC.

During the period of captivity, Babylon was overcome by the Persians. Seventy years after the Jews had been sent into exile, the Persian king Cyrus issued a decree that all Jews so desiring could return to their homeland, to rebuild the city of Jerusalem and its temple. In "troublous times," as the book of Daniel had prophesied (Dan. 9:25), the restoration project was completed. The Old Testament ends with the prophets looking ahead to the much-anticipated coming of the Messiah.

Even this much-abbreviated version reveals remarkable continuity. When this skeleton is sinewed and fleshed-in with the painstaking details that make up the OT, the suggestion that this might be the final product of an artificial construct seems absurd. As a conglomeration of events linked together in an unbroken chain, this record seems unassailable. Yet a certain German school of biblical scholarship, riding the popular wave of naturalism in the latter half of the nineteenth century, would have none of it.

Of course, loose theories of non-Mosaic authorship of the Pentateuch could be traced back to the mid-1700s. Yet this German school under the direction of Julius Wellhausen would take the lead in building a new narrative upon this old framework, tying "independent source documents" together within the prevailing evolutionary view of history. Wellhausen's contribution was to separate these various "sources" based on chronological placement. That is, degree of sophistication of phraseology and "higher concepts" was the determiner of which source was being employed in each book, chapter—or even, in some cases, verse.

Although the story told in the Bible interlocked various characters, events, and themes in an irreducible narrative, Wellhausen, because he was committed to an evolutionary model, was predisposed to reject the single authorship of the Pentateuch. In his mind, the four distinct styles he believed he uncovered reflected at least four different authors who wrote, for the most part, in ignorance of each other. These four sources were labeled (in their chronologic order) J (the Yahwist), E (the Elohist), D (the Deuteronomist), and P (the priestly writer). This would become known as the Wellhausen theory, or the documentary hypothesis.

At least six foundational presuppositions factored into the documentary hypothesis:

1. No supernatural intervention was possible; all religions developed along a universal evolutionary pattern.

2. The Jewish religion grew naturally out of environmental and geographic conditions. Religious ideas were borrowed from surrounding pagan religions.

3. Abraham and his descendants were untrustworthy and unhistorical.

4. The second commandment prohibits making and worshiping graven images. The Jews of Moses' day *did* worship images; thus, this commandment could not have been given at this time (1500–1400 BC).

5. The laws, moral tone, and social level of Leviticus and Deuteronomy were too developed and sophisticated to have been written during Moses' time.

6. No writing in Israel existed at the time of Moses.

In accordance with these six foundational presuppositions, it was reasoned that Abraham to Moses were simply fictional legend intended to instill tribal pride in larger-than-life characters. Moses to David were likely a blending of mostly fiction with history. From David on, Bible history was perhaps fairly reliable.[3]

Yet if these different authors wrote at different times in history with, in some cases, no specific knowledge of each other, then how was Wellhausen to account for such precise intermingling of these independent accounts, such that the parts came together to form an uninterrupted whole? And who were the individuals responsible for taking the various sources and "fitting" them into this final form that certainly, at least to the average reader, had the appearance of an indivisible story?

The answer to all the above was to be found in the ingenious employment of "redactors"—assumed to be a group of Jewish editors who took upon themselves the task of combining the various written sources of Jewish legend and history into the final Pentateuchal form around 400 BC. The redactors proved a most convenient solution to any problem the documentary hypothesis might otherwise find intractable. Wellhausen thus presumed to reconstruct the "actual" history of the Jews.

Whatever may have existed of an actual Jewish identity and presence in the mid to early part of the second millennium BC, it was assumed, simply mirrored neighboring tribal customs. That is, a chief tribal deity (with his vast entourage of subordinate gods) was concocted with all the elaborate accompanying myths and legends, all for instilling pride and creating a rallying (or controlling) point of orientation for the people. Again, in imitation of cultures the Jews contacted, heroic characters were woven into epic tales that featured these mighty men prevailing despite impossible odds. As writing would scarcely have existed among such a crude and mostly nomadic people, these legends were passed down verbally through the generations, each succeeding predictably embellishing that which it had received from the previous. Near the end of the second millennium or early part of the first millennium BC, the loose strands of Jewish nomads had coalesced into a nation, a real historic entity whose movements in relation to other nations of the region could reasonably well be charted.

About 850 BC, the "J" writer committed important national legend to scrolls. Yet his writing was from a political perspective that reflected the division of kingdoms. His chief objective was to place the center of true Judaism in Jerusalem, to establish through an embellished history that Judah (the southern kingdom) was the rightful inheritor of covenantal promises. The "E" author, writing near 800 BC, responded from the northern kingdom's perspective, presenting a parallel history which countered J's claim to exclusive governmental and religious legitimacy. Sometime in the seventh century BC, Israel achieved its greatest degree of legal sophistication in the form of the Deuteronomic code. This marvelous achievement left its record in the writings of "D," which concerned themselves mostly with religious reform, possibly in response to the gross excesses of Manasseh—an attempt to restore lofty principles established by Moses. After the end of the northern kingdom, the J and E documents may have been combined by an early redactor, about 650 BC; it is believed that the D author was probably familiar with both J and E. During the fifth century BC, Jewish religious thought reached its pinnacle with the emergence of the priestly class. The "P" writer combined worship around the temple with the loftiest concepts of the Law, making it impossible to separate the two from this point forward.

Finally, about 400 BC the final and most important group of redactors, apparently possessing these "sources" (J, E, D, and P), conspired to create a story of the Jews—a seamless retrogression at least a thousand years into the past for promoting a false chronology of Jewish history. Apparently, it was decided by these "ancient editors" that the very survival of the Jewish race depended upon a reconstruction of the past, an ingenious never-before (and never-since) accomplished fusion of legend and history.

As is evident, the documentary hypothesis is considerably at odds with the traditional approach to examining the straightforward presentation contained within the pages of the Old Testament. Concepts that are laid out in an intertwined, contemporary, and complementary manner in the Bible are ripped apart by time, differing literary style, and evolving complexity (within Wellhausen's view). Yet it must be stressed that the documentary hypothesis, for all the prestige and pageantry surrounding it, remains afloat only to the extent that the above presuppositions are justified. What if it should turn out that not one of these presuppositions is "seaworthy"?

For instance, Wellhausen suggested that writing at the time of Moses, according to an important documentarian assumption, was relegated only to the most necessary of government functions. Thus, it is considered doubtful that Moses (allowing he is even a real historic figure) and his band of nomads would have had any such capability. As early as 1935, however, this notion was thoroughly discredited. At least five different scripts were shown to have been in common and widespread use in the regions occupied by the Jews several centuries before their existence: Egyptian hieroglyphs, Accadian cuneiform, the Sinaitic alphabet, the cuneiform alphabet of Ugarit, and a form of hieroglyphs employed by the Phoenicians. Writes Cyrus Gordon, an authority on the tablets discovered at Ugarit, "Prose and poetry were already fully developed. The educational system was so advanced that dictionaries in four languages were compiled for the use of scribes, and the individual words were listed in their Ugaritic, Babylonian, Sumerian, and Hurrian equivalents. . . . The notion that early Israelite religion and society were primitive is completely false. Canaan in the days of the Patriarchs was the hub of a great international culture."[4]

In the book of Genesis, documentarians believe they can point to one of the earliest evidences of multiple sources, with the divine names "YHWH" and "Elohim" occurring in close proximity. Elohim, it was maintained, represented a distinctly differing strain of thought within Israel's religious development. Predictably, Wellhausen (and his present-day defenders) chose to ignore the unfolding implications of Genesis that would have easily explained the different usages. The names are in fact not interspersed interchangeably reflecting preference of individual authors but follow a consistent pattern—"YHWH" when the theme is related to covenant, "Elohim" in all other instances. The use of these two names does not suggest disagreement of style or level of sophistication, but makes the vital distinction between the shadowy concept of God (which even pagans held) and the very *personal nature* of God. To further illustrate where the term "Yahweh-Elohim" occurs it can be understood "Yahweh is God."

Supposedly, God (in the Jewish "myth") did not reveal Himself as YHWH until His visitation with Moses on Mt. Sinai (Exod. 6:3). Thus, all prior occurrences of this word prove that the J and E documents were combined to give a more full-bodied presentation. Yet documentarians are again guilty of sliding past the obvious to embrace the obtuse. The covenant established at Sinai brought the nation into a more personal relationship with the Almighty than ever previously known. The Jews became privy to an unprecedented intimacy with the Creator of all heaven and Earth. The idea is that this far and away surpassed the knowledge of God revealed to the Patriarchs.

Documentarians would like to have it both ways. The names Yahweh and Elohim are said to be indicative of alternate (and distinct) source passages. Yet if Yahweh showed up in what is deemed an E source passage or Elohim in a J source passage, the "redactor" is said to have either made a mistake in intermingling the different sources, or simply went with the appellation of his preference. Thus, the redactor is simultaneously clever on an unprecedented scale *and* sloppy (or far too cavalier) with his "clever" intermingling of source materials.

Yet the real question is this: If the redactor is guilty of altering the original source (and not merely blending) materials in *any* case, why should we suppose he hasn't done this frequently? What sort of test can we employ to see if he's monkeyed with an original source, and how do we determine the direction in which his error lies? Is it not peculiar that the entire case for the Wellhausen theory rests on the reliability of certain individuals who are *presumed* to have acted fallaciously?

The Deuteronomic code and the priesthood are not entities capable of meaningful mutual exclusion any more than a human heart and its arteries. The Deuteronomic code and the priesthood were immediately and intricately tied up in covenant relationship, forming the method/mediation by which the Jews might enter and keep covenant. The violation of Yahweh's mediation ordinances, in turn, formed the basis for which prophets inveighed against the sins of the people (such as "thou shalt not have any graven images"). This assumes "the people" have some prior knowledge of a Law which they have been accused of violating. This also means the prophets cannot represent some imagined early strand of Jewish religious thought, existing independently of the Law and serving as a forerunner to the priesthood.

As the primary responsibility of a prophet was to call the people to repentance for national sin, how could his office come into existence if no standard (the Law) yet existed to *be* violated? Not surprisingly, prophets throughout the Old Testament and in every age made frequent allusions to the Law. Since the central purpose of the Law was to demonstrate to the people how utterly unapproachable a holy God was by any human devices or personal striving, what could have been the purpose of entering a covenant with this God if no means were present for the people to uphold their side of the equation? Without the existence of the mediating priesthood, this would have exactly been the case. Clearly, these (prophets, law, priesthood) form a unit; no one part has any useful function without the presence of the other two.

Interestingly, if we allow the Bible timeline—that the Law and priesthood were concurrent developments originating between 1500–1400 BC—the omission of the city of Jerusalem is precisely expected. At the institution of the priesthood and the Law (during the forty-year wilderness wandering) Jerusalem was not yet a Jewish settlement. Again, regarding the priesthood, those items missing in the postexilic period (a period covered in the OT writings of Ezra, Nehemiah, Haggai, Zechariah, and Malachi) are either out of vogue by this time (500 BC), no longer possible to comply with, or have become, for all practical purposes, nonexistent (such as the ark of the covenant and its contents, including the Ten Commandments, with the Babylonian destruction of the temple in 586 BC). As to the assumption that the D and P writers feature themes that are too sophisticated for the purported time of

Moses, Josh McDowell writes: "The Ras Shamra tablets (1400 BC) which contain a large amount of Ugaritic literature render the Wellhausen postexilic concept void. Many of the technical sacrificial terms of Leviticus were discovered in far-removed Canaanite-speaking Ugarit (1400 BC). Such P terms include: (1) ishsheh: 'offering made by fire' (2) kalil: 'whole burnt offering' (3) shelamin: 'peace offering' (4) asham (?) 'guilt offering.'"[5]

The details *lacking* in the Jewish journeying round the Eastern Mediterranean are also significant. Not only is the beloved city of Jerusalem (the very seat of Jewish identity) omitted, but there is not even a whisper regarding the divided kingdom. If these writings were compiled within the framework documentarians project, it seems unthinkable that such vital and current themes would have been absent.

Those things that *are* mentioned, however, are equally weighty. The geographical picture of mid-second-millennium Moabite country is far too fleshed-in to discount eyewitness testimony. Deuteronomy, following closely on the pattern of typical treaties of this period (Hittite suzerainty treaties, in particular) is already long out of vogue for the time documentarians ascribe its writing (seventh century BC). The priestly code of the Jews was presumably too complex to have been compiled in Moses' day—yet the very complex Code of Hammurabi was written at least a few hundred years before the time of Moses. Moreover, though there are some superficial similarities between the two, there is no compelling evidence establishing the Hebrew code's dependence upon its Babylonian predecessor; the former is set in rigid religious injunctions with the latter entirely a civil standard.[6] What all of this means to documentarians is that their cherished herculean friends, the redactors, would have required an unparalleled keenness, an ability to capture their contrived history in an uncannily accurate depiction of the customs and literary forms for which they were backward casting. Surely in this sense, the redactors possess an element of the divine.

If the biblical account is simply taken at face value, then it must be admitted Moses was eminently qualified to have authored the Pentateuch. Raised within the Egyptian royal court, he would have been exposed to the finest in the arts and education available in the entire Mediterranean world. With the forty years he spent in the royal court, the forty years in the Midian desert, and the forty years in the Sinai wilderness, Moses would have had the time, training, and knowledge to display a detailed, accurate record of customs, seasonal variations, and geographical descriptions so prominently featured (in fact) within the Pentateuch. Moses would have likely as well been informed of oral traditions from his natural mother (his court-appointed nanny) as well as any existing written Hebrew histories. Moreover, if Jacob (several centuries earlier) *had* brought written traditions with him in the Jewish relocation from Canaan to Egypt, it is quite possible that these records had been confiscated in conjunction with the servitude to which the Jews had eventually become subject. Again, as a high-ranking member of the royal court, Moses would have had access to all Egyptian vaults and libraries. Thus equipped, he would have been in the best possible position to edit (perhaps through divine inspiration) the earliest traditions, now placed at his disposal, and to dovetail with his own eyewitness testimony.

Because the Bible is *a priori* determined a cultural artifact, a reflection of unfolding tribal superstitions, it is not allowed to be examined on its own terms. Any evidence of diversity or repetition of themes is instantly Exhibit A of internal tampering. Documentarians routinely ignore the testimonial nature of the Bible, that repetition is evidence of intent to validate the authenticity of the message. Repetition and parallelism is a frequent feature of Hebrew poetry, as Hebrew grammarians point out. There is a certain majestic style that is woven into the Scriptures—indeed, a sublimity of communication unmatched in any other literary work. Yet documentarians, in effect, penalize the Pentateuch for its breathtaking style, maintaining, through some contorted logic, that evidence of the highest known level of literature equals fraud.

Documentarians set out with an inflexible attitude; obvious explanations that were readily available were commonly passed over for imaginative, exotic, just-so sketches. To be sure, it is not an axiom but a philosophical assumption that internal diversity is evidence of multiple sources. Different word usages and styles can simply reflect differing subject matter. Even within the same subject, it is no violation of logic to allow for different styles to indicate different emphases. To deny this is to deny any writer a multifaceted personality. Are any modern works confined to such a rigid one-dimensional, colorless presentation? If the critic will entertain the notion, for even a moment: if the Old Testament truly did represent a message from the transcendent Creator, wouldn't it stand to reason that record would evince an unsurpassed richness of expression? If God is indeed animating the subject matter, shouldn't we rightly expect to see multiple devices communicating this message— diverse literary forms, parallelism, repetition, differing genres, and subtle nuance conveying an unequaled sublimity of depth and breadth? By what logic can this lofty language be assumed as evidence *against* a divine unifying presence?

Documentarians have presumed they are better equipped from the confines of an occidental culture—removed at least 2,500 years (and possibly more than 3,500) from the object of investigation—to interpret an *oriental* culture than its actual inhabitants. In other words, though examining a culture consisting of language nuances, philosophical assumptions, customs, and wide-ranging milieu to which documentarians are foreigners, they nevertheless believe a projection of their own cultural biases will render a more faithful construction of actual facts than their ancient counterparts, who were deeply embedded in the culture in question and lived in much closer chronological proximity to events described.

The Pentateuch, in bold defiance to the claims of documentarians, exhibits remarkable evidence of an organic outworking. The so-called "multiple sources" do not lend themselves to the suggestion of independence but appear fundamentally integrated and complementary, providing specifics to generalities. Comments W. J. Martin:

> Genesis possesses all the characteristics of a homogeneous work: articulation, the unwitting use of forms and syntactical patterns which indicate the linguistic and geographical milieu of the writer . . . in particular the definite article passing through the stages from demonstrative to definitive, as well as here the fluid state of grammatical gender. . . . No man now would dream of deducing from diversity of style diversity of authorship; diversity is part of the very texture of genius. It is not in the uniformity of diction or style but in the uniformity of quality that unity is discerned. It is easier to believe in a single genius than to believe that there existed a group of men possessing such preeminent gifts, so self-effacing, who could have produced such a work.[7]

The basic problem with the literary critical method (or source criticism) is that once employed, it can only continue to wander in the direction of the subjective. Though possibly confined to only certain questionable passages initially, in time there is no passage that escapes hyper-skeptical reconstruction. This is especially true when the archaeological evidence is sparse. The temptation to be the first to issue just-so scenarios can be overwhelming. After all, there is little fear of a challenge in the form of concrete evidence. Yet these scholars might be expected to show a little humility when the state of the art significantly expands, and the unthinkable happens—hard evidence reduces clever painstaking reconstructions into foolish drivel—"mythical" persons and events suddenly taking on substantial form. The lack of scholarly humility within radical criticism, however, can be traced back to its chief proponent.

Wellhausen never bothered to revise his conclusions when new information, especially in the field of oriental scholarship, cast his opinions in a dubious light.[8] The record of history would not support the notion that many gods were gradually reduced over time until few or only one remained. The reverse was demonstrably the rule, with the several gods multiplying into many more. Yet Wellhausen turned a blind eye to this pattern and ignored something even more damaging to his theory: Only Judaism featured a genuine monotheism radically departing from its "sister" religions, embracing not only a much more pronounced and complex version but one existing on a *national* basis as well. A vast gulf existed between the ancient Israelites and their pagan counterparts that could not be explained away by ingenious reconstructions. The Jews remained the anomaly that would not fit the mold. In the face of mounting conflicting evidence, Wellhausen remained unmoved. It is as though the story of the Jews was not permitted to be a factual historical account.

The internal formula (an *assumption* of evolutionary development) that drives documentary hypothesis amounts to a baseline no more rigid than documentarians' own limitless imaginations. This has produced a situation where no amount of additional new "sources" can be ruled out of bounds. If an esteemed scholar believes he has divined the presence of yet another independent source, on what grounds might his new finding be challenged? How does one rebut scholarly intuition without bringing the whole house of cards crashing down?

Incidentally, the discovery of the Dead Sea Scrolls in 1947 placed at scholarship's disposal a cache of documents of varying length, some of which date to just over two hundred years removed from the purported final compilation of the redactors. Included in this enormous find are fragments of various length of thirty-eight of the thirty-nine books (Esther the exception) of the OT and numerous commentaries, many on these very books. Nowhere to be found in these or any documents recovered from the ancient world is a single scrap of an "independent source document" (J, E, JE, D, or P). There is not even a *reference* to any "source material."

When pressed, documentarians will concede the relative weakness for the Wellhausen theory if the criteria are interrogated in relative isolation. Nevertheless, "The strength of the critical position is mainly due to the fact that the same conclusions are reached by independent lines of argument."[9] This might be compelling if these "independent lines" were grounded in any hard external, objective evidence. As each of these exists in the realm of the imagination and is directly dependent upon certain *a priori* assumptions, the number of so-called independent lines is irrelevant. As Kenneth Kitchen once wrote: "[I]t is a waste of time to talk about the 'cumulative force' of arguments that are each invalid; 0+0+0+0 = 0 on any reckoning."[10]

The burden of proof is upon Bible critics to decisively establish by a preponderance of the evidence that the Pentateuch could not have been written by a single author, and in the timeframe it purports. This, by any reasonable standard, the Wellhausen theory has failed to do. The presuppositions upon which the documentary ship sets sail leave a hull riddled with gaping holes. In the end, the only thing this theory has proven is its unflagging commitment to preserving its own self-serving agenda.[11]

CHAPTER 15

DANIEL: HISTORY OR PROPHECY?

M essrs, Freke, and Gandy, not wishing to be left out in this critique of Old Testament reliability, treat us to an exotic recasting of history that even Wellhausen and peers would not have dared. Our authors rely on ultraliberal "scholarship" that extends quite beyond the pale of higher criticism to build their case. That case is summed up in "the Hasmonean theory":

> In 161 BCE the Jewish leader Judas Maccabeus made an alliance with the Romans and led a rebellion against the Jews' Greek rulers. . . . Maccabeus and his sons established the Hasmonean dynasty that ruled Judea for the next century. In 164 BCE the temple in Jerusalem was rededicated, after which a whole new era was declared, a new calendar created, and a military programme for the expansion of Jewish territory began. During this period, the collection of texts we know as the Tanakh (a.k.a. Old Testament) was written, compiled and extensively edited, to serve as the mythological justification for the Hasmonean desire to rule all of Palestine. The Hasmoneans constructed a history that portrayed themselves...heirs of King David, who had once ruled over both northern and southern Palestine. . . . It is in this [Hasmonean] period that the term 'Israel' first acquires a political and religious connotation.[1]

So, whereas the documentary hypothesis places the final form of the Pentateuch at about 400 BC, Freke and Gandy put it no earlier than 164 BC. In fact, state the authors, "[T]here was no such thing as the Tanakh until as late as the first century BCE. . . . Far from developing as a coherent whole over a period of centuries, the Tanakh appeared as an incoherent mishmash of texts, cobbled together by a bunch of religious extremists in a few generations."[2] Suffice it to say that the enormous tension placed on the Wellhausen theory to artificially compress a two-thousand-year history into no more than about five hundred years, and all the resulting sticky entanglements, is now multiplied enormously. Freke and Gandy presume to pull off in but "a few generations" what serious criticism has failed miserably to accomplish in a considerably expanded historical grid.

If the redactors of the Wellhausen theory possessed uncanny abilities that bordered on the divine, what are we to make of the evil religious extremists "cobbling together an incoherent mishmash of texts" but somehow avoiding any appearance of contrivance? How are we to explain the most brilliant compilation of literature ever assembled is nothing more than the incidental (or accidental?) product of incoherent texts thrown together willy-nilly? Since this considerably later dating obviously complicates matters for those wishing to discredit the OT, why not leave well enough alone?

The answer is tied up in the book of Daniel. This OT book purports to have been written about 600 BC. Because of the predictive elements of this book, portraying with uncanny accuracy events four hundred or so years into the future, it is attacked almost as enthusiastically as the Pentateuch. The dating of Daniel and the final compilation of the Pentateuch are two separate issues, but Freke and Gandy have chosen to tie the two together: "Although *Daniel* claims to be written in the sixth century BCE, it was actually composed centuries later. The Pagan scholar Porphyry first demonstrated this in the third century CE. Using careful textual analysis, he demonstrated that *Daniel* was written in the second century BCE, during the Jewish Maccabean revolt."[3]

It is astounding the authors would predicate their case against Daniel on the suggestion their imaginary scenario begins during the Maccabean period. If it is so that the book of Daniel was authored in this timeframe, we would surely expect the emphasis to be on the central event and *key* character of that time. Freke and Gandy are either deliberately ignoring or are simply ignorant of the direct cause of the Jewish uprising. Let's have a little closer look.

The breakup of the old Persian Empire, after the death of Alexander the Great (323 BC), resulted in the division of the empire among his generals. Egypt was then ruled by the Ptolemies and Syria by the Seleucids. In Daniel 11:31, a prophecy is given concerning a coming Syrian ruler, Antiochus IV, also known as Antiochus Epiphanes, who will profane the temple: "And arms shall stand on his part, and they shall pollute the sanctuary of strength, and shall take away the daily sacrifice, and they shall place the abomination that maketh desolate." History records the reign of this man and of his act of abomination that occurred about 168 BC. The apocryphal books 1 and 2 Maccabees give considerable information about this man, including his placement of a sow on the altar to desecrate the temple, clearing the way for worship of pagan gods. From the historic record, we glean several key points confirming the identity of this man, clues that so closely verify the detailed accuracy of Daniel's prophecy that secular historians insist this book must have been written after the fact. (Note: While Freke and Gandy can probably find no shortage of secular historians who agree that Daniel was written as history and not prophecy, few would share the extreme view that the entire Old Testament was composed essentially in the first century BC.)

It is a matter of record that Antiochus made an agreement with the Jewish high priest Jason which he then proceeded to break, putting the more corrupt and politically malleable Menelaus in his place. Again, in accordance with prophecy, Antiochus dealt more punitively with the Jews than any of his forebears, attacking the very foundation of Judaism. To this end, he forbade observance of the Sabbath and any traditional Jewish feasts. He did away with sacrifices and forbade the reading of the Law of Moses. Especially abhorrent to Jews, he outlawed the practice of circumcision, *the* practice which most set Jews apart from all others, and a requirement without which Jews could not enter covenant with God. Even the placing of an unclean animal on the temple altar (in the Holy of Holies) would not be Antiochus' final act of deliberate profanity against the Jewish God. The last straw would be the setting up of an idol in the Jewish temple, followed by the temple's rededication to the Greek god Zeus. It is this last act that would finally initiate the bloody protracted Jewish revolt.

These events are all part of the historic record, disputed by no serious scholar, secular or otherwise. It is clear, then, that the Jewish uprising was not only definitely provoked but an act of desperation against one of history's most repressive and vicious tyrants. Yet Freke and Gandy make no mention of this, and try to create the impression that this rebellion was a conscious and deliberate power grab inaugurated by ruthless villains driven by political aspirations. They never bother to mention why the temple was rededicated in 164 BC. They would like their readers to simply tie this into some grand conspiracy to inaugurate the "Hasmonean Dynasty." The fact is, though, if Freke and Gandy were to include this little overlooked fact, their entire Hasmonean theory would fall. This would mean that the Law of Moses, which spelled out the duties of the priesthood, ordinances, and prohibitions concerning the temple, was already in existence before this uprising— a most inconvenient fact for the authors, since this is not supposed to be compiled until the first century BC.

It isn't just that Freke and Gandy omit key information that is damning to their theory; they also fail to explain why the author of Daniel—who, according to their timeline, wrote during the Maccabean revolt—gives an account of *contemporary events* that does not comport with Antiochus's reign. Why is the brutal figure who stands behind this entire event only vaguely mentioned in the eighth (possibly) and not in detail until the eleventh of twelve total chapters in a *future* context?

Yet there is something even far more significant about Daniel's reference to Antiochus IV that Freke and Gandy conveniently ignore. Remember in Daniel 11:31, we read those chilling words that anticipated one of the key offending actions, "the abomination that maketh desolation" placed in the Holy of Holies. Daniel 11:36–39 forms an intriguing transition between 11:21 and the end of the book (12:13). From 11:21–34, there is consensus among secular historians that these events and descriptions were literally fulfilled in Antiochus IV. There is a division of opinion, however, over verses 35–39. Yet with verse 40 to the end of the book, there is again consensus that this has no historic correspondence to Antiochus IV. However, these later verses seem to flow very naturally—to grow organically, as it were, from the previous part. It is as though the deliberate intent is that we should see that individual fulfilling the first part and the individual fulfilling the second as being eerily similar (kindred spirits joined at the hip, as it were), yet undeniably distinct. In fact, when we consider the bridge connecting these two reigns, it seems the two persons are mystically merged into one.

Now consider this: Two hundred years *after* Antiochus IV, in the Gospel of Matthew (24:15–16), Jesus Christ takes up this same theme echoing the words of Daniel: "When ye therefore shall see the abomination of desolation, spoken of by Daniel the prophet, stand in the holy place, (whoso readeth, let him understand:) Then let them which be in Judaea flee into the mountains." Christ is issuing a stern warning to His listeners about a yet-future character at the time He is speaking, who will commit atrocities strikingly similar to Antiochus IV and who will feature prominently in the final act of Israel's history. This mystery person is later referred to by the apostle Paul as "the son of perdition; who opposeth and exalteth himself above all that is called God, or that is worshiped; so that he as God sitteth in the temple of God, shewing himself that he is God" (2 Thess. 2:3–4).

What is so significant about all this? This "villain of the ages" to whom Christ alludes, and by which it is implied all others by comparison pale, is directly modeled on Antiochus IV. And it is Christ who makes this connection. Of all the evil men in history, there is only the one Christ specifically references as the prototype for what Christian theology describes as the Antichrist. If the author of Daniel were a contemporary with Antiochus, as Freke and Gandy maintain, it is inconceivable that no mention of the three- or four-year war with this evil despot is made, nor of the twenty-four-year war with the Seleucids to win independence from Syria. Shouldn't this have been the *theme* of Daniel?

What of the charge that "a military programme for the expansion of Jewish territory began"? While it is true that an expansion took place under the Hasmonean kingdom, this would hardly qualify as an aggressive campaign of conquest as Freke and Gandy imply. Our friends would like to tie this period of brief Jewish independence (142–63 BC) into a quest for empire. But modest gains attained under this period would pale when set against, for instance, the Greek Empire from which Jews had won independence. The Maccabean military campaign was not nearly so much about conquest as it was about protecting Jews throughout Palestine from physical danger, establishing defensive fortifications due to the aggressive Hellenization program inaugurated by Antiochus IV. Moreover, as skirmishes with the Seleucid Empire in outlying lands would continue virtually to the end of the Hasmonean period, those territories taken served mostly as a protective buffer. The "brutal" tactic of forcing those in these lands to be circumcised and observe the Torah (of which Freke and Gandy complain) was not unusual for these times. It was quite common for the conquerors of any land to insist on some act or acts of allegiance as a requisite for new citizenship. Those opposed were free to flee.

It is ironic that the Hasmonean dynasty which began as a revolt against aggressive Hellenization would in fact be marked by its concessions to Greek culture. It is laughable that Freke and Gandy refer to Hasmonean leader Alexander Jannaeus' murder of "liberal Pharisees." The Pharisees would find themselves at odds with the Hasmonean leadership precisely *because* the former were of a particularly observant (literalist) sect.[4] The Hasmoneans, on the other hand, rather quickly became notorious for politicizing the priesthood, filling the office of high priest with their own leaders rather than the legitimate Levitic-Aaronic-Zadokite priest-line recognized by staunchly observant groups like the Hasidim/Pharisees.[5] To cast "literalism" as the oppressor, making a reference to "the fanatical Jewish Literalism of the Hasmoneans"[6] while simultaneously referring to "liberal Pharisees," requires a reversal of historic facts.

Yet what is so grievously absent in Freke and Gandy's treatment is the immediate context. Even if the Hasmonean dynasty had boasted wide-reaching conquests, these would have occurred within the context of what any fair-minded observer would concede as a just war. The Jews were not only under the yoke of an oppressive regime but forced to surrender their sacred religious heritage. The Jews were victims of what liberals would today call "ethnic cleansing."

Let us return to the dating of the book of Daniel. The mention of Belshazzar (son of Nebuchadnezzar, according to the Bible) in Daniel is said to be problematic. Belshazzar, once considered a fictional character until archeological evidence confirmed his existence, nevertheless cannot be a son of Nebuchadnezzar according to the historical record. The father of Belshazzar (Nabonidus) was the son-in-law of Nebuchadnezzar. The charge that follows: Daniel (or whoever is the writer of this book) is so many centuries removed from these events that he doesn't know the true historical royal lineage. This, however, overlooks the fact that the terms "father" and "son" are often used figuratively in the OT.

The reference to Darius the Mede in Daniel 6:28 is also said to raise a red flag. Darius, according to critics, is fictional. The Bible names Darius as the conqueror of Babylon, yet Persian records identify Cyrus the Great as this conqueror. It is possible, however, that this person is known by both names, Darius and Cyrus, Darius emphasizing the Median heritage of his mother and Cyrus the Persian heritage of his father, as well as his Persian rule. An alternate theory suggests Gubaru (a Persian), the provincial governor of Babylon put in place by Cyrus, is possibly the one referred to as Darius the Mede. In support of this view, it is known that subordinate rulers were sometimes referred to as kings.[7]

Perhaps the greatest refutation of the above complaints, though, is the question of motive. If Daniel were written in the second century BC, there is no reason for the writer to insert erroneous information when the facts would have been well known. Even in Josephus' day, histories of the Persian Empire were in circulation as well as the time of the Maccabean Period (Herodotus, Berosus, etc.). Other OT books even specifically named Cyrus as the conqueror of Babylon (Isaiah 45:1; 2 Chron. 36:20–23). Thus, the alternate explanations are most reasonable.

An early date for Daniel is objected to by its use of Greek and Persian words that are not in vogue in Palestine until after the conquest of Alexander the great (332 BC). J. P. Holding comments:

> We are solemnly told about the presence of "Greek and Persian words" in Daniel that require us to late-date it—but you would never know: a) the Persian words are only 15 in number, and largely government and administrative terms; b) the Greek words are only THREE in number—and all refer to instruments (*kitharos, psanterin,* and *sumphonyah*)! This tactic is utilized by Katz ("McDowell in the Critics Den," *The American Rationalist,* July/August 1982) and by Calahan (*Bible Prophecy? Failure of Fulfillment?* Millennium Press 1996, p. 151), who writes solemnly of "a number of Greek and Persian words" that are "salted" throughout the text—never once telling his readers what they are, or how many there are! Is this an honest way to present one's case?[8]

Regarding the occurrence of Persian words in Daniel, Archer writes:

> [C]onservative scholars do not maintain that the book of Daniel was composed, in the final form at least, until the establishment of the Persian authority over Babylonia. Since the text indicates that

Daniel himself lived to serve, for several years at least under Persian rule, there is no particular reason why he should not have employed in his language those Persian terms (largely referring to government and administration) which had found currency in the Aramaic spoken in Babylon by 530 BC.[9]

Concerning Greek words, Whitcomb adds:

> Perhaps the most important point to consider in this great controversy is that the book of Daniel would have been saturated with Greek terms if it were written as late as 167 BC, in Palestine, where Greek speaking (Hellenistic) governments had controlled the entire region for more than 160 years. Instead of this, we find just two or three technical terms referring to obviously foreign cultural objects.[10]

Daniel's primary languages are Aramaic and Hebrew. The presence of Aramaic is said to be indicative of a late date. States Archer:

> It was formerly asserted that the Aramaic of Daniel is of the Western dialect and hence could not have been the case if the sixth-century Daniel was its real author. Recent discoveries of fifth-century Aramaic documents, however, have shown quite conclusively that Daniel was, like Ezra, written in a form of Imperial Aramaic, an official or literary dialect which had currency in all parts of the Near East. Thus, the relationship to the Aramaic of the Elephantine Papyri from southern Egypt is a very close one, inasmuch as they too were written in the Imperial Aramaic.[11]

Archer further explains that the Maccabean date hypothesis was given before the Genesis Apocryphon was found at Qumran. No Aramaic document previously existed from the third century BC with which to compare Daniel. The Apocryphon demonstrates linguistic tendencies consonant with a later stage of development than Daniel.

Events that portray the rise and fall of the world empires, if written in the time Daniel purports, would admit for an unacceptable element of the supernatural—thus, the priority for discrediting this dating. However, the description of the four major empires in Chapter 2 and again in Chapter 7 of Daniel cannot be forced into a Maccabean grid. In Chapter 2, four metals are used to symbolize four separate coming kingdoms: Babylon—gold head; Medo-Persia—silver chest and arms; Greece—brass thighs; Rome—iron and clay toes. These four empires are also later distinguished by animal associations: Babylon—lion; Medo-Persia—bear devouring three ribs; Greece—leopard with four wings and four heads; Rome—ten-horned beast.

The Maccabean hypothesis indicts the writer of Daniel with erroneously concluding that Media and Persia represent separate kingdoms. But the reference to the devouring of the three ribs is an important clue. The historic conquest of the Medo-Persian Empire incorporated Babylon, Lydia, and Egypt. Daniel 7:5 also makes mention of the dominance of one side with respect to the other. This anticipates a similar idea we see in 8:3, with one horn of the ram featured more prominently than the other. This seems an indication that the Persian component of the empire would command greater importance with respect to the Median element. Critics maintain the writer of Daniel asserts the Medes were conquered by the Persians; Daniel 6:8, however, makes clear the writer sees the two as a united kingdom from the outset.

Besides Rome logically defaulting to the last description (iron and clay/ten-horned beast), this also represents the most natural summation of that empire. The iron sword and breastplate, as many have noted, became synonymous with the might of Rome. Additionally, the ten toes that were part iron and part clay describe the peculiar nature of the Roman Republic—partly strong due to its monarchy, and partly weak (in terms of absolute power) due to its forms of representative government. The ten toes also have a prophetic significance with respect to a ten-nation or ten-kingdom confederation that will make up the revived Roman Empire in the last days.

CHAPTER 16

HIGHER CRITICISM
AND THE NEW TESTAMENT

The assault that began on the reliability of the Old Testament would not
be content until it had exhausted its resources on the New Testament as
well. Higher criticism could only accept the historicity of Jesus of Nazareth
if He were deconstructed in much the same fashion as the Pentateuch. The four
Gospels—Matthew, Mark, Luke, and John, which presume to present the life
and ministry of Jesus of Nazareth—would bear the brunt of the new criticism.
After World War I, German scholars, following on the work of Wellhausen and
others, would piece together imaginative theories resulting in a New Testament
perhaps even more radically reconstructed than the OT of their forebears. As with
the documentary hypothesis, each gospel would find itself carved up according to
structure and form, as dictated by the rules of literary analysis. The quest to uncover
"the real story of Jesus" would again make use of source criticism, as well as a new
subdiscipline called form criticism.

Source criticism sought to reconstruct the earliest parts (independent sources)
that came together to form each gospel. To that end, a "Q Source" was discovered
within the pages of two of the synoptic gospels (Matthew, Mark, Luke). That is,
within Matthew and Luke there appeared to be a body of material which was
common to each. Because this body (Q) was presumed to be limited to the sayings
of Jesus, it was considered the earliest document to have circulated among the
early Christian church, before accretions attached. The gospel of Mark (believed
the earliest gospel composed in its present form) supposedly served as an additional
source for Matthew and Luke. Narratives and various other embellishments that
would make up the final gospel forms were assumed later developments and thus
not historically reliable. John, composed considerably later than the other three,
was believed to represent an independent line of transmission. Though bearing

some merit, the "Q source" is, to a degree, the NT equivalent of the Pentateuchal J, E, D, P Sources. As with its OT counterparts, no copy nor fragment of Q has ever been found; it exists solely as a theory. In the case of the Gospels, the evangelists are cast in the role of the redactors, editing, combining oral and written traditions, and inserting useful details after the fact into the gospel narratives.

Form criticism concerned itself with the twenty-or-so-year gap that separated the death of Jesus of Nazareth (between AD 30–33) from the first NT writings. It sought to go back beyond the earliest written sources to the earliest traditions, recovering the isolated oral fragments which would coalesce into patterns before finally captured on papyrus. If source criticism seemed to lend itself to imaginative speculations, form criticism would submit to no boundaries. "Higher critics" of the NT, unlike those of the Old, did not have the luxury of the vast time span with which to introduce myriad independent and isolated factors affecting the reliability of the biblical account. Because the period under examination was highly con-strained, critics needed to cast the contrivances that had produced the Gospels in an accelerated climate pressured by rapidly changing exigencies. Rather than a con-scious conspiracy of a relative few, an almost unconscious collusion of community would participate in the emerging narrative. Instead of centering the motivation for religious innovation in national themes as with the story of the Jews, the story of Jesus (concocted by a small subset within Judaism) was set, at least as far as higher critics were concerned, in something called the *sitz im leben*.[1]

Form critics employed this term (literally translated "life situation") to sum up the needs of a budding Christian community with respect to those things judged necessary first for worship and secondarily for survival; from establishing a unique religious identity to refuting charges of heresy. As certain problems arose, new aspects of Jesus were suddenly "discovered" engendering the necessary "faith" to meet each unfolding crisis. Form criticism thus made a distinction between "the Jesus of history" and "the Jesus of faith"; the latter a composite of superstitions, myths, sayings, parables, and narratives—a spontaneous mutation fleshed in and energized by the changing (and sometimes desperate) needs of the community of believers. Higher scholars would, of course, see it as their task to peel away the lay-ers of embellishment (the Jesus of faith) and recover the "real" historic figure.

Form criticism, because its very foundation rested on the *assumption* the Gospels could not be factual, cast its reconstruction in much the same one-dimensional mold as its OT counterpart. Followers of Jesus were but docile sheep so wedded to a superstitious world that critical examination of certain claims would have been near to unthinkable. These primitive beings lived in such an emotion-charged, moment-to-moment existence that material concerns with preserving some sort of accurate historical record would have been almost as out of place as expecting them to give any thought to retirement plans. Thus, it is a mistake for us to assume the inquisitive spirit that dominates the modern mind would have had any place in the world of demons and spirits. Early Christians were little more than children desperately needing to believe in happy-ending fables. Heaven someday coming to Earth was not a rational expectation but an emotional hope that all the cruelty and injustice the powerless suffered was not just what it in fact appeared to be—meaningless.

The Jesus divested of the *sitz im leben* turns out to be a teacher and prophet in the tradition of OT seers who forecast the coming rule of God over all the earth. He is a radical figure whose anti-establishment agitation finally results in his arrest and crucifixion at the hands of the Roman government. For believers, Jesus emerges as a larger-than-life character to which the downtrodden can relate. He is wise and good, yet defiant of the power structure, and in death, will prove even more troublesome. He now gives voice to an otherwise voiceless people. He has become the self-fulfilling and self-sustaining prophecy. The growing nuisance his resurrection myth creates induces the power structure to crack down on his followers. Yet persecution has the unintended consequence of growing the myth to even greater proportions, prompting still further persecution. The growth of the movement has the effect of legitimating the myth, "If Jesus has not in fact resurrected, then why is he perceived such a threat?"

Perhaps the most renowned proponent of form criticism was Rudolph Bultmann, whose approach, as with the Wellhausian, reversed the normal method of interrogating literary forms. Such forms were not taken at face value, representing a desire on the part of recorders to faithfully portray certain facts. Literary forms were assumed to contain little objective information but believed to hold clues to the climate in which narratives were nurtured. Getting back to the "real Jesus" first required uncovering the true *sitz im leben*, the precise circumstances that necessitated the additions.[2] Once this was established, the scholar would then be in the best possible position to peel away accretions, leaving us with an unadorned Jesus and a reliable principle upon which to extract a "true" account of Jesus from the remainder.

Bultmann was committed to an anthropological template, that all religions follow a similar pattern of development. Bultmann sought to remove the concept of a preincarnate Christ, miracles, the ascension, and any other supernatural element that placed the Christ experience outside a purely existential plane. Within the new naturalistic worldview, religion could not be permitted to assert itself as a way to arrive at ultimate truth. Whatever amount of imaginative trimming were required, Christianity would be stuffed into the standard mold. For reasons inexplicable, Bultmann was convinced the composers of the Gospels could not have seen themselves as transmitters of some factual account of an actual historic figure. They knew their readers would have held no such expectation either. They were, after all, merely appropriating a powerful historic figure for *religious* purposes; whatever promoted myth overrode any other concerns.

Bultmann, as a "Christian theologian," believed that true faith in the Christ could not be experienced until one had first exorcized the supernatural from the story. Thus extricated, faith need not place itself at the tenuous disposal of any mortal flawed being, nor at the mercy of "highly improbable events" (miracles). Faith, the new liberating variety, could now rest in an ideal that need not fear the pronouncement of unyielding facts (science). The Christ could now be experienced as a rallying principle, a striving toward the higher standard for which one's life would be immeasurably better. This faith was also superior in that failure to reach and maintain its lofty ideals need no longer carry the stigma of eternal damnation.

Though higher criticism rather quickly descended into extreme antisupernaturalism, it did at least begin with a kernel of legitimacy. Because the Gospels make claims that are far removed from the ordinary and because they are not written from a detached perspective, it is fair to approach these claims with a healthy skepticism. It is not fair, however, to dismiss any possibility of literal accuracy simply because the writer is invested in a story for which we possess no analogue. I am aware of no serious reporters who refused to present the Apollo moon landing as a factual event simply because something of this sort had never occurred and because those involved in the actual event (from planning to execution) had an emotional attachment. Even that most trusted and revered of icons, Walter Cronkite, was openly emotional in his reportage. I do not recall, as a result, any challenges to the objectivity of Mr. Cronkite at that time or since.

According to Hume's formula of skepticism, however, this should have been rejected as factual due to its high statistical improbability against the record of history. The fact that there was a clear context from which this event could be investigated would not have been allowed to factor in. For instance, a pattern of increasing technological advances through numerous trial-and-error experiments would have been available to show that all previous obstacles to this event's plausibility had each (though formidable) been meticulously removed. Again, though, if one followed the rules of rigorous skepticism, the moon landing should have been explained away as a fanciful myth. Yet no serious investigator would dare deny the compelling context for this unprecedented historical event.

Those who reject the Bible's fantastic claims invariably do so by refusing to consider the context in which they are presented. Historically, critics have taken cover under the rubric of "neutrality." Neutrality is translated as an *a priori* rejection of any supernatural component. The objective investigator, we are often reminded, must necessarily limit his examination to natural phenomena. "That which falls outside these confines belongs to the realm of faith." This proceeds from the premise that natural laws, rather than describing what is normal, must be causal *and* limiting for all legitimate knowledge. This flows from no test tube so must be imposed philosophically and self-servingly. The resurrection, though a supernatural event, was deliberately placed within a *naturalistic setting* where it intentionally and provocatively erected the most serious physical barriers and *then* submitted itself to the canons of investigation.

For a nonbelieving scholar to concede that mounting circumstantial evidence seems to support the probability that a phenomenon has occurred which has no apparent naturalistic explanation does not *ipso facto* transform the scholar into "a man of faith." It is simply an honest acknowledgment of fact. Those who read the scholar's findings are free (including the scholar himself) to view this as evidence in favor of the supernatural or to conclude that a natural explanation will at some future point emerge. To pretend, however, that ruling out the supernatural as a matter of course is the position of neutrality is a farce and a violation of basic intuition. Whatever the circumstance, if any investigator wishes to retain credibility, neutrality, or objectivity, the initial question cannot be "Why did these people set out to invent these myths?" but "Is the evidence on a par with the claims?" If after thoroughly examining the evidence the answer is no, then and only then is it proper to ask why the story was concocted.

To suggest all in the ancient world were either incapable of or simply did not care to separate fact from fiction is a philosophical position not consonant with any known facts—a position displaying not a little arrogance. Form criticism creates an artificial reality that precludes any possibility the gospel narratives might represent faithful reportage of events surrounding the life (or death) of Jesus of Nazareth. To wit, only that body of material which does not serve some specific need of the early church may pass the legitimacy test. Since Christ's purported mission is specifically to meet the most basic hunger in human beings (the *foundation* of the church), the fix is in. Note that form critics do not take the context of mission to determine if the weight of available data point toward or away from validation, but the allusion to mission itself as justification for denying the evidence any hearing. This is like saying we can only accept that part of the moon landing as authentic which does not involve the actual mission of getting a man to the moon and back.

Inconsistent with the reconstructed view, early Christians did not insulate their claims from investigation. To the contrary, they welcomed all such inquiries, convinced of the unassailable quality of their message within the verifiable space/time continuum. The claims of Christianity (as with Judaism) are distinguished from all other religions in that they are deliberately made out in the open and linked to numerous specifics which are subject to refutation. One of the most repetitive themes in the Gospels is a constant allusion to eyewitness testimony. This is a clear anticipation that certain challenges will be made to the veracity of unusual claims. This also serves notice that the gospel writers are intentionally and formally submitting all claims, no matter how unbelievable on their face, for intense scrutiny. This is completely at odds with the presumption that these people had no interest in historical accuracy. While it is true they were not historians in the strictest sense we now apply the term (nor was anyone in the ancient world, as all wrote from the favorable perspective of each's respective nation sponsor), one cannot ignore the repeated determination to ground fantastic claims in verifiable settings. The writers *knew* they were making out-of-the-ordinary assertions. If the motivation behind the Gospels was simply emerging spiritual utility, then how do we explain the meticulous efforts to preserve a record that was intended to survive the most thorough interrogation, including the test of time?

Before the twentieth century, virtually no liberal scholar put any of the original NT writings any earlier than the mid to latter part of the second century. The weight of archeological discoveries, however, in Egypt, Syria, and Palestine forced them to abandon long-cherished assumptions such as the Tubingen theory. This theory was based on the Hegelian presumption of progress through the clash of opposing forces. In this case, it was the Jewish Christians led by Peter pitted against the Gentile Christians championed by Paul. Though accorded high praise and prestige for a time, it was fully discredited before the close of the nineteenth century. So much for the certainty of scholarly pronouncements arrived at through the most sophisticated and scientifically unimpeachable methods. Yet the late dates assumed by the Tubingen theory did not easily give up the ghost.

In the late 1870s Sir William Ramsay, a staunch supporter of the Tubingen theory, set out to prove that the book of Acts could not have been written any earlier than AD 150. After many years into his archeological work, he was compelled to reverse his initial assumptions. His conclusions have been recorded:

> Luke [the writer of the gospel by that name and of Acts] is a historian of the first rank; not merely are his statements of fact trustworthy; he is possessed of the true historic sense; he fixes his mind on the idea and plan that rules in the evolution of history, and proportions the scale of his treatment to the importance of each incident. He seizes the important and critical events and shows their true nature at greater length, while he touches lightly or omits entirely much that was valueless for his purpose. In short, this author should be placed along with the very greatest of historians.[3]

A central problem that form critics ignore is the very Jewish backdrop to nascent Christianity. Remember that Christianity is set forth as merely another of myriad religious alternatives, following the usual pattern of anthropological evolution. Critics, however, look past the immense complexity of a new religion that simultaneously makes bold departures from the mother religion *and* consciously, deliberately, and deeply imbeds its incredible claims within the structure of its parent. There is a symmetry connecting the New Testament to the Old that is striking. Consider this condensed intimate correspondence with the nation of Israel and Jesus Christ: Both are sent down into Egypt and later brought back up from it; Israel is sent into the wilderness for forty years in preparation for her entrance into the Promised Land—Christ is in the wilderness for forty days in preparation for His salvific ministry which promises entry into a heavenly land; Israel made up of twelve tribes—Christ's inner circle made up of twelve disciples; Israel baptized in the Red Sea crossing—Christ baptized in the Jordan River, and so on.

More than one hundred messianic OT prophecies would find precise fulfillment in Jesus (manner of birth, place of birth, time of birth, betrayal, manner of death, descriptions of His trial and crucifixion, etc.). Finally, the six objects within the holy temple (the altar of burnt offering and the basin in the courtyard; the golden lampstand, the table of showbread, the altar of incense in the Holy Place; and the ark of the covenant in the Holy of Holies) together formed the pattern of a cross. These items did not merely prefigure some aspect of Christ but anticipated the very altar where the perfect sacrifice was to be offered up, some 1,400 years after the atonement program was first instituted. At that time, crucifixion would not come into existence for nearly another one thousand years.

Yet another problem for liberal critics is that the compilers of the New Testament (as with the "redactors" of the Old) must interchangeably exhibit the characteristic of being too hopelessly simpleminded *yet* extraordinarily clever to pull off the necessary sleight of hand. The resurrection is not exactly the kind of myth one advances hoping to attract new converts. This sets the bar at a level that ensures failure unless the claimants are prepared to meet the most unforgiving demands. The Jewish religion was by its nature so exclusive that it reflexively resisted novel accretions or pagan alternatives. Notes historian Michael Grant: "Judaism was a milieu to which doctrines of the deaths and rebirths of mythical gods seems so entirely foreign that the emergence of such a fabrication from its midst is very hard to credit."[4]

While it may be true that some Jews of this time dabbled in pagan excesses, leadership did not embrace core pagan principles or concepts (worshiping multiple gods, fusing the divine with the temporal, denying the reality of the natural world, etc.) which were 180 degrees out of phase with Judaism. This puts budding Christianity in the most tenuous position of having to compete with the entrenched religion for potential converts with claims deeply offensive to Jewish sensibilities (God taking on human form; resurrection of a physical body *before* the last day—especially of a perceived blasphemer; the first day of the week replacing the last day—the Sabbath—as the preeminent day of worship; circumcision replaced with baptism—a recapitulation of Christ's death, burial, and resurrection—as the new means of covenantal entry, etc.) while not actually setting itself up as an alternative. Frankly, it's hard to imagine who the "inventors" of this new religion expected to appeal to. It's hard to envision a scenario under which their hopes for attracting and growing such a belief system could have been any more doomed. These claims were not just offensive, they were shocking. The man who would become known as the apostle Paul is a good example of the intolerant nature for "wild claims" perceived at variance with the establishment. He so despised Christianity's "heretical" departure from the faith that he formally requested authorization to round up and execute what to him was a sect of criminals. Yet unless we allow for an extraordinary event, something so far removed from the expected, we are at a loss to explain Paul's dramatic 180-degree turn.

CHAPTER 17

WAS JESUS TRULY RESURRECTED?

The resurrection of Jesus Christ is, of course, the most hotly contested position within Christianity. As much as this event is resisted, discounting the resurrection altogether has proven problematic. That something happened which had a tremendous transforming effect is undeniable. Something changed these pitiful cowering disciples of Jesus into bold proclaimers of a new vision—and in a remarkably short span. Whether one chooses to take the route of "faith" and accept the historicity of the resurrection, some explanation must be provided for such a dramatic shift. The problem is, nothing short of the magnitude of resurrection is sufficient to account for this degree of change. This compels critics, however grudgingly, to concede that the disciples were somehow or other deluded into believing their master had come back to life. There are four basic alternatives that are set forth: the swoon theory, the theft theory, the hallucination theory, and the mistaken grave theory.

According to the swoon theory, Jesus did not actually die on the cross but fell into a deep coma where his faint breathing was imperceptible. Medical knowledge of that day lacking our present sophistication, soldiers inspecting the body would have pronounced His death prematurely. Once laid in the coolness of the tomb, Jesus would have revived and made His way to His disciples to proclaim victory over death. Regrettably for critics, there are certain insurmountable obstacles to the theory. Medical experts agree that the primary cause of death by crucifixion was asphyxiation. In the sagging position, the victim's diaphragm swells due to the inability to expel the buildup of oxygen. Relief is achieved only by pushing against the nail through the feet to raise the body sufficiently to release the pectoral and intercostal muscles. A crucifixion victim, conscious or otherwise, could not hang for long before death would become a certainty. The spear thrust in Jesus' side is also a serious obstacle. The apostle John records blood and water came forth. Medical experts say this is a likely indication of heart failure induced by hypovolemic shock.[1] This would have resulted in the buildup of fluid in the membrane surrounding the heart as well as the lungs.

Even if we suppose Jesus clinging to life as He lay in the tomb, the idea that He could have long survived the totality of His brutal ordeal is absurd. By this time, He had not eaten nor drank in at least fifty-five hours. His back was torn open, flesh hanging in ribbons from a savage Roman scourging. On the cross, His body had undergone severe trauma ranging from searing waves of whole body tetany to bone-grinding agony (each time He pushed against the nail through His feet) to excruciating nerve damage from the wrist nails impinging on the medial nerves (anyone who's ever had an exposed nerve due to a toothache, for instance, can testify to this most indescribable pain) to repeated episodes of near-asphyxia. Added to this was the very serious internal wound inflicted in His chest.

In the tomb, He would have also been wrapped in about seventy (American) pounds of burial spices. The spices, besides acting as a preservative, would have served to glue the various strips of linen, making it very difficult (if not impossible) for the victim to extricate himself. But we can take it still further: If Jesus had revived and mustered the strength to cast off His burial clothes, He would have still faced the problem of removing the slab cover, a feat for which three healthy women considered themselves inadequate. *Had* He managed this and even slipped past the tomb guard unnoticed, He would have had to walk at least several miles on nail-pierced feet with multiple joints out of socket. If these incredible obstacles are overcome, we must still try to imagine this most pitiable sight of the naked, wretched body of their master inspiring a belief that Jesus had "resurrected."

The theft theory maintains that the disciples stole the body during the night while the tomb guard slept (based on Matthew 28:11–15). This simply leaves us with no way to explain how a cowering band huddled in frightful expectation would suddenly be emboldened to either oppose or sneak past the Roman guard commissioned to secure the tomb. Considering it would have cost them their lives, it's not credible that trained disciplined soldiers would have been asleep at their post. The Jewish Sanhedrin was aware that prior to His death Jesus had forecast His resurrection after three days in the grave. In this politically charged climate, a missing body would now pose a most serious problem for both Jews and the Roman government. To be sure, none of this would have been lost on those directly responsible for preserving extremely sensitive interests. We are then left to conclude that a small band of despondent fearful civilians overpowered a military guard, such that they could enter the tomb and steal away with the master's body.

Even if we allow this as a possibility, we are again confronted with the question of motivation. Why would they do this? What could they hope to gain from such a suicidal risk? Why would they then proceed to proclaim a patent lie that they would willingly die for? None of this even addresses the strong aversion to unburied bodies within Judaism. Not only would this violation of the sanctity of grave have constituted a flagrant dishonoring of the master but would have rendered the perpetrators ceremonially unclean. If, as others have pointed out, the story the soldiers were bribed to tell were true (that they were asleep, and the body stolen) then how would they know this to be so? Finally, the Romans and the Jewish Sanhedrin had a powerful interest in keeping Jesus' body in the tomb. Had either party been responsible for removing the body, we should have expected them to readily exhibit the corpse in the most public manner to definitively lay such rumors to rest.

Is it possible that the visions of Jesus Christ were group hallucinations? Is it plausible the followers of Christ were so emotionally distraught and incapable of dealing with the unexpected death of so beloved a leader that their minds constructed the reality for which their hearts were desperately pleading? In fact, it is not. To begin with, after His resurrection, Christ deliberately submitted Himself for examination to the full range of senses. He *spoke* to His followers; He challenged them to *handle* Him to see that He was not an apparition; He *ate* with them; the time He spent with them was not limited to fleeting moments but sustained over several weeks. Clearly His post-resurrection activity anticipates objections to the physical aspect of His reanimation, the kneejerk tendency to write this off as an experience disconnected from space/time reality. These acts are not consistent with the nature of hallucinations. A hallucination must first have a strong expectation of the event's imminence. Hallucinations induced solely by stress and emotional trauma are very rare and do not typically manifest in multiple sensory planes.[2] The disciples had zero expectation of seeing their crucified master again in the physical world. His death was not met with any sense of eager anticipation but of incomprehensible and humiliating defeat. Remember that the initial reaction by Christ's disciples to the claim He had risen was *disbelief*.

The chance of two persons sharing the exact same hallucination at the same time is extremely remote. Because practically unlimited unique variables are present in each, the insertion of each additional person decreases the possibility of a shared identical hallucination by an astronomical factor. There is virtually no court of law that would ascribe the consistent, highly detailed, and unshakeable testimony of ten persons to a group hallucination. This would either be seen as a conspiracy to fabricate, or a record of the truth. Even maintaining a highly controlled environment from day one where the ten are sequestered and subject to the exact same nourishment, stimuli, etc., and the identical hallucinogens induced, the differing personalities introduce an insurmountable obstacle. How does one control for variables that would take a lifetime trying to identify?

In the case of the Jesus visions, more than *five hundred* in a single setting experienced the exact same set of multiple sensory perceptions, claiming to witness Jesus alive after His passion. These people would have come from widely divergent backgrounds. Moreover, the normal pattern for hysteria generated visions or for any sightings of an unusual nature (UFOs, for instance), is for reported sightings to increase in frequency and to vary widely in description. A saturation point is reached, followed by a gradual lessening of sightings. Yet the sightings of Christ ended just as abruptly as they had begun—no tailing off, as might be expected if this were psychologically manufactured.

The weak argument that the women went to the wrong grave that Sunday morning can be dismissed with this simple logic: If Christ were still dead but His body lay in some other tomb, the Jewish Sanhedrin, once again, would have produced the corpse to put an immediate end to all such politically subversive resurrection talk.

The circumstantial evidence alone for the resurrection is formidable. First, women were not considered reliable witnesses, yet the Gospels feature women as the first to affirm the resurrection. A contrived tale in the ancient world would not have begun with the testimony of women. The inclusion of this inconvenient fact is evidence of the writers' desire to relay a faithful presentation regardless of accepted customs. A second point, all ancient treatments of the resurrection assume the empty tomb. The question of whether the grave was unoccupied was never dealt with, only why. Additionally, as noted by J. N. D. Anderson, the sepulcher of Jesus never became a place of pilgrimage for believers. Christians would have naturally gravitated to this last remaining point of contact with their founder. Why did they not turn this into a sacred shrine?[3] Beyond these questions, the conversion of James (the half-brother of Jesus) and Paul are inexplicable in terms of either a *sitz im leben* or a conspiracy. James was decidedly hostile to Jesus and Paul to His followers until something literally transformed each.

An enduring obstacle for critics is that the central tenet of the NT, the foundation upon which it rests, is an irreducible event. It cannot be explained in terms of gradual accretions. Its unique nature (the reanimation of a human corpse) and the setting in which it resides makes it impossible to peel apart "resurrection layers." The earliest Christian creeds formulated before the first NT writings powerfully affirm the resurrection. "For I [Paul] delivered unto you first of all that which I also received, how that Christ died for our sins according to the scriptures; and that He was buried, and that He rose again the third day according to the scriptures" (1 Cor. 15:3–4). Concerning the above verses, Gary Habermas writes, "it is likely that the creed is organized in a stylized, parallel form, thereby providing a further indication of the oral confessional nature of this material."[4] Habermas continues:

> Paul's conversion would have occurred shortly afterwards [Christ's crucifixion], about AD 33–35. Three years after conversion (AD 36–38) he visited Jerusalem and specifically met with Peter and James (Gal. 1:18–19). . . . [T]he probability [is] that Paul received this creed from these apostles when he visited them in Jerusalem. Another possibility is that Paul received this material in Damascus immediately after his conversion, which would make it even three years earlier. . . . A Jerusalem location would date Paul's reception of the creed at about five to seven years after the crucifixion. . . . Since the tradition would actually have been formulated before Paul first heard it, the creed itself would be dated even earlier. . . . Therefore, we are dealing with material that proceeds *directly* from the events in question and this creed is thus crucial in our discussion of the death and resurrection of Jesus.[5]

Yet early creedal confessions did not merely affirm the resurrection; they deliberately and intimately tied this event to Christ's *deity*: "And without controversy great is the mystery of godliness: God was manifest in the flesh, justified in the Spirit, seen of angels, preached unto the Gentiles, believed on in the world, received up into glory" (1 Tim. 3:16). The dual nature of Jesus—fully human yet fully divine— was also developed from the central resurrection tenet. For Christ's death to be married to the OT redemptive program, His atoning sacrifice required more that the mere merits of even the greatest most moral man who ever lived; a component had to be present that transcended sinful humanity. Yet if the component of humanity were absent, then He could not have truly experienced death. Sacrificial death, however, as offered up even by the multitude of innocent OT animals could not remit sins, only temporarily cover them in anticipation of a future event which would finally definitively satisfy the full demands of justice. The resurrection constituted the definitive declaration/validation that Jesus had both tasted death in all its evil facets, and that He was indeed divine.

One of the most oft-repeated fallacies is that outside of the Bible, there is no historical mention of Jesus of Nazareth. In fact, the existence of Jesus is independently attested more than any other figure of antiquity. Were it not for the threatening implications that attach to this man, the question of His existence would never arise. All scholarship agrees that the Jewish historian Josephus, writing in the latter half of the first century AD, affirms His existence, though there is legitimate disagreement over disputed portions of his "Testimonium" (*Antiquities*, XVIII, 33).

F. F. Bruce makes mention of Cornelius Tacitus (born between AD 52–54), considered the greatest Roman historian, and a statement the latter makes about the famous fire Nero was rumored to have instigated:

> Therefore, to scotch the rumour, Nero substituted as culprits, and punished with the utmost refinements of cruelty, a class of men, loathed for their vices, whom the crowd styled Christians. Christus, from whom they got their name, had been executed by sentence of the procurator Pontius Pilate when Tiberius was emperor; and the pernicious superstition was checked for a short time, only to break out afresh, not only in Judea, the home of the plague, but in Rome itself, where all the horrible and shameful things in the world collect and find a home.[6]

In his book *The Historical Jesus*, Gary Habermas lists several persons of antiquity who either affirm the historicity of Jesus of Nazareth or the hostility of Christians to emperor worship: Suetonius, Thallus, Pliny the Younger, Emperor Trajan, Emperor Hadrian. In addition, Habermas points out the hostile witness from the Jewish Talmud (compiled between AD 70 and 200) found in *Sanhedrin 43a*, "on the eve of Passover Yeshu was hanged. For forty days before the execution took place, a herald went forth and cried, 'He is going forth to be stoned because he has practiced sorcery and enticed Israel to apostasy. Any one who can say anything in his favour, let him come forward and plead on his behalf.' But since nothing was brought forward in his favour he was hanged on the eve of Passover."[7] We see a decidedly hostile Jewish orthodoxy unwittingly corroborate several key NT claims: Jesus was both crucified and His execution took place on the eve of Passover; His ministry was inherently threatening to the Jewish power structure and the orthodox position; mysterious deeds outside of the natural realm are ascribed to Him; finally, at His trial, no one spoke up on His behalf.

In summary of the testimony of *nonbiblical* voices from the first century AD, Dr. Norman L. Geisler notes that from Greek, Roman, Jewish, and Samaritan sources we see these facts in complete agreement with the NT: 1) Jesus was from Nazareth; 2) He lived a wise and virtuous life; 3) He was crucified in Palestine under Pontius Pilate during the reign of Tiberius Caesar at Passover time, being considered the Jewish king; 4) He was believed by His disciples to have been raised from the dead three days later; 5) His enemies acknowledged that He performed unusual feats they called "sorcery;" 6) His small band of disciples multiplied rapidly, spreading even as far as Rome; 7) His disciples denied polytheism, lived moral lives, and worshiped Christ as divine.[8]

In light of these facts, let's reconsider the premise of higher criticism. The Jewish followers of Jesus are invited to exchange the stringent and relatively secure confines of their ancient tradition to embrace an unsubstantiated story. Their reward will be a life that eschews any self-serving component. The lifestyle the Christian is called to not only runs counter to the natural grain but will make increasing demands more personally exacting than any other religion in existence. They are invited to center their lives in a fiction for which they will be reviled by both fellow Jews and the Roman government, held in highest contempt, imprisoned, tortured, and ultimately (in many cases) exposed to the most horrific deaths. Because this story is simply an invention, there is no reason to believe the brutal deaths many will suffer will have any significance. Even if we allow that most of those martyred truly believe that Christ is risen and that they genuinely anticipate (foolishly) a wonderful afterlife, how do we account for those who *know* that Jesus' body still lies in corruption somewhere—that the resurrection is a fiction? Of Christ's inner circle and all the writers of the NT, only the apostle John would escape martyrdom. Who would *willingly, knowingly* not only send scores of friends and loved ones to their deaths but surrender their own lives for an outrageous lie? Some sort of romanticized "spiritual resurrection" could not have produced the overwhelming sense of conviction that something truly unique and world-transforming had occurred.

While projecting an imaginary context in which Christianity could "flourish," critics willingly ignore the actual context. Christianity clearly took root in a climate that was altogether hostile to any resurrection-centered religion and is the more remarkable for the impossible circumstances it would overcome. Again, and again, the explanation demands a cause proportionate to the effect. If universal rules of scholarship exist, are scholars bound by those rules to check as much as possible their own biases, to divorce themselves from preconceptions as to what the story *should* mean—to step *outside* of their own cultural influences and assumptions to be in the best possible position to apprehend not a preferred, but *the* cause of the all-too-evident effect?

Do the original storytellers reserve the right to tell their story within their own context and on their own terms? If they do not, then higher critics have not merely cleverly "deconstructed" layers of ancient myth; they have deconstructed language itself and laid waste the idea of any meaningful communication from one culture to another. Indeed, if language is this fluid, this imprecise, is it not the concept of *any* sort of communication that has been reduced to a mere myth?

If, on the other hand, such a universal code as mentioned above is recognized, and travelers of another period permitted to speak and be received on their own terms, then it must be admitted that form critics have failed to show any compelling reason why the "Jesus of faith" should be separated from "the Jesus of history." For no matter how many "layers" we peel away, we never arrive at a Jesus who is less than supernatural. Never do we arrive at a Jesus who is not hopelessly entangled in messianic implications.

CHAPTER 18

JESUS: JUST ANOTHER
"DYING/RISING GOD-MAN" MYTH?

The problems with denying the resurrection are formidable, to understate the matter. But Freke and Gandy do not shrink from this challenge. They take these obstacles head-on, systematically and courageously taking apart one argument after another by—removing a historical Jesus from the equation altogether! That's right: Jesus of Nazareth simply never existed. Again, from a purely historical perspective, there is probably no person of antiquity as well attested as Jesus of Nazareth, and from such diverse and reliable sources. Many are the characters of history with far less attestation yet whose existence has never been questioned. Freke and Gandy not only dismiss a vital historic record but, predictably, make no effort to address the thornier hostile witness.

Their justification for sidestepping the evidence for Jesus' historicity is based on a popular and frequently cited argument—Jesus was just another of the many "dying-resurrecting god-men" seen in almost every ancient culture. Since the similarities between all these other pagan myths and the Jesus myth are so striking, it should be obvious, according to Freke and Gandy, that the latter is borrowed from the former and thus no more historically reliable. These parallels leave readers to conclude that Jesus is surely a composite of, or at least heavily influenced by, the Isis cult and the various Mesopotamian and Greek mystery cults. Yet this argument is valid only to the extent that some sort of ground rules are set that can reasonably effectively screen out similarities that are only superficial. There must be a threshold that distinguishes incidental similarities from obvious borrowed ideas. Charles Penglase explains:

> It is all too easy to run eagerly after superficial parallels which cannot really be sustained under a closer scrutiny. Accordingly, the parallels

must have similar ideas underlying them and, second, any suggestion of influence requires that the parallels be numerous, complex and
detailed, with similar conceptual usage and, ideally, that they should
point to a specific myth or group to related myths in Mesopotamia.
Finally, the parallels and their similar underlying ideas must involve
central features in the material to be compared. Only then, it would
seem, may any claim stronger than one of mere coincidence be worthy
of serious consideration.[1]

Before even looking at any "connections," it is noteworthy that for pagans, the
trustworthiness of pagan myths was never an issue. Questioning the reliability of
tales concerning cultic hero-gods would have been puzzling to the pagan mind.
Why? Because their gods were so inseparable from nature that even dying and rising, in some sense, would have been identified *with* natural cycles, not definitively
defeating death with finality. Accretions were expected to attach, since these mythic
figures *lived* in allegories; the inspiring symbolism of their deeds far more significant
than any substance. To all practical purposes, the symbolism *was* the substance.

The Christian emphasis on preserving an accurate record stands in sharp relief.
Jesus Christ has something that none of these god-men have—a two-thousand-year
complex and highly detailed Jewish context to step into. It is his personal identification with that context that makes any peripheral similarities (even if numerous),
incidental and irrelevant. Christ's death and resurrection are central to His identity
and the vindication of His claims—to be the fulfillment of the Jewish context. And
this is central *immediately* to the Christian community. Jesus' teaching, in comparison to mythic figures, is eschatological. Rather than serve as some temporary source
of comfort or even inspiration, His teaching embraces the whole of history and
foresees an outworking of the divine plan in history that touches each individual
soul intimately, eternally and *transcendently*. To try to build a case against Christianity based on its relationship to Egyptian, Greek, or Mesopotamian myths is to
at best betray a glaring lack of knowledge about Judaism. While critics scour the
record for external influences, Judaism remains the all-too-conspicuous elephant in
the room.

If a fair comparison of Jesus and all these other myths is to be made, He must
be represented from the earliest and most trustworthy sources that describe this
man—the four Gospels of the New Testament. Too often, these comparisons are
based on the embellishments of later Christian organizations that consciously
sought to cast the Christ story, at least parts, in the line of mythical heroes, perhaps
to make Christ more palatable to pagan sensibilities. Such was the case following
Constantine's conversion and the influx of new converts. Christian authorities

would suddenly find themselves overrun by pagan numbers too great to assimilate, and pagan influences impossible to resist (at least in their entirety). Leaders would have to choose which battles to fight while reluctantly conceding to the masses those practices that seemed comparatively benign. Since this was too widespread to rein in with limited resources, an emphasis was placed on trying to fill the pagan praxis with some sort of Christian alternative, whether festivals, sacred days, venerated objects, or intercessory patrons. This would have, of course, generated many artificial similarities *after the fact* that did not previously exist in any form. For instance, December 25 is not a birth date extracted from the New Testament, which is silent on this question.

After ensuring we are making a legitimate apples-to-apples comparison (i.e., against the Christ of the NT and not of later embellishments), we must then be willing to dig past the surface to ensure that the apples do not turn out to have peach or plum cores. What appear to be parallel practices must involve implications that are central to the faith and not merely peripheral. For instance, the practice of baptism cannot be represented as a close parallel to pagan ritual washings if the two imply such vastly different things. In Christianity, baptism is not just an initiation sacrament; it is the summation of the gospel and closely associated with the conversion experience.

"Virgin birth," we are reminded, is a rather common theme in these stories of mythic figures. But this is misleading. Again, if we look past the general similarity, we see that the Christ story is fundamentally different in its conceptualization. Apart from the Christ story, all these accounts have this in common—the impregnation, no matter how exotic, explicitly involves a sexual union. None of these "virgin births" were in fact virginal at all. The Christ account is completely absent a sexual component. Moreover, God, in the Jewish framework, is never portrayed, as in the common pagan motif, exhibiting sexual (and lustful) characteristics. The "overshadowing" of the Holy Spirit upon Mary, which results in the Christ child placed within her womb, is a concept that occurs elsewhere in the NT and never implies sexual union.

Commonality of words and terms between Christianity and pagan religions is cited as evidence of borrowing. It might be helpful, though, to remember that early Christianity was surrounded by paganism. The very concept of language necessitates a commonality of terms and word usages within the larger culture to which every Christian was as well immersed, like it or not. Context, however, is always the key to arriving at a specific meaning of one of these common terms in any given instance. *If* the context of Christianity closely mirrored its pagan counterparts, *then* it would be reasonable to further investigate individual word linkages. Yet when Christianity consistently and on so many levels distinguishes its context from any other (save for Judaism) then getting hung-up on word similarities is straining at gnats while ignoring whole camels. Christians were presenting their case in contrast to paganism. Is it unreasonable that they would have expressed their challenge in terms familiar to the pagan world? Glenn Miller puts this in perspective: "[T]he issue is not one of what *individual* words, symbols, or motifs are used, but rather (a) the underlying concepts and systems of concepts; (b) the intensity of the parallels (e.g., numerous, complex, detailed); and (c) the 'unexpectedness' of the parallels."[2]

Most submitted candidates for the dying/rising god motif can be such only with certain assumptions filling in considerable gaps, which are ambiguous at best and even under the most favorable assumptions bear only the faintest resemblance to the Christ story. This is true of Adonis, Baal, Tammuz, Attis, Marduk, and Osiris. Turning any of these into a dying/rising parallel with Christ requires a considerable reduction of the concept of coming back to life from the dead. For instance, we must be willing to see Zeus' keeping Attis' body from corrupting and permitting hair to grow on his little finger, and Osiris' body parts reconnected that he might become lord of the underworld, on a par with resurrection. Except for Jesus of Nazareth, there is no clear claim to the dying and reanimation of any ancient figure. Professor Jonathan Smith weighs in: "All the deities that have been identified as belonging to the class of dying and rising deities can be subsumed under the two larger classes of disappearing deities or dying deities. In the first case, the deities return but have not died; in the second case, the gods die but do not return. There is no unambiguous instance in the history of religions of a dying and rising deity."[3]

Now that we have established something of a baseline for meaningful comparisons, let's look at a favorite of those who believe Jesus Christ is a ripoff of the savior-godman myth, and possibly the one most frequently alluded to as the model for Christianity: Zoroaster. All of the following descriptions/ideas encompass the ministry of Zoroaster, we are told, and were borrowed by Christianity: 1) born of a virgin and "immaculate conception by a ray of divine reason"; 2) baptized in a river; 3) astounded wise men in his youth with his wisdom; 4) tempted in the wilderness by the devil; 5) began ministry at age thirty; 6) baptized with water, fire, and "holy wind"; 7) cast out demons and restored sight to a blind man; 8) taught about heaven and hell, and revealed mysteries, including resurrection, judgment, salvation, and the apocalypse; 9) had a sacred cup or grail; 10) was slain; 11) his religion had a eucharist; 12) he was the "Word made flesh"; 13) his followers expect a "second coming" in the virgin-born Saoshyant or Savior, who is to come in 2341 AD and begin his ministry at age thirty, ushering in a golden age.

The following is a summation of Christian apologist J. P. Holding's findings about the above assertions, point for point: 1) the only source (the Avesta) that gives some support to this (though vague) is *later* than Christianity; 2) no record this was ever claimed; 3) Zoroaster is actually a *prodigy* to a wise man; 4) vague but basically so; 5) true but lacking relevance, since thirty was the recognized coming of age; 6) no existing evidence in support; 7) the demon reference is vague, not *out* of per se but drove something away, and the blind man reference is actually from a tenth-century AD document, not in any earlier existing source; 8) of these, resurrection comes closest to paralleling the Christian take (more on this later); 9) not found in any record (though actually irrelevant—the NT places no emphasis upon this); 10) apparently supported but nothing to indicate *murdered* (possibly killed in battle, possibly by lightning, etc.); 11) not supported by extant evidence; 12) not supported by extant evidence; 13) apparently supported but uncertain whether this will be Zoroaster or a descendant.[4]

We simply do not have historic documentation for many of the close (asserted) approximations to Christianity. States Holding:

> Our main source for details on Zoroaster is the Avesta, a collection of sacred texts which was put in writing from AD 346–360 and of which we have manuscript copies only as early as the thirteenth century. Some of the material probably comes from a time before the Christian era, but most of this is reckoned to be hymns and some basic information that was part of the oral tradition. The rest seems likely to have been added later.[5]

Considering the lateness of the sources, there is more reason to suspect that any borrowing is likely in the opposite direction. Even if Zoroastrianism does represent a bona fide development of resurrection thought, this in no way makes Judaism dependent upon it. The fact remains that a strain of resurrection theology exists throughout the history of the Jews. Though not solidified till the Babylonian/Persian period (600 to approx. 300 BC) this is a clear organic development that flows from central and early Judaic themes. The whole life/death drama is played out through history on the macro level in the story of the Jews. Key events in their unfolding history are metaphors for a dynamic that is, bit by bit, fleshed out on a personal level. Jewish journeying down into Egypt and subsequent bondage and misery—a metaphor for hell or at least the enslaving effect of sin; the forty-year wilderness journey—the tension between God's call and the pull of the pagan world (the lusts of natural man); entry into the Promised Land—a type of heaven; exile into Persian captivity and restoration to the Promised Land—death and resurrection.

In the field of ancient studies, the assumption that Christianity borrowed resurrection from the Persians is called the Zoroastrian hypothesis. Says N. T. Wright:

> [This] account, which remains popular in some quarters despite being regularly refuted, attempts to trace the emergence of Israelite belief in resurrection to ancient Zoroastrianism, pointing out that the belief seems to have emerged in Israel around the time, or shortly thereafter, that Israel was exiled in the parts of the world—Babylon, then Persia— where Zoroastrianism was the official religion of the Persian empire. This proposal has been debated for well over a century, hampered not the least by our radical uncertainty (because of the lateness of the primary sources) as to what ancient Zoroastrianism actually consisted of.[6]

In the footnotes, Wright adds, "Hengel, in company with some others, suggests that the line of probable influence runs from Jewish and Christian conceptions to the more developed Iranian ones."[7] Isaiah, writing at least one hundred years before the captivity, would give considerably more clarity to implications that had been converging in this direction since the dawn of Jewish history (Isa. 26:19). According to Wright:

> That is where, supremely, the hope for the nation and land becomes focused on an individual, or at least what looks like an individual; even if this is a literary code for the nation as a whole, or for a group within the nation, there are signs in the text itself, as well as in subsequent interpretation, that at least some of the "servant" passages in Isaiah may have an individual representing the nation, in mind [see Is. 53 for instance].[8]

National restoration in the face of unthinkable odds gives a much clearer and personal meaning to Isaiah's words in conjunction with the latter vision of Ezekiel featuring "the valley of dry bones" (Ezek. 37, predating the 539 BC Persian conquest of Babylon). This does not, viewed within an expanded context, require any borrowing from the Persians. There is a rather obvious clue that is too often overlooked: Whatever influences Persia may have exerted are dwarfed by the monumental reality that the Jews were delivered from this captivity! It is this dramatic fact that allows the Jews to look back and see all the pieces of resurrection theology that have suddenly coalesced. Says Wright, "[T]he meanings of 'bodily resurrection for dead humans' and 'national restoration for exiled/suffering Israel' are so closely intertwined that it does not matter that we cannot always tell which is meant, or even if a distinction is possible, in relation to particular passages; that is part of the point."[9]

Generally regarded the most esteemed scholar and unimpeachable authority in the field of Zoroastrian studies, R. C. Zaehner has this to say:

> The case for a Judeo-Christian dependence on Zoroastrianism in its purely eschatological [the outworking of history especially in relation to the soul's destination] thinking is quite different. And not at all convincing, for apart from a few hints in the Gathas and a short passage in Yasht 19.80–90 in which a deathless existence in body and soul at the end of time is affirmed, we have no evidence as to what eschatological ideas the Zoroastrians had in the last four centuries before Christ. The eschatologies of the Pahlavi books, though agreeing in their broad outlines, differ very considerably in detail and emphasis; they do not correspond at all closely to the eschatological writings of the intertestimentary period [the non-canonical Jewish writings of the 450-year span between the testaments] nor to those of St. Paul and the apocalypse of St. John. They do, however, agree that there will be a general resurrection of the body as well as soul, but this idea would be the natural corollary to the survival of the soul as a moral entity, once that had been accepted, since both Jew and Zoroastrian regarded soul and body as being two aspects, ultimately inseparable, of the one human personality.[10]

The "god-man" Mithra is notable for being the chief competitor with Christ for new converts during the first century AD. The more popular version of Mithra is derived from the so-called Hellenic mystery religions, generally known as the Roman Mithra, a version differing widely from the earlier Iranian presentation. So radically different is the Roman version that there is almost no continuity between the two. The Roman Mithra myth does not actually take shape until *after* the completion of the NT.

Whatever the "god-man parallel," the pattern seems clear. Most similarities are too superficial to command any significance. In those cases where the possibility of borrowing does emerge, the evidence indicates it is *from* the Judeo-Christian tradition. Proposed parallels are all too often based in misappropriate use of terms, giving an illusion of similarity when the connection is vague and irrelevant—for instance, attempting to cast essentially *any* afterlife scenario as the equivalent of resurrection while ignoring the very specific meaning given this word within a very specific and extended Judaic backdrop and refusing to address related vital questions. What impact, to begin with, does the resurrection/new life have on the eschatology, if any? Is this concept central or merely incidental? Rounding off terms to create an impression of sameness will not do, especially when resurrection and pagan disembodied afterlife schemes set side by side contrast such irreconcilably different meanings. What's more, in comparison to Jesus Christ, all dying/rising myths fit exactly into the normal pagan immersion into the cycles of nature.[11] Says Glenn Miller:

> It must be remembered that SOME general similarities MUST apply to any religious leader. They must generally be good leaders, do noteworthy feats of goodness and/or supernatural power, establish teachings and traditions, create community rituals, and overcome some forms of evil. These are common elements of the religious life—NOT objects that require some theory of dependence. . . . The common aspect of *homo religiosus* is an adequate and more plausible explanation than dependence.[12]

It is ironic that the Jesus story again and again demonstrates that it cannot be fit into the cut-and-paste mold alleged by critics. It is all these "parallel" accounts that so closely resemble a patchwork quilt, and often owing a considerable debt to Christianity.

Finally consider this: Of all these ancient religions that supposedly represent precursors to Christianity, most are now long since defunct, with a residue existing only in obscure enclaves. They inform none of the social or political discourse and are effectively irrelevant. Moreover, these have all fallen by the wayside without having ever faced the full onslaught of Enlightenment thought.

CHAPTER 19

THE NEW TESTAMENT: THE TEACHINGS OF JESUS, OR POLITICAL REACTION TO GNOSTICISM?

Regrettably, a century and a half of hostile scholarship regarding the authenticity of the New Testament has left its mark on an increasingly uninformed and uncritical public. From time to time, popular mini-movements spring up which promise a novel reexamination of Christianity. Yet the "novel" approach almost always follows a very familiar theme. Practically without fail, the scenario involves "alternative Christianities" which purportedly existed side by side with (some say before) the orthodox view from the very beginning, but somehow became lost. The spotlight is directed at Gnostic Christianity, the most prominent of these alternatives, exposing a view of Jesus radically different from the orthodox position. Until about the middle of second century AD, Christianity (so goes the tale) existed in a fluid state, with no strain reaching for ascendancy. Each Christian was free to decide which version he or she was more comfortable with, and little antagonism existed between the various strains until about the late second century. Enter the early Church Fathers, the Emperor Constantine, and the Roman Church, the predictable villains of the plot. The popular book *The Da Vinci Code* by Dan Brown is but the latest regurgitation of "a fresh new look at Christianity" (more on this later).

Because the Roman Church is widely regarded as the custodian of the NT, there is an assumption held by many that the Catholic Church was the original controlling force on the selection of books that make up the present NT. Additionally, because the church was to emerge as the dominant political force of the Middle Ages, it is suspected of political intrigue. First, it made all competitors void by declaring them heretical and aggressively removing all such subversive literature. Second, it changed or deleted much of the original message of its own recognized canon of Scripture which shared too close a kinship with other strains of Christianity. A third possibility is that the early Church Fathers did not merely draw out scriptural implications but *invented* the canon, creed, and hierarchy. Gnosticism, its chief competitor, was thereafter denied a hearing and eventually faded with the dying embers of history. Fortunately for mankind, preserved copies of Gnostic "gospels" have recently been unearthed, and the opportunity to recover ancient "truths" is again within our grasp. Such ideas, admittedly intriguing, cannot be sustained by the facts.

It is true that no original recordings of the words of Jesus Christ exist today. How then do we know that what we now have accurately reflects those words, especially almost two thousand years removed from the source? The problems inherent to message transmission tell us it's unreasonable to think the original message has not been compromised. The NT consists of twenty-seven books. Why not twenty-six? Why not twenty-eight? After all, are we not told that many other writings of that time were claiming to be the true sayings of Christ? Some of those writings were at considerable variance to those that became the official canon. Did God place a special stamp on these twenty-seven? If not, then some group of mere mortals (with all their prejudices and manifold fallibilities) took it upon themselves to decide what should and should not be part of official church dogma.

The above questions and problems represent what the average lay critic sees as sufficient grounds for dismissing the Bible as wholly authoritative. Let's consider the first problem: The original recordings of Jesus' words are no longer in existence. This is not a situation that is unique to the NT writings. There are *no* ancient writings (secular or otherwise) from the early Christian era that have survived to this day in their original form. Most great works from this period have come down to us in copies that are removed from their original source an average of about seven to nine hundred years and only in fragmented form. For instance, the oldest surviving copy of Caesar's *Gallic War* (58–50 BC) dates to nine hundred years after the original; the earliest books of Livy's *Roman History* (59 BC–AD 17) to about four hundred years; surviving *Histories of Tacitus* (AD 100) to about eight hundred years; the *History of Thucydides* (460–400 BC) and the *History of Herodotus* (488–428 BC) both to about 1,300 years from their original writings.[1] Yet no classical scholar doubts the authenticity of any of these works, though they are so far removed from and represent but a small portion of the originals.

The actual uniqueness of the NT writings lies in the very short time interval between originals and our earliest existing copies. The Codex Vaticanus is the earliest manuscript containing nearly the entire New Testament. Housed in the Vatican Library, this copy dates between 325–350. The Codex Sinaiticus, located in the British Museum, dates to about 350 and contains almost all the NT and more than half of the OT.

But the writings of the NT do not distinguish themselves from all other writings of antiquity solely on the basis of time interval between original and existing copies. There are more than five thousand partial or complete Greek handwritten manuscripts of the NT from the second through the fifteenth centuries. There are more than ten thousand Latin Vulgate copies. When we add to this more than nine thousand early versions written in various languages (from Ethiopic to Persian) we have nearly 25,000 manuscripts of the NT that date from the Middle Ages to no more than a century removed from living eyewitnesses to Jesus Christ. To this impressive number can be added numerous papyrus fragments, sixty-six from the gospel of John dating to about the mid-second century and one (the John Rylands papyri containing verses 31–33 and part of verse 37 of chapter 18 from the same gospel) dating to AD 130. To illustrate the significance of this number, of all documents of antiquity, Homer's *Iliad* comes in second with 643 manuscripts that still survive.[2]

Since we have nearly complete NT books and extensive fragments of books that date to the second century (and the one fragment to AD 130), it's a given that the originals must date still earlier. Conservative scholarship has placed the writing of Paul's letters (epistles) between AD 50–66; Matthew between AD 70–80; Mark between AD 50–65; Luke somewhere in the early 60s; John between AD 80–100. Liberal scholarship (which, as should now be evident, has long demonstrated a strong animus toward the entire Bible) has dated Paul's letters between AD 50–100; Matthew between AD 80–100; Mark about AD 70; Luke between AD 70–90; and John between AD 90–170.[3] Incidentally, the late dating for John represents an extreme position that few liberals agree with today and feel can be supported by existing evidence. Even with this late dating, however, what the above means is that there is unanimous agreement that those who recorded the words of Jesus did so within living memory of His life.

Long before there was anything called the Catholic Church, long before any structured church councils met to settle (or even discuss) the matter of NT canon, there was a circulating body of writings that was accepted as trustworthy and authoritative by the early Christian community. The four Gospels and the thirteen Pauline Epistles were given favored status almost from the very beginning; recognized as inspired and bearing the power of God. This body formed something of a baseline for the criteria by which all other writings would be judged.

The prolific writings of the apostolic fathers or early Church Fathers (available today in a ten-volume set called The Ante-Nicene Fathers) attest to the intricate structure, the high Christology (i.e., Jesus both human and divine), and the vigorous and lucid defense of the faith, existing as early as the beginning of the second century. Moreover, to the problem of ever-present persecution was added the new and growing problem of factions within the ranks who were playing fast and loose with the Scriptures. Especially problematic was the heretic Marcion who broke ranks because of his contempt for the God of the Old Testament (Marcion, as earlier suggested, may have been a kind of prototype Gnostic). To Marcion, the proper thing was for the Church to sever all connections with the Jewish faith. To that end, he produced his own NT canon, about AD 140, consisting of a "purged" edition of Luke's gospel (Luke being the only Gentile author and his the least Jewish of the Gospels), and ten of the Pauline epistles.

According to Dr. Darrell Bock, the notion that the Church of the first century was faced with a choice between radically differing views has no basis in fact. There simply were no competing circulating (Christian) documents that challenged the basic accepted truths of the orthodox position. Questions at this time involving inclusion were not based on which views of Christ were to be accepted; there was but the single view. The question centered on *inspiration*. The earliest possible strands of anti-orthodox views cannot be seen until the beginning of the second century. It was not until the mid to latter part of this century that the church would find itself having to consciously separate itself from "alternative Christianities." It was about this time that a new mystical *anti*-literalist approach called gnosticism (from the Greek word *gnosis*, meaning "knowledge") would begin to define itself, appropriating Jesus Christ as a focal point. The new threat made it more important than ever that believers understand the non-negotiable basics of the faith.

Gnosticism's own view of the actual historic personage of Jesus was rather loosely held. If He *had* been a real person, it was certain He had not actually died on the cross nor bodily resurrected. For the Christ, it was held, could not have come in the flesh. As the idea of the divine intermingling with human flesh was anathema, at most Jesus had perhaps taken on the appearance of human form. What was of greatest importance was the *symbolism* that all these supposed events and sayings related to Jesus represented. These were all "spiritualized" into metaphors that signified a new emerging period in a spiritual evolution. Because the Gnostics took such a dim view of the material world, concerns for historical facts carried little weight in any of their writings. "Truth" could not be found in material events but could only be apprehended in the realm of the spirit. This view justified the writing of countless "gospels" as each initiates' own experiences dictated. In other words, they were free to put whatever words in Jesus' mouth they deemed appropriate, unfettered by time/space/material constraints. As such, no gospel held (nor *should* hold) any claim to be superior to any other, including the four NT Gospels.

As we examine the writings of the early Church Fathers we find numerous polemics to the claims of schools of Gnosticism. Writing in the latter part of the second century, Irenaeus (a disciple of Polycarp, who was in turn a disciple of the apostle John) voiced this frustration over his efforts to press Gnostics for the authority behind their claims:

> When, however, they are confuted from the Scriptures, they turn round and accuse these same Scriptures, as if they [the Scriptures] were not correct, nor of authority, and assert that they [the Scriptures] are ambiguous, and that the truth cannot be extracted from them by those who are ignorant of tradition. For they [Gnostics] allege that the truth was not delivered by means of written documents. . . . And this wisdom [which Gnostics believe that they alone are privy to] each one of them alleges to be the fiction of his own inventing, forsooth; so that, according to their idea, the truth properly resides at one time in Valentinus, at another in Marcion, at another in Cerinthus, then afterwards in Basilides, or has even indifferently in any other opponent, who could speak nothing pertaining to salvation. For every one of these men, being altogether of a perverse disposition, depraving the system of truth, is not ashamed to preach himself.[4]

It could be said that Gnosticism anticipated the Wellhausen/Bultmann reductionism of language, showing that aggressive efforts to deconstruct the Gospels dates as early as the second century AD. Gnosticism presented such a distorted picture of God, an ambiguity that overwhelmed the examiner with an endless maze of convoluted pathways, that understanding its essential reality was nearly impossible. Yet Irenaeus committed himself to this task. The vigorous protest and defense by Irenaeus shows the immediate and sharp divergence between the apostolic tradition and Gnosticism from the time the latter first began to emerge. As Bock sums up Irenaeus' pointed responses, "Irenaeus was not the creator of orthodoxy; he was created by it."[5]

Frankly, extant Gnostic writings show the same antagonistic attitude toward the apostolic view. So much for the notion that these different views originally peacefully coexisted. Gnosticism did not offer some purported fuller complimentary portrait of Christ; it proposed something radically at odds with the traditional view, such that if one view was correct the other *must* necessarily be false. Moreover, whereas the apostolic writings closely agreed with and were deeply rooted in OT Judaic tradition—its concept of God and redemption from sin—Gnosticism could scarcely have been more contemptuous of this tradition.

At the core of Gnosticism was a concept called dualism: Physical matter was considered evil, whereas ideas (which were thought to have originated in the spirit realm) were generally good. Again, in common with all paganism, we find the highest God is unknowable and ineffable. The physical plane, with its multitude of flaws, is the result of lesser gods (called aeons) who have done a poor job of creating, introducing all sorts of problems due to misunderstandings and improper emotional outbursts. The God-force, consistent with pagan themes, is inherently flawed, the universe the product of a mistake that He/it is either powerless or does not care to prevent. The God of the Old Testament is evidently the most corrupted of these lesser gods and called the Demiurge. Salvation has nothing to do with redemption from sin but is about placing oneself in position to apprehend the "secret knowledge" that can enable one to overcome the ignorance that separates man from spiritual freedom. The physical world is so deficient that it is beyond redemption; it must be escaped. Jesus Christ is presented as but another of these aeons. He of course, ceases to exist in any mediating role and is reduced to a warm, fuzzy spirit guide. As with all non-Christian religions which seek in some fashion to make Him one of their own, He is altogether superfluous.

Having delved deeply and exhaustively into their claims, Irenaeus would conclude that the difference was not something to be measured in degrees, but expressed as opposites; the mundane cast against sublime royalty:

> Such then, is their system, which neither the prophets announced, nor the Lord taught, nor the apostles delivered, but of which they boast that beyond all others they have perfect knowledge. They gather their views from other sources than the Scriptures; and, to use a common proverb, they strive to weave ropes of sand, while they endeavour to adapt with an air of probability to their own peculiar assertions the parables of the Lord, the sayings of the prophets, and the words of the apostles, in order that their scheme may not seem altogether without support. In doing so, however, they disregard the order and the connection of the Scriptures, and so far as in them lies, dismember and destroy the truth. . . . Their manner of acting is just as if one, when a beautiful image of a king has been constructed by some skillful artist out of precious jewels, should then take this likeness of the man all to pieces, should re-arrange the gems, and so fit them together as to make them into the form of a dog or of a fox, and even that but poorly executed; and should then maintain and declare that *this* was the beautiful image of the king which the skillful artist constructed, pointing to the jewels which had been admirably fitted together by the first artist to form the image of

the king, but have been with bad effect transferred by the latter one to the shape of a dog, and by thus exhibiting the jewels, should deceive the ignorant who had no conception what a king's form was like, and persuade them that that miserable likeness of the fox was, in fact, the beautiful image of the king.[6]

All available Gnostic sources, including the "gospels" of Thomas and Judas, emerge as a later and deliberate *reaction* to the orthodox view of Jesus Christ. If early Christianity were so fluid, so lacking in any kind of structured principles (even if only in rudimentary form), how could we account for the intense and near universal persecution that sought out believers so early on? The Gnostic version of Christianity would have required tremendous imagination to uncover anything that might be interpreted as subversive. In fact, this form of Christianity would have been right at home in this accommodating ancient Roman environment, taking its place among the ever-increasing pantheon of religions already openly practiced. Whatever their diversity, they shared this commonality—all obediently avoided any claims or implications that might challenge the sovereignty of the almighty state. On the other hand, the orthodox view that a new order had been instituted which established Jesus, not Caesar, as the sovereign head of the world, explains the tension very well.

In the end, Gnosticism succumbed to the apostolic tradition neither because of political subterfuge nor ruthless intimidation, but because it could not compete with the promise of real substantive life as ratified by the resurrection. Those who had tasted the fruit of eternal life knew that Gnosticism, no matter how cleverly it tried to repackage an old idea, had no capacity for answering that deepest hunger in man. At best, it could only mock his despair by concocting a grand pretense that anguish, heartache, and death weren't real. Those who had the hunger met could never settle for a cheap imitation, let alone consider laying down their lives for multiple layers of bluster.

Laying aside the issue of "gnostic gospels," it would be misleading to say that none of the books that became canon were ever in dispute. But by AD 200, about twenty books were widely accepted with very little dissent among orthodox congregations (those following the apostolic tradition, as opposed to advocates of radical departure). "Origen (185–254) mentions the four Gospels, the Acts, the 13 Paulines, 1 Peter, 1 John, and Revelation as acknowledged by all; he says that Hebrews, 2 Peter, 2 and 3 John, James and Jude, with the 'Epistle of Barnabas', the *Shepherd of Hermas,* the *Didache,* and the 'Gospel according the Hebrews' were disputed by some."[7]

By the time of Constantine's Edict of Toleration (311), the New Testament canon, certainly key doctrinal positions, was, for all practical purposes, already settled. Through a process somewhat akin to attrition, these books had proven through trial by fire that God's stamp was indeed upon each of them. All of this had occurred in an environment of intense persecution before there was anything to be gained politically or materially, and everything to be lost. Most of the elders who met at the Council of Nicaea in 325 to discuss doctrinal issues (*not* canonization) bore the scars of persecution that had just ended.

The first council regarding canonization did not meet until 393 at Hippo Regius (North Africa). This was still probably a hundred years before the early stages of what would become *the* Catholic Church (as politically distinct from the church catholic, small c—a term which had simply been employed from the second century on as a shorthand way of distinguishing the universally accepted apostolic tradition from rogue groups nipping at the edges). The next such council took place four years later at Carthage. Neither of these imposed anything new on Christians. They merely made official by decree what Christians everywhere had long since recognized as official in their hearts and minds (*and* practices). In fact, Athanasius had named the twenty-seven as *alone* canonical in a letter written in 367. Incidentally, Christianity did not become the official religion of the state until 381 under the reign of Theodosius.

Regarding the NT record we possess today, neither the Catholic Church nor Constantine has been a factor. When Martin Luther nailed his ninety-five theses to the church door at Wittenberg, he was not protesting the church's alteration of the Scriptures whether by addition, subtraction, or any other manipulation. He was protesting *church* practices that were occurring despite the Scriptures; *church* doctrine that had no scriptural support and, in some cases, was completely at odds with Scripture. The Catholic Church did attach several apocryphal (of doubtful origin) books to the Old Testament (which Luther also spoke against), but did not bestow full canonical status on these until 1546.

CHAPTER 20

SYMBOLISM VS. LITERALISM

.

A final word on the "literalist" interpretation of Scripture that Freke and Gandy inveigh against: If one assumes license to construct new narratives out of whole cloth, then adding a completely new twist to old plots should not be off limits. Though critics most often lay the blame for the "intolerant" orthodoxy that would emerge from Christ's teachings at the feet of the austere apostle Paul, Freke and Gandy don't quite see it that way: Our friends decided it would be neat (and certainly novel) to cast Paul, instead, as a champion of *Gnostic* Christianity. As this is a complete departure from the usual hostile approach, we expect some reasonable explanation. Not wishing to confuse their readers with or otherwise entangle them in mundane minutia such as, well, evidence, Freke and Gandy substitute this clever and charming tact: Where Paul's epistles plainly refute the Gnostic position, they are obvious forgeries. When they don't directly disparage Gnosticism, they are of course authentic. So Paul vindicates their view completely, and anyone who denies this irrefutable formula is just being blockheaded.

The first imposing obstacle to their preferred view of Paul is that he was originally *hostile* to Christ and His followers; he was zealously persecuting the faith. It is not possible Paul that could have been preaching a Gnostic Jesus when he was (according to the historic record upon which all reputable scholarship agrees) a strict, observant Jew and of a particularly rigid sect of Pharisees. Unless he had a split personality, Paul would not have surrendered his proud Jewish pedigree for a pagan would-be Messiah. The thrust of Gnosticism was the antithesis of all that Paul held sacred. His acquiescence to Jesus could only happen if he were convinced by some overwhelming new evidence or event that Jesus was the Christ, the fulfillment of Judaism. As there would be an adamant *denial* of any such event by Gnostics there is then no occasion nor explanation for such a drastic transformation. Yet his change was so profound and so abrupt that Christians were skeptical, dubious, and guarded (and certainly suspicious) of and toward a man who now professed

172 Kingdom of God or Pagan Empire?

such a radically different message. Paul's great missionary zeal, publishing far and wide the gospel, would have also been out of character with the Gnostic tendency toward the secretive.

Freke and Gandy also overlook Paul's involvement in the first Christian council in Jerusalem, convened to settle a particularly sharp contention between those believers who continued to stress the Law of Moses (which some scholarship sees James at least sympathetic to) and those believers (whose view Paul represented) who stressed the grace that had come through Jesus Christ. All the major players were present, including James and Peter. How easy it would have been for James, Peter, or Paul to each consider himself uniquely qualified to convey Christ's message, with all its new implications, to the masses. James was a devoutly observant Jew, first bishop of Jerusalem, and the actual blood brother of Jesus. Peter could point out that he was not just a chosen apostle of Christ but that he had directly been given the authority and privilege of preaching the first gospel message to the Jews on Pentecost and later to the Gentiles. He could remind him that he (James) had not been a believer until after Christ's resurrection. He could also remind Paul that not only was he (Paul) not an original apostle but of how he had so brutally once persecuted Christ's church. Paul was a Johnny-come-lately. On the other hand, Paul could make the case that he had a very personal one-on-one encounter with the risen Lord on the way to Damascus. His zeal for God's righteous implementation of His kingdom, coupled with his lofty education in Jewish eschatology, uniquely qualified him to draw out the implications of new profound complexities. He could certainly remind Peter of his betrayal of Jesus, whereas Paul had always been fearless.

If early Christianity truly were so fluid (as goes the current popular notion) we should have expected to see three (possibly four, if we weigh the unique role and contributions of the apostle John) distinct Jesus movements emerge in that first century. The central element that holds these divergent positions together, however, is the very element *missing* from the new Jesus movements that spring forth in the second century—the centrality of the resurrection. In the earliest Christianity, even though there are pronounced contentions over doctrinal matters, the spirit of unity and conciliation prevails among these strong-willed leaders. And though Paul's mission is most prominent, taking the gospel beyond the narrow borders of Jewish Palestine, each of these three is vital in taking a local religion to the world without losing the essential link with the Old Testament paradigm. It is not possible to address the contribution of any one of these without the complementary role of the other two. This is a little indivisible trinity. Alone, any one of these would have been insufficient to the overwhelming task. Three distinct personalities, styles, and sets of weaknesses intermingled with eminent qualifications. Yet God would use this diversity to achieve ultimate unity—weaknesses counterbalanced against strengths. In this, God's signature is most evident: "For with God nothing shall be impossible" (Luke 1:37). Freke and Gandy cannot arbitrarily transform Paul into some convenient caricature without leaving the rapid spread of apostolic (orthodox) Christianity completely inexplicable. Moreover, they cannot hijack Paul while ignoring James and Peter. Like it or not, the three are a package deal.

Though it is absurd to plug Paul into a Gnostic role in first-century Christianity (the time frame for all thirteen Pauline Epistles), Freke and Gandy do not easily give up the ghost. Commenting on Paul's letters, "Why does Paul never mention an historical Jesus in his letters?"[1] What about 1 Corinthians 15:3–8 (which all reputable scholarship attributes to Paul) where Paul mentions the message of the death and resurrection of Jesus that he had received and was now passing on? But the authors' premise is itself fundamentally flawed, and completely disregards the context of Paul's writings. The historicity of Christ is well known and attested at least orally throughout the community of believers. Paul clearly sees his mission is to examine and draw out the Jewish redemptive implications of His life, death, and resurrection. And though his mission is distinct from the gospel writers, this hardly makes Paul disinterested in Christ's historicity.

Freke and Gandy continue: "There is no mention of any miracles. No water into wine, no walking on water, no miraculous meals or extraordinary catches of fish."[2] Oops again: They must have forgotten about the resurrection. Of course, our friends intend to get around this by giving the word a new meaning: "The only elements of the Jesus myth that Paul mentions are Christ's death and resurrection, which Paul understands as symbolizing the process of initiation. By sharing in Jesus' death and resurrection initiates symbolically die to their 'old self' and resurrect 'in Christ.' Paul reminds his students 'the person you once were has been crucified with Christ.'"[3] So here is the solution, then: Resurrection must be understood to have meaning as a *symbol*. If only the authors could learn to leave well enough alone.

Literalists do not deny that crucifixion and resurrection are powerful symbols, but symbols of *what*? Do symbols ever take on meaning without a literal referent? If a symbol has no concrete anchor, then it can mean anything, which is to say it essentially means nothing. When Jesus says He is "the door" in John 10:9, His statement is filled with meaning. Why? Obviously not because we picture Him in rectangular form suspended by hinges swinging fore and aft. His statement has meaning because we immediately relate the concrete experience of a literal door separating one chamber from whatever lies on the other side. Had we never been exposed to a literal door and the concept of unknown possibilities beyond this side, His statement would be indecipherable gibberish.

Casting symbols as the opposite of the concrete or literal is just the sort of fallacious premise on which Freke and Gandy routinely predicate their positions. The power of symbols is in their ability to immediately and dramatically draw *literal experiences* together in a single moment and instantly yield multifaceted meaning or project their myriad implications. A symbol minus the concrete referent would fail to represent anything; therefore it cannot *be* a symbol. A policeman's badge sums up the authority of the entire US Constitution and the numerous complexities contained in its multiplicity of laws. Absent that code of authority, that badge is only a little hunk of metal. A hundred-dollar bill without the backing of the US Treasury is but a thin piece of worthless paper. An American flag stirs the passions of the citizen who has not only acquainted himself with the sacrifices of past generations but has put his own life on the line to secure and preserve the unprecedented freedom and opportunity that flag represents. Those who have no knowledge nor appreciation of those sacrifices, and have never had to leave their comfort zones to uphold that freedom, will see that same flag as little more than the sum of the cloth and dye which constitutes it.

With these things in view, what sort of symbolism could the cross have engendered in a *Gnostic* sense? In Paul's own words, the cross was weakness (shame) to the Jews, and foolishness (a stumbling block) to the Greeks. Why would a Gnostic Paul have used the most repulsive act of human cruelty to both pagans and Jews (crucifixion) to impart an uplifting message, to sell a mystical concept of spiritual "initiation"? Remember, the cross was already a powerful symbol in the first century AD. It was the most direct, the most visceral summation of Roman oppression for Jews. Who would have had the audacity to try to transform that symbol into one of hope and triumph? Would a Gnostic Paul, who as a Gnostic would have had an even greater aversion to anything material and despised any physical sacrifice, have used the cross to represent a *spiritual awakening*? Could he have chosen any less appropriate symbol?

Imagine right after World War II, selling to the Jews the idea the Nazi flag has now become a symbol of hope and triumph. How many Jews would have willingly laid down their lives for this proposition? Martyrdom aside, how many Jews would have looked at the Nazi flag as a new symbol of spiritual enlightenment? That Paul would center his entire message in this abhorrent act can only be rationally explained if his premise is that this act is *itself* the agent of change. If, however, we divorce the symbolism of "crucifixion in Christ" from the historic act, what sort of message are we left with? Apart from the literal crucifixion and resurrection of Jesus Christ, what sort of passions could the terminology of crucifixion stir up in the world of that day? Only the most negative and contemptuous. For Paul to zero in on "the cross" meant something had to have transformed that most despised form of execution into something radically different from any previous perception. And, incidentally, there is nothing in any of Paul's writings to support the idea that he identified the concept of "being crucified with Christ" as some kind of "initiation." There can be no doubt Paul is speaking about a *transformation* offer extended to *all*, which has nothing to do with acquiring "secret knowledge."

CHAPTER 21

THE DAVINCI CODE

The *Da Vinci Code* is an intriguing novel that unwraps an exciting mystery of conspiracy involving the highest levels of Christendom, reaching back through history to the time of Christ. The unfolding implications threaten to reduce a two-thousand-year monolith to a mound of rubble. As a work of fiction, *The Da Vinci Code* is an entertaining excursion into the fanciful world of "what-ifs." Though author Dan Brown does not pretend his characters or plot are real, he does make a curious statement in the preface of his book: "Fact: The Priory of Sion—a European secret society founded in 1099—is a real organization. In 1975 Paris' Bibliotheque Nationale discovered parchments known as *Les Dossiers Secrets*, identifying numerous members of the Priory of Sion, including Sir Isaac Newton, Botticelli, Victor Hugo, and Leonardo da Vinci. . . . Fact: All descriptions of artwork, architecture, documents, and secret rituals in this novel are accurate." With these provocative statements, Brown leaves no doubt that though his story is cast in a make-believe plot, he fully intends that the not-so-subtle implications fleshed out through fictional characters should be taken as unimpeachable fact.[1]

With Brown's heavy reliance on the work of scholarship in the vein of the Jesus Seminar (which is to say, almost no scholarship) and Gnostic sources in particular, his radical challenge to traditional Christianity is already on shaky ground at best. Nevertheless, considering he obviously intends to challenge well-substantiated claims that find support on so many levels and from such varied angles, one would expect Brown to zealously guard against overplaying his hand. Rather than blunt head-on assaults of specific points (where refuting Brown's assertions would be too easy) we might expect a vast multitude of facts to be bent just ever so slightly. Weaknesses could be disguised with clever rhetoric and just enough innuendo to create the impression of plausibility. In other words, Brown might have taken Gnosticism itself as his working model, where the art of subtlety and ambiguity leaves critics scrambling to find a handle. This would have afforded Brown considerable cover and placed those refuting his assertions in the frustrating position of having to painstakingly sort out numerous inaccuracies, in a culture that already boasts perhaps the shortest attention span in history. Meanwhile, *The Da Vinci Code* could enjoy practically free reign to propagandize a substantial (and growing) segment that eagerly swallows any theme which fuses the sensational with the conspiratorial.

Inexplicably, Brown has apparently chosen instead to model his approach after an infamous statement by Hitler's minister of propaganda, Joseph Goebbels: "If you tell a lie big enough and keep repeating it, people will eventually come to believe it." The thrust of Brown's novel, though many consider it groundbreaking, is not exactly original: The church (collectively represented by Roman Catholicism) is responsible for perpetrating the most far-reaching and socially irresponsible fraud in history. Jesus Christ, we learn, never claimed divinity and was not received as such in the ancient world until the council of Nicaea in AD 325, convened and closely controlled by Constantine. The church, purging any memory of "the Divine Feminine" from the record, set about to replace traditionally accepted matriarchal society with a new extreme and oppressive patriarchy. Women were subjugated to demeaning roles of hapless servitude.

Sexuality, the ancient conduit to the divine, became repressed by the church and recast as an evil. What's more, the church concealed the fact of Jesus' marriage to Mary Magdalene. Its greatest sin, though, is its deliberate suppression of the truth concerning the *child* this union produces. Secret documents hidden away somewhere in Europe not only bear conclusive evidence of this truth but also of the royal French Merovingian line descending from this child. The plot Brown unfolds chronicles the various secret organizations that formed for the sole purpose of protecting these documents from the ruthless efforts of the church to find and destroy at any cost. The Priory of Sion (mentioned above and reportedly founded in 1099) is perhaps the most important secret organization dedicated to the preservation of this hallowed truth.

These are intriguing propositions to be sure; yet what is Brown's solid source for such a tradition-shattering premise? The answer can be traced to a Frenchman by the name of Pierre Plantard. In 1956, a small group of friends formed a recreational club called "the Priory of Sion." Soon disbanded, the group was reformed as a political entity a year later, under the direction this time of Plantard. In the late 1950s or early '60s, Plantard caught wind of a delightful local tale. According to the story, in the late nineteenth century, a young French parish priest found ancient coded parchments (which allegedly contained information about secret bloodlines and the like) while his church building was undergoing renovations. Muzzled by the Catholic Church, the priest was discredited and died in obscurity in 1917. As the legend left no trace of any actual authenticity, it was suspected by most that the story contained but a grain of truth (the existence of the parish priest perhaps the only verifiable item), the remainder likely a publicity gimmick intended to spruce up the local flavor for tourists.[2]

Apparently suffering from grand delusions, Plantard coopted and embellished the tale of the parish priest. Plantard forged writings purporting to be the secret parchments of the priest. He not only created a fiction that these papers related information about secret organizations but proceeded to identify his own group as one of these ancient organizations and invented documentation which seemed to establish Plantard as a descendant of the royal Merovingian Line, a line he traced back to Jesus Christ, Himself. In his fiction, the Priory of Sion boasted an unbroken line of "grand masters" from near to its inception to the present. Plantard listed among these grand masters such key historical characters as Isaac Newton, Botticelli, Victor Hugo, and of course, Leonardo Da Vinci. The next step was to plant these forged documents in the Bibliotheque Nationale in Paris where they could innocently be "discovered." The hoax was brought to light as early as 1973. Yet it would not be for another twenty years, with Plantard brought before a court of law because of his possible involvement in the death of an identified grand master, that he would fully admit to the fraud. In 1996, the BBC (hardly a propaganda organ for conservative Christianity) exposed the hoax along with the full story in a documentary.[3] Other news organizations and publications followed suit.

The above revelation carries serious and troubling implications. To begin with, this means that Dan Brown is either deliberately perpetrating a fraud of his own, or his investigative and research methods are extraordinarily lazy and sloppy. Since a thoroughly discredited fiction forms the bedrock of Brown's contentions, there should be no logical reason to examine or consider any other claims. Da Vinci could not be a member of an ancient secret organization that never existed; no secret documents are left to protect; no more unimpeachable historic evidence the church is involved in some cover-up, and so on. The clever lengths Brown has gone through to "decipher" coded paintings are all deprived of a basis in reality. From this point forward, it is nothing short of a mystery that so many apologists were, nevertheless, not only willing to extend credibility to Brown but to laud his work as some remarkable breakthrough.

In 2004, *U.S. News & World Report* devoted a special collector's edition to the phenomenal success of the *The Da Vinci Code*. Though it pointed out a number of serious factual errors, it nonetheless gushed over the book's success and the excitement Brown had stirred, many now having to rethink old assumptions. It was as though the lack of historical accuracy was irrelevant. Wrote Amy D. Bernstein: "Despite its patently fictional content and glaring factual inaccuracies, *The Da Vinci Code* has been the subject of endless cocktail party chatter and water-cooler discussion."[4]

Bernstein went on to quote Harold Attridge, dean of the Divinity School at Yale, and then to add her own comment: "'Though you gag at the historical claims in it' [Attridge] says, he spoke on every occasion to packed houses of Yale alumni 'who sat with rapt attention.' Why the rapt attention from Ivy League graduates, no less? The secret lies in the novel's potent convergence of elements that entertain, enlighten, and empower the reader."[5]

Rather than rhapsodizing over the new iconoclast on the block, shouldn't the buzz round the water-cooler have been centered on Brown's blatant *fraud* and how he'd stigmatized himself as a propaganda hack? How is one empowered and enlightened by assertions so divested of the most basic element of truth—especially when those assertions specifically claim to *represent* that truth?

It is hardly a secret that Dan Brown relied considerably on earlier conspiracy yarns such as *The Templar Revelation* and *Holy Blood, Holy Grail*. Commenting on the latter (and the authors' approach) in this same special edition was Laura Miller: "Sources such as the New Testament are qualified as 'questionable' and derivative when they contradict the conspiracy theory, then microscopically scrutinized for inconsistencies that might support it. The authors spin one gossamer strand of conjecture over another, forming a web dense enough to create the illusion of solidity. Though bogus, it's [*Holy Grail*] an impressive piece of work."[6] Dan Burstein, enthusiastic cheerleader for Brown, offered this generous appraisal:

> Some saw *The Da Vinci Code* as highly derivative of books like *Holy Blood, Holy Grail* and *The Templar Revelation*—books Brown cited by name in the text of *The Da Vinci Code* and credited on his website as important to his research . . . *Holy Blood, Holy Grail* . . . has its own credibility issues: it is generally considered to be an occult stew of myth, legend, and outright hoax, mixed in with some very intriguing historical details. Finally, the secret sect that first started it all off, the Priory of Sion, has been exposed as a fraud. But . . . there are enough other historical issues, controversies, and implied secrets to keep most readers satisfied anyway.[7]

Satisfied about *what*? That truth *can* be spun out of gossamer strands of conjecture? That if the illusion is elaborate or clever enough, it has the *right* to supplant truth? This would be the equivalent of Orthodox Christians conceding the resurrection is based on deliberately planted phony documents that have been thoroughly debunked, maintaining nonetheless, "there are enough other historical issues, controversies, and implied secrets to keep most readers satisfied anyway" that the NT record, though not terribly accurate or reliable, is nevertheless impressive enough that the Orthodox view is fully justified.

So, what about these "other historical issues and controversies" to which Burstein alludes? Even if Brown has cast his tale injudiciously, surely there must be something legitimate in his claim. Well, let's consider a sampling. Assertion: Jesus' divinity was not established until the Council of Nicaea in 325. "'Hold on. You're saying Jesus' divinity was the result of a *vote*?' 'A relatively close vote at that' added Teabing.'"[8] The actual vote was *316 to 2*. What's more, the issue involving the nature of Christ was not even over whether He was divine. The issue involved the nature of His universally accepted divinity—that is, was He of a similar divine substance (though created), or of the same eternal essence as God? The majority vote, squeaker that it was, favored Christ's coeternal divinity. Additionally, there are no known *Gnostic* sources that denied the divine nature of Jesus. Gnostics denied His *human* nature. Consider Saying 77 from the Gnostic Gospel of Thomas, where "Jesus" said, "I am the light that is over all things. I am all: from me all came forth, and to me all attained. Split a piece of wood; I am there. Lift up a stone, and you will find me there."

Assertion: The church conspired to eliminate "the divine feminine" from religion and transformed society from its former matriarchal structure to an oppressive patriarchy. "The Priory believes that Constantine and his male successors successfully converted the world from matriarchal paganism to patriarchal Christianity by waging a campaign of propaganda that demonized the sacred feminine, obliterating the goddess from modern religion forever."[9]

The idea that the Gnostic version of religion placed femininity in an exalted role is not immediately evident in any Gnostic literature. The divine feminine in Gnosticism was Sophia, the goddess of wisdom. Sophia occupied the bottom rung of thirty or so lesser deities (aeons), produced by the unknowable, inexpressible, ultimate, unbegotten. Sophia is almost directly responsible for the botched creation, succumbing to base passions due to an unrequited desire to know, to experience the unbegotten Father in a manner for which she is not equipped. Her extreme vexation of spirit manifests itself in her offspring, Acamoth.

Acamoth, composed of baser passions, has come into existence without benefit of a male parent. Fluctuating emotions over her isolation and possible reconciliation with the unbegotten manifest in the creation of the material universe as well as the Demiurge, an altogether degenerate entity. The Demiurge, as the direct offspring of Acamoth, is so hopelessly engulfed in ignorance that he does not even retain knowledge of his mother. He imagines himself Supreme Being and creator of all, not knowing he is but the agent through which his mother creates, nor that an entire higher divine order transcends him including the Ultimate One. The Demiurge, the new bottom rung in the hierarchy of deity becomes, to all intents, an impediment to those created souls trapped within the material universe. Escaping the material will require overcoming this being. Thankfully, help becomes available in the form of arcane societies, spirit guides, and esoteric knowledge for those bold few who desire to reach beyond religion for *spirituality.* Not very surprisingly, the Demiurge is identified as the "repressive" God of the Old Testament.[10]

Is there something in the above that *empowers* women? Saddled with responsibility for a very messy creation does not seem inherently flattering. Dan Brown's assertion notwithstanding, in the theology of Gnosticism, Jesus Christ has come not to celebrate "the sacred feminine" but to overcome "the degenerate feminine." Notice the words of "Thomas," Saying 114: Simon Peter said to them, "Make Mary leave us, for females don't deserve life." Jesus said, "Look, I will guide her to make her male, so that she too may become a living spirit resembling you males. For every female who makes herself male will enter the kingdom of Heaven."

Cultures that have promoted goddess worship have shown no necessary correlation to the elevation of women in society. As earlier pointed out, paganism generally afforded women a status barely higher than barnyard animals—in some cases, lower. For all Hinduism's veneration of the divine mother, its cultures have exhibited some of the highest contempt for women's rights. Women, on the other hand, are prominently featured in both the Old and New Testaments—Mary, for instance, the vessel through which divinity comes into the world. Women are portrayed as the only followers of Christ who did not abandon Him during His passion. Remember also that women were the first witnesses to Christ's resurrection. Though Christianity has sometimes been conscripted to give cover to gross mistreatment, on balance it has reversed the historic role of women in society. The age of chivalry, holding women in highest esteem, was a direct reflection of Christian concepts.

Assertion: Christianity transformed sexuality into a loathsome expression of depravity. "For the early Church . . . mankind's use of sex to commune directly with God posed a serious threat to the Catholic power base. It left the Church out of the loop, undermining their self-proclaimed status as the *sole* conduit to God. For obvious reasons, they worked hard to demonize sex and recast it as a disgusting and sinful act."[11] To the contrary, Christianity provided a specific zone where sexuality, rather than reduced to primal unrestrained release, found synthesis in a multidimensional experience that encompassed mind, body, and soul in transcendent intimacy. Sexuality was not transformed into an evil but rescued from the common and then sanctified (literally, set apart for a higher purpose). Sexuality was made *sacred.* It would be difficult to make the case that sexuality was sacred under paganism when it permeated every facet of culture. Christianity is often mistaken for Victorianism, where even marital sex had a negative connotation. A reading of the Bible's Song of Solomon will put to rest any idea of a Bible-based sexual animus.

*   *   *

The authors of *The Jesus Mysteries* treat readers to their soul-stirring journey from confining traditional Christianity to liberating Gnosticism. The following excerpts from their book appear in the special collector's edition of *U.S. News & World Report*: "[H]ow could Gnosticism be the original Christianity when St. Paul, the earliest Christian we know about, is so vociferously anti-Gnostic? And is it really credible that such an insular and anti-Pagan people as the Jews could have adopted the Pagan Mysteries? And how could it have happened that a consciously created myth came to be believed as history."[12]

These are excellent questions. Finally, authors who seem to have a serious appreciation for the considerable obstacles that must be surmounted before one can simply anoint an alternate view as the authentic version. Cautiously, we read on, "All these difficult questions would have to be satisfactorily answered before we could wholeheartedly accept such a radical theory as the Jesus Mysteries Thesis." Marvelous. The authors are serious about this.

> As we pushed farther with our research, the traditional picture began to unravel completely all around us. We found ourselves embroiled in a world of schism and power struggles, of forged documents and false identities, of letters that had been edited and added to, and of the wholesale destruction of historical evidence. . . . It was becoming increasingly obvious that we had been deliberately deceived, that the Gnostics were indeed the original Christians, and that their anarchic mysticism had been hijacked by an authoritarian institution which had created from it a dogmatic religion and then brutally enforced the greatest cover-up in history.[13]

Alas, the mystery men behind the curtain turn out to be our old friends Freke and Gandy. *The Jesus Mysteries* is but an earlier incarnation of *The Laughing Jesus*— same tired tortured logic, ad hominem attacks, obfuscation, unsubstantiated charges of serious transmission error (mostly deliberate of course), evil revisionists demonstrating something approaching divine capability, massive coverup conspiracies, and cliched arguments *reductio ad absurdum*. As usual, the coronation of a preferred position is assumed to transform a great deal of special pleading into reality. While a mountain of internal, external, and circumstantial evidence is ignored, we are subjected to parlor tricks.

We open one of these bold volumes (whether by Freke and Gandy, or any other of these sensationalist peddlers) expecting to see *something* substantive. Instead we get the same old shell game. Time and again we are teased with something big but just as the fog begins to lift, we're whisked away and sent down another dimly lit corridor. The irrefutable proof that we've been promised seems always, mysteriously, just out of our reach. It exists, we are assured, yet some evil organization has somehow suppressed or concealed it. We never quite get to see it for ourselves. Presumably, we are expected to believe the sheer volume of passages we've traversed, the sum of nebulous sightings, *must* add up to something tangible. In the meanwhile, a plethora of simple but serious questions are left unanswered and apparently presumed irrelevant, such as: Just why would so many willingly die for a "resurrection myth"?

Chapter 22

Misquoting Jesus

Not all criticism directed at the reliability of the NT comes from the pen of pseudoscholars or con artists. Against this lineup of rabble-rousers stands Bart D. Ehrman, representing a 180-degree departure. Ehrman has an impressive command of the Bible and surrounding issues and is highly esteemed in his field of studies, textual criticism. Having formerly been in the role of *defending* controversial Christian positions, he is well acquainted with any weaknesses in the case for NT authenticity. Thus, when this gentleman writes a book (*Misquoting Jesus*) explaining his sober journey from committed believer to agnosticism because of serious NT credibility issues, we must assume this is a matter of utmost gravity, a far cry from the frivolous theme-park joy ride of Freke and Gandy.

Because Ehrman has an odd habit of making what appear to be very provocative assertions, only to then effectively retract any apparent significance, it's sometimes difficult to understand his intended purpose. Is he arguing there is, or is not, new information that will revolutionize our understanding of Scripture? Frankly, Ehrman seems himself unsure what his point should be. Embedded within his text are two apparent themes not in obvious agreement that do little to dispel the sense of confusion. His first premise is that there are many textual variants among the many extant New Testament manuscripts, but that the overwhelming majority has no effect on traditional theological/ doctrinal issues. There are, however, a very small number, radical alterations, that *do* bear on these issues. His second premise—any change, no matter how minor in nature, *is* radical.

What is also most odd is that Ehrman does not even seem to be aware that either of his premises represent any challenge to the conclusions of his colleagues, or that there is any reason why they should. Responding to objections by Bible scholars to his book, he offers the following:

> What has most struck me about this objection is that it has to do with the *impression* left by the book, rather than about anything I actually *say* in the book. In fact, in the book I regularly point out the facts that the very scholars who raise the objection want to emphasize—for example, that most of the textual variants in the manuscript tradition of the New Testament are of no real importance: they don't change the meaning of the text or have any bearing on its interpretation.[1]

Well if he did not intend to leave this impression, then he had nothing new to say. So why then did he write a book that essentially agrees with the status quo and provocatively title it *Misquoting Jesus*? Just four sentences below his earlier statement, Ehrman says, "Where I differ from some critics is on the other differences, the ones that do matter. Some of these are in fact highly significant."[2] So, let's see, is it possible that Bible scholars got the *impression* Ehrman is contending that there are serious problems with textual variants because he has actually *said* this? Is it possible they were left with the *impression* that Ehrman intends his alleged "highly significant" changes compromise theological or doctrinal integrity because this is what he repeatedly, and not very demurely, *implies*? If, as he says, most textual variants do not change the meaning of the text nor bear on its traditional interpretation, then we can only conclude he is implying the "ones that do matter" *do* (at least potentially) affect meaning and interpretation. In which case, the latter category must also impact upon theology. If he is *not* implying this, then why do these matter?

Let us first consider Ehrman's second premise: Any change is radical. "The fact that we don't have the [original verbatim] words surely must show, I reasoned, that he [God] did not preserve them for us. And if he didn't perform that miracle, there seemed to be no reason to think that he performed the earlier miracle of inspiring those words."[3] As a Bible scholar, Ehrman knows he is casting the generally recognized doctrine of "inspiration" in a way that is misleading. He is making the concept of inerrancy so rigid, that ancient NT manuscripts which are shown to contain less than absolute agreement become the proof that the claim of divine inspiration is false. Actually, inerrancy means that though diverse personalities of flawed human beings are used, who may exhibit a wide range of perspectives sometimes introducing variations at the margins, no contradictions are found concerning central truths. In fact, if different writers all recorded the exact same words in account after account, would this not raise suspicions of collusion? That we do find differences (insignificant) in reporting the same facts is evidence of independent and honest attestation. As Timothy Paul Jones puts it in *Misquoting Truth*, the proper question is not "Does everything in Scripture and in the biblical manuscripts agree word-for-word?" The correct question, though humans with manifold flaws are employed in the transmission process, is "[A]re the available copies of the New Testament manuscripts sufficiently accurate for us to grasp the truth that God intended in the first century?"[4]

Now to his first premise: There are changes in NT manuscripts that seem to compromise the traditional presentation of Jesus Christ and His actual message. In *Misquoting Jesus*, Ehrman maintains that the differences in variation between the more than five thousand NT manuscripts we possess may feature as many as 400,000 such examples. "There are more variations among our manuscripts than there are words in the New Testament."[5] This staggering number seems to suggest there was no such thing as a uniform presentation of Christ's life and teachings. According to Timothy Paul Jones, however, "more than 99 percent of the 400,000 differences fall into this category of virtually unnoticeable variants."[6] Nor, as Jones points out, does the remaining 1 percent constitute a possible challenge to core doctrinal issues. Even Ehrman admits, "Most of these differences are completely immaterial and insignificant."[7] He also agrees that transmission of the earliest Christian texts was mostly a process not of innovation but conservation.[8] Still we must wonder, since the amount of actual variations relevant to this discussion are minuscule, why does he throw this gargantuan number out there? If it is not his intention to massage a particular impression, why mention this vast number at all?

Where any questions remain as to which textual variant represents the earliest version, the science of textual criticism can establish the earliest manuscript traditions. Ehrman concedes as much:

> I continue to think that even if we cannot be 100 percent certain about what we can attain to we can at least be certain that all the surviving manuscripts were copied from other manuscripts . . . and that it is at least possible to get back to the *oldest* and *earliest* stage of the manuscript tradition. . . . This oldest form of the text is no doubt closely (*very* closely) [parenthetical insertion and emphasis in original] related to what the author originally wrote, and so it is the basis for our interpretation of his teaching.[9]

So Ehrman is, in effect, telling us that textural criticism is a definite science that is very reliable in taking us back to the original message.

Ehrman points to John 7:53–8:12 as an example of a now-familiar passage not part of the original manuscript:

> When Jesus had lifted up himself, and saw none but the woman, he said unto her, Woman, where are those thine accusers? hath no man condemned thee? She said, No man, Lord. And Jesus said unto her, Neither do I condemn thee: go, and sin no more. (John 8:11)

By Ehrman's own admission, most scholarship has concluded this was part of the oral tradition that had attached itself to this manuscript early on. As such, at some point it was written in the margin of the text for readers to decide its value. Later, a scribe thinking it was *meant* to be included copied it within the text. Even if this truly represents an addition that was not part of the original story, at worst this is an honest mistake.

A similar addition is cited in the last twelve verses of the gospel of Mark (16:9–20). This passage includes Jesus' appearance to Mary Magdalene after His resurrection, His upbraiding of the eleven apostles for their unbelief at her proclaiming this event, and Christ's Great Commission and prediction of confirming signs (casting out devils, speaking with new tongues, etc.). Comments Ehrman: "The verses are absent from our two oldest and best manuscripts of Mark's Gospel, along with other important witnesses; the writing style varies from what we find elsewhere in Mark."[10] Again, though, this is part of early oral tradition. None of this addition leads to some *new* inference that is not already established in the text (i.e., 16:1–8 of Mark, which has already established the witness of Mary Magdalene) or conflicts with the other three gospels.

Despite this, Ehrman feels compelled to issue this remark: "This is a textually oriented religion whose texts have been changed, surviving only in copies that vary from one another, sometimes in *highly significant ways* [emphasis mine]."[11] Just what does Ehrman mean by "highly significant"? This deliberate wording by someone so intimately acquainted with the Scriptures conveys very strong implications. We naturally expect such highly charged language to be followed by serious thought-provoking elaboration—specifically, about how this affects theology or doctrine. Yet nothing of the sort is forthcoming. Neither of these examples affect any doctrinal position, even mildly, nor do they represent collusion to invent some new self-serving doctrine.

His next tact is to find evidence of disharmony between the four NT Gospels. "[D]ifferent scholars come to different conclusions—not only about minor matters . . . but also about matters of major importance, matters that affect the interpretation of an entire book of the New Testament."[12] This is again misleading, because none of the three textual variants Ehrman cites live up to this bold assertion. Ehrman strains to produce significant differences separating Mark from Matthew and Luke. "I have indicated that whereas Matthew and Luke have difficulty ascribing anger to Jesus, Mark has no problem doing so."[13] And this, "Luke never explicitly states that Jesus becomes angry. . . . Luke portrays an imperturbable Jesus."[14]

It isn't just that Ehrman has exaggerated peripheral differences to try to cast an artificial conflict between gospels, but his very argument lacks integrity. Even if we exclude Luke 22:39–46 (whose authenticity Ehrman doubts) we still have many passages which at least implicitly suggest a Jesus we would not exactly characterize as docile—Luke 12:13–14, 20, 49, 51–53; 13:27–28, 34–35 (Jesus prophesying the coming destruction of Jerusalem); 14:26 ("If any man come to me, and hate not his father, and mother, and wife, and children . . . he cannot be my disciple); 19:27 (parable: "those mine enemies . . . slay them before me"), 19:45–46 (casting the money changers out of the temple, "My house is the house of prayer, but ye have made it a den of thieves," v. 46); chapter 21 (the coming destruction of Jerusalem). Luke 11:40–53 features six woes Christ pronounces upon the Pharisees and lawyers for various offenses. In verse 50 we read, "That the blood of all the prophets, which was shed from the foundation of the world, may be required of this generation." Admittedly, it's difficult to know just what Ehrman means by an "imperturbable Jesus," but we would tend to associate this with passivity. Frankly, it's hard to imagine a passive Jesus in verses that contextually portray a most *agitated* Jesus.

Nevertheless, Ehrman continues to work this theme. "At no point in Luke's Passion narrative does Jesus *lose control* [emphasis mine]."[15] Remembering that Ehrman discounts the garden of Gethsemane scene and the "great drops of blood" (Luke 22:39–46), this statement is apparently meant to imply that Christ *has* lost control in other narratives. It's hard to understand how a bona fide scholar like Ehrman could engage in such disingenuous casting of terms. We expect this from Freke and Gandy, not from an esteemed student of the Bible. Equating emotional displays by Christ with lack of control is a self-serving proposition that cannot be extracted from any biblical texts.

Jesus was not exempted from emotions. To the contrary, "For we have not an high priest which cannot be touched with the feeling of our infirmities; but was in all points tempted like as we are, yet without sin" (Heb. 4:15). Remembering that Jesus is also fully human and that this is the defining moment of history, why would His emotions *not* run the gamut, ebbing and flowing in conflict: tranquility, doubt, sanguinity, horror, circumspection, exuberance, lucidity, mind-numbing agony, betrayal, abandonment (even the Father must turn His back on the crucified Christ for a time). That Christ demonstrates a wide range of emotions does not measure up to "losing control." A real loss of control would be evident were He to allow any of these emotions to keep Him from His appointed destiny, including all prophecies concerning His death. But in fact, Christ fulfills all righteousness, *even in* the throes of agony. He retains His dignity and the presence of mind to leave no jot or tittle unfinished.

Ehrman introduces some of the divergent groups of the second and third centuries who were associating themselves with Christianity. He makes mention of the already-discussed Gnostics, as well as the "Adoptionists" (the Ebionites in particular) and the "Docetists." As we recall, Gnostics (at least most) believed that Jesus Christ was fully divine but not truly human. Some Gnostics believed there were two separate beings called Jesus, one fully human and the other fully divine. Accordingly, the divine Jesus departed from the human manifestation at the cross. Adoptionists believed Jesus was a nondivine human being who God "adopted" as His son at Christ's baptism.

Docetists believed that Jesus had only a divine nature (though He "appeared" to have a human nature as well) and was sent by the "highest" God to rescue some from the Jewish God of the OT. The Jewish God (the Demiurge), apparently convinced that Christ's sacrifice was real, accepted this as a perfect atonement for sins and anyone believing this would be delivered from the enslavement of this brutal God— apparently by the supposed Supreme Being who rules over all lesser deities, though it's not clear why the *Gnostic* God employs the mistaken assumption of the Jewish God as the vehicle through which souls escape the latter; neither is it clear how the Jewish God would fool *Himself* into thinking a Jesus sent by some other source is *His only begotten Son*. Docetism probably represents an early strand of Gnosticism. Ehrman refers to the group who held that Jesus was both fully human and fully divine (the inheritors and preservers of the apostolic tradition) as "proto-orthodoxy."

Says Ehrman, "All these groups claimed to be Christian, insisting that their views were true and had been taught by Jesus and his followers."[16] This is the old "one religion is as valid as any other" argument. Should this argument be applied to all fields where truth is at stake? Should we approach science in this manner? Should a claim that Mars is made of dark chocolate receive equal weight with the theory of relativity? Should the scientific community cheerfully concede an unsubstantiated assertion is just as valid as one that can be backed by reams of evidence? Making a claim requires nothing more than imagination. Supporting and *validating* a claim may require a great deal, depending on the depth and breadth of the claim. If this is axiomatic and never questioned in scientific inquiry, why should this principle find itself so easily abandoned with respect to religion? Why should religious claims that make almost no effort to achieve validation through accepted rules (indeed are contemptuous of any rules of investigation) be placed on a par with specific claims that demonstrate multifaceted support?

"To be sure, all the books of the New Testament had been written by this time, but there were lots of other books as well, also claiming to be by Jesus's own apostles—other gospels, acts, epistles, and apocalypses having *very different perspectives* [emphasis mine] from those found in . . . the New Testament."[17] There can be no doubt Ehrman knows the *earliest* of these noncanonical writings were written nearly a century after Christ's death. It is also a well-established fact of scholarship that the NT writings were already circulating in the first century AD. No "alternative gospels," etc., show up until at least the early second century. And Ehrman offers no new evidence, nor even attempts to make the case that this picture has changed. The best he can do is to create an impression that all these diverse "Christianities" (at their point of origin) are contemporaries by using wording like "the views of this [non-canonical] group are clearly reported in our early records."[18] What he of course fails to do is to tell us *how* early.

Ehrman casts doubt on the institution of the Lord's Supper recorded in Luke 22:17–19. "Despite the fact that [the words] are familiar, there are good reasons for thinking that these verses were not originally in Luke's Gospel but were added to stress that it was Jesus's broken body and shed blood that brought salvation 'for you.'"[19] Even if this is so, Paul, writing no later than about AD 55 (in 1 Corinthians 11:23–26, which Ehrman himself does not dispute) has already received the Lord's Supper tradition in the exact formula presented in Luke. This means the tradition is sometime earlier still. All indications are that this is a very early component of the oral tradition. Thus, even if the Luke verses are later additions, they clearly reflect the earliest Christian beliefs.

The effort to drive a wedge between Luke and other NT gospels continues:

> In fact, on the two occasions in which Luke's source (Mark) indicates that it was by Jesus's death that salvation came (Mark 10:45; 15:39), Luke *changed* the wording of the text (or eliminated it). Luke, in other words, has a different understanding of the way in which Jesus's death leads to salvation than does Mark (and Paul, and other early writers). . . . Jesus's death is what makes people realize their guilt before God [and] . . . drives people to repentance, and it is this repentance that brings salvation.[20]

Apparently Ehrman does not believe logic need play much of a role in his conjectures. Luke states plainly in the opening verses of his gospel that he is putting together a record of information delivered to him by eyewitnesses. Were Luke a direct eyewitness himself to these events, it is unlikely he would have placed such stress on his sources. Luke, as was noted in an earlier chapter, is a meticulous investigator, a "details man." His conclusions are the result of thorough, careful, painstaking research culled from many sources, primarily the apostles no doubt, and most certainly Paul to which he was a frequent companion. And as it is generally conceded that Luke borrowed at least from the gospel of Mark, the evidence adds up that Luke saw his role as a consolidator of authoritative firsthand testimony. Why, then, would Luke have a *different* understanding than those from which he received all this? It is out of character for one so given to the preservation of the authentic record to arbitrarily follow touchy feelings or some other gut instinct.

Ehrman disputes the originality of Luke 24:12: "Then arose Peter, and ran unto the sepulchre; and stooping down, he beheld the linen clothes laid by themselves, and departed, wondering in himself at that which was come to pass." Comments Ehrman, "[if not original,] it is a striking addition, because it supports so well the proto-orthodox position that Jesus was not simply some kind of phantasm, but had a real physical body."[21] What Ehrman mysteriously overlooks is that Luke has just testified (in the previous verses) that *Jesus is risen*! Ehrman knows that "risen" (resurrected) from a Jewish framework was intricately tied into corporeal reanimation of a human corpse. Luke 24:12 was not needed to convey an idea that all readers would have already derived from the previous text. Though he is speaking to a mostly Gentile audience, he is using language that is intimately rooted in a *Jewish* context. To suggest a need to stress the "physical nature of resurrection" is like saying there might be a need to stress the physical nature of breathing.

Ehrman suggests the familiar words "My God, my God, why have you forsaken me?" may be an early strand of Gnosticism. After all, this would capture perfectly the human Jesus' sense of betrayal at the separate divine nature suddenly departing from him in this most agonized hour. Accordingly, adds Ehrman, "After Jesus' death, though he [the divine Jesus] raised him from the dead as a reward for his faithfulness, and continued through him to teach his disciples the secret that can lead to salvation."[22] But this would make resurrection nothing more than an afterthought—the more incredible because Paul makes resurrection the centerpiece of his teaching: "For I determined not to know anything among you, save Jesus Christ, and him crucified" (1 Cor. 2:2). This grueling shameful execution can only have meaning as it is wedded to resurrection, which Paul makes plain in 1 Corinthians 15:3–4. Beyond this, though, why would divine Jesus resurrect human Jesus if the truth is that the material world is evil and must be escaped? In the Gnostic scheme, this would be a cruel *punishment*.

There is this little inconvenient fact as well: The resurrection is closely tied into the theme of miracles, the obvious embodiment of this theme's ultimate expression. Most miracles either restore or temporarily correct some physical imbalance. Miracles point to a rift in the material world that needs repair. They represent a tiny preview of the final restoration of the physical order. Thus, miracles by their very nature validate the original goodness of the physical as well as the need and intent to bring it back to its former (non-sin-cursed) state. Every time Jesus performed a miracle He was consciously, deliberately identifying with and sanctioning the Jewish redemptive program. Resurrection was the beginning and iron-clad *guarantee* of this ultimate reordering. Thus, the concept could not be any more at odds with *any* form of Gnosticism.

"By this you know the Spirit of God. Every spirit that confesses that Jesus Christ has come in the flesh is from God; and every spirit that does not confess Jesus is not from God. This is the spirit of anti-Christ" (the oldest form of 1 John 4:2–3). By Ehrman's own admission, "This is a clear, straight forward passage: only those who acknowledge that Jesus really came in the flesh (as opposed, say, to accepting the doecetist view) belong to God; those who do not acknowledge this are opposed to Christ (anti-Christs)."[23] This means that the counter to Gnosticism existed in written form and was very early, well before fully developed Gnosticism emerged. Yet Ehrman can't resist a parting shot at proto-orthodoxy by pointing to what he admits is a late variant of the above verse. The words "that does not confess Jesus" are changed to "that looses Jesus."[24]

The apparent significance for Ehrman is that this is meant (by orthodox scribes) as a shot across the bow of those who would try to divide Christ into separate entities. Ehrman concludes, "Once again, then we have a variant that was generated in the context of the Christological disputes of the second and third centuries."[25] Ehrman is willing to execute cartwheels to create the impression that the NT has been inordinately shaped by the conflict of "Christological disputes." Again, and again, he willingly and conveniently omits the key and overriding fact: This competition did not *begin* until the second century; well after proto-orthodox traditions were set!

"[S]cribes sometimes modified their texts in light of the adoptionistic, docetic, and separationist Christologies that were vying for attention in the period."[26] But the fact remains, all examples of modification do not refute the central view of Christ. These passages, even without the modifications, could still be harmonized with the balance of Scripture even if not lending direct support. Even Ehrman admits, "[S]cribes occasionally altered their texts to make them say what they were already believed to mean. This is not necessarily a bad thing, since we can probably assume that most scribes who changed their texts often did so either semiconsciously or with good intent."[27] The scribes were at worst guilty of trying to ensure more ambiguous passages could not be twisted to support these later *challenges* to what was already well established. This, we can readily agree, was a mistake. The important point, though, is that none of these passages in their original unembellished form could be easily reconciled to any Gnostic, Docetist, or Adoptionist view.

What Ehrman actually shows is that proto-orthodox views existed in oral and written form from the very earliest traditions. No matter how you slice it, this puts the orthodox position in the catbird seat. Ehrman is aware of this, and though he does not directly address this in this book elsewhere assails the value of the oral tradition. His case is built upon the notorious unreliability of oral transmission in our own day. Even simple messages, as all know, can be considerably altered if circulated in just a relatively small gathering. As a scholar, Ehrman should know better than to automatically impose modern tendencies on an ancient and foreign culture.

Today, messages of import intended to be preserved for any appreciable time are not passed orally. They invariably find their way into any number of convenient retrieval systems. Culturally speaking, we have no incentive to place any special value on orally preserving long tracts of information. My wife is very careful to limit any information she hopes to relay through me—exceed my rather sensitive threshold, and the accuracy of the transmission is severely jeopardized. Such was not the case in the ancient world where relatively few could read or write. A premium was placed upon faithfully preserving oral sayings, and nothing was more valued than eyewitness testimony. Writes Timothy Jones, "In some cases, first-century folk may have been *less likely* to trust written records, because they couldn't speak personally with the individual telling the story!"[28]

Ehrman maintains that the writers of the four NT Gospels are unknown. Though names are affixed to each gospel, they were simply put there many years after the fact as a way of imparting apostolic legitimacy. And what is Ehrman's evidence for this position? Ancient manuscripts of the four Gospels display many different titles. On the face of it, this again looks damning. Once more, though, it is what Ehrman *omits* that is most telling:

> Despite many variations, *every title that's ascribed to the Gospel* [Matthew] *identifies Matthew as the source.* And this happens not only with the gospel according to Matthew but also with the other New Testament Gospels . . . and this unity in titles isn't limited to one region of the Roman Empire—examples of this unity may be found in manuscripts from the western portions of the ancient empire all the way to North Africa, Egypt and Asia Minor.[29]

Even if we concede Ehrman's contention that the supposed authors of the Gospels were all illiterate, professional scribes were available in the first century for this task (though it is certainly plausible that a tax collector, Matthew, and a physician, Luke, would have been literate). And even if the first written records of Christ's words were not compiled until three decades after His crucifixion, those who did write (even if not those ascribed) had at their disposal both eyewitness testimony and well-established oral history. Eyewitnesses would have served the dual role of correcting inadvertent errors, as well as refuting deliberate deceit.

We are entertained with still more conjecture:

> [I]n Matthew 24:36, where Jesus explicitly states that no one knows
> the day or the hour in which the end will come 'not even the angels of
> heaven nor even the Son, but the Father alone.'. . . . A significant num-
> ber of our manuscripts omit 'nor even the Son'. The reason is not hard
> to postulate; if Jesus does not know the future, the Christian claim that
> he is a divine being is more than a little compromised.[30]

So, we are to suspect monkeying with the text because a Jesus who doesn't know the future casts doubt on claims of divinity. Once again, Ehrman chooses an exotic explanation, when the simple answer is provided within the Scriptures. Philippians 2:5–8 is probably a very early church hymn encompassing basic and high Christology in its most primitive form: Jesus' full equality (in every aspect) with God the Father; His divesting Himself of divine glory and (at least some) power though retaining His essential deity; His voluntary and complete submission to the Father's will; His taking on in its every facet a human nature. Thus, Christ's divinity was well established completely apart from Matthew 24:36. As for Christ's not knowing the future, taking the fact of his voluntary emptying and numerous gospel allusions to His empowerment by and submission to the Holy Spirit, we may conclude Christ is willingly limiting Himself. Frankly, if He can retain His divine essence while submitting to physical death, is it any more fantastic that He could be divine, yet agree to wield only that power and knowledge which the Holy Spirit chose to dispense during His earthly ministry? Remember, He has come to be the perfect *servant* of God the Father and to demonstrate faith in action. Faith necessarily requires an element of the *unknown*.

Now Ehrman begins to bring his case to its radical climax:

> I realized just how radically the [NT] text had been altered over the
> years at the hands of scribes, who were not only conserving scripture
> but also changing it. To be sure, of all the hundreds of thousands of

textual changes found among our manuscripts, most of them are completely insignificant, immaterial, of no real importance for anything
other than showing that scribes could not spell or keep focused any better than the rest of us. It would be wrong, however, to say—as people
sometimes do—that the changes in our text have no real bearing on
what the texts mean or on the theological conclusions that one draws
from them. We have seen, in fact, that just the opposite is the case.[31]

This is a rather helpful illustration of Ehrman's methodology in miniature. First,
he employs the term "radical," alerting us to be ready for some explosive revelation. Barely have we moved to the edge of the seat and we are again deflated—most
of the radical changes, alas, are "of no real importance." But, we are upbraided, it
would be wrong to think these insignificant radical changes have not significantly
affected the theology. In fact, as Ehrman is quick to remind, we have *seen* this to
be so! And since he has not made a single convincing (or even plausible) argument to this effect, we are evidently expected to *believe* it is so, why, because he
says it is. In reality, what Ehrman *has* shown, in spite of himself, is that *the changes
have no real bearing on what the texts mean or on the theological conclusions drawn
from them.*

Commenting on Ehrman's premise, Timothy Jones gives the following: "[D]
espite the sensational title of *Misquoting Jesus*, I find only a half-dozen times when
Jesus *might* have been misquoted, and most of these supposed changes simply echo
ideas that are found elsewhere in Scripture."[32]

Ehrman concludes his effort to sow seeds of discord between the four Gospels
with this:

> The point is that Luke changed the tradition he inherited. If [Mark and
> Luke] are not saying the same thing, it is not legitimate to assume they
> are—for example, by taking what Matthew and John say and melding
> them all together, so that Jesus says and does *all* the things that each of
> the Gospel writers indicates. Anyone who interprets the Gospels this
> way is not letting each author have his own say . . . he or she is making
> up a *new* Gospel consisting of the four in the New Testament, a new
> Gospel that is not like any of the ones that have come down to us.[33]

If Ehrman is serious about this, then he is guilty of making up a new linguistics that
has no foundation in logic. To insist it is "illegitimate" to form a composite picture
from four different but clearly *complementary* perspectives of the same subject is
counterintuitive and *surely* spurious.

The most Ehrman has shown is that while each author shares a core and considerable periphery with the other three (especially the Synoptics), each nevertheless chooses to emphasize different aspects of Jesus and surrounding minutiae—a conclusion few doubted before Ehrman published his findings. Yes, out of personal preference, one author may choose to include where another may choose to omit some detail, but *not one* of the differences places any perspective at odds with any other. No author ever introduces a detail that necessarily or even potentially renders another's account *false*. Yet it seems Ehrman would have us pretend that differing stresses equals *contradictory accounts*.

Despite his use of terms like "radical" and "highly significant," the insinuations throughout his book that he is about to reveal substantive examples either of collusion or disharmony among NT writers, we never see anything that places central doctrines in question. His revelations are a tempest in a teapot, stirred by artificial categories, "in control," "apart from God," "by the grace of God," "Christ's atonement," etc., imagining a conflict that simply isn't there. Says Ehrman, "It is obviously important to know whether Jesus was said to feel compassion or anger in Mark 1:41; whether he was calm and collected or in deep distress in Luke 22:43-44; and whether he was said to die by God's grace or 'apart from God' in Heb. 2:9,"[34] challenging the original meaning of these verses.

Even if the original word was "anger" and not "compassion," the fact remains that the *healing* was itself an act of compassion. Ask any caring parent if the two are mutually exclusive. Is it possible Jesus could have faced the cross and vacillated between calm and deep distress, knowing the physical horror that awaited yet the indescribable victory on the other side? Is it possible Jesus could have died by the grace of God and *apart* from God, since the Father would at least momentarily turn His back on the Son? What is obviously important to know is *why* Ehrman chooses to cast these terms as either/or when they are all quite easily both/and, without any contradiction. Ehrman can only try to pull off some appearance of disagreement by restricting Christ to an entirely static one-dimensional figure. Despite his protestations, the four Gospels "meld together" precisely *because* no unnatural tinkering, no contrivance nor compulsion is necessary. The same cannot be said for his static portrayal.

To be sure, Ehrman is not quite done. The above is only a segue to his far more provocative bottom line:

> The idea that Luke changed the text before him—in this case the Gospel of Mark—does not put him in a unique situation among the early Christian authors. This, in fact, is what all the writers of the New Testament did—along with all the writers of all the Christian literature

outside the New Testament, indeed writers of every kind everywhere. They modified their tradition and put the words of the tradition in their own words.[35]

Finally, we come to the motivation for this book. It is essential to create lines *separating* the NT Gospels so as to *blur* the lines that separate proto-orthodoxy from the Gnostic "gospels" and all other "Christian" writings. The unity of the NT Gospels must be deconstructed so that a bridge may be built connecting first-century Christianity to the strikingly different "Christianities" that pop-up in the second.

If the NT Gospels really do represent an unwieldy blending of irreconcilable differences, then why were these same defenders of the faith so staunchly opposed to Gnostic interpretations? If altering texts was this fluid and commonplace, why did it suddenly become an issue with the Gnostic version? How did they come to believe the ideas in the four NT Gospels formed a perfect unity, and that such a profound gap separated these four from *all* Gnostic versions that they were willing to die for this conviction?

Let us take Ehrman back to an important statement he makes in his book, a statement to which he would do well to pay closer attention: "The one thing that nearly all scholars agree upon, however, is that *no matter how* one understands the major thrust of Jesus's mission, he must be situated in his own context as a first-century Palestinian Jew. Whatever else he was, Jesus was thoroughly Jewish, in every way—as were his disciples."[36] How can Ehrman make this admission, and then whisk past its enormous significance? It is this exact fact that so unifies the NT Gospels. They are each deeply entrenched in this *precise* Jewish environment. And it is this fact that so dramatically separates them from any Gnostic writings. All agree that Christ's mission entailed the *fulfillment* of the OT redemptive program. And no matter what latitude each author may take, it is this complex context that *constrains* definite boundaries. Jesus can only take on a significantly different character (His mission, His nature, etc.) if these intensely rigid OT barriers are broken down. This is precisely why all alternative "Christianities" placed such a premium on disconnecting Christ (through whatever way necessary) from His Jewish environment!

In concluding, Ehrman shares with readers the great truth that his lifetime of study has yielded:

> The only way to make sense of a text is to read it, and the only way to read it is by putting it in other words, and the only way to put it in other words is by having other words to put it into, and the only way you have other words to put it into is that you have a life, and the only

way to have a life is by being filled with desires, longings, needs, wants, beliefs, perspectives, worldviews, opinions, likes, dislikes—and all the other things that make human beings human. And so, to read a text is, necessarily, to change a text.[37]

And so, a most enigmatic book comes fittingly, we suppose, to an enigmatic close. Ehrman seems to be saying that human beings, by their inherent fallible and corrupting nature, are incapable of receiving any written communication (presumably oral as well) without so distorting the original intent, that meaningful transmission is essentially impossible. The way in which each will interpret that message is so profoundly different that any author's desire to transmit his ideas, to convince through a carefully constructed point-by-point case, or to establish a unique system of thought, is an utterly hopeless quest. To which we can only reply, why has Ehrman bothered to write this book?

Ehrman has placed himself in the untenable position of having to prove his case by proving it is impossible to prove any case. If, on the other hand, he does believe it is possible to retain the primary thrust of some original message, even though personal nuances may alter some specific wording in the transmission, his entire argument is pointless. Either way, the strain of incoherence that underlies his methodology is exposed.

At the beginning of his book, Ehrman crafts the impression it is scholarship and intellectual honesty that have brought about his soul-stirring and painful transformation. Perhaps he truly believes this. But his arguments have failed to convey any sense of proportionality to his crisis of faith. If Ehrman is earnestly looking for evidence of the trustworthiness of the New Testament, I recommend he look no further than his own book. For here he will find the case of a learned Bible scholar who "knows where all the bodies are buried." He will find a determined man who has marshaled all his rhetorical skills and impressive scholarly resources to discredit the reliability of Holy Writ. He will see that despite giving it his best shot, the case for inerrancy is, if anything, more conspicuous for its unassailable character. Is it not the more astounding— indeed, *miraculous*—that Ehrman's own evidence testifies to the nearly pristine preservation of the original message *despite* flawed human agency? Certainly, as a hostile witness, he has left no doubt that the essence of that message is intact within our present-day New Testament, *despite* human nature's tendency to modify, embellish, and remold to suit political agendas. Something very powerful indeed must be preserving that message.

One can scarcely escape the distinct impression that Scripture is not the source of this "unraveling of faith." Suspicions are heightened when Ehrman leaves an important clue: It would seem the real problem is with the God these Scriptures portray. Evidently Ehrman could believe in God if He acted according to Ehrman's ethics. In this Ehrman shares a common thread with the entire range of Bible critics. It is not so much the record of His presence nor plan of salvation but God *Himself* who is found wanting. In common with all Enlightenment thought, Ehrman makes himself judge of God. In a special question-and-answer feature at the back of his book, Ehrman has this to say:

> The big issue that drove me to agnosticism has to do not with the Bible, but with the pain and suffering in the world. I eventually found it impossible to explain the existence of evil so rampant among us—whether in terms of genocides (which continue), unspeakable human cruelty, war, disease, hurricanes, tsunamis, mudslides, the starvation of millions of innocent children, you name it—if there was a good and loving God who was actively involved in this world . . . at the end of the day, I don't know how we can say that God exists, given the senseless pain and suffering in this world.[38]

Ehrman could have saved himself a great deal of ink and needless argument had he cut to the chase early. It is not to his credit that this line of reasoning smacks of a high-school debating team (or our good friends, um, you know who). Pointing to the existence of evil as the proof of God's nonexistence has always struck me as odd, even during the period of my life (late teens through mid-twenties) when I was trying to understand who or what God might be and how or if His/its existence was relevant to my own. With all due respect, how do we account for the existence of evil *apart* from the existence of a Supreme Being? If this Being is not real, then everything that happens in the universe is the product of purposeless blind chance. Human beings are reduced to a mass of electrical wiring and chemical impulses. "Good" can only exist as a utilitarian imperative (constantly subject to redefinition by the powerful), not as an absolute. If God is rejected, then nature is all we are left with to try to model some approximation of right versus wrong. Nature tells us the ultimate good is survival, with pleasure perhaps a close second.

But here is where the problem gets sticky: We see no example of the "unspeakable cruelty" in the animal kingdom that Ehrman mentions above. Animals kill only to survive. Why are humans the only creatures on the planet to engage in the most horrendous, heartbreaking acts against their fellow man that have no connection whatever to basic survival? Interestingly, Ehrman has no trouble or hesitation calling these senseless acts exactly what they are—evil. Yet the question is, *how* does he know this is evil? Because he has a sense of justice? But how is the complex, abstract concept of justice consonant with basic survival instincts?

Something so obviously transcendent in its fundamental recognition of intrinsic human worth is mysteriously conspicuous in a setting that consistently rewards strength and punishes weakness. Do we see any examples of justice existing in the animal kingdom (i.e., do weaker animals have "rights" recognized and respected by the mightier)? Is it mere coincidence that those nations and systems that happen to *deny* the existence of God also consistently display the lowest regard for individual justice? How does Ehrman determine that his chemical impulses are sufficient to stand in judgment of the chemical impulses that have directed a child rapist to commit his acts?

Ehrman's acknowledgment of evil—and indeed, his bitter denunciation of it—betray his intuitive knowledge of justice. But justice can only exist if there is an ultimate judge who will *ultimately* balance the scales. And yes, admitting God's existence does not make natural disasters and cruel acts of inhumanity any less painful in the moment. We may glimpse only the faintest shadow of His purpose behind heartbreaking events. But His existence means there is an expectation of eventual understanding (however limited) and of justice rendered. Furthermore, specifically acknowledging the God of the Bible means that evil *does* have an explanation (the fall) that neither impugns this God's character nor makes a mockery of our pain by insisting we pretend it isn't real.

What could be more cruel or *senseless* than to disconnect all pain and suffering from any purpose whatsoever; to remove all hope that justice *will* eventually have its day? To deny the existence of the Judeo-Christian God is to do precisely this. How, then, do you explain the existence of evil, Mr. Ehrman?

Section III

INTO THE GARDEN OR BACK TO THE WILDERNESS?

CHAPTER 23

THE EARLY STRANDS OF CONSERVATISM

Much Western political thought after the start of the French Revolution embraced some form of progressivism. Talk of the rights of man and sentiment for egalitarianism was sweeping through Europe. Class distinctions were viewed with increasing suspicion and private property was coming to be seen as the source of all evil. It appeared that the momentum of Jacobinism (making whole societies over, emphasizing autonomous rights, universal equality, etc.) would leave a radically altered Western world in its wake.

Perhaps no single individual would be as instrumental in turning back this mounting tide as Edmund Burke. Born in 1729, Burke's *Reflections on the Revolution in France*, published in 1790, soberly and systematically examined the unintended consequences of ideas not only divorced from practical experience but which made assumptions that ran counter to basic human nature. Burke dissected the arguments of the so-called intellectually enlightened of his day.

Jean-Jacques Rousseau (1712–1778), as would his famous pupil Marx, saw everything in terms of class struggle. "Rich" and "poor" were fixed conditions one was locked into by a static economic hierarchy. A chief architect of the French Revolution, the core thrust of Rousseau's writings was simple: Nature should be the supreme model for human interactions. His writings emphasized a return to the primitive state, a period of human innocence prior to the modern civilizing structure. This was a time, of course, when men were free to blithely follow sexual impulses, and the unnatural division created by private property did not exist. One could be free to pursue base impulses without agonizing over consequences. True to his core convictions, Rousseau fathered five children illegitimately, condemning each to conditions not even fit for hardened criminals.

Jeremy Bentham's utilitarianism reduced societies to mathematical formulas, balancing pleasure against pain. Societies could be strained through "pleasure filters" to right actions. Bentham did not see humans as complex creatures but motivated by basic needs and desires. The problem with philosophers like Rousseau and Bentham was that for all the talk of rights, these rights did not exist in raw nature—only brute force. To the extent rights existed at all, they descended from a divine order and were manifest through self-sacrificing men who first recognized duty to God. Natural rights, as envisaged by Rousseau and others, inescapably reduced man to an instinctive creature where justice was not possible, only assertion and sanction of natural *wants*. Man was thus denied any nature distinct from beasts.

A unifying, civilizing, moral order could not be extracted from abstract reason, economic equality, or utility. Burke insisted that moral order could only be nestled in *principle*. And principle could only be derived from divinity. Burke was suspicious of progress as the result of some natural force, preferring to ascribe this to Providence.[1] The state, held Burke—in a complete repudiation of the popular sentiment—was the outworking of that very Providence. Burke wholly supported equality of justice but argued that equality of outcome/circumstances was not just a denial of reality (recognizing differing abilities, drives, intellect, industry, etc.), but a goal in which implementation (or even an attempt to) could only produce tyranny. Burke demonstrated that civil order was not the outworking of natural impulses, but an intuitive admission that men needed a structure that might protect them from impulse.

Concerning natural rights, Burke was guarded, and conceded the concept of natural law only insofar as the concept was restrained within transcendent (Christian) assumptions of divine order and grounded in that body of knowledge carefully accumulated through millennia of practical experience. Morality was not a quality that could be derived from any aspect of brute nature.[2]

Classes of men could be said to have separated and distinguished themselves as a result of "natural" endowments. This, argued Burke, had given rise to aristocracy. Forbidding the cream to rise to the top could only deny society the benefit of learned, introspective, deliberative resistance to kneejerk innovations. To deny a natural distinction could only ensure that the "better angels" of men would forever be extinguished, society denied a nobler station to aspire to.

Through the efforts of men like Edmund Burke, a movement called conservatism (though Burke himself never used the term) took shape. This is often portrayed as a counter-ideology to the various popular ideologies of Burke's day. This notion is not only inaccurate but fails to acknowledge the core of this movement. First, conservatism takes the world as it is, not as it would prefer. It does not look at man through rose-tinted glasses but soberly acknowledges his dual nature—for good if restrained by a high moral standard, for the most brutal evil if unfettered. It weighs ideas on the scales of practical experience; it eschews emotional appeals that have no basis in fact; it respects that body of knowledge that has come to us through the ages by costly lessons. An "ideology," on the other hand, derives from an intense passion to support a belief that is at odds with truth. Because reality intrudes again and again on ideological ambitions, truth must somehow be circumvented through ever more clever means, usually resulting in a system bereft of consistency and sustained only by the most monstrously contorted logic. Conservatism is the antithesis of an ideology.

Some have referenced a television to make the analogy.[3] Suppose some well-meaning soul decided he wanted to convert his set from a black-and-white picture to color. Though a laudable goal, one small problem stands in the way: The determined individual has only the most elementary knowledge of electronics. Because he is dealing with a dynamic system, any change he makes will not be isolated to that single modification but will affect the overall unit. Because his knowledge is so limited, it is far more likely his modifications will result in disastrous unintended consequences than success in his intended goal. *Successfully* pulling off this conversion would require the expertise of one who is well acquainted with all aspects of the system and is thus able to anticipate the outcome of all necessary changes.

When dealing with a complex dynamic system, one must have a serious appreciation for the effect of even modest tinkering. In comparison to a television set, the conglomeration of diverse individuals we refer to as "society" is indescribably complex. Society is so exceedingly complicated that no mere mortal (or group) could ever possibly possess the necessary knowledge to anticipate all possible consequences of trying to change it. If lack of knowledge is almost certain to produce unintended consequences with something as relatively simple as a television set, the odds are astronomically greater that unintended consequences will result from tinkering with something as unwieldy as society. But because "society" is so vast and non-homogeneous in its myriad aspects, unintended consequences will be so many times more far-reaching and devastating in scope. Unfortunately, ideologies, which instinctively propose sweeping changes, usually justify themselves based on intent rather than outcome.

*   *   *

Although no Western nation probably displayed a greater natural resistance to the radical spirit overtaking Europe, certain factions within the United States were nevertheless falling sway to the new romantic ideals of universal equality. Thankfully, Burke's influence would extend beyond Europe to reach into the political mainstream of American thought, especially views on constitutionalism.

Political parties in America, dating to the late 1700s and early 1800s, arose spontaneously as the result of the sharp divergence between Thomas Jefferson and

Alexander Hamilton. Despite the strong sense of internal unity and mutual concern for those forces (mostly European) that threatened the new nation, Americans were divided over how best to preserve that union. Federalists, headed up by Hamilton, believed in the strong assertion of government, that it should take an active role in promoting the common good. Hamilton and his party believed there were *implied* powers in the Constitution. Republicans, taking their cue from Jefferson, took a very suspicious view of government. The best form of government was that which governed least. Further, the Constitution should be construed in the strictest sense. Rather than eyeing the Constitution as an open-ended grant, it was to be treated as higher law. Jefferson and company did not oppose the idea of change per se. Change, however, must come through the amendment process to preserve the basic framework and resist the common law tendency to reduce the Constitution to an ever-evolving standard. Only those things specifically enumerated were at the disposal of government. Anything that reached beyond this would ensure the eventual irrelevance of the Constitution itself.

Though there were considerable differences in approaches, little difference existed with respect to principles of freedom and the recognition of the basis for that freedom. The same Christian foundation and axioms animated both parties. Even Thomas Jefferson, who was not a Christian in any orthodox sense, neverthe-less believed in a sovereign God and divine providence. Though he did not accept the doctrine of Christ's divine Sonship, he believed that the standards set by Jesus were faultless and a perfect model for right living.[4]

The strength of Jefferson's personality and the unassailable quality of his ideas would eventually leave the Federalist Party obsolete. Restrained, lean government became the national norm for most of the nineteenth century (the notable excep-tion being that period immediately following the Civil War called the Reconstruc-tion, after which the country would see a return to constitutionalism). In 1828, Jefferson's Republican Party divided up into competing factions now represented by the Democratic and Whig Parties. Kentuckian Henry Clay's interest in mer-cantilism (establishing a favorable trade balance by exporting far more goods than importing) was perhaps a chief cause of division. The original Democratic Party, as it emerged under Andrew Jackson, modeled itself after Jefferson's strict construc-tion of the Constitution, states' rights, and free trade. The Whig Party was largely shaped by Henry Clay and his ideas. The Whigs came to adopt a position similar to the former Federalist Party.

In the 1850s the Whig Party would be replaced with the new Republican Party. The politics of the Republican Party did not cater to Southern sensibilities. The party practically molded itself into a *reaction* to the monolithic hold of the South. The effect, not surprisingly, was to cause Southerners to identify more than ever with the Democratic Party. A major issue, and perhaps the chief cause of the War between the States, involved tariffs (taxes on imports). These the Republican North favored, while the Democratic South remained staunchly opposed. The inevitable war that followed put a severe strain on strict construction. Abraham Lincoln would take the lead in violating Constitutional rights, from suspending the writ of habeas corpus to running roughshod over any concept of states' rights. With the end of the Civil War, states had been reduced to little more than appendages of a vast Federal entity. Thomas Jefferson's great fear had become reality. The Constitution was now seen more within the framework of common law—an evolving standard based on precedent rather than viewed as higher law.

After the Reconstruction, some semblance of constitutional restraint was restored but the genie had been let out of the bottle. Crises, real or manufactured, became the vehicle for sweeping measures that had little relationship to any enumerated powers.

CHAPTER 24

TWENTIETH-CENTURY CURRENTS AND HITLER'S AKTION T-4

A s the twentieth century dawned, it had become apparent to the more radical agents of change that the charitable nature of man, believed to have been a natural attribute, was simply a holdover from Christian morality. Not only was this not intrinsic to man but (in some ways) an impediment to building a new better society. Freud would declare Christian morality a straitjacket that restrained the natural man who was crying for liberation. Religion, in general, was a neurosis of all humanity.

The early twentieth century also found America having once again to resist popular radical currents—this time, various socialist ideas emanating from Marxism. To be sure, socialism had made definite inroads into the Western world. Featured most prominently in this scheme was the redistribution of wealth. The state had come increasingly to take on the role of an Almighty God. In parallel, "the people" were finding themselves viewed with suspicion—obstacles too often interfering with progress and government's role as the ultimate remedy.

Socialism was the predominant political theme of the new century, but not all approaches were necessarily in agreement with their Marxist parent. John Stuart Mill (1806–1873) had taken up the utilitarianism of his predecessor Bentham and promoted "the greatest good for the greatest number" as the new morality. This represented a particularly soft and sentimental kind of socialism. But because self-sacrifice was surely at odds with such a principle, there was nothing here ennobling or inspirational. Who would be left to pay the costs demanded of freedom? At the other end stood the great contribution of German Enlightenment thought, *realpolitik*. Under this system, raw power and utility were the determiners of morality.

Realpolitik would be the fleshing-out of Nietzsche's unsympathetic, incisive philosophy. Unlike most Enlightenment philosophers, Nietzsche did not try to put a cheery face on the staggering implications of Darwinism. He looked at this soberly, showing no patience with those who wanted to pretend that this represented some great liberation of the human condition. If Darwinism is true, reasoned Nietzsche, then we have tragically lost an essence that has inspired men through great struggles to achieve magnificent ends. Recognizing the reality and refusing to retreat to some artificial sentiment, his "God is dead" pronouncement was an emphatic closing of a cherished era and recognition that if life was to retain meaning, men of valor had to somehow summon within themselves a will that inspired greatness on a wholly new stage.

Nietzsche railed against utilitarianism and its emphasis on eliminating personal discomfort. He could only imagine a society of pampered, weak men who could never exhibit the courage and character to aspire to any sort of greatness. Robust Christianity, whatever its shortcomings in Nietzsche's mind, had at least recognized and promoted the view that nothing of worth had ever come without great suffering and willingness for self-sacrifice. If it were now certain that a Supreme Being did not exist, then some men would have to ascend to a position approximating this. If not, then no one had any hope of any purpose ever being restored to their lives. Even the most hapless peasant completely exploited by this new ruling aristocracy could at least find a measure of meaning otherwise impossible. Even if sacrificed, the peasant could take comfort in his death serving to glorify the drive for nobility. The only other option was for all to sink into hopeless despair.[1]

As with the radical forces sweeping through Europe after the French Revolution, America would again exhibit a natural resistance to popular notions of socialism, though it seemed to be taking hold everywhere else. It was becoming apparent that in its stark nature, this economic view would not gain currency in the US. Proponents understood it would require considerable repackaging to sell it to the freedom-loving American intellect. Socialism would find its greatest opportunity for advancement if it could attach itself to one of the major American political parties.[2] There was also a new appreciation for the long view. Success would eventually be achieved through patient incrementalism.

In America, "socialism" would be replaced with more palatable terms like "progressive," "democratic," and finally "liberal." The use of this last term required the reinventing of a word that, in its classic sense, had always been associated with the cause of freedom and *resistance* to government intrusion. This was done by making the quest for democracy (equality) synonymous with the quest for liberty. But "true liberty," the new liberals understood, could only come about by deemphasizing America as a constitutionally federated republic, since this directly impeded vital egalitarian measures. Private property was, again, very much in danger. The great problem of socialism was that, at its heart, it required theft. Just to create the illusion of government benevolence, the state had first to steal from some to bestow the most meager blessings on others. Yet even this would come at a cost—the death of human dignity.

Both major political parties made concessions to Marxist thought in the early twentieth century under the rubric of "reform" (or *change* the great virtue of the nineteenth). But progressives would find their ideals more in line with those of the new Democratic Party, especially since the US South was solidly Democrat and filled with resentment and mistrust for a government that had robbed it of both its wealth and its dignity. Using the strategy of divide and conquer, the Democratic Party would recognize a distinct advantage to structuring itself as the champion of the little guy, battling a faceless exploitative giant. With Marx' dialects in view, class envy would become the party's most effective tool.

Implementing progressive ideas, of course, meant that government had to grow itself to greater proportions, its reach ever extended. Bigger government required greater revenue, thus the Sixteenth Amendment was ratified in 1913 to levy a tax on personal income—a tax strictly *prohibited* by the Constitution. The Federal Reserve Act, passed in this same year, created and authorized a central bank to print money as expediency required, enabling the government to inflate the currency and redistribute wealth. This would prove most useful to the (Franklin) Roosevelt administration.

Enlightenment apostles John Dewey and Maynard Keynes would spearhead the socialist incrementalism in the public education system and economics respectively. In 1896, American philosopher and educational reformer Dewey founded and directed the University of Chicago Laboratory School. For the first half of the twentieth century, his teaching curriculum would exert an unfettered influence over the American public education system. A disciple of Darwin, Dewey moved the emphasis away from traditional values to the inculcation of humanistic utility. As a bold reformer, he rejected transcendent authority and absolutes (God as the ultimate source of truth) and emphasized democratic ethics, meaning the integration of the individual into the whole, where truth was presented as an evolving concept, determined by the needs of community. Rather than equipping each student with a classical education structured in fixed concepts of right and wrong—challenging and honing the intellect while demanding the pursuit of personal excellence—the classroom was to be a social model in miniature, social efficiency the shared goal. The intent was to ensure a homogenized predictable product—the forerunner of today's "outcome-based education."

English economist Keynes responded to the Great Depression with his work *The General Theory of Employment, Interest and Money*, published in 1936. According to Keynes, it was morally imperative for government to promote full employment, even if it meant deficit spending. Keynes made his refutation of orthodox economics, somewhat presumptuously, analogous to Einstein's overthrow of Newton's classical physics. Orthodox economists believed the free market was self-correcting and, if left to its own natural mechanisms, would always move toward full employment. Keynes disagreed, insisting unemployment was the inevitable effect of the free market with its economic inequalities separating the business class and wage-earners. Apparently, the tendency of entrepreneurs to hoard personal capital (during economic downturns) short-circuited the only factor that seemed to matter—investments. Thus, the need for government intervention to "stimulate consumer demand" through artificial manipulations, "temporarily" borrowing wealth from a future generation. Of course, the idea was to pay back the debt when markets recovered.

Keynes was right to correlate reduced consumer demand with recessions. But this was the *effect* rather than the *cause*. Recessions were not caused by lack of consumption but lack of real *income*. And it was not consumer demand per se but unobstructed *production* that generated wealth. Yet it was production that debt and government manipulation *stifled*. Somehow, all those principles (industry, thrift, self-sacrifice, prudence, self-discipline, staying within one's means) that were hailed as virtues by community and associated with the accumulation of personal wealth, no longer applied on a *national* level. By some mystical force, government profligacy was transformed into selflessness and now economically responsible. Yet, several months after the stock market crash of 1929, the unemployment rate (before government came to the rescue) was far lower than the 11.7 percent of the early 1920s. Ignoring his advisors at that time, President Warren Harding refused to interfere with market corrections, and within two years the rate dropped to 2.4 percent. He did, however, reduce *government* spending significantly.[3] Nevertheless, ever since World War II, the Keynesian model, but for short-lived interruptions, has been dominant in both major political parties, contributing to the creation of the welfare state.

The Roosevelt Administration of the 1930s increased the scope of federal government far beyond even the most ambitious plans of any previous administration. A precedent was solidly established, and a not-so-subtle understanding had entered the field; merely overseeing and protecting the integrity of numerous transactions was now an antiquated role. Armed with so many resources, government had a moral obligation to go beyond managing primitive market corrections; it must fashion itself into the agent of salvation.

The Great Depression would serve as the vehicle for massive new manipulations. In April of 1933, FDR took the US off the gold standard. Shortly thereafter, he began arbitrarily setting the gold price each morning, with no rhyme or reason. Agencies and acts were put in place to create remedies, regulate prices, and pressure higher wages, showing no thought for unintended consequences. Whereas businesses had a long-view appreciation for the balance between supply and demand, state planners treated the economy in a *static* way, seeing only the immediate effect.

Because prices and wages were artificial and did not reflect actual *market* value, and because the flow of capital was so severely restricted by ever growing regulations and new taxes, few had money to invest, and those who did had no idea where the sound investments lay. The stability, the *predictability* that would have been vital to bringing health back to the economy, was systematically *stifled* by the Roosevelt Administration. Only the outbreak of World War II would begin to end this event. Nevertheless, the template was set. Hereafter, "compassion" would be defined as government intervention, even if disastrous. The Democratic Party was now the champion of the working man, and the Republican of the privileged.

Unfortunately, FDR's most enduring and harmful legacy has been the proliferation of so-called "administration agencies." Comments Clarence Carson:

> [T]he outstanding feature of these regulatory agencies is that they tend to join together what the Constitution puts asunder. That is, the Constitution separates and generally accords different spheres to the legislative, executive, and judicial functions. These powers tend to be joined in a single body in regulatory agencies. By their interpretation and decisions, they make what is now called 'administrative law'; they ordinarily enforce—i.e., execute their laws—; and they have courts which perform judicial functions.[4]

*   *   *

World War II would provide an opportunity for the world to see some actual fruit of the Enlightenment, especially that strain which emerged from Darwinism. It is a little ironic that some such as Freke and Gandy try to tie Hitler's Nazi experiment to Christianity. Hitler was most contemptuous of Christianity, believing it to be directly responsible for artificially sustaining the weak. Employing the popular eugenics movement (championed by Margaret Sanger, founder of Planned Parenthood) and following Nietzsche's model, the Nazi Party placed its stress on the preservation of the race—in this case, the Aryan race.

This was not some abhorrent strain that grew in a vacuum. The subtitle to Darwin's *Origin of the Species* was in fact (the seldom-mentioned) *On the Preservation of the Favored Races in the Struggle for Life*. Eugenics was actually considered (until Hitler) a much-respected field of scientific endeavor (even in America), which traced its foundation directly not just to Darwinist implications but to Darwin's own specific words: "There is reason to believe that vaccination has preserved thousands, who from a weak constitution would formerly have succumbed to small-pox. Thus, the weak members of civilized societies propagate their kind. No one who has attended to the breeding of domestic animals will doubt that this must be highly injurious to the race of man."[5]

As far as Hitler was concerned, capitalism and Marxism were merely two sides of the same Jewish coin.[6] Both were the result of a Jewish plot to prevent that superior race from assuming its rightful place. Jews were thus cast as a planetary virus that stood in the way of racial evolution. So long as Jews existed, the health of the collective organism was in danger. Further, only the perfecting of the race could engender the kind of national pride that would rekindle the self-sacrificing spirit that had seemingly succumbed to Darwinism. Good and evil must not be measured by any previous set of absolutes, but by the achievement of the desired ends. The world would learn that working toward that "noble end" would entail the murder of six million men, women, and children.

Because the component of hatred is so prevalent in Hitler's extermination of the Jews, there is a tendency to write off this shameful episode as an aberration that really cannot be fairly linked with Darwinism. There is, however, a seldom-mentioned side to the perfecting of the race that shows no apparent animus: Before implementation of the so-called "Final Solution," nearly the entire scientific and medical community of Germany were already engaged (through "health courts") in an "experimental" sterilization program aimed at purging the German population of inferior stock. In just a few years, this bold eugenics experiment would metastasize into the shocking eradication of those citizens deemed burdensome to the "progress" of the nation. Confined in the early stages to the terminally ill and the disabled, its reach would respect few boundaries. "Unplanned groups and individuals were murdered: welfare wards, asocials, wayward children, healthy Jewish children or those of mixed blood, homosexuals, political offenders, elderly wards of nursing homes, sick and healthy Eastern workers."[7]

Possibly the most disturbing feature of this entire program (called Aktion T-4) would only emerge at the Nuremberg trials—Karl Brandt, a personal physician of Adolph Hitler and charged with T-4's implementation, perhaps best represented and most eloquently demonstrated the mindset for its *justification* in his final statement. Continuing to affirm innocence from any "criminal" behavior, he did not deny responsibility. His greatest sense of despair seemed to lie with a world that judged his actions apart from the context in which they had occurred. Implicit in his testimony, remarkably moving and sincere under the circumstances, was the idea that he had summoned the courage to put his *personal* feelings aside to act in the best interests of humanity. His actions, he insisted were not motivated by economics but by pity.

It is difficult to accept that the director of the T-4 program would have held with such a disparate motive from that which was almost uniformly demonstrated at every level by those who *carried out* the program—the elimination of "useless eaters." Brandt's willing accomplices never doubted they were taking Darwin's "survival of the fittest" to its logical conclusion. Purging the race of its "unfit" was never equated with a crime but a sober, thoughtful, and altogether rational *service* to mankind. Yet even if we take Brandt's statement at face value, there is something terribly perverse about a "pity" that would entail busloads of helpless patients dragged away weeping, screaming, and pleading in the face of what they knew was certain death. Nevertheless, even as the gallows loomed large, Brandt could say with deep conviction, "In my heart there is love of mankind, and so it is in my conscience."[8]

The question the world wanted answered was, *how* could this have happened in a modern "enlightened" society? How could 200,000 innocent citizens, many contributing including veterans and children, be sent to such merciless deaths by a profession entrusted with *preserving* life? There is a saying that placed in a heated pot, a frog will immediately leap to safety. If cool, however, the frog will remain even if heated to the extreme, if the application of heat is in minute, carefully measured increments—to its eventual death. Obviously, some process of desensitization is necessary for any creature to act in a manner contrary either to its basic nature *or* its social conditioning. In human beings, desensitization entails the breaking down of inhibitions, personal as well as societal. The greatest inhibitor of human action (as well as motivator of altruistic behavior) has been acquiescence to a moral code bequeathed by a transcendent, unchanging Supreme Being.

Sanctity of life—the belief that all human life is precious and that all reasonable efforts are to be vigorously pursued to preserve it, totally without regard for one's relative societal value—is inescapably tied into the belief that each human being possesses a unique individual soul created in the image of that Supreme Being and endowed by that Creator with a sense of purpose, dignity, and intrinsic value. With the denial of this transcendent reality and the subsequent vacuum of absolute morals, sanctity of life eventually erodes into the Enlightenment alternative, *quality* of life. In theory, this amounts to those in authority seeking to do the most "good" for the greatest number at a given time. While this may have surface appeal, the reality is otherwise.

Elevating "quality" to *the* defining societal ethic presupposes the possibility of *failing* to measure up to its specifications. What is to be done with those who do not meet its criteria and may represent a hindrance to the success of others seeking to attain? There is nothing sinister— indeed, avoidable—in a society dealing seriously, and where necessary, harshly with those who refuse to conform to the rules of harmonious coexistence. But what about those whose nonconformity is restricted to physical or mental handicaps, unacceptable speech, or even thought patterns? Will they be forced to comply, extended special assistance in overcoming nonconformities, or will they eventually be declared a detriment and thus expendable if they will not or *cannot* comply?

It is true that the event in Germany did entail many factors which intersected in just the right timeframe, but the effect of Darwinist thought in circles of higher learning cannot be minimized. This was not merely one of many, but the key factor, without which all other elements combined, could not have catalyzed the horror that was to occur (T-4, or the Holocaust).

There is also an important footnote to the T-4 program: Though government institutions had largely abandoned theistic principles due to evolutionist implications, this was not the case among the German citizenry. Christian values still significantly influenced the social psyche. In fact, under great personal peril, the German clergy led the charge to stop this government-sponsored assault on its citizenry, once it became apparent what was taking place. The role of clergy, far from minimal, was most directly responsible for the public outcry and outrage that finally brought this nightmare to the surface, forcing Hitler to officially end T-4 in 1941, two years after it was initiated.

Unfortunately, the culture of death spawned by T-4 did not go away. Physicians would continue to voluntarily put the unfit to death, right up to the war's end. And though perhaps not directly responsible, this culture certainly made it easier to implement the program that would murder 6 million Jews.

CHAPTER 25

THE FRANKFURT SCHOOL

Possibly the most pernicious source of leftist influence to infiltrate American culture would manifest in something called the Frankfurt School. The Frankfurt School was a German think-tank of Marxist intellectuals residing at Goethe University. Founded in the early 1920s, with the rise of Hitler to power in the 1930s, a contingent of these gentlemen fled, eventually settling at Columbia University in New York City in the mid-'30s. Rather than exposed for the dangerous moral deviants they were, these men were embraced as probing thinkers with exciting new ideas, who were perhaps a bit eccentric but otherwise harmless.

Now ensconced in its new home, the Frankfurt School quickly set about its strategy for systematically tearing down alienating American institutions, employing an approach called "critical theory." This spelled out the methods for undermining Western institutions in general, pillars of American strength and greatness specifically. All previous institutions (especially religious) had been put in place to control the masses. The Frankfurt School, having liberally incorporated Freud, would shift the Marxist emphasis from economics to cultural change. The initial attack would begin against the fundamental elements: the traditional nuclear family, powerful sexual mores, and of course, the *source* of those inhibitions, the Judeo-Christian ethic.

Everything had to be cast in terms of a great struggle—and it had to be of a nature that eclipsed the individual's historic, heroic battle against the easy default path of least resistance. This new higher struggle had to be framed in terms of "us vs. them," where individual identity and personal responsibility were swallowed up in a new group consciousness. Thus, the old Marxist theme of dividing humanity into "oppressor vs. oppressed" was again placed at the center of the budding revolution but with an important tweak. Because the attack on American institutions had to be comprehensive, new "injustices" had to be found (invented, in fact) for political exploitation.

Marx had originally formulated his theory of class struggle along a single fault line—the ruling class vs. the exploited peasantry, or, the bourgeoisie vs. the proletariat. It would be necessary to create numerous new fault lines based on special identity categories—black, female, Hispanic, homosexual, and so on. Eventually, all would become official exploited minorities in need of special protection from the oppressor class. Everything that had represented normalcy was merely a social construct of the oppressors. The assumption of well-delineated natural boundaries was to be replaced with the iron clad assertion reality was fluid. Nothing would escape the long reach of critical theory, including (and especially) gender roles.

Perhaps the most influential of the Frankfurt School was Herbert Marcuse. It was Marcuse who astutely recognized the advantage of using minorities as a special weapon for assaulting the foundations of America. Marcuse and his band very cleverly used the sacred American principle of tolerance and dissent to *undermine* American principles. Once leftist ideas were fully inculcated, such primitive notions could be discarded. In 1965, Marcuse published *Repressive Tolerance*. The very point of tolerance, insisted Marcuse, was to deny tolerance of those things deemed oppressive.[1] Any voice opposing the revolution was (conveniently) evil by definition, thus disqualified from the conversation. Marcuse's ideas also highly influenced the sexual revolution of the '60s.

"Harmless" these men were not. As for bold, courageous pioneers of penetrating, groundbreaking analysis, their siren song was a particularly vapid regurgitation of ancient anarchy, seducing with the same old worn promise the serpent made to Eve in the garden. In so many words, that serpent told Eve not to believe any of the information her senses, her intuition, was relaying. Everything was a "social construct" devised by a diabolical mind to keep her in chains. Yes, on the surface it certainly seemed she was living in paradise—but it was just a grand conspiracy, and surely her superior intellect could see through the evil pretense.

Whether the Garden of Eden, the French Revolution, Marxism, or the Third Reich, so the satanic invitation to mass suicide has always been: dispense with "the lessons of history," dispense with your own faulty senses, dispense with God-centered reason—or, to borrow the underlying theme of the Frankfurt School, question authority. If the goal is to pursue truth no matter the cost, this is sound advice and, in the words of the apostle Paul, "worthy of all acceptation" (1 Tim. 1:15). But if there are no absolutes, as the Left often insists, then there is no truth and we are left with self-serving assertions. A questioning attitude has less relevance than scratching an itch.

But to whatever extent the Left chooses (self-servingly) to assign significance to this catchy slogan, the question remains: Why would this not apply to the icons of the movement? What is the unimpeachable source of their own moral certitude? If, as they assert, all of history is a record of white men following their natural greedy impulses to exploit, how has nature suddenly produced a class of white men wielding disproportionate influence who act only out of altruism? If their motives are pure and their ideas liberating, wouldn't they submit their entire range of argument for the most microscopic examination, in fact *insist* on it? Why would they instead *exempt* themselves from that which they demand of all others?

More than any single source, the Frankfurt School sowed the seeds for today's progressive movement and its determined drive to implement full-blown statism. A distinction should probably be made between progressivism, liberalism, and statism. Progressivism represents those most extreme and deliberate efforts to undermine American institutions, liberalism a socialist bent intended to modify certain perceived injustices while generally upholding basic Constitutional freedoms. Statism is that form of government where the religious superstructure and corresponding set of morals is entirely based in materialist, naturalist assumptions, admitting no transcendent (Christian) morals in conflict. For all practical purposes, the state fully assumes the role of God.

Progressives do not, in principle, object to the story of good vs. evil working through history to find eventual resolution in an ultimate all-powerful savior. Nor do they object to that story culminating in some form of heaven. The Religious Right and the Religious Left's stories of redemption differ only in the details—the cast of characters, the evil tempter, the mystical forces at play, the definition of morality, and of course, the location. The power of the Right's redemptive narrative is in its subtlety, its almost imperceptible intrusion into the human psyche *despite* a natural resistance. It is because its organic pathways seep relentlessly into every facet of intuition that it is especially haunting and intractable.

The Left's redemptive narrative, because it contains no organic component, can only be sustained by a constant intentional bombardment of the senses. Without a consistent expression of rage against some imagined injustice, the subtle, detestable stirrings of the old narrative creep back in. Only a conscience "seared with a hot iron" (definitively rejecting love's last call) can finally silence the subtle stirrings. Thus, narratives to the Left can never merely serve as a grounding, an underlying point of orientation. They must be dominant and ostentatious in every waking moment, bloody bludgeons employed early and often against the evil opposing progressive utopia. But the all-consuming exercise is enervating, eventually leaving an emaciated soul where once stood a vital human being.

The traditional Western narrative has always had an element of self-examination and the self-sacrificial, even if certain strains did not fully embrace the explicit Judeo-Christian code. Leftist narratives have no place for self-sacrifice; the vigil is always for more scapegoats to vilify and exact revenge upon. Loathe to self-examine, leftist narratives must be held with absolute conviction. To even allow the possibility of some flaw is to usher in the unraveling of the leftist universe.

The ideas of the Frankfurt School took hold in the 1960s. By now, the teaching of Marx and Darwin were aggressively promoted on college campuses, the lofty path of the intellectual illuminati. No other decade featured so many major transformative events, so powerfully impacting the culture. The assassination of President Kennedy in 1963 was particularly significant, a severe loss of innocence inflicted on the nation. Yes, other presidents had been assassinated and the nation thrust into a time of mourning. But no other president had been so young, glamorous, handsome, charismatic, and seemingly so courageous in battling injustice. And surely no president had ever been the recipient of such passionate infatuation from the press. We would find out later President Kennedy was a very fallible man. Yet during his presidency, this man was the personification of every ideal, and he and his lovely wife treated as American royalty—his presidency, larger than life.

We as a nation took this loss *personally*. If possible, the media took it even more personally. In their grief, the media made a point of bringing every facet of sadness directly into our homes; the slow funeral procession, Jackie courageously hold-ing onto her dignity despite her overwhelming grief, little John-John saluting his father's flag-draped casket, and so many exquisite expressions of sadness. Perhaps nothing could have so emphatically placed an exclamation point on this monstrous injustice than to now be reminded that Lyndon Johnson had been sworn in to com-plete the slain president's term. To say this added insult to injury is an immeasur-able understatement. The contrast between the two could not have seemed greater.

The perfect storm was brewing. The palpable loss of innocence would lead to a general sense of disillusionment, especially among young people. The disillusion-ment would spark a growing suspicion and mistrust toward all forms of authority. The Frankfurt School, and the Left in general, could not have hoped for a better climate for promoting an alternate worldview. In just a few years, talk of "revolu-tion" was on nearly every college campus. A counterculture sprang up challenging old institutions. Kids were "dropping out," rejecting the values of their parents, looking for alternate paths to ultimate purpose, turning on to drugs and exploring Eastern mysticism to tap into the new spirituality.

Not everything associated with that time was necessarily bad. In fact, for some time the media had served to protect the interests of government, seeing it as their duty to preserve the public trust in the institution at all costs. This surely was at odds with the Framers' intent that a free press should function primarily to protect the public from government abuses. Indeed, for much too long, government had taken advantage of the loyalty of Americans. It had become axiomatic that a true patriot simply answered in the affirmative when his country called. Now people were asking, "Is this really a just war? Is our national security really at risk? What is the real reason we are in this fight?" The '60s saw the press now leading the questioning, determined in its investigation of every dubious government activity, and assuming the role it was intended.

There is something in human nature that cries out for an explanation equal in magnitude to an enormous event. A larger-than-life figure such as President Kennedy practically demanded an extraordinary explanation to his untimely end. It offended, indeed inflamed the senses that some little obscure speck of humanity, Lee Harvey Oswald, could have taken down this monumental person and snuffed out the light he had brought to an entire nation. Surely, only something of gargantuan proportions could have accounted for this seismic event.

It was not until many years after this national tragedy that I decided to look deeply into the matter myself, considering the arguments and evidence of each side. As I have a close family member who was directly involved in New Orleans DA Jim Garrison's investigation in the late '60s, up to this time I had leaned toward the conspiracy side, assuming the numerous problems so often cited with the lone-gunman theory had to equal a high probability of conspiracy. I was surprised to find that whatever problems a single assassin may have posed, these were miniscule in comparison to problems inherent to the various conspiracy theories. In many cases, nothing short of intervention bordering on the divine could have overcome serious obstacles. If one set aside an emotional investment in a particular outcome and simply followed the scientific method, the case for Oswald acting alone was overwhelming.

Yet there was something about the investigative methodology virtually all these conspiracy theories shared, something that just didn't seem quite right. Like all legitimate investigators, these authors gathered facts, analyzed data, sought eyewitness testimony, and so on. But what suddenly became apparent was that they had turned the classic investigative process on its head. Conspiracists had not begun with known facts (the inductive method), set up competing explanations to see which could best unify all facts, and proceed to systematically eliminate possible scenarios till the weight of evidence left only the one most plausible explanation standing. Instead, conspiracists *began* with an assumption and a conclusion, and then worked backward, looking for evidence to fit the only permissible outcome. Truth was measured by whatever preserved the theory, because it was inconceivable the theory might be wrong.

If intransigent facts intruded upon assumptions, then and only then were these acknowledged. Yet these were not explained through recourse to consistent rules of investigation, allowing alternate explanations. They were dealt with by invoking special circumstances, associations of collusion, and abilities far outside the range of normal physical constraints or human behavior. Their key premises were weak on facts but overflowing with speculation and conjecture, huge extrapolations routinely made from the flimsiest evidence. Because this was about looking for "the justice President Kennedy deserved," it was okay to set aside the normal dispassionate approach.

This "cult of conspiracy" would reverberate far beyond swapping intriguing tales. It would make the concept of an evil underlying structure of oppression much more mysterious, sinister, immediate, and personal. It would serve to validate the message of the Frankfurt School, especially the sacred duty to question authority and expose the conspiracy. Every form of repressive traditional authority could now be summed up in just two words: "the Establishment" (also synonymous with "the system," which of course was rigged against the oppressed). In short, a new kind of virtual reality was emerging which would coincide with the death of critical thinking.

The "cult of conspiracy" would fuel a new paradigm that could be described as the New Left. This paradigm not only employed the inverted scientific method above but constituted a preemptive strategy; treating its causes as self-evident truths not open to debate, investing every element of the human condition (and soon nature itself) with a political component, and justifying the quest for "social justice" through any means possible. This construct ensured that the quest would necessarily move away from thoughtful, reasoned discourse toward intolerant moral outrage. This entire approach would eventually be summed up with the words "political correctness." But of course, the inverted scientific method was not new, having, more than a century earlier, breathed life into Marxism and Darwinism, and later higher criticism and Freudianism. What was new was a willingness to use this in a full-court press against any political opposition.

By the late 1960s, the message coming out of American universities was that America was no longer to be hailed as a great beacon of hope to the world but to be disparaged as perhaps the leading cause of the world's poverty. The belief in American exceptionalism had given way to American exploitation. The steady drumbeat had now produced a generation of revolutionaries who held little in common with either political party, seeing both as hopelessly locked into an establishment mentality. Wildly optimistic, these young revolutionaries were fully committed and understood the kind of change needed could only come about through social upheaval.

This would unleash a new kind of "journalist." Unlike their predecessors who may have been sympathetic to a socialist vision but generally remained faithful to their duty to report the facts, these new journalists were committed to an *ideology* and were convinced their vision was synonymous with truth. As such, they would rather quickly lose any sense of objectivity, abandon their mission as journalists, and become crusaders for the new revolution—political activists. Some wanted the revolution to be violent, bloody, and brutal (after the French and Bolshevik models). The side that would win believed the most effective way to advance the revolution would be by taking hold of the organs of power through the political process. Thus, a whole new class of candidate would be taking up the flag of the Democratic Party.

Prior generations of Democrats had fought for Socialist-leaning policies, but most stopped short of endorsing the full-blown Communist model. Some were even intensely patriotic and valiantly opposed Communism. But the new class of Democrat enthusiastically embraced Marxism and viewed American patriotism with grave suspicion. To their credit, these young revolutionaries understood the value of gradual, deliberate, incremental infiltration of Marxist ideas into the body politic. The belief was that by the time Americans realized what had happened, it would be too late to do anything about it.

The United States could not have been birthed by Hindu pantheism, atheism, Islam, or humanism. Only those specific biblical principles prominently displayed in our Constitution could have produced this nation. With the emergence of the New Left, it was understood that Marxist thought could not make significant inroads into American government unless the Constitution was subverted, gutted, negated, or otherwise rendered irrelevant. But this could only happen if the Judeo-Christian worldview were boxed in. Political correctness (PC) would be the trojan horse that would affect that war on Christianity and disconnection from our founding documents. The key to employing PC effectively would be to take those special identity categories ("minorities") and portray them as victims of discrimination of a white advantaged majority.

Only something as multitentacled as PC—invoked tenaciously, passionately, and constantly—could be equal to the daunting task. But PC could only be effective if nestled within its own special setting. Because the progressive gospel is based in a lie (that it is driven by compassion and that America as founded is inherently evil), it could not lay out its vision in the open and submit to honest scrutiny. It could only make its case within carefully constructed "political narratives." For the Left, these were invented stories that, though they bore only the faintest connection to reality (or none at all), were aggressively promoted with the intent that the combination of constant repetition and righteous indignation would create an impression they *were* true, and their defenders, the most moral of persons. Left unchallenged, political narratives became self-justifying concepts.

This political narrative set up a "higher morality" based on "compassion" that not only superseded Christianity but set out to show Christian principles to be the invention of unenlightened, superstitious, and the most intolerant exploiters of all time, while raising "diversity" and "multiculturalism/inclusiveness" to a sacrament. It made "tolerance" and its fully ripened fruit "acceptance" the measure of all compassion. Thus, any religion/morality that excluded and exhibited intolerance toward special protected groups was guilty of hate. For a Christian, "intolerance" is calling the practice of homosexuality sin, even though that is what the Bible has called it since the days of Abraham and Lot. Likewise, questioning leftist policies that have decimated black families made one a racist. This worked equally well with the pseudoscience of "global warming," where one is put on par with a Holocaust-denier for questioning its "science." The Left thus positioned political correctness as the highest form of morality.

But because it is rooted in a lie, its power lies entirely in its ability to extort. It can exert control only to the extent its illusion is left unchallenged. But unlike the story of the naked emperor, where the illusion is burst as soon as the innocent eyes of a child proclaim the simple truth, PC does not relinquish its illusion or power at this point. It unleashes the fury of hell, certain the challenger will back away long before the smoke clears. Indeed, the instant howls of hysteria and shrieks of derision coupled with the determination to inflict maximum, sustained personal pain, hate-filled venom and humiliation has proven a most effective silencer of any who might be thinking of saying "but I can't see any clothes."

This brings us finally to the *goal* of progressives, "social justice." This is the message, the mantra, and the mission. The very term carries the implication that justice in America is being systematically denied by an inherently racist nation that is structured to keep minorities from succeeding. Because the Constitution is designed to "preserve the interests of people of privilege," it is an enemy of the revolution. Social justice envisions a future idyllic state where all are equal, living in perfect harmony, with that pernicious tempter (capitalism) vanquished and no more "hateful" religions (especially Christianity) poisoning the minds of citizens. While equality of *opportunity* is guaranteed in the Constitution, nothing short of equality of *outcome* is acceptable under social justice. In practice, this means taking from those who have, by force if necessary, and giving to those who do not. In short, social justice is the progressive quest for heaven—excepting of course, that it is all accomplished here on Earth without divine intervention.

CHAPTER 26

MODERN AMERICAN ENLIGHTENMENT FRUIT

The 1960s would also see Christian theism—the worldview that animated US jurisprudence since the founding period—overpowered by naturalism, the state of reality described by Darwinism. Cowed by the authority of "science," universities (which almost all, ironically, had been founded to promote Christian values) and seminaries abandoned all references to the supernatural, since all such talk had no place in the "rational" world according the new rules of science. This made much of Christianity, almost unbelievably, complicit in its own increasing irrelevance as well as in the burgeoning influence of naturalism.

By the time scientific naturalism *was* ready to assume the mantle, no surreptitious well-coordinated coup under cover of darkness was necessary. Indeed, naturalism ascended the throne with neither a shot fired nor hardly a whimper of resistance. All its basic assumptions had already been accepted in all major universities, including many still claiming *Christian* affiliation. These assumptions were most evident in the US Supreme Court's ruling of 1947 (Justice Black's invocation of separation of church and state). With John Dewey having inculcated humanist ideas into standard public education, capitulation to Marx and Darwin in higher education, and the highest court disposed toward a neopagan interpretation of the Constitution, there could be no doubt naturalism now held a monopoly on the levers of political thought.

Proponents thus ensconced, pretensions of obeisance to Christian ethics (which, by now, were clearly seen as an obstacle to a socialist vision) were no longer necessary. At last, the Christian emphasis on the internal could be set aside for the Enlightenment/progressive emphasis on the *external*. Best of all, this could be done now without having to contend with the messy business of reconciling two opposing worldviews, even cosmetically. From this time forward and in a staggeringly short time, Christian theism's opportunity to influence the culture would be negligible, where permitted at all.

The 1960s would prove most pivotal in implementing bold, innovative social experiments. These were all a reflection of that overwhelming progressive desire to tinker with externalities, especially wholesale reforms intended to radically alter the face of that vast entity called society. The disdain for unintended consequences would be evident within fifteen to thirty years after their implementation. In his book *The Vision of the Anointed*, economist Thomas Sowell identifies the typical pattern of socialist intervention from beginning to eventual denial in four general stages: 1) The Crisis; 2) The Solution; 3) The Results; 4) The Response.[1]

In the 1960s, the anointed (Sowell's name for elitist social engineers) decided the time had come to intervene with respect to soaring crime rates. This involved a joint effort by the chief justice of the US Supreme Court (Earl Warren), the US attorney general (Ramsay Clark), and the chief judge of the Circuit Court of Appeals for the District of Columbia (David L. Bazelon). The disproportionate emphasis placed on punishing criminals, it was decided, was archaic and not consistent with the latest scientific information derived from psychiatry and psychology. Rather than seeking revenge on criminals, the root causes that precipitated antisocial behavior needed to be addressed and a new emphasis placed on rehabilitation. In other words, a "compassionate" judicial system was the key to eliminating the sense of oppression and hopelessness that drove the powerless to lash out at society.

High-ranking members of the Democratic Party hailed this progressive innovation as an important breakthrough. Several rulings were issued that set out specific procedures for the apprehension of criminals. The violation of any detail could literally mean the overturning of a conviction. The 1966 Miranda decision, in particular, which required a reading of constitutional rights to those incarcerated at the moment of arrest, and its complementary rulings would actually make it harder to prosecute criminals, thus making criminal activity *more* attractive than ever. If the vision of the anointed was correct, statistics should reflect a drop in crime rates, and this eventually be borne out by hard data. The merits of this approach did not need to be confined to intellectual musings any longer. The results would speak for themselves.

So, what were those results? Sowell writes:

> Crime rates skyrocketed. Murder rates suddenly shot up until the murder rate in 1974 was more than twice as high as in 1961. Between 1960 and 1976, a citizen's chances of becoming a victim of a major violent crime tripled. The number of policemen killed also tripled during the decade of the 1960s. Young criminals, who had been especially favored by the new solicitude, became especially violent. The arrest rate of juveniles for murder more than tripled between 1965 and 1990, even allowing for changes in population size.[2]

229 Julien Stanford 229

Such stark results not only should have ended any debate as to whether this approach had any merit, but should have served to sufficiently embarrass proponents away from any longer defending a vacuous approach. However, rather than admitting the utter failure of this social experiment, the anointed chose to make it morally reprehensible to speak of the escalation in crime, since crime rates were higher among blacks. So, as would become the norm, the *failure* of a cherished socialist experiment, rather than being acknowledged and scrapped, was exploited for political gain. The disproportionate rise in crime by blacks had to mean we were a more racist society than even previously suspected. More socialist intervention, of course, would be necessary to address the pervasive racism in America.

Similar experiments would be conducted in the '60s, with the "war on poverty" and sex education, with specific programs instituted to remedy these "crises" as well. With respect to the compassion aimed at ending poverty, Sowell writes, "Senator Barry Goldwater predicted that these programs would 'encourage poverty' by encouraging 'more and more people to move to the ranks of those being taken care of by the government.' Nor did he expect expanded social programs to lead to a more harmonious society, for he saw their underlying philosophy as an 'attempt to divide Americans' along class lines, to 'pigeon-hole people and make hyphenated Americans.'"[3] As Goldwater predicted, a huge new dependency class was created, along with a new sense of entitlement simply as a birthright. "Responsibility for personal accountability" also became a code term for racism. America became more divided than ever. Sex education likewise resulted in a sharp increase in unwed pregnancies and transmittable diseases. Concludes Sowell, "The relationship between theory and evidence was simply not discussed. The vision was axiomatic."[4]

*   *   *

In 1962, the Supreme Court definitively severed the religious faith of our forefathers from the government they had instituted. The establishment clause of the First Amendment, interpreted for nearly two hundred years as a restraint on government (including by the Founders themselves) was now turned on its head and "interpreted" as a restrainer on *religion*. Nothing would so clearly establish the willingness and audacity of the Supreme Court to legislate from the bench—a power that constitutionally had been restricted to the (elected) legislative branch of government, not the (unelected and essentially unaccountable) judicial.

Even if we accept the Warren Court's novel reading of "separation of church and state" (a phrase nowhere existing in the Constitution), this ruling represented a most egregious coupling of church and state *and* an assault on the establishment clause of the First Amendment. The wording of this clause expressly *prohibits* the establishment of a *government-sponsored national religion*. Yet it is precisely the religion of progressivism (complete with all its moral imperatives and injunctions), to the deliberate exclusion of all others, that has now been established and guarded by federal government sanction. In violation of individual conscience, we are now forced (with our tax dollars) to worship around the altar of this imposed national religion. Nowhere is the zeal of the ACLU more evident than with its determination to preserve the monopoly of progressivism's chief cornerstone, the theory of evolution, in the public-school system. Whatever the cost, impressionable students must not be exposed to its inherent problems, no matter how compelling the evidence (more on this later).

The backlash against the judicial activism of the courts would propel conservative candidate Barry Goldwater to the Republican nomination in the 1964 presidential election. To be sure, the Republican Party proper, especially the historically entrenched country-club monolith, never embraced the conservative movement very warmly. Ronald Reagan's ascendency in 1980 would prove particularly inexplicable to the party's "blue-bloods." Rather than seeing this as an inspiring movement and a yearning on the part of the electorate for a return to sound principles of governance (and especially *reigning in* government), the Republican monolith chose to view this as an aberration, and conservatism as a movement that could not be sustained on a national level.

In the meanwhile, progressivism was becoming not only the dominant voice but an increasingly radical voice of the Democratic Party. By 1972, the party would nominate as its presidential candidate George McGovern, an unabashed hardcore leftist who made no effort to conceal his radical agenda. McGovern's colossal defeat, however, would not approximate the effect of Goldwater's equal and earlier defeat. Whereas the conservative movement was largely viewed within the Republican Party as an embarrassing stepchild, the Democratic Party became more committed to a socialist agenda than ever. The lesson taken from defeat: from this point on, progressive candidates would have to disguise their intent and pretend to support mainstream views. Because the electorate would not give its assent to socialism through the ballot box, the radical agenda would have to be implemented by the courts. The courts, of course, were safe from the outcry of ordinary citizens. Thus, the imperative for stacking the courts with progressive judges who had no qualms about shredding the very Constitution they were "entrusted" with upholding.

Traditionally and constitutionally, Federal courts had authorization to *apply* law to specific cases, acting within rigid negative confines, striking down legislation judged unconstitutional. No power to *invent* law was delegated constitutionally, yet was taken by progressive activist courts. Decrees were being issued in "the name of the people." Yet the contempt for "the people" could not have been more evident when the primary organ of redress of the people (local autonomous government) was being hemmed-in on every side. Since the '60s, judicial activism has produced some of the most tortured rulings. In 1973, Harry Blackmun, in delivering the majority opinion in *Roe v. Wade*, made it clear that he had divined a constitutional right to abort a baby, and even tied this into, of all things, a right to privacy. Where might such a "right" be found in the Constitution? Apart from its barbarous aspect, this ruling voided anti-abortion laws in forty-six states.[5] Whatever breaking effect states had still exercised over the federal government was now void as well.

The Democratic Party's growing association with Marxism would necessitate the demonization of big business, specifically "evil corporations." A recurring them in defense of progressive policies has been the fear that, if not for a constant vigil, one day the ultimate corporation will rise to become that all-powerful monopoly; hapless citizens forced to comply with its unyielding dictates. Yet while this has become an almost unquestioned certainty in the minds of many, in the entire history of the world we have yet to see this become *reality*. This "logical conclusion to capitalism" exists *only* in theory. On the other hand, the threat of the all-powerful *state* is something that does not merely exist as a possibility, but has manifest as cruel reality numerous times.

To be sure, corporations can become exploitative, and it is certainly legitimate to check potential abuses. But notice that the greatest abuses we see involve those instances where, once again, unrestrained *government* insinuates its presence, reaching deep with its tentacles producing that aberrant and insidious strain called crony-capitalism. This is the direct result of government changing the rules for certain favored businesses. These "deals" invariably empower government bureaucracies, introducing confusing regulations that strangle those businesses that might otherwise compete with the favored. Thus, business policies that are hurtful to consumers are insulated from a free market which would otherwise eliminate inferior products and services. In such cases, it is clear the state is not acting on behalf of the common man but its own selfish interests.

Corporations, when relatively free from the reach of government (whether favored with special privileges or handcuffed with harsh regulations) generate tremendous productivity, and thus wealth that has a ripple effect throughout countless levels and communities. They are also constrained by real-time and real-world conditions. Because it is generally the pursuit of profits and not a drive for issuing vague pieties about ultimate purpose that animates their existence, free-market corporations must yield to fixed economic laws. Statist governments (in their inevitable socialist forms), because they seek to define morality while refusing to recognize a higher superintending *source* of morality, bow to no bounds set by reality.

Where, we must ask, is the sense of proportionality? We have the freedom to work for another company or corporation if we so choose. We can even pool resources and start up an alternate corporation if one proves particularly oppressive, insensitive, or exploitative. How do we choose or start up an alternate government if our present government holds all the levers of power, and citizens no place for redress? Statist government encroaches on freedoms, generates zero wealth, confiscates wealth through taxation, and consistently creates disincentives to productivity. If the *corporation* should be closely monitored because of potential abuse, shouldn't the zeal be so many times greater when it comes to the *state*?

To the extent the rich are demonized, the poor are also seemingly championed by progressive elites. Those who have enjoyed great blessings should indeed feel a burden for those less fortunate but defining what constitutes "the poor" can be a slippery thing, as with many politically charged terms today. Most often the poor are presented as a static class locked into an economic status with no hope of escape. "The poor" is an arbitrary category based on some percentage of all income-earners, usually in the lowest 20 percent of that scale. Consider the following as an illustration of just how relative terms like "rich" and "poor" are: In 1971, of *all* classes, one-third had air conditioning, less than half had a color TV, and less than one percent owned a microwave. In 2001, of those officially listed among the *poor*, 75 percent had air conditioning, 97 percent had a color TV, 73 percent owned a microwave, 98 percent had a DVD player, and 72 percent owned at least one vehicle.[6] In most other countries today, or even *this* country forty or fifty years ago, those in this class would have been the *rich*.

Even if the state's motives were genuine and this was not about political exploitation of an entire class of "underprivileged," the state could never possess the resources to make important distinctions that might elevate the truly needy. Yet no matter the motive, the state's intrusion has effectively destroyed community. As recently as the mid-sixties, neighbors all knew and helped each other. There was a distinction (even if no one thought of the terms) between the "worthy poor" and "unworthy poor." The worthy poor were those who, through no fault of their own, had fallen on hard times. Some event—whether a spell of bad weather, a lengthy sickness, or the death of the breadwinner—had depleted a family's resources, making it impossible to meet the most basic needs. Neighbors would rally around this family and give food and help with the crop or whatever the need, until the family could get back on its feet. Churches also took an active role in helping, and took a personal interest in overseeing the spiritual welfare of the affected children. Yet those same afflicted families took the greatest role in becoming self-sustaining as soon as possible; it was simply a matter of pride. Because it was understood that no help would come to those who were otherwise healthy yet simply refused to be responsible, there was no incentive to be part of the unworthy poor, and these were very few by comparison.

Because the state cannot possibly know each case individually (as community can), it chooses to make a blanket presumption about anyone below an arbitrary economic number. In so doing, it lifts few and instead creates a large dependency class where no incentive and no pride exists to drive people toward a better state. It also obliterates the concept of neighbors thinking of each other as their brother's keeper. Each becomes ever more isolated, assuming it is someone else's responsibility to care for the destitute neighbor down the street. Of course, there will always be those who truly have special needs that are not easily accommodated by community. There is a role for government intervention in such cases, but the more local that government the more likely those specific needs will be met and the less likely the system will be abused.

*   *   *

The Democratic Party's association with Marxism has also produced a sharp shift in religious values. Today, there is no discernible movement or cause embraced by the national Democratic *structure* with any connection to Christian theistic principles. Apart from the *talk* of compassion (which always manages to spread the misery), there is no evidence a Christian conscience any longer drives any of the party's agenda, only expediency. To be sure, however, the tiny spark of conscience within the Republican Party is on life support, and only because the party still pays lip service to the Christian conservative movement.

CHAPTER 27

THREE TWENTY-FIRST CENTURY PRESIDENTS

The first president of our nation to emerge from the crucible of the 1960s would be Bill Clinton. The coming of Mr. Clinton portended something truly sinister. The ascendancy of this man to this office signified that the very radical element of the Democratic Party (first emerging in that fertile decade) was no longer relegated to the kook fringe. The decision by the Democratic Party to circle the wagons around Clinton no matter what meant that the radicalization of an entire political party was now complete. Whatever "ideals" the Democratic Party may have once represented, it was understood now that the party had crossed the Rubicon. What had become evident to the Democratic Party had become just as painfully obvious to conservatives: Truth and justice had become irrelevant to leftists. It was now all about the acquisition of power, and nothing (no matter how ruthless) was out of bounds.

Apart from his scandal-a-month administration, his complete lack of sexual restraint, his deconstruction of the English language (the meaning of "is"), his lack of integrity and honor (looking the American people in the eye and lying with a straight face, *and* lying under oath in both civil and criminal proceedings), Clinton's primary legacy has been an open assault on the rule of law. The most dramatic demonstration of his contempt for the American people was evident in a Department of Justice that was (until President Obama's) the most political, compromised, and corrupt in the history of the presidency. The Clinton DOJ was either an active accomplice or looked the other way in declaring war on American citizens (Waco), *legal* businesses (tobacco industry, gun manufacturers, pharmaceutical companies, software makers, etc.), and in confiscating nearly one thousand highly sensitive background files of Reagan and Bush administration officials. These files provided a convenient blackmail database against all political opposition—especially useful against impeachment hearings.

The most egregious example of Justice Department corruption, obstruction, *and* contempt for the rule of law would be Attorney General Janet Reno's absolute refusal (no matter the amount of evidence) to appoint an independent counsel to investigate Clinton-Gore fundraising abuses, even though she was strongly urged to do so by FBI director Louis Freeh and her own senior aide Robert Litt, a Democratic Party loyalist.

Ever since the Clinton presidency, the standard by which progressives impart "morality" to an individual is based solely upon that person's support for the "proper causes." Personal behavior is irrelevant. In other words, one may be an adulterer, liar, thief, rapist, or even murderer, and still be a moral person simply by standing on the right side of the issues. By this standard, Bill Clinton is unquestionably a moral person (and so was Harvey Weinstein and company, until very recently).

On the other hand, the man who would follow Clinton, George W. Bush, though he violated no constitutional law (the unending efforts of his detractors to *manufacture* a violation notwithstanding) was guilty of a crime against the natural order of things. Democrats, by their right standing on issues of compassion, could not possibly be out of power because the people had rejected their ideas. This was unthinkable and an absurdity. The only possibility is that the people were duped by vile, scheming Republicans. As the one who presided over this "culture of deceit," it was morally just, a moral imperative that Bush should be hounded as the personification of evil.

What made this so ironic is that Mr. Bush was far from a conservative. That he was deeply infected with the spirit of progressivism was evident through his unprecedented expansion of government and an illegal immigration policy that was at odds with his war on terrorism. Sadly, Mr. Bush's last days in office would find him overseeing and endorsing a massive bailout bill that was the most ill-conceived policy of his entire administration. But because he was not fully committed to socialism and even defended traditional values, to the Left he was irredeemably evil.

Ostensibly, at the heart of the Left's ceaseless tirade against Bush is the deceit he perpetrated to manipulate us into an unnecessary and obscene war. Bush willingly misled not only the American people but the Democratic Party as well. According to the charge, Bush knew there were no weapons of mass destruction in Iraq but deliberately sold this lie that he might proceed to topple the government of Saddam Hussein.

To be sure, there is indeed a party that acted with duplicity in all this, but it was not the Bush administration. The Democratic Party, though having access to the same intelligence and reaching the same conclusions as the Bush administration, once it became expedient double-crossed President Bush and insisted he had massaged the intel. This implies that any intel disseminated first had to be filtered through the administration before anyone else could draw conclusions. It also implies the position that Iraq posed a grave threat to national security was hatched in the Bush administration. To the latter, Norman Podhoretz responds:

> But the consensus on which Mr. Bush relied was not born in his own administration. In fact, it was first fully formed in the Clinton administration. Here is Bill Clinton himself, speaking in 1998: 'If Saddam rejects peace and we have to use force, our purpose is clear. We want to seriously diminish the threat posed by Iraq's weapons-of-mass-destruction program'. Here is Secretary of State Madeline Albright, also speaking in 1998: "Iraq is a long way from [the USA], but what happens there matters a great deal here. For the risk that the leaders of a rogue state will use nuclear, chemical, or biological weapons against us or our allies is the greatest security threat we face."[1]

Regardless of squabbles among the two major political parties, no matter how intense or heated disagreements may have been, it was always understood that politics ended at the water's edge. When external threats surfaced, ranks immediately closed. The Democratic Party apparently decided that the acquisition of power was more important than national security. To that end, this party actively and consistently sought to handcuff our nation's efforts to defeat our common enemy.

Mr. Bush's action, unlike the kneejerk reaction as it is so often characterized, followed eleven years of warnings and seventeen UN resolutions calling for Hussein to allow inspectors unimpeded access of his nation's facilities or face the consequences. Whatever mistakes the Bush administration may have made after (or the universal failure of intelligence before) the invasion, there is nothing, despite never-ending charges, to indicate that Mr. Bush did not believe the threat was real and grave.

To defeat perhaps the most ruthless and abstract enemy our nation has faced in its history, Mr. Bush had to overcome an unprecedented set of circumstances. This included not just the unconventional tactics of an implacable and asymmetrical enemy, but the obstacles erected by our "allies," the dominant leftist media's negative portrayal, and even a major American political party that consistently undermined the successful prosecution of this war and demoralized not just the American population but the very soldiers Democrats voted to put in harm's way. The sad and sobering truth: the Democratic Party positioned itself where good news in Iraq was bad news for the party. Thus, the party had a definite stake in either disrupting the US war effort or at least casting any successes in the worst possible light. In the bluntest terms, for the reacquisition of power, the Democrats literally invested in America's defeat.

Though the Iraq war certainly formed a conspicuous profile on the progressive radar, one suspects the greatest motivator of "Bush-derangement-syndrome" was the charge that Bush had "stolen the 2000 presidential election from Al Gore in Florida." Nowhere was the venom so lethal, forgiveness so anathema. This would forever be the proof of Bush's illegitimacy. This event was most illuminating in that it featured at least three of the four primary organs of the Left working in concert to circumvent the will of the people, as well as the rule of law. Of the four key organs, the Democrat Party, the courts, the media, and academia, perhaps only the last was not an active, obvious, enthusiastic, and shameless participant in this episode.

When the US Supreme Court finally handed down its ruling, effectively ending all recounts, the American Left went into conniptions. "This was a scandalous naked power grab by a Supreme Court dominated by Republican appointees." Bush had been elected by judicial fiat, and many similar charges were flying fast and furious. The amount of outrage, however, would turn out to be as selective as had the reportage of facts. The Left buttressed its case on an undeniable fact—seven of the nine Supreme Court justices had been appointed by Republican presidents. Missing from this "unassailable" piece of evidence was the actual *ideological* leaning of these seven appointments with regard to interpreting the Constitution. Of the number, only three, Renquist, Scalia, and Thomas consistently adhered to a strict construction of the Constitution. Kennedy and O'Connor were "swing votes" who frequently joined in the tortured rulings of ultra-activist justices Breyer, Ginsburg, Souter, and Stephens. Far from conservative, the Supreme Court was at *best* divided. But philosophical leanings were not even relevant in this case.

What the Left also selectively omitted from the story was the all-important fact that the Supreme Court (in a 7–2 vote) had acted entirely in accordance with the rule of law to restrain a lower court that had consistently displayed an open contempt for *any* legislated law; that very law which was put in place by elected representatives of *the people*. Moreover, various recounts were conducted by a determined media in the months that followed who were going to find the real winner. A seldom reported fact: in *each* of these recounts, no matter who conducted it and whatever the final margin of victory, George Bush emerged the victor. Despite every effort by the media, the Democratic Party, and Florida judicial activism, by every measure Bush was the clear and undisputed winner.

*   *   *

The central leftist narrative, the one from which all subnarratives flow, has always been that America is inherently racist. One might have thought that the election of Barack Obama in 2008 to the world's highest office by a white majority would have made it impossible to sustain that illusion any longer. Yet in a wholesale rejection of anything approximating logic, Mr. Obama and his associates would take the occasion of his administration to *highlight* American racism and to insist it was more pervasive than ever.

No single person in the history of America ever occupied such an ideal position to unify and heal deep wounds. Instead, Mr. Obama's Justice Department chose to politicize every instance where white-on-black violence occurred and to declare war on law enforcement officials. Mr. Obama chose to consistently divide, promoting the narrative of racial injustice and to deliberately engage in the most inflammatory rhetoric. This did not abate the rush to judgment, though in an overwhelming number of cases police were exonerated when facts finally filtered through the manufactured hysteria. This was not inconsequential. Not only did it produce an environment of polarization that had not existed since the 1960s but led to a disturbing increase in cop murders. This would result in police pulling out of neighborhoods most in need of their presence.

But President Obama's war on Americans and attempt to divide would not be limited to police or racial issues. Christians would come directly into his crosshairs, with his JD deciding the right of a "transgender" male to enter a women's bathroom was more important than the psychological trauma this might inflict on some little girl. Small Christian businesses would suddenly be subject to huge fines, not for refusing to serve homosexual couples but for refusing to violate their conscience by participating in the *sanctioning* of homosexual marriage. Mr. Obama would turn the IRS into his personal Gestapo wing, targeting conservative advocacy groups, denying tax-exempt status, and using IRS goons to intimidate and harass. All this was encouraged under the banner of "social justice."

Mr. Obama turned a deaf ear to Americans' plea that he examine the true insidious nature of Islam and see that those perpetrating acts of barbarity were not violating their religion. While it's true that most Muslims are not terrorists, this is despite the Koran and simply because murdering human beings is appalling to human nature in general. Yet Obama was so ideologically driven that though Americans were being murdered in the name of Allah, we were constantly lectured that "we must not surrender our 'values'" and back away from bringing as many unvetted Muslim refugees here as possible. As the Constitution is not a suicide pact, it's clear the "values" Mr. Obama spoke of were progressive values dear to him, but utterly anathema to any freedom-loving strain.

President Obama ignored Congress and ruled by executive edict, making a shambles of the Constitution, secure in the belief no one in the Republican Party would dare challenge his end-arounds for fear of political-correctness backlash. Republicans would not disappoint. The one thing Republicans could consistently be counted upon was to assume the fetal position if the president threatened any overreaching action. Even when the Obama administration was caught in the middle of scandals such as the gun-running operation "fast and furious," where 2,500 assault weapons were knowingly allowed to slip into the hands of the Sinaloa Cartel in Mexico; or Benghazi, where national security advisor Susan Rice was trotted out on Sunday news shows to repeat the known phony narrative that an American ambassador and several brave Americans were murdered because of a spontaneous uprising in protest to a video, the Republican Party could be counted on to "moderate" its investigations so as not to appear racist.

Of course, Obama's signature accomplishment would be "Obamacare." Aside from the monstrous precedent—government could now force all to buy private goods and services—there was never any doubt of the law's intent. With insurance companies required to insure patients with already-existing conditions, insurers would have been forced to raise premiums to levels where it would be impossible to compete in the free market. In the face of this planned collapse, the government would have ridden to the rescue with its single-payer plan, effectively putting in place full-fledged socialized health care.

Once implemented, the most ominous effect would have seen government with an absolute stake in regulating every action of every American citizen. Numerous new laws would be enacted to ensure "healthy behavior," along with multiplied thousands of new bureaucrats and special "health police" to enforce new regulations. Because the strain would be so great on enforcement agents, special incentives (moved up to the front of the line, etc.) would no doubt be offered to citizens to turn in neighbors not in compliance. And yes, "death panels" would have had to decide where precious resources were now best applied.

Fortunately, an election took place that derailed what certainly *would* have happened. Yet, as predicted, and despite President Obama's constant assurances, millions would lose their primary health care physicians, millions more would face skyrocketing premiums, and still many others, forced to surrender full-time for part-time jobs as a direct result of this law.

Though you would scarcely have known it by the media, Barack Obama has a past that would have predicted the radical course he would take as president. Everything he did while in office was completely consistent with ideals that were nurtured from his earliest days and the singular trajectory his life has followed. His father was a radical Marxist, writing in a 1965 paper published in the *East African Journal* ("Problems Facing Our Socialism") that property should be communally owned and confiscated where necessary.[2] It is not coincidence that the younger Obama titled his book *Dreams from My Father*. It was a steady diet of his father's ideals he was spoon-fed by his equally radical mother up to the time she abandoned him in his teens. In his book, the younger

Obama would write "it was into my father's image . . . that I'd packed all the attributes I sought in myself."[3]

At age sixteen, Frank Marshall Davis became Obama's mentor. Davis was a member of the Communist Party USA. The House Un-American Activities Committee accused Davis of involvement in several communist-front organizations. Years later, Alice Palmer picked Obama to succeed her in the Illinois State Senate. She would introduce him to the radical elitists of Chicago in the home of Bill Ayers and Bernadine Dohrn in 1995 and endorse Obama's candidacy. The FBI records that she served on the board of the US Peace Council, a communist front group.

Bill and Bernadine were once on the FBI's Ten Most Wanted List for a string of bombings they committed in the US when part of The Weather Underground. Their slogan was "Kill the rich people." They remain unrepentant. Bill's father, Tom, had been a very wealthy and influential figure in Illinois politics, at one time the CEO of Commonwealth Edison. With his father's wealth and connections, and a plan to destroy the capitalist system from the inside, Bill Ayers would be a key enabler for Obama.

Every important person to touch the future president's life was hardcore left-ist. We all remember Obama's "spiritual mentor" whose teachings he sat under for twenty years, Jeremiah Wright. Wright's black-liberation theology mirrored Marxist thought, its quest for "social justice" through class struggle, *ad nauseam*. When the hate-filled rants of this man were brought to light, the leftist media kept the lid on, insisting Obama's religious convictions were a personal matter that should not be dragged into the campaign. The same sensitive media had no qualms about thoroughly investigating and publicizing Mitt Romney's Mormon beliefs.

Obama's mentors made a point of placing into his hands the revolutionary tactics of Saul Alinsky. Mr. Alinsky, often hailed as the father of modern American radicalism, was a community organizer who modeled his tactics after the Frankfurt School. Alinsky's "Rules for Radicals" were enthusiastically promoted throughout the eight years of the Obama Administration. Consider Rule 13: "Pick the target, freeze it, personalize it, and polarize it. Cut off the support network and isolate the target from sympathy. Go after people and not institutions; people hurt faster than institutions."

The question is not where is the evidence that Obama was (and remains) a hardcore Marxist with a smoldering contempt that could only be soothed by reducing the United States perhaps to just above third-world status? Where is the evidence he had *departed* from the dreams of his father? Where is the evidence that he was *not* actively working to overthrow the capitalist system his father despised (overseeing the loss of our AAA credit rating); that he did *not* share the core belief that America must be punished for the poverty it has caused (in his mind) throughout the world?

Where is the evidence that he did *not* faithfully follow the Marxist playbook of divide-and-conquer through class warfare, constantly pitting groups against each other over matters of race, religion, economies, and even sexual orientation?

It may be that a single event, shortly before he left office, best captures the essence of incoherence, insanity, inconsistency, deliberate polarization, and the cruelty of the Left's virtual reality. In August of 2016, a massive storm that showed up without warning left one of the greatest flood disasters Louisiana had ever known. With Louisianans rolling up their sleeves, fighting the sense of despair and seeking desperately to find hope in the face of so much heartbreak, they were delivered yet another blow. President Obama's response was to issue a stern warning to Louisiana "not to engage in discrimination." It would be hard to imagine how Mr. Obama could have more effectively executed the perfect cheap shot or poured acid into an already gaping wound.

Without bothering (evidently) to view any of the numerous videos or pictures of diverse ethnicities standing shoulder to shoulder and lending a helping hand (including police officers selflessly engaging in endless rescue missions while continuously placing themselves at great peril), Mr. Obama chose to do what he always reflexively did—politicize. While the people of Louisiana were literally up to their necks in the harsh elements of the *real* world, Mr. Obama was firmly entrenched in his pretend world of forcing human beings into distinct pigeonholes, assuming superficial differences equaled a fundamental divide that overrode any common human bond (casual commonalities like "how do I recover from this devastation; where will our family stay in the meantime; how do we replace things that took a lifetime of sacrifice to acquire; how will my family survive if the economy continues to worsen," etc.).

But it wasn't just that this was deeply offensive to Louisianans who were making no distinction at all, seeing only neighbors in desperate need; it was downright bizarre. One need only try to picture this stern directive applied in the midst of all the chaos to get some sense of the inverted reality. Would this mean that one needed to keep a scorecard handy, a careful check of ethnicities already helped before venturing into the next home? And if it turned out that next home would violate the proper ratio, did that mean this family would have to be bypassed (and any other "ineligible" ethnicity) until the scorecard was properly balanced again? And if no eligible ethnicity could be discovered reasonably soon, would the rescuer have to "undo" whatever help was given?

Just one year later (with Obama no longer president) this pattern of Americans ignoring personal politics, creeds, ethnicities, or any other distinctions to selflessly and bravely help each other in the wake of widespread devastation would repeat, this time in Texas and part of Louisiana. If average Americans are really the hate-filled monsters of the leftist narrative, here was yet another grand opportunity to expose those deep-seated passions. Instead, once again, Americans showed that when they are removed from the make-believe crises of the Left and thrust into the most savage, desperate, heartrending real-world/real-time crisis, it is the Left's ideology that is exposed for its utter irrelevancy, its upside-down human model, and dearth of compassion.

This brings us to the religious convictions that animated President Obama's stern warning. We can only take Mr. Obama at his word that he professed Jesus Christ as his savior. One can only imagine he felt the compassion promoted by his ideology was in essential agreement with all Christ taught and modeled. But I don't recall Jesus ever defining compassion in the way Mr. Obama did. While Jesus did certainly stress the need for concern over the less fortunate, He consistently emphasized salvation from personal sin over salvation from personal circumstances (within the context of normal everyday life, of course). In fact, His teaching implied that negative circumstances, even if not always caused by, were always exacerbated by personal sin.

President Obama's ideology consistently whittled away at the concept of personal sin; preferring to view personal *circumstances* as the cause of negative behaviors. But because Jesus came *specifically* to save from sin, to heal a personal heart problem, leftist ideology leaves Him with no significant role. Yet removing the Savior's role means sin continues unabated, which in turn, leads to the proliferation of sin's *effect*. It is precisely to this effect Mr. Obama, and those of his ideological bent, have worked tirelessly to assume the role of that Savior they have, by an endless array of policies, systematically denied those who need Him most.

One of the most vital challenges Christ leaves His followers is to live the self-examined life. No other way of life calls its followers to such an exacting demand—to honestly assess our motives and actions in the most sobering and unflattering terms. It is a call to be willing, after a careful examination of all the evidence, to let go of even some of our most cherished assumptions simply because they do not measure up to *Christ's* standard. There is no place in the self-examined life for a refusal to recognize that no matter how sincere, we just may be wrong.

There is something curiously at odds with Obama's confession of faith in Christ and the deep religious convictions he has tenaciously clung to. As he surveyed the Louisiana flood, there was never a possibility he might pause to rethink his assumptions. Acknowledging and praising the spirit of cooperation among all ethnicities would have seriously undermined the narrative of his ideology that deep divisions among groups are the natural state of things, and that only *its* prescriptions can heal that divide. Thus, within the secure confines of his golf course, the first thing that came to mind to most effectively impart all the inspiration and compassion of his ideology was to emphasize the very worst in humanity—while those to whom his words were directed, and who were trapped in the very midst of tragedy, were *exemplifying* the best.

CHAPTER 28

GLOBAL WARMING

To sustain its noble quest for social justice, the progressive movement must center itself in a tangible and sacred object of worship. That sacred object is on full display in the modern global warming (or "climate change") movement. Anyone suggesting the science that drives the present global warming hysteria is incomplete is likely to find himself the immediate object of the most contemptuous ridicule. For the modern Left, it is neither permissible to deny the *fact* of global warming or (even if one concedes a climate-warming trend) its *source*. We are indisputably living in a warming period and human beings (especially greedy capitalistic humans) are the reason. Anyone attempting to cite credible research conducted by some of the most eminent scientists in the world in refutation is, nevertheless, equivalent to a Holocaust-denier. In other words, considering the evidence (no matter how thorough or thoughtful it might be) is not necessary, because a global-warming denier is the epitome of evil, guilty of committing a crime against humanity.

For some years now, we have been hearing the popular slogan "We must save the planet." Yet without fail, the not-very-subtle implication following is that human beings are the object from which the planet must be saved. The US, of course, is responsible for the most egregious assault on the environment. The political solutions to the impending crisis, we can't help noticing, always seem to involve some form of socialism. Likewise, capitalism is the scourge of the planet that must be rooted out.

Thinning of the ozone layer was one of the first "concerns" to receive attention. Ozone, an important filter for ultraviolet radiation, is formed from oxygen in the upper-earth atmosphere. Ozone thinning was first described in 1956 by Gordon Dobson of Oxford University when CFCs (chlorofluorocarbons, the supposed source of thinning) were not widely used. The "hole" in the ozone layer was understood to be a predictable phenomenon that lasted three to five weeks,

245

occurring at the end of the Antarctic winter when certain conditions were present.[1] This was a *natural* phenomenon not attributable to any manmade causes, and thus not some dire pattern that was reason for concern—that is, until it became politicized. In 1987, the Montreal Protocol banned CFCs. As with all socialist solutions, noble intentions seldom allow for actual consequences.

Lawrence Solomon has profiled a wide range of eminent scientists whom, even if some of those he lists agree there is a discernible warming trend, nevertheless vigorously dispute the conclusions of the powerful global warming advocacy. These "deniers" as the radical advocacy derisively dismisses them, are not (at least those Solomon cites) dilettantes nor part of a conservative think tank. They carry impressive resumes that boast of some of the most respected positions at some of the most prestigious institutions from all over the world. Some of these "deniers" even have a history of activism within the environmental movement. Solomon is himself part of an environmental group called Energy Probe, an anti-nuclear establishment. Yet Solomon was driven to write his book out of a growing concern that the champions of global warming have so politicized the issue that vital and honest serious debate is becoming almost impossible. Science is being held hostage to politics. Solomon sums up the situation soberly: "Most laymen, most citizens, owe most of what we think we know about global warming not to science directly, but to science as mediated by the media and by political bodies, especially the UN and our governments."[2]

For the American Left, the collapse of the Soviet Union left an unexpected void in the universe. The world was, inexplicably, left without a standard for reigning in the evils of rugged individualistic capitalism and denied a model now for "true compassion" and "fairness." The Left was in desperate need of a cause to justify its existence. For a constituency that was already committed to the idea that the material universe was the sum of all reality, the preservation of the environment was a natural stage. The man who would become most responsible for promulgating the new vision would be none other than Bill Clinton's visionary vice-president.

Throughout the years of the Clinton administration, Al Gore would prove his mastery of artful Clintonism. In 1996, Gore attended a fundraising event held at a Buddhist monastery in California. When word got out that Chinese operatives John Huang and Maria Hsia had staged the event, Gore immediately denied that the event was a fundraiser or that any campaign finance regulations had been violated. He preferred to describe it as a "finance-related" event or the more innocuous "donor-maintenance" event, proving himself every bit as adroit at the art of language deconstruction as his mentor, Clinton. Had Mr. Gore been caught in the very act of murder, we might have expected he would have sought to explain away his act as a single insignificant wounding to the heart followed by an unfortunate coincidence of too many body systems failing in rapid sequence.

As things would turn out, Mr. Gore's "taking responsibility" meant the very same for him that it meant for Clinton when he took responsibility for Monicagate and for Ms. Reno when she took responsibility for Waco—which is to say, it meant nothing. Not only was Gore not investigated, but, in typical Clintonian fashion, he managed to turn his own unethical behavior into political advantage. Clinton and Gore were involved in shady campaign schemes and possibly selling out the nation not because of any *personal* character flaws but because campaign finance laws were flawed! And true to form (when the issue was raised in the run up to the 2000 election), only a man with the integrity and insight of Al Gore could be trusted to address this serious deficiency and enact the proper reforms.

Yet whatever their similarities, there is something that makes Al Gore more dangerous than Bill Clinton. Clinton was a spoiled, undisciplined adolescent let loose in a candy store and hopelessly bound to gorge himself on its goodies *and* to deny his guilt even with chocolate smeared all over his face. Mr. Gore, on the other hand, was and remains a determined ideologue driven by deep religious convictions shaped by a commitment to the global implementation of what can only be described as a pagan worldview. Consider Gore's vision, presented in his own words:

> [T]he prevailing ideology of belief in prehistoric Europe and much of the world was based on the worship of a single earth goddess, who was assumed to be the fount of all life and who radiated harmony among all living things. . . . The last vestige of organized goddess worship was eliminated by Christianity as late as the fifteenth century in Lithuania . . . [I]t seems obvious that a better understanding of [goddess worship] could offer us new insights into the nature of the human experience.[3]

> On the other hand, politically conservative theologians and clergy have inherited a different agenda, also defined early in this century. The "atheistic communism" against which they have properly inveighed for decades is, for them, only the most extreme manifestation of a statist impulse to divert precious resources—money, time, moral authority, and emotional labor—away from the mission of spiritual redemption and toward an idolatrous alternative: the search for salvation through a grand reordering of the material world. As a result, they are deeply suspicious of any effort to focus their moral attention on a crisis in the material world that might require as part of its remedy a new exercise of

248 Kingdom of God or Pagan Empire?

something resembling moral authority by the state. And the prospect of coordinated action by governments all over the world understandably heightens their fears and suspicions.[4]

Translation: Bible-believing Christians need to get over their suspicious and irrational view of unrestrained government—a view that stands in the way of global material salvation. Christians also need to be able to make the distinction between "evil" Communist statism and a benevolent and benign New World Order that only *resembles* statism. So, Bible-believing Christians not only hold no solution to the world's problems; alas, they are the problem.

> The Pacific Yew can be cut down and processed to produce a potent chemical, taxol, which offers some promise of curing certain forms of lung, breast, and ovarian cancer in patients who would otherwise quickly die. It seems an easy choice—sacrifice the tree for a human life—until one learns that three trees must be destroyed for each patient treated.[5]

> [S]omething like . . . a Global Marshall Plan . . . is now urgently needed. The scope and complexity of this plan will far exceed those of the original; what's required now is a plan that combines large-scale, long-term, carefully targeted financial aid to developing nations, massive efforts to design and then transfer to poor nations the new technologies needed for sustained economic progress, a worldwide program to stabilize world population, and binding commitments by the industrial nations to accelerate their own transition to an environmentally responsible pattern of life.[6]

> What does it mean to make the effort to save the global environment the central organizing principle of our civilization?[7]

The bottom line: per the socialist/progressive playbook a crisis, real or imagined, is the window of opportunity to advance a radical agenda that otherwise would not survive to see the light of day. In creating a global environmental crisis that borders on hysteria, progressives have hit upon the perfect scheme to empower government to intrude into every life, family, kitchen, and bedroom to save the earth from extinction. And Al Gore, that paragon of virtue, has selflessly consented to serve as pied piper for this most noble cause. So, it is not spiritual transformation through Christ, or the pursuit of human liberty and dignity, nor federal republicanism following that wildly successful American model, nor even free-market capitalism, but the *rescue of the environment* that is this man's "central organizing principle for civilization."

The above illustrates the problem for Solomon, and for anyone wanting reliable information about climate change. "Global warming" is heavily encased in a *religious view*, the solemn worship of nature. Mr. Gore also makes it clear that the movement is, more than anything, about assuming *control*. Even if we were to concede the sincerest motives to Gore, it is apparent that anything approaching the implementation of his vision would require massive taxation on an unprecedented scale and something approaching absolute authority for those responsible for its execution. If we are even going to consider surrendering our most cherished freedoms, shouldn't we first want to know just what the real evidence for and against impending environmental doom is? Likewise, shouldn't we want to know what the actual consequences of such draconian policies might be? How do we know (assuming the trend is real) humans are responsible? And if we truly are facing worldwide catastrophe, do we have any reasonable assurances that any of these policies will make the slightest difference? And if we do not, then *why* should we obligingly comply like lambs led to the slaughter? Unfortunately, because the issue has been so demagogued (not the least by its self-appointed leader Al Gore), these are questions not deemed worthy of a response.

So, what precisely is the evidence for human-induced warming? As far as the global warming advocacy is concerned, the smoking gun is the increase in greenhouse gases, especially CO_2 (carbon dioxide). The issue first took on the status of the new orthodoxy with the famous "hockey stick graph." According to paleoclimate specialist Michael Mann, for the last one thousand years a steady decline is evident in global temperatures until the beginning of the twentieth century. From that point on, a sharp rise can be charted, which clearly coincides with a massive expansion of industrialization, especially the burning of hydrocarbons. What's more, the 1990s (according to the hockey stick graph) was the warmest decade in this thousand-year period and 1998 *the* hottest year in this span.

But how did Mann construct his graph? The answer is, he used selective information. For one, he excluded the medieval warming period that just preceded the "Little Ice Age" which ended about 1700. A rising temperature trend has followed since. Were this factored into the graph, the "apparent" sharp rise resembling the blade of a hockey stick would cease.[8]

Perhaps no single piece of propaganda was as instrumental for imprinting a public mindset as this graph. The media embraced it without any critical examination. But many well-respected professionals were suspicious and demanded to know Mann's methodology. Rather than answering serious criticisms with compelling evidence and argumentation, Mann chose to attack his critics. This would become the standard response to any criticism directed at the "settled science" of global warming, even when dissenters had a history of having previously supported government intervention on a wide range of environmental issues.

Dr. Edward Wegman, acting under the direction of the US Congress, investigated Mann's graph. Wegman's final report repudiated the hockey stick graph and agreed largely with McIntyre and McKitrick's earlier objections to Mann's approach. Solomon quotes Wegman, "[T]he paucity of data in the more remote past makes the hottest-in-a-millennium claims essentially unverifiable."[9] Solomon discloses Wegman's most important finding gleaned from his inquiry: Paleoclimate specialists largely exclude the vital input of mainstream statisticians. This practically ensures a fundamentally flawed methodology. "All this was devastating enough. But then Wegman asked another question: why didn't the peer review process work? Why didn't the third-party reviewers catch the errors in Mann's work? The answer is disturbing. . . . What Wegman discovered is that the real problem in the field is *too much consensus*, especially in the peer-review process."[10]

So that oft-cited qualifier, that global warming is established by a *consensus*, turns out to be its Achilles heel. While consensus may be desirable in certain areas, good science is not nor ever has been about consensus. Consensus is the stuff of *politics*, where it occurs it always comes at the expense of fundamental scientific principles—among them the falsifiability principle. Consensus is hostile to disconfirming evidence, tending to ignore or explain away through ever more ingenious flights of fancy. Although the hockey stick graph is no longer trotted out by the UN's Intergovernmental Panel on Climate Change (IPCC), the psychological damage has already been done. The emotion unleashed has generated an irresistible momentum. Yes, once more, the inverted scientific method is fully deployed by the Left.

The more recent bulwark erected by the global warming advocacy is a 600,000-year graph which purports to show the undeniable relationship between the rise in CO_2 and the rise in global temperatures. Since human activity (especially in the last century) has greatly increased CO_2 levels, and since temperatures *have* risen in concert, so goes the argument, the cause could not be more evident. This has served as the centerpiece for Al Gore's "inconvenient truth."[11] But earth's atmosphere is subject to many other factors besides CO_2, including effects of the sun and clouds that are little understood at present. If the earth's temperature is indeed rising, which factor, or combination of factors, is responsible? Professor Nir Shaviv (who concedes global warming) believes that the sun may account for as much as 80 percent of the warming trend of the past century. Mars shows a warming trend, but has neither a capitalist economy nor industrial complex. Why should we assume that the most likely source of recent Earth warming is not the same likely source as

Martian warming—cyclical solar activity? If Martian warming, which seems to run parallel to Earth's, can occur without those notorious sources, why must we assume they are the culprits on Earth?[12]

With the above in view, why has the "consensus" settled on CO_2 as *the* factor of record? The answer lies in ice-core data. The climate modeling derived from this data is, however, based on a convenient assumption. That assumption is that polar ice cores represent a closed system which "precisely preserves the ancient air, allowing for a precise reconstruction of the ancient atmosphere. . . . [N]o component of the trapped air can escape from the ice. Neither can the ice ever become liquid. Neither can the various atmosphere gases trapped in air bubbles in the ice ever combine or separate."[13] Because none of these necessary conditions are possible to maintain, we cannot possibly know (at least based on this record) what ancient CO_2 levels were like. Yet the global warming advocacy points to the higher levels of CO_2 in our present atmosphere in comparison to levels present in ancient ice core data as the indisputable proof of a record of a recent rising trend. Again though, because there are so many factors that permit the *escape* of CO_2 from ice cores, it is not surprising these should feature disproportionately lower levels in comparison to that in our present atmosphere. This is to be *expected.*

We are often told that the focus on global warming is necessary because the consequences are so potentially devastating. Even if the science does not conclusively establish man and modern industrialization as the cause, we must take immediate action based on this assumption, this being the more "cautious" approach. But, absent any real compelling science (all things considered), is this truly the most reasonable response? In fact, the extreme measures called for would have the most devastating effect on the world's poorest. What's more, these prescribed measures, as with the proposed Kyoto Protocol, tend to override national sovereignty.

Danish economist Bjorn Lomborg is a friendly witness for the prosecution. Lomborg does not even question the science of global warming. He is fully on board with the fundamental premise that humans are responsible for an increase in CO_2, and that this has contributed to a warming trend. But he does question the inflated proportion it is given in relation to equally valid concerns. Specifically, he questions the *solutions* set forth by the global warming advocacy. As an economist, Lomborg insists that proposed climate-control measures are not even close to the most efficient way to deal with the potential problems this change might cause.

Solutions for the radical advocacy, as with virtually all socialist schemes, treat the problem as though it can be isolated from the much greater dynamic (remember our attempt to convert the TV?). But what about the *adverse* effect these solutions have on numerous other important issues, such as the loss of technology to combat world hunger and diseases ranging from malaria to HIV?

The Kyoto Protocol, signed in 1997 (though not ratified by the US) is a multi-national initiative aimed at reducing atmospheric CO2. Mostly this is to be accomplished by limiting industrial emissions. Lomborg is critical of the approach: "With Kyoto we can avoid about 140,000 malaria deaths over the century. At one-sixtieth the cost, we can tackle malaria directly and avoid eighty-five million deaths."[14] The protocol's strategy for addressing global food shortages also comes under fire: "For each person saved from malnutrition through Kyoto, simple policies—like investing in agricultural research—could save five thousand people."[15]

For all that Kyoto and like-minded initiatives try to give the impression they are comprehensive in outlook, they suffer a debilitating myopia:

> The money [for R&D to address potential warming problems] should be spent on research of all sorts, exploratory and applied; pilot programs to test and demonstrate promising new technologies; public-private partnership to incentivize private-sector participation in high-risk ventures (just like those now used to get pharmaceutical companies to develop tropical-disease vaccines). . . . Such a massive global research effort would also have potentially huge innovation spin offs, from energy-storage research giving us better cell-phone batteries to the truly unexpected finds that dramatically improve our world.[16]

In other words, solutions (if they are really needed) are more likely to come from a competition-based environment than a socialist template. Unfortunately, the global-warming advocacy is as monolithic in its approach to solutions as it is determined to ignore any dissension as to how evidence for or against climate change may be interpreted.

"Cost-benefit analysis" is a phrase that frequently sends progressives over the top. Pitting a well-intentioned policy aimed at saving human lives against the *cost* of implementation is indicative of the heartlessness in the core of the free market, or so we are told. Yet, arriving at the most streamlined cost has proven in a whole host of ways to *save* the most lives. More resources left over means avenues are available for treating other survival concerns.

Even *without* knowing any of the science or considering any of the consequences surrounding this subject, isn't there something very curious about all this? Isn't there something that strikes an intuitive chord and causes one to detect a certain fishy odor? What about, for instance, the arrogance of an advocacy that deliberately invokes perhaps the most contemptible, emotional charge of the modern era to describe those who even mildly question the science—Holocaust denier? After all, it is not the critics but Al Gore and company who are faithfully following the template of Adolf Hitler: demagogue the issues; cut-off any debate; maintain a monopoly over the public megaphone; smear, malign, and marginalize critics (make them "the enemy of humanity"); create a climate of fear and intimidation where dissension is immediately met with vicious condemnation; find a convenient scapegoat to assign blame for the present crisis; finally, achieve consensus.

The "consensus" among the academic, medical and scientific classes of World War II Germany was that Aktion T-4 was a progressive vision; deciding Jews were a virus on humanity that could justifiably be eliminated required no major philosophical shift. Today, global-warming consensus preaches that dissenters, no matter the credentials or how compelling the arguments, are defined out of the debate by their denial of the only permissible interpretation. Many reputable scientists are now afraid to speak, for fear of the instant vitriol to which they will be subjected. One's career is placed in jeopardy and a lifetime of careful research suddenly delegitimized if a whiff should ever get out that he is "one of those."

CHAPTER 29

THE GOD DELUSION

No comprehensive worldview can be complete without a creation myth. Thus, the theory of evolution (or, scientific materialism) doubles as that myth *and* as the cornerstone for the entire leftist universe. *The God Delusion*, by Richard Dawkins, remains possibly the classic refutation of superstitious religion when set against Enlightenment Darwinism. Dawkins' book is a call for nothing less than the dismantling of organized religion, especially the fundamentalist type. Though critical of Islam, he quickly leaves no doubt that the real target of his rant is Judeo-Christianity; as he gleefully lampoons and harpoons a belief system which has inspired billions. You see religion, Christianity especially, is a pathology that has caused irreparable harm to humankind. A sampling of Dawkins' incisive, thought-provoking, and penetrating objections follows. Be forewarned, with respect to the question of God, religion, and any implications, this man will spare no expense to prove he is hopelessly out of his depth.

"For most of my purposes, all three Abrahamic religions [Judaism, Christianity, Islam] can be treated as indistinguishable."[1] This is a fair illustration of Dawkins' skill in religious studies and appreciation for substance, a skill which shall be on parade throughout his tome. "For my purposes the differences matter less than the similarities."[2] Sadly, that is the problem. The differences turn out to be immeasurably more significant than the similarities.

Dawkins does little to elevate his sustained rant to thoughtful argumentation when he caricatures the God of the Old Testament and shows almost no consideration for a context that is immensely complex and multifaceted. The gist of his case against God seems to be that the deity does not live up to Dawkins' lofty standards. How dare God set a standard and then actually expect it to be upheld? How dare He assign consequences to violations of His standard? How dare He demand a balancing of the scales? To sum up Dawkins' complaint, God shows what a beastly ogre He is by establishing absolute justice. A touchy-feely God who, to be sure, frowns at sin but who would never think to endanger fragile human self-esteem is much closer to the proper kind of deity. Moreover, God cannot establish His love for mankind on His own terms. Placing *Himself* on the altar to atone for mankind's sins, providing a passageway out of sin's consequences and into eternal life is not enough. God, if He really is "loving," should be willing to demonstrate it by hoisting a few with the boys after work. Apparently, we may infer that Dawkins can accept God if He agrees to limit Himself to being something *less* than God.

Dawkins' rigorous "test for God" consists of throwing Him up on a cosmic roulette wheel and declaring "Sorry, it looks like God is improbable." Sorry, Mr. Dawkins, for noticing that the rules by which God is deemed improbable seem suspiciously to *assume* that outcome. Rather than the non sequitur "the universe is already highly improbable, thus God (Whom would have to be even far more complex than the components of the universe) must be immeasurably more improbable," how about, instead, the logical deduction: An improbable universe demands an *essential* God?

Dawkins' gift for obfuscation aside, if he is serious about his pronouncement, he might want to make an argument that bears some similarity to the scientific method—something, perhaps, like showing us a universe where God *does* exist and one where He does *not*. And of course, show us from the scientific method how he has constructed each model. Then we would know just what to look for in either instance, and if our universe is found lacking fundamental God elements, then yes, His existence it must be agreed, is improbable. But if Dawkins is not prepared to make this comparison, his exercise is not only self-serving but farcical. Yet we suspect this is not intentional. Dawkins is so hemmed in by the Enlightenment box that it never occurred to him God might exist outside of his narrow thought processes.

Dawkins' assessment of morality turns out to have about as much rigor as his case against God. There seems no subject for which Dawkins is unwilling to invest an impressive amount of shallow thought. "If you agree that, in the absence of god, you would 'commit robbery, rape, and murder', you reveal yourself as an immoral person, 'and we would be well advised to steer a wide course around you.'"[3] This, admittedly, is a breathtakingly shortsighted view of the situation. Dawkins is free to explain its existence through whatever contorted naturalistic scenario strikes his fancy, but the fact remains that most people, whether professing religious convictions, possess an inborn conscience. There is an intuitive sense of right and wrong. A human conscience, however, is constantly in tension with natural appetites. Either a conscience will subdue appetites or appetites will achieve ascendancy. A conscience firmly in control gives birth to principles that transcend mere individual survival. From this we derive selfless virtues of honor, duty, self-sacrifice. A conscience's ability to inform one's behavior, though, is only as effective as the standard to which it is calibrated.

Dawkins goes on to reveal (unwittingly) one particular slippery slope strain of the godless society when he approvingly quotes psychologist Nicholas Humphrey:

> "Freedom of speech is too precious a freedom to be meddled with." But he then went on to shock his liberal self by advocating one important exception: to argue in favor of censorship for the special case of children. . . . "Parents . . . have no God-given license to enculturate their children in whatever ways they personally choose. . . . In short, children have a right not to have their minds addled by nonsense, and we as a society have a duty to protect them from it. So we should no more allow parents to teach their children to believe, for example, in the literal truth of the Bible or that the planets rule their lives, than we should allow parents to knock their children's teeth out or lock them in a dungeon."[4]

We suspect Mr. Humphrey's "liberal self" was not exactly *shocked* by his open advocacy of absolute state control. Maybe mild stupefaction would be a better description. Nevertheless, there is something that sounds suspiciously familiar about this. Wasn't something like this tried on a massive scale in, let's see, just this last century, and didn't it have something to do with assuming humans were nothing more than overgrown worker bees? Wasn't this bold experiment about the virtue of inculcating right thinking from the earliest possible stage? And wasn't it paramount both to do away with the outmoded idea of God and to ensure that the imperatives of the state superseded any parental oversight? And what exactly were the *results* of this grand utopia? A system of "mutual fairness" where the only remaining right was the right to worship the state; a soulless society where human life no longer held any value, finally imploding for lack of any ennobling principles. The upside, though, was that no children were irreparably harmed by any insidious supreme-being idea. Thank God.

Before leaving the subject of morality, there seems a curious inconsistency worth pointing out: Without even asking, we can be certain that Dawkins and the overwhelming majority of his materialist peers view the brutal act of rape as a monstrous violation of the most sacred trust. We wonder why. To be sure, Christians share this sense of outrage, but ultimately tie this into the concept of absolute justice. Yet it is difficult to conceive of any single act which so perfectly captures the essence of the driving impetus within evolution—dominance of the weaker by the stronger (survival of the fittest) and producing as many offspring as possible. Why isn't the act of rape celebrated as the ultimate expression and fulfillment of the evolutionary process? If materialists are serious about their convictions and consistent, should we not expect to see festivals, parades, parties, and banquets featuring this theme? Indeed, we would look far and wide to find a more appropriate grand marshal for the festivities than the esteemed Mr. Dawkins. Since the outrage Dawkins would express is a complete repudiation of the most sacred tenets of evolution, we can only suppose this is another example of materialism *borrowing* from the Judeo-Christian worldview to salvage a little credibility.

On why the actions of Hitler and Stalin are not intrinsically tied into their religious atheistic convictions: "What matters is not whether Hitler and Stalin were atheists but whether atheism systematically *influences* people to do bad things. There is not the smallest evidence it does."[5] The point is not that it necessarily *influences* as much as it clears the way. It *excuses* abhorrent behavior because there is no longer any standard or higher authority to answer to. What is relevant is not whether progressive butchers were avowed atheists but that they imbibed the Enlightenment wine which dulled the senses to ultimate judgment. Furthermore, Hitler did not appeal to Scripture for justification; his appeal was to Darwin. Perhaps David Berlinski puts it most eloquently: "What Hitler did *not* believe and what Stalin did *not* believe and what Mao did *not* believe and what the Gestapo did not believe and what the NKVD did *not* believe and what the commissars, functionaries, swaggering executioners, Nazi doctors, Communist Party theoreticians, intellectuals, Brown shirts, Black shirts, gauleiters, and a thousand party hacks did *not* believe was that God was watching what they were doing."[6]

Dawkins on why vigilance must be maintained for any sign of those pernicious "miracles" that undermine the pillars of civilization: "I suspect that alleged miracles provide the strongest reason many believers have for their faith; and miracles, by definition, violate the principles of science."[7] Miracles, evidently, do not violate scientific principles when it comes to natural selection. Let's eavesdrop as Dawkins recites a cherished creedal confession (no doubt from his knees) just before he turns in for the night: "Natural selection is the champion crane of all time. It has lifted life from primeval simplicity to the dizzy heights of complexity, beauty, and apparent design that dazzle us today."[8]

Like a frightened visitor to Dracula's castle waving his crucifix at every moving shadow, this is Dawkins' instinctive response when the evil question of evidence threatens to insinuate its grotesque presence. It is positively criminal that evidence intrudes on Dawkins' sublime recitation. It's nowhere apparent in the geological record (the Cambrian explosion) that natural selection ever operated anywhere except within a given kind (basic type). There are no observations within living kinds since (or before) Darwin of natural selection taking a simpler type and transforming it over time into a more complex and obviously different kind (a reptile to a bird, etc.). Yes, natural selection (NS, hereafter) does allow for certain *limited lateral* change within kinds, but the very DNA within each organism functions primarily to *preserve* those distinct characteristics, to *resist* innovation.

As a biologist, Dawkins is aware of this. He also knows *why* innovation is resisted—because, overall, it *weakens* an organism. While it might confer, under the most favorable circumstances, an advantage with regard to a specific obstacle, this is accomplished at the expense of *reduced* ability to contend with many other challenges. In other words, overall survivability is *lowered.* This is the insurmountable problem for NS: The kind of innovation that can even induce the brand of vertical change that could lead to higher complexity requires an invasive assault on the whole DNA *conservation* matrix. All observed mechanisms that produce these mutations unfortunately (for Dawkins) produce no new information and often a net *loss.*

Higher complexity would require a genetic information increase. Gene duplication is often forwarded as a solution to the need for more information. This is where an extra "unemployed" gene is available for nature to tinker with. But supposing these non-expressed genes provide material for mutations to work on that is free of selection pressure is a nonstarter. Dr. Jonathan Sarfati explains: "This 'idea' is just a lot of hand-waving. It relies on a chance event, genes somehow being switched off, randomly mutating to something approximating a new function, then being switched on again so natural selection can tune it."[9]

A more fundamental problem is that information cannot be explained in naturalistic terms. It is neither mass nor energy. So how might it be generated through any recourse to nature? Since at no point does Dawkins try to explain *how* NS overcomes this devastating termination, his assertion is nothing less than a demonstration of his unwavering faith, much like the faith he ridicules Christians for. It would be false, though, to place the Christian creed of, say, the resurrection, on par with Dawkins' sacred creed. The resurrection was attested to by more than five hundred witnesses. There are zero witnesses to Dawkins' article of faith.

Dawkins' materialist atheism is truly remarkable in that it places blind faith in a process that *smears* the coding (imagine shaking a simple constructed sentence on a scrabble board and getting a more complex message) of a DNA sequence which is already exceedingly complex and specified. The DNA in each human cell contains about one thousand five-hundred-page books of information,[10] making DNA the most efficient storage/retrieval system in the universe.[11] More problematic than extracting new information from a blurring effect, this physical impossibility would have to be overcome countless multiplied millions of times.

Dawkins is of course, logic notwithstanding, free to confer all sorts of magical properties on NS. He is free to believe that regardless of the laws of physics, somehow NS finds a way. There is no limit to the amount of faith he can place in NS because he is, after all, a believer. And according to today's rules, if a respected highly credentialed materialist speaks *ex cathedra*, then it becomes holy writ in what today passes for "science."

Dawkins' colleague and fellow atheist, the late Stephen Jay Gould, however, simply could not muster this kind of blind faith. For Gould, it was easier to believe in a relative few "naturalistic miracles" (saltationism) of enormous proportion than endless smaller successive miracles. The geologic period known as the Cambrian was especially troublesome. If the "geologic column" truly was a representation of the assumed evolution process, then "for billions of years," to quote the heading in a *Time* magazine article, "simple creatures like plankton, bacteria, and algae ruled the earth. Then suddenly, life got very complicated."[12] "Nearly every major branch in the zoological tree," fully formed, emerged in no more than ten million years, some putting the period at half that.[13] This may seem a lot of time, but in evolution terms this is the blink of an eye. This collection included everything from classes and orders to families, genera, and species. There are no transitions leading to this astounding complexity. What's more, this incredible phenomenon has been observed all over the world, meaning the explosion of complexity occurred in, for all intents, the same instant of geologic time. In fact, the Cambrian period is commonly referred to as "biology's big bang."

Gould was quoted as referring to the life forms of the Cambrian as "weird wonders" in his 1989 book *Wonderful Life*. Transitional fossils should have been plentiful if classic Darwinism were true. None of the explanations were satisfactory. The idea that transition fossils would have mostly consisted of soft body parts and thus would have eluded preservation did not hold up. The fossilized remains of soft-bodied marine creatures were remarkably well preserved in sandstone beds featuring well-delineated species. Moreover, in the Cambrian, "Preserved were not just the hard-shelled creatures familiar to Darwin and his contemporaries but also the fossilized remains of soft-bodied beasts like *Aysheaia and Ottoia*. More astonishing still were remnants of delicate interior structures, like *Ottoia's* gut with its last, partly digested meal."[14]

Rather than abandon the theory of evolution, Gould offered what he believed to be the only way to salvage the theory: The fossil record did not contain any bona fide transitional candidates because change, when it occurred, was taking place in leaps too rapid to be captured in the record (a revisiting of Goldschmidt's old "hopeful monster theory"). Ever since Gould proposed his "punctuated equilibrium" in the early '70s, both sides have held the other in derisive contempt. Each has painstakingly demonstrated (from the scientific method) the utter absurdity of the other's position.

More illumination of Dawkins out of his depth: "Ever since the nineteenth century, scholarly theologians have made an overwhelming case that the gospels are not reliable accounts of what happened in the history of the real world. All were written long after the death of Jesus."[15] Yes, and the overwhelming case Dawkins refers to is, much like the current case for evolution, based on overwhelmingly unproven (as shown in previous chapters), highly biased, preferred, and thoroughly *discredited* assumptions. "I shall not consider the Bible further as evidence for any kind of deity."[16] What a scholarly approach to examining the evidence. Dawkins simply sweeps aside enormous obstacles to his position then says, "What obstacles?" Lest we should accuse him of a less than rigorous methodology, though, he does cite the work of Bart Ehrman[17] and that scholarly giant Dan Brown.[18]

"The argument from improbability, properly deployed, comes close to proving that God does *not* exist. My name for the statistical demonstration that God almost certainly does not exist is the Ultimate Boeing 747 gambit."[19] This is a play on Fred Hoyle's famous tornado-in-a-junkyard metaphor. It is also a non sequitur. Dawkins overlooks just one little inconvenient matter: He is placing the determiner of God's probability squarely within the evolution/materialist paradigm. If God exists then He, according to Dawkins, would had to have come about through random, accidental, purposeless processes. Dawkins ignores the fact that the postulation of God is the *termination* of infinite regression (the uncaused first cause). *Something* must exist that did not require being brought into existence. Either this is an external Creator God, or some physical force contained within the universe. Whatever the uncaused first cause, it *cannot* be a product of its own creation.

Dawkins continues in this vein: "Seen clearly, intelligent design will turn out to be a redoubling of the problem. Once again, this is because the designer himself (herself/itself) immediately raises the bigger problem of his own origin. . . . Far from terminating the vicious regress, God aggravates it with a vengeance."[20] Dawkins is again projecting on the theist the evolutionary paradigm in admonishment of the God-theory. Note to Mr. Dawkins: "God" is presented as an *alternative* to the evolution story (actually, the other way around). Again, something must exist from all eternity that is self-sustaining and has no prior cause, that is not *contingent*, or we and the universe would not be here. This is a given, whether theist or atheist. There is nothing in physics that allows something to come from *no thing*!

Dawkins likes to harangue intelligent-design advocates for, as he sees it, conjuring up the ghost of old Paley and his "God of the gaps." This is intriguing. Between emphatic assertions such as "natural selection is the unassailable mechanism of biological change" and "the evolution of simpler organisms to more complex is a *known fact*," etc., exists, well, a gap. The gap consists of the following: no idea how life ever got started; no observation of NS facilitating new kinds; no unambiguous transitional fossils though the record consists of millions uncovered comprising some 250,000 species; no examples of *living* intermediates (bridging kinds) observed in nature; no credible explanation how a mutation which frequently *reduces* information might lead to greater complexity; no explanation why the Cambrian layer suddenly explodes with life in its myriad and highly complex forms; no explanation why humans and apes, though morphologically remarkably similar, are separated by an intellectual unbridgeable gulf that remains fixed, no matter how many efforts are made to engineer some tiny step toward closing the gap.

Though materialistic assurances proliferate, the gap between assertion and evidence grows ever wider. Thus, we presume we are to interpret Dawkins' upbraiding of ID specialists as a critique of degree and not of kind. These fellows are simply guilty of thinking too small; worshiping the God of the gaps when they could join Dawkins on the high road and worship the God of *the* gap.

In defense of less-than-fully-formed organs or limbs and their usefulness to an organism, Dawkins offers:

> Half a wing is indeed not as good as a whole wing, but it is certainly better than no wing at all. Half a wing could save your life by easing your fall from a tree of a certain height. And 51 per cent of a wing could save you if you fall from a slightly taller tree . . . there must be a smooth gradient of advantage all the way from 1 per cent of a wing to 100 per cent.[21]

But what about the distinct *disadvantage* a slight wing protrusion would initially pose? Whatever gliding advantage gained would surely not compensate for the loss of agility and speed vital in the most routine functions. A prototype wing would have to be well advanced to achieve a useful tradeoff for the loss in aerodynamics. Yet this would require NS *preserving* these protrusions (though a decided nuisance) through numerous gradations, anticipating a future advantage. Natural selection, however, by Dawkins' definition anticipates nothing; it works only in the immediate, under the intense pressure of ceaseless competition. Rather than conferring gliding advantages, the most primitive protrusions would far more likely result in increased drag and thus *reduce* vital jumping ability. We notice that in Dawkins' examples, he always imagines an idealized state where real-world practicalities may not intrude. In the idealized world constrained by nothing but imagination, it is indeed as Dawkins says, "easy."

According to Dawkins, it's a sign of intellectual laziness to deem certain biological or chemical machinery "irreducibly complex" just because the subtraction of some of the parts would render one of these machines useless and thus likely to be eliminated long before it achieved functionality. "The speedy resort to a dramatic proclamation of 'irreducible complexity' represents a failure of the imagination."[22] When did "imagination" become the cornerstone of science? What about quaint things like evidence, testing, observation, making predictions that are falsifiable? When were these cast aside in favor of a contest to see who could conjure up the most fantastic game of make-believe? Wasn't the Enlightenment mission all about exorcizing the ancient tendency to appeal to the imagination in favor of a rational, empirical reality? Indeed, wasn't the *modern scientific method* about discovery triumphing over imagination?

It's one thing to use imagination as a highly constrained tool while keeping oneself firmly grounded in empirics. It is another to make imagination the foundation, giving it free rein while only occasionally referencing observed phenomena. The problem with assigning primacy to imagination is that its hypotheses eventually break down into something remarkably difficult to separate from ancient pagan creation myths.[23]

CHAPTER 30

THE GOD DELUSION, PART II

Dawkins continues, as he winds through his book, to hammer home his case on why scientists must not allow a divine foot in the door. Not only does His admittance terminate scientific inquiry but at no point is His postulation *necessary*. The elegance and superiority of natural selection is that it does away with the need for both design *and* chance. Christianity exhibits its dearth of sophistication in that its basic tenets can pop up anywhere, at any time, especially in the most primitive societies. And, as a bonus, Dawkins graciously shares a little pearl with his readers: Christianity is not an alternate explanation to the universe at all; it is itself no more than a quirky little evolution mutation.

"Such work [scientific investigation] would never be done if scientists were satisfied with a lazy default such as 'intelligent design theory' would encourage. Here is the message that an imaginary 'intelligent design theorist' might broadcast to scientists. . . . Dear scientist, don't *work* on your mysteries."[1] This is, of course, another non sequitur. At this very time, materialists are working feverishly to find a "unified theory of everything"—one that would provide an elegant, simplistic explanation to all the various phenomena of the universe. This is that explanation which would terminate the need for further explanations. If such a theory should ever be uncovered, does this mean science would cease? And if so, then doesn't this mean science is right now actively working toward its own demise?[2] If this is not a necessary conclusion, then why in principle should the postulation of an Intelligent Designer (a *personal* terminator to the question of origins) represent the death of science?

Moreover, this oft-repeated charge has never been validated by actual experience. If the assumption that the universe is designed and overseen by a sovereign being is a nonstarter and a "lazy default," how do we explain the breathtaking breakthroughs by scientists who completely embraced just this proposition? Since Dawkins is scorn to soil his hands in any kind of *study* of religion, actually seeking to investigate religious claims rather than regurgitating tired clichés, we might expect he would at least try to learn something about the modern scientific method we presume he holds sacred, and in particular, its *source*: Christian theism.

Even the Greeks, who achieved advances in empirics beyond their contemporaries, were constricted by their inability to recognize both transcendence and immanence existing in a sovereign, Supreme Being. They could conceive of "God" as an impersonal principle of pure actuality. But this left God unknowable and with no significant role. It also left evil unaccounted for and (presumably) reaching for its own potential. Greek thought could do no better than default to some variation of the philosopher-king as the ultimate interpretive principle.

But since knowledge is derivative, and *exhaustive* knowledge cannot reside in any man, reality was always subject to changing nature—nature was fluid, thus truth was fluid (essentially the model for Hegel's "breakthrough" idea of replacing being with becoming). For knowledge to exist as a *possibility*, it must reside somewhere exhaustively. If there is no source of exhaustive knowledge, then one set of conclusions about reality is of no more value than any other. Knowledge dissolves into cerebral convulsions. Truth ceases, and reality is but a shifting kaleidoscope of absurdity and chaos—nihilism.

It was specifically the revelation of *the* Supreme Being through Jesus Christ that brought to the world a new realism that would eventually subdue the demon-haunted world (to borrow a Carl Sagan phrase). The universe did not yield its secrets because man had suddenly reached a plateau of reason, but because of the revelation of ultimate truth, Christ. Revelation of *the* Absolute put man in position to optimize reason. As man has rejected revelation, so too have his reasoning faculties diminished, perhaps precipitously.

If ultimate truth is conceded, then man *cannot* be the measure of all things. If ultimate truth does not exist, then neither does knowledge. Thus, to reject the existence of a transcendent (yet immanent) all-knowing, sovereign God is to reject any basis for reason. It is regrettable that Aquinas borrowed Aristotle's model to infer that God's existence could be apprehended through reason. This puts it exactly backward. We come to reason *because* of God. Reason exists because God *first* exists. When God is denied, reason unravels with nothing left to anchor to, and truth is replaced with chaos as the starting (and eventually end) point.

"If the history of science shows us anything, it is that we get nowhere by labeling our ignorance 'God.'"[3] Another empty assertion. It assumes a history that has never existed. No theistic scientist since Copernicus/Galileo has labeled ignorance "God." It has been the *assumption* of God and the underlying order of His creation that spurred scientific inquiry. The question was always framed "*How* has God integrated these systems and *what* are His laws that guide the universe, etc.?" As to the fear of too easily defaulting to "God," isn't the better question, how do we get anywhere by labeling our ignorance "chance"? And though Dawkins tries to deny this is the only alternative to design, his version of NS is imbued with magical properties that in fact owes an immense debt to chance.

"To suggest that the first cause . . . is a being capable of designing the universe and of talking to a million people simultaneously, is a total abdication of the responsibility to find an explanation."[4] *Why*? How is positing a cause sufficient to explain the observed effect either irrational or irresponsible? If God is the ultimate truth, what will come of a process that seeks to uncover truth by denying it at its very source? As God is defined *out* of the process, there remains no check, no device to reel it back from what can only become an ever more contorted, convoluted enterprise that cares naught for science (the advancement of *knowledge*) but acts only to preserve its own religious convictions.

Our suspicions are heightened when we see explanations that, if presented under any other circumstance (than the desperate need to get around God), would surely be a source of embarrassment. If no evidence is ever allowed to weigh in *favor* of God's existence, then nothing in principle exists to check an assumption that may be wrong. This ensures that the process must move *away* from truth, order, knowledge, meaning, etc.—a one-way proposition entirely. Christianity, unlike Darwinism, has dared to make claims that are subject to refutation by physical and circumstantial evidence. It did not (and does not) seal its claims from examination, invoking the special privileges of evolution "science."

Dawkins rhapsodizing over the efficiency of nature in comparison to cumbersome religion: "Religion is so wasteful, so extravagant; and Darwinian selection habitually targets and eliminates waste. Nature is a miserly accountant . . . punishing the smallest extravagance."[5] Like, for example, a protrusion that will one day become a wing?

Dawkins of course bristles at the idea that the only two possibilities are design and chance. According to Dawkins, there's a third, far-too-often-overlooked choice: natural selection. Natural selection does away with the need for chance because it works relentlessly along a path of utility. It slowly engineers great machines through addressing one small (and immediate) necessity at a time. Even if we accept his premise, he has of course omitted an important bit of information: Natural selection only works on organisms already in existence. It has no power to bring inanimate matter to life. No matter how many experiments are conducted, we never see life spring from non-life. In fact, we are no closer today to understanding how life (from a naturalistic view) might have started than in Darwin's day. Experiments and expanding knowledge have not yielded pathways to a solution, but have only erected more and far greater obstacles than ever imagined. What has become exceedingly clear is that the phenomenon we call "life" would require an immense long shot, a very rare (there's that pushy word) *chance* event.

As life has never been observed arising spontaneously from non-life, the odds are incalculable. But the prospect, however remote, becomes even more muddled when we consider some of those "obstacles." Even in its most primitive form, a living organism requires more than the right ratios of various chemicals stirred and catalyzed in a warm little pond. If just the right combination of necessary events, chemicals, environment, alignment (including all left-handed amino acids and right-handed nucleic acids), spark, etc., converged in the same moment of time to miraculously send life winging on its way, this would indeed be remarkable.

As improbable as this is, it only addresses the hurdles that must be crossed to get life *started*. *Keeping* life going is exponentially more formidable. *Reproduction* of the original "simple" organism is more daunting still. If life is to progress along some evolutionary pathway, several major parallel systems, each addressing radically different but vital functions, must come into existence in a single organism *at the same time*. The processes of life require the execution of highly complex and specific instructions. But something even far more complex also must exist to decode or "read" the instructions. For instance, a book represents a very complex arrangement of information, but the human *reader* of that book is more complex beyond any measurable factor.

The issue of reproduction introduces mind-numbing problems all its own. Reproduction makes no contribution to individual survivability. It speaks of teleology—that nature has some *interest* in promoting life in the future. The reproductive system thus must come into existence simultaneously with all these other major systems, the absence of any one resulting in the immediate cessation of life. Each one of these systems, itself immeasurably complex, must not simply be present—it must *coordinate* with every other system, interacting, communicating, and facilitating smooth transitions. This means that brand-new, highly complex systems that are complete strangers not only *anticipate* precise sequential handoffs but somehow understand they are involved in a concert that is bigger and more important than any one. But what is to keep these primary systems from ganging up on the reproductive system that is contributing *nothing* to the organism's survivability? None of this even addresses the innumerable ancillary systems that must be present for each primary system to function.

If it seems the above may not be quite as daunting as it sounds, "Even the simplest known true self-reproducing organism, *Mycoplasma genitalium* (a parasite bacterium) has 482 genes with 580,000 'letters' (base pairs). But even this appears not to be enough to sustain itself without parasitizing an even more complex organism."[6] In the state of nature, the tendency is not to integrate radically diverse systems but to resist integration (try meshing a toaster with a TV). Diverse systems don't just glom on to each other. They tend to short-circuit each other's operations, interfere with delicate timing, and gum up the works.

If chance finds a way to bring breathtaking diversity and complexity into a single organism and stumble upon a yet-unknown spark of life, all components must fire simultaneously in perfect concert or life never leaves the launch pad. Lest we think chance is out of the equation from this point forward, though, its role is paramount every additional step of the way. The available candidates that NS will choose from will be decided by the generation of mutations (copying errors), dispensed from an immeasurable hopper. The far greater likelihood is that poor choices will be available which would terminate the process, than candidates that enhance the march to greater complexity and survivability. In fact, Dawkins gives the game away: "Biologists acknowledge that a gene may spread through a population not because it is a good gene but simply because it is a lucky one."[7]

Dawkins' dissertation on "faith": "Faith (belief without evidence) is a virtue. The more your beliefs defy the evidence, the more virtuous you are."[8] This would make Dawkins a virtuoso of virtuousness. This also reveals another gross failure of Dawkins to apprehend basic Christian concepts. Faith, in the Bible, is never presented as something set against evidence. Faith is essentially *grounded* in evidence. The test of faith is to trust in the *demonstrated* pattern of God's dealings with mankind and to believe that the same God responsible for that pattern will fulfill His promises. If God was willing to validate His own existence and ability to save to the uttermost by physically coming to earth, dying for the sins of mankind, and resurrecting, it can hardly be said this belief in God demands a blind faith. The issue is not, as Dawkins predictably miscasts it, God/faith vs. evolution/science, but *reasonable* faith (God) vs. *unreasonable* faith (evolution).

To demonstrate how ridiculously easy it would be to initiate a Christian-like religion, Dawkins shares the delightful tale of an island of primitive inhabitants and the poignant legend that grew out of an unexpected encounter. According to the story, an American named John Frum once visited the island and made such an impression with his mastery of magical gadgets (such as a radio) that this was taken to be a sign of his deity. Purportedly, Mr. Frum announced an approaching time of great upheaval followed by unprecedented prosperity. The legend grew that John had promised he would return someday bearing wonderful gifts. The expectation of this glorious return produced sightings, unexpected trances and the like, and of course, an annual religious ceremony marking the date of the promised return. Though years pass with no return, the fervor and absolute commitment to this belief does not waver. Pressed to explain this sacred belief in spite of the years, a native responds, "If you can wait two thousand years for Jesus Christ to come an'e no come, then I can wait more than nineteen years for John."[9]

We are expected, of course, to see this as a parallel to the Christ story. Except the implication is that Christians are bigger rubes than these poor island natives, holding to an irrational faith which even these simple souls would likely have abandoned long ago. This does illustrate very nicely, however, what passes for reasoned argument in Dawkins' mind. If the approach sounds a little too familiar, it is because it closely mirrors the line of reasoning Freke and Gandy take with their "dying/rising god-man" hypothesis: Assume superficial similarities equal central and fundamental connections.

Yes, the John Frum story does bear *some* resemblance to the Christ story, but let's consider a few significant differences. More than one hundred prophecies were given concerning Christ's first coming, many very specific. *All* were fulfilled. I don't recall any prophecies mentioned with respect to Mr. Frum's first coming. Christianity, in comparison to the island legend, didn't arise from almost nothing; it was intricately woven into a complex two-thousand-year history and a unique, exacting religious code. Jesus Christ performed miracles, died a brutal crucifixion death, and ratified His audacious claims through His resurrection. John Frum, in a striking parallel, "left the island."

In contrast to an isolated area where the John Frum religion could prosper unmolested, Christianity took shape in an environment intensely hostile, where Christian identification often meant death. Finally, the influence of Jesus Christ revolutionized the entire world, even though the revolution was often carried out by terribly flawed followers. What has been the effect of John Frum's influence? Only a mind as selectively engaged as Dawkins would see a meaningful parallel.

"But the moral superiority of Jesus precisely bears out my point. Jesus was not content to derive his ethics from the scriptures of his upbringing. He explicitly departed from them, for example when he deflated the dire warnings about breaking the sabbath."[10] More embarrassing ignorance of context. Jesus referred to the extenuating circumstances of David to make a point, that the Sabbath was made for man and not the reverse. The point of the Sabbath was, above all else, to honor God. Condemning an act of compassion and generosity on the Sabbath was, itself a violation of the Sabbath's intent. Jesus, incidentally (that radical fellow, as Dawkins sees Him), *kept* all the Law. He did not depart from it. He *fulfilled* it.

"What kind of ethical philosophy is it that condemns every child, even before it is born, to inherit the sin of a remote ancestor?"[11] How ethical is it that genetics should pass on *physical* characteristics in a purely materialistic world? "Augustine's pronouncements and debates epitomize, for me, the unhealthy preoccupation of early Christian theologians with sin. They could have devoted their pages and their sermons to extolling the sky splashed with stars, or mountains and green forests, seas and dawn choruses."[12] Yes, I suppose they could have. But human beings were not in desperate need of redemption from stars, mountains, or green forests.

"The historical evidence that Jesus claimed any sort of divine status is minimal. . . . A fourth possibility [to the trilemma—lunatic, liar, or lord?], almost too obvious to need mentioning, is that Jesus was honestly mistaken."[13] Unfortunately, He then compounded His error by rising from the dead. But Dawkins, to his credit, graciously concedes it was an honest mistake.

"We believe in evolution because the evidence supports it, and we would abandon it overnight if new evidence arose to disprove it. . . . I know what it would take to change my mind, and I would gladly do so if the necessary evidence were forthcoming."[14] This is bold talk and certainly gives the impression of genuine open-mindedness; most commendable. Yet perhaps Dawkins needs to share the scenario under which he would abandon evolution. Considering that the laws of physics pose the most serious obstacle to any evolution process, exactly what would it take to change his mind? Since Dawkins' belief in and defense of evolution resides almost entirely in the realm of imagination, there is no reason to suppose that any amount of empirical evidence could compete with a faith that insulates itself from any possibility it might be false.

"There are, then, people whose religious faith takes them right outside the enlightened consensus of my 'moral Zeitgeist.' They represent what I have called the dark side of religious absolutism, and they are called extremists."[15] This sounds a great deal like a moral distinction. But how can Dawkins inveigh against Christians who, by his reasoning, are a product of evolution and NS? Can NS make *mistakes*? Can it be possible to stand in judgment of nature? By what standard is one version of nature called good and another evil? By the standard of "consensus"? If so, then it must be morally just for 51 percent of a population to imprison, rob, or exterminate the other 49 percent.

Dawkins hypothesizes that just as genes pass on biological characteristics, there is a sort of gene (he is pleased to call it a "meme," though it exists *only* in conceptual form) that passes on psychological characteristics. Since he is loath to place any phenomenon outside the reach of evolution and *assumes* that religion and especially the appeal to a Supreme Being is irrational, there must be some type of inherited unit that, though NS would likely eliminate it were it to come into existence individually, when it exists in concert with numerous other such units (making up a "memeplex") is far more likely to resist elimination. The various irrational but *integrated* and mutually supportive (and this is key) beliefs/virtues that make up a religion are a perfect example of such a memeplex. A memeplex is more likely to be selected when an entire community finds its mutual survivability enhanced by like-minded belief. Thus, is explained the origin of religion—not a deep yearning for a reunion with the Creator, not a result of perhaps many years of searching and investigation, but a curious short-circuiting of what represents normal survival instincts.

Does Dawkins really want to pursue this line of thinking? Is this maybe not a case of trying to prove too much? How might one ever *know* if one of these regressive memes has infected his thinking? How would Dawkins know he had not been infected with an "I-think-I-alone-possess-exhaustive-knowledge-which-is-blinding-me-to-the-truth" meme? How would he or anyone know that the very articles of faith that make up the evolution story is not one of these memeplexes? By what standard would it be possible to differentiate rational from *irrational* thought? Wouldn't one have to stand *outside* of nature to make ultimate judgments *about* nature?

In fact, this whole evolution of psychology that has become the latest fad in Darwinism seems to be locking *all* human behavior into some form of genetic determinism. But, interestingly, Dawkins denies that he is a prisoner to his genes. If Dawkins and his peers are free, as David Berlinski puts it, to tell their genes "to go jump in the lake," then his entire argument on psychological origins for religion is useless. Again, Berlinski says it best, "On current views, it is the gene that is selected by evolution, and if we are not controlled by our genes, we are not controlled by evolution. If we are not controlled by evolution, *evolutionary* psychology has no relevance to the origin or nature of the human mind."[16]

"But how can there be a perversion of faith, if faith, lacking objective justification, doesn't have any demonstrable standard to pervert?"[17] Precisely the question we would pose to Mr. Dawkins. Christians have a very stringent and demanding standard established in no less than Christ Himself. Where exactly *are* those boundaries of imagination (the foundation of evolution) that might be violated? Judeo-Christianity has made numerous predictions that have come to pass *verbatim*. What has Darwinism predicted that has been validated? That change takes place over time? Who could have guessed? Why would we *not* abandon Christianity and any semblance of civilizing principles for something with this much explanatory power?

"Maybe if you repeat something often enough, you will succeed in convincing yourself of its truth."[18] Such as, evolution is a *fact*? "Maybe our prayers for the dead really *are* pointless. To presume the opposite is to presume the truth of the very conclusion we seek to prove."[19] And maybe God *does* exist. And to presume the opposite is to presume the truth of the very conclusion we seek to prove.

"Not explaining science seems to me perverse" [quoting Carl Sagan].[20] Not anchoring science in an eternal unchanging absolute that exists outside of the *decaying* material universe seems to me not just perverse but a logical absurdity. Absent this, how can there be any such thing as science?

"Miracles are events that are extremely improbable. A statue of a Madonna could wave its hand at us . . . the jiggling atoms in the hand *could* all just *happen* to move in the same direction at the same time. And again. And again . . . but the odds against are so great that, if you had set out writing the number at the origin of the universe, you still would not have written enough zeroes to this day."[21] Dawkins can't seem to resist mixing worldviews. Miracles, as portrayed within religious themes, occur to validate the existence of a reality *outside* the material universe, a reality not governed by physical laws. Nevertheless, even if we indulge Dawkins' propensity for mixing opposing views, the waving hand of a Madonna statue (by physical coincidence) is still infinitely more probable than something emerging from nothing. It is also far more probable than life arising spontaneously in violation of the laws of physics.

"We considered the improbability of the origin of life and how even a near-impossible chemical event must come to pass given enough planet years to play with; and where we considered the spectrum of possible universes."[22] From a purely naturalistic standpoint, Dawkins is unwittingly arguing that the resurrection was inevitable, especially since all the complex systems are already in place in a deceased human. Reanimating a human corpse would surely be an immeasurably easier feat for nature than having to bridge all the mind-boggling gaps and surmounting the dizzying array of obstacles to bringing all this staggering complexity into a single organism and *then* producing that spark of life. We wonder, then, why Dawkins steadfastly resists the evidence for resurrection when it is so overwhelming and, according to his reasoning, should have occurred at least once "given enough planet years to play with" and when "considering the spectrum of possible universes."

When we consider the reverential awe with which Dawkins bows before the irresistible force of natural selection or chance or whatever mystical naturalistic urge he is willing to bet the farm on, this simple reanimation should be (in Darwin's word) "easy." Regarding physical reality, Dawkins does a little hand-waving of his own. Why would the introduction of time (no matter how much we agree to concede) *reverse* physical laws? And if time *can* reverse natural processes, what happens to evolution—to *science*? Wouldn't this represent a far greater threat to the uniformity of science than those despised occasional miracles?

Dawkins on the indescribable ecstasy of being fully surrendered to one's God: "But perhaps you need to be steeped in natural selection, immersed in it, swim about in it, before you can truly appreciate its power."[23] There's something about this that bears striking resemblance to worship. Unfortunately, those masses of unwashed, those who have never been spirit-filled with the holy unction of natural selection, who are less than convinced by materialist assurances that all is well, can't help wondering at times if Darwinists really take themselves seriously. There is just so much special pleading, circular reasoning, just-so scenarios, and tongue-in-cheek platitudes ("we must not default to appeals that are beyond the realm of testability") that we half-expect materialists to pull back the curtain with a collective and resounding "Gotcha!"

> Think about it. On one planet, and possibly only one planet in the entire universe, molecules that would normally make nothing more complicated than a chunk of rock, gather themselves together into chunks of rock-sized matter of such staggering complexity that they are capable of running, jumping, swimming, flying, seeing, hearing, capturing and eating other such animated chunks of complexity; capable in some cases of thinking and feeling, and falling in love with yet other chunks of complex matter. We now understand essentially how the trick is done, but only since 1859.[24]

And what precisely is that essence of understanding to which Dawkins can barely contain his exuberance? What is that monumental discovery that has laid bare the profound complexity and interaction existing, as far as we can see, nowhere else in the universe? What is the essence of the breakthrough that has purportedly disproved Christianity and decided it is an evil; that has sought to restructure an entire culture in devastating ways, declared parents a greater danger to their children than a jealous state, aggressively implemented an entirely new value system, and, finally, coronated Darwinism the cornerstone of all reality? Oh yes, "change takes place over time." Why don't you think about it, Mr. Dawkins?

CHAPTER 31

THE IMPLICATIONS OF
DARWINIST-MATERIALIST THOUGHT

On now to the casual skeptic, who can be heard voicing a common complaint: "But if only God could do something to reveal Himself." Indeed, this is one of Dawkins' pet peeves—that only some perverse God would engage in this silly game of hide-and-seek. "Why does He have to make His existence so obscure that we can never know for sure?"

Let's consider this. We have a book that purports to be a revelation of God to mankind. This book records events that date to at least four thousand years ago and include a Supreme Being's plan of salvation for the world as it is brought forth through a specific people. Dramatic, detailed prophecies of coming events are given sometimes hundreds (sometimes thousands) of years before the fact. These prophecies are found to be uncannily accurate with the unfolding of history. The predictive element of prophecy speaks of some ability that is beyond the bounds of nature. Since all these prophecies (the negative as well as the favorable) come to pass, the indication is this is a power that is trustworthy.

"Okay, all that stuff is fine, but why doesn't this supposed God do or say something to let us know that He cares about us *personally* and that He's not just some sadistic monster out to take revenge the moment we step out of line?" Let's think about this: Suppose He were to *leave* His throne in heaven and just become one of us? Suppose He went further and came to live among His own in very humble circumstances, subjected to the same poverty, hurts, frustrations, injustices, and petty jealously as the least of us? What if He spoke words of wisdom and demonstrated selfless giving such as the world had never before or since seen? Suppose He performed miracles to show His mastery over nature—that He is not beholden to *any* of its laws? And what if, knowing that we were hopelessly incapable of lifting ourselves from the enslaving power of sin, He sacrificed *Himself,* submitting to the most grueling form of death, to *break* that power? Would that say something about a genuine depth of love for mankind? Now, what if He were to then perform His greatest miracle of all: to literally rise from the dead three days after His death, thus demonstrating the power to *recreate*, a power that could only be reserved for the *Creator Himself*?

And what if all these events were encased within circumstances that made it impossible to refute, though an innumerable company would line up to attempt this very thing almost from inception, attacking from every conceivable angle? Suppose more than one hundred prophecies were given concerning this Messiah's first advent and all were fulfilled *precisely*? Of this number, let's just consider the likelihood of fulfilling eight that are specific: 1) place of birth; 2) time of birth; 3) manner of birth; 4) betrayal; 5) manner of death; 6) the crowd's reaction at His trial and crucifixion; 7) piercing; 8) burial. The odds of fulfillment have been calculated at one in 10^{17} (one, followed by 17 zeroes). This conclusion has been arrived at through a rigorous methodology that has been submitted for peer review by a committee of the American Scientific Affiliation. The executive council of this same group has concluded that in general, the methodology is sound, and the figure arrived at reasonably accurate. In practical terms, 10^{17} silver dollars would cover the entire state of Texas to a depth of two feet. The likelihood that one man could fulfill all eight of the above prophecies by chance are equal to the likelihood that a blindfolded man dropped into Texas would be able to grab a special uniquely marked silver dollar with only a single pick.[1]

When we consider forty-eight specific prophecies, the odds soar to one in 10^{157}![2] As a matter of interest, mathematicians have arrived at a "probability threshold" below which the chance of occurrence is so infinitesimal as to be declared "zero probability." Most set the limit between 10^{50} and 10^{110}. In other words, an event that has less chance than one in 10^{110} of occurring cannot happen. A French mathematician, George Salet, stated the principle thus: "A phenomenon whose probability is sufficiently weak—that is, below a certain threshold—will never occur, 'never' meaning here within the limits of space and time at our disposal, that is to say within the limits which it is possible to repeat the trials, for as long as a world, all of whose known dimensions are finite, allows."[3]

Would the above constitute reasonable grounds for validating this person's claims, as well as this book's claim to represent the revelation of God? Suppose, moreover, that the claims and major events in this book's unfolding are presented within the space/time continuum where they are not only open to but *invite* investigation? What if there is also conspicuous circumstantial evidence that just won't go away?

Let's take all this still further: What if the effect of this person's life and recognition of His work of regeneration by, admittedly, exceedingly flawed followers who fail far more often (sometimes grievously) than succeed at His standard, nevertheless leads to unprecedented advances in the arts, science, charity, and government, culminating in a freedom revolution never before known? And finally, what if the most insidious, ingenious, and pernicious mode of human thought ever assembled, the "Enlightenment," were to bring its full weight to bear against the above belief system in a sustained open assault for more than two hundred years? What if every facet of Enlightenment resourcefulness from literature to materialistic science, to academia to political philosophy, to an entire entertainment industry and its awesome power to influence, took turns subjecting every element of this belief system to a perpetual microscopic exam, casting in the worst possible light?

What if over the course of this two-hundred-plus year period, time and again some definitive finding would pronounce the inaccuracy of the Bible, only to find with more evidence that its claims are vindicated? What if despite all this concerted never-ending effort to discredit this belief system, it continues to thrive and radically transform millions while its ancient competitors have all now either disappeared or been relegated to practical irrelevance? Would all the above constitute reasonable grounds for conceding God *does* exist, does have a *personal* interest in His creatures, and has given us a way to know what He expects of us?

Remember, the key word here is "reasonable." Even a court of law, where the stakes may literally be life or death, concedes that even the most meticulously constructed and airtight case cannot eliminate all doubt. Thus, the qualifier, *reasonable* doubt. Has a high enough degree of *probability* been established that any remaining doubt can no longer command serious consideration?

"Yeah, all right. I suppose all this does add up to a pretty compelling case. But if God really wants to reveal Himself, why does He have to make it this long, drawn-out process where we have to put all those pieces together? A lot of people are put off by this having-to-negotiate-a-maze stuff. I mean, rather than having these numerous religions and examining their competing claims, why can't God simply reveal Himself right here and now *directly*, take all the mystery out of it and do away with feuding religions?"

This seems a reasonable request, but what would the practical effect be? There is also the question of what it might take to satisfy hardcore skeptics (Darwinists). It would obviously require something that is so improbable that it would be absurd to defer to naturalistic explanations. The problem is we already have numerous examples of things (such as the dazzling specified complex language in DNA) that overwhelm naturalistic explanations, but skeptics remain unmoved. "Yes, it has the *appearance* of intelligent design to be sure, but we are confident there is no connection." So even if God were to project His awesome appearance all over the world simultaneously and thunder specific commands, would skeptics be convinced? After all, wouldn't it be presumptuous to deem this unusual phenomenon "God" without first investigating the atmospheric conditions that might well be responsible for this event? In fact, we are duty-bound to initially *assume* a naturalistic explanation since (as we have heard ad nauseam) "the admittance of God into the universe is the death of science." So, if we are to attempt to investigate the *possibility* of God, we must first assume His *impossibility* (is it only me or does the game seem rigged?).

As we can see, God would have to do quite a bit better than this. So, what if God were to project His appearance every day at precisely the same hour where the whole world could receive His audible instructions? What if every person who failed to carry out His commands verbatim for that day received the same form of retribution—say, painful sores all over the body that disappeared at precisely midnight? Meanwhile, no obedient person, for any given day, would experience sores that day. No doubt skeptics would be intrigued, but would they attribute this to God? Remember, if one cannot, by *definition*, have an inquisitive mind while entertaining the notion of a supernatural God, then there *must* be some other explanation. And "though we are completely at a loss to explain these extraordinary coincidences and improbable phenomena *at this time* we must resist the cowardly impulse to default to the 'God must have done it' mode of thinking. After all, in a universe this vast and this old, almost *any* cycle of recurring phenomena is bound to happen at least *once*! Moreover, we have every reason to suppose that a naturalistic explanation, perhaps in the far future, awaits our discovery."

The likelihood, sadly, is that though the number of people who would openly acknowledge a Creator God as the result of the above scenario might rise appreciably, this would produce such a radically different dynamic, it's hard to imagine any actual net increase in *worshipers*. Those previously undecided would now likely believe, but their "belief" would now be fundamentally different from anything it had meant before. At any rate, there is no reason to suppose religious materialists would abandon their faith under any circumstances.

But let's suppose the above did persuade everyone, Darwinists and all, to acknowledge the supernatural Supreme Being. Suppose everyone perfectly *obeyed* His unyielding commands. There remains a profound difference between belief as the effect of wooing by the Creator coupled with a desire by the creature to know and be reconciled to his Maker through diligent searching, seeking, knock-ing, whatever obstacles may be present, and belief by *compulsion*.

If we accept the (highly dubious) premise that seeing would automatically produce believing, then under this scenario there would no longer be a place for faith as there would no longer be anything left to *doubt*. Thus, there would be no framework for the kind of conflicts that cause human beings to reflect, learn, seek, and grow in understanding and character, no diligent journey of discovery. There would be no way to establish the desire of any "believer" to know his Creator, let alone to test his love for God. In fact, love would cease, unable to determine that any seeming altruistic actions were motivated by genuine caring, duty, honor, or simply fear.

There would no longer, of course, be any evil left in the world (at least practiced) because the threat of instant retaliation would compel even the worst reprobate to toe the line. But the far greater evil, to those whose belief and obedience exist only under the threat of force, would be this ever-present and imposing God who effectively short-circuits any sort of choice process.

The objection has nothing to do with God's mode of revelation but with His refusal to abdicate His throne to natural man. Equally evident, reason (as with conscience) is only as reliable as the standard to which it is calibrated. There is no mystery concerning the fact of His existence. God has made this evident through His general revelation (see Romans 1: 19-20) which natural man tacitly acknowledges each time he progresses through logical thought patterns, necessarily *assuming* the infallible, exhaustive, transcendent ground of truth upon which he is trespassing.

The mystery has to do with *Who* God is. But this is a quest that, though supplemented by intellect, must begin with a humble heart response. Absent this, rationalization quickly hollows out "God" to a *deus ex machina*; an exalted, intricately gilded shell barely obscuring the hubris it enshrines.

I happen not to believe in the Easter bunny any longer. Yet, mysteriously, I have never entertained the notion of writing a book expressing my contempt for this nonentity and expounding the dangers of those who do take the Easter-bunny hypothesis seriously. This has never even occurred to me (well, until now). Typically, one does not expend a great deal of time and energy (or thought) on things that pose no threat, especially if one is convinced the *source* of the "threat" doesn't exist. It's hard to accept that Richard Dawkins spent more than four hundred pages ranting against something he believes isn't even there. In fact, he goes through considerable pains to express his undying hatred for the being he has set out to *prove* is but a figment of imagination.

As for Dawkins' charge that religion (especially Christianity) has been a bane to the world, this is demonstrably false. Any fair assessment of history shows that belief in the Judeo-Christian God, especially as manifest in Christ, has introduced far more good into the world than the evil produced by its very worst representatives. Moreover, this evil always required a grave departure from the very Scriptures for which they feigned allegiance. It can be shown that Dawkins' atheistic worldview *has* produced unprecedented evil in a remarkably short time, not by departing from but faithfully *adhering* to its basic tenets:

> Mao killed about 72 million human beings from 1948 to 1976. When we add the 40 million Stalin is responsible for, we come to a number of 112 million. Throw in Hitler's 15 million (not counting the devastating war he started!), and we come to about 127 million. Add other killings by other atheistic and totalitarian states—as a result of their atheistic ideology—you come up with more than 130 million. . . . Using the most exaggerated criteria and numbers, one could come up with no more than 17 million people killed by professing Christians "in the name of Christ" in *twenty centuries* of Christian history.[4]

Those who have committed atrocities under the banner of Christianity cannot be excused. This ugly black mark, though again, done in *repudiation* of Christian principles, cannot be swept under the rug. But from a pure numbers comparison, the evil directly produced from Enlightenment atheism (and this does not even address the more than 1 billion aborted unborn babies in the last century) is light years beyond the evil due to even the shakiest Christian association. Yet this has not put the tiniest dent in Dawkins' faith. Thus, this is a non-issue and can be eliminated as a legitimate concern.

To be sure, no one would think to impose on Mr. Dawkins a form of worship for which he is uncomfortable. He is of course entirely within his rights to choose instead to worship that mystical naturalistic force in defiance of rational explanation and to call it whatever he likes—Buddha, Odin, Marduk, natural selection, the Force, the Easter bunny, Peter Pan. He is even free to *imagine* (his apparent preferred exercise) that someday Tinker Bell will reveal to him those esoteric mysteries of natural selection. But he ought to be honest enough to admit that the sacred reverence he gives to his belief system is sheltered in *religious conviction*. Frankly, it would be easier to take Dawkins seriously if, instead of ostentatiously strutting the hallowed halls of science where echoes of heroes like Kepler, Galileo, Copernicus, Linnaeus, Mendel, Pasteur, and Einstein still linger, he donned a necklace of talismans and danced the fertility two-step of his pagan ancestors. His faith would still be blind superstition but, one hopes, not so caustic. Couldn't we sum up Dawkins' entire case for evolution and against Christianity with these words: "There is no God but natural selection and Darwin is its prophet (and Dawkins its present high priest)"?

*   *   *

The danger of theism, we are often reminded, is the temptation to invoke the "God must have done it" explanation. This, alas, would be the death of science. But what does a Darwinist do when he comes to an impasse, a sticky reality that is hostile to evolutionary assumptions? "There must be numerous other universes where laws act differently from the universe we occupy. Something in those unobserved, unknowable, untestable universes (forever sealed from our investigations) *may* have engineered our universe." Why is this "theory" proposed?

Because nothing in our universe will permit its own creation. In effect, Darwinists are conceding they have no idea how to explain our present reality in terms of *any known laws of physics* or even how a fish can become a man, but they are confident that "the grand multiverse (the landscape) must have done the former" and "natural selection must have done the latter." Yet we can no more observe the landscape creating than we can God. And though we can observe NS, we have never actually seen it perform except in a *conserving* role.

These two presumed miracle workers are no less a starting assumption than God. How then are we advanced in our knowledge by invoking a mystery? Especially since this mystery requires ever more ingenious just-so tales that exist only in the realm of imagination, safe from any sort of empirical testing or refutation. Either invoking a mystery is the termination of science, or it is not. If science can proceed from an assumption that can never be verified, there is no reason in principle why the acknowledgment of God should stifle the desire to know the details of His creation. In fact, creationists can point to tremendous advances that have come about under just this assumption. Darwinists are not just invoking an unknown; they are appealing to a faith that violates all experience and intuition.

For all that materialists have sought, at least in theory, to expand horizons of understanding, to conjure up multiverses, their own universe continues to collapse around them. Their shrinking sphere is evident in the reductionist reality to which they bind themselves and insist we all follow suit. No longer is it permissible that something might exist which is greater than the sum of its parts (love, mind, life, courage, duty, valor, self-sacrifice, knowledge, justice, etc.). Had natural selection taken just a slightly different path, instead of pursuing these inspiring qualities we might have had nothing greater to aspire to than incessant belching and tap-dancing (simultaneously). Thus, we are left with Dawkins' hedonistic model, "If it feels good, do it . . . as long as no one is harmed." But what if "harm" is more than an obvious outward manifestation? What if the inward psychological damage of human reductionism turns out to be immeasurably harmful? What if that which civilizes us is at stake?

As we make our final assessment of the whole naturalistic/materialistic paradigm, it seems fair to ask, what has been the whole point of evolution? What could possibly urge a struggle for survival when extinction is a foregone inevitability and survival only *prolongs* the misery of a meaningless existence? "But others will live on, and things will improve." So what? If they do, what is the net gain? Knowledge? Experience? Of *what*, and to what *end*? That life is a vanishing vapor and whatever body of knowledge accumulated, even vast libraries (allowing a purposeless universe can contain knowledge), will one day be indistinguishable from the ashes of the wino's bottle? As many have pondered, would the most exhaustive comprehensive knowledge of what *is* ever yield a clue as to what *ought* to be? Just why *should* something have existed instead of nothing?

Indeed, if NS really were about conferring an "advantage" and motivated by selfish interests, wouldn't it be *advantageous* to extinguish life in its incipient moments, to short-circuit the long track of a meaningless, worthless, useless, pain-racked struggle we call life? If the God of Judeo-Christianity is, according to Dawkins' caricature, contemptible and sadistic, what does this make the god of natural selection? What could be more cruel and reprehensible than to create an illusion of transcendent experiences we call love, duty, and honor, only to pull the rug out and gleefully shout "Surprise, only kidding!"? What could be more despicable than to impart a sense of conscious self-awareness, a desire to *want* to survive, to *want* to love and pursue beauty, to *want* to gain knowledge—only to be reminded in the end it was all just a grand cosmic joke, just another chemical process no more significant than passing gas?

Healthy skepticism of biblical claims is not unwarranted, but what about healthy skepticism of atheistic materialism? Is it okay to doubt the monolithic faith Darwinists place in things that are counterintuitive? Is there a point where it *is* okay for skeptics to be suspicious of theories that exist only because the alternative is unacceptable to religious materialists? At which point is it okay to assume that a threshold exists where science ceases, and there remains only a proposition devoted to dismantling aspects of reality deemed loathsome? Or should we all just pledge blind allegiance to something *called* science and worship around its altars no matter how speculative, fanciful, culturally suicidal, or irrelevant evidence becomes? Isn't this the objection materialists have hurled at "religion," and the very reason "incorruptible" science was proclaimed the path of the enlightened?

Darwinism has long and successfully employed the strategy of tying its fate to the whole scientific community. It has vigorously promoted the notion that philosophic materialism's demise will be the demise of all science. In this, it has at best grossly overestimated its importance. Darwinists are working feverishly to, perhaps more than anything, keep themselves from becoming the laughing stock of the scientific world. Holes are popping out everywhere.

History appears poised to render its verdict, and it is not favorable. It has become evident this is an enterprise almost entirely financed on credit *from the beginning* and the debt it has piled up against such meager returns has become crushing. When this house of cards collapses, however, the structure (science) over which Darwinism has superimposed itself will still stand. Why? Because *that* edifice stood tall and proud long before Darwinism huffed and puffed but mostly *bluffed* its way to a hegemony.

On its face, what exactly has Darwinism contributed to any *operational* science? Are there any technologies, whether medical, aeronautical, astrophysical, industrial, or otherwise, that would even notice Darwinism's collapse? Where has Darwinism's chief contribution to civilization actually manifested? Has it really contributed anything, apart from a vacuum of meaning and cultural disintegration?

CHAPTER 32

THE WORST GENERATION

The chickens that were loosed in the 1960s have come home to roost. Today we can see the destructiveness and incoherence of progressive thought everywhere. Those Americans who made incredible sacrifices (both abroad and at home) to overcome the forces of tyranny in World War II are often referred to as "the greatest generation." If this is an apt description then my generation that followed, the baby-boomers, can with some justification be called "the worst generation." Traditionally, adolescence has been a rite of passage; a time for testing the waters in preparation for adulthood. Taking one's place in the community as a responsible contributing citizen was not a thing to be despised but eagerly and impatiently anticipated. Being a mature adult was a sign of success, of having come into one's own.

Among its sterling contributions, my generation decided that youthful rebellion against authority need not be restricted to the teen years but could be institutionalized into a lifelong vocation. As such my generation invented an entirely new youth culture where adolescent drives, tastes, and ideals could be maintained into one's forties, fifties, sixties, and beyond. The worst generation was the first to disregard context when it came to facing serious issues. The assumption was that this was a special generation endowed with a cosmic wisdom which the world had never been prepared to receive. This generation would finally show the courage to lead the way—to throw off that oppressive yoke that had led to all those nasty wars. Reason had been taking a beating since the French Revolution. The worst generation definitively displaced reason with "feeling." The most lamentable casualty in the war on God: wisdom.

My generation was the first to conclude that keeping one's own sorry rear end alive was more important than making sacrifices to preserve a freedom that all previous generations intuitively understood *had* to be made. In fact, it was now assumed that freedom was the natural order, a given if greedy capitalists could be kept in their proper place. It never occurred to the cosmically endowed that against the record of history, freedom was an aberration. Perhaps the greatest failing of my generation is that it failed to pass on much of a structured value system (apart from emotional sloganeering) to its children. Not too surprisingly, having abandoned "enslaving traditional morality," about the only thing offspring could extract from their self-absorbed parents was there are no absolutes; truth is whatever each decides, and never let consideration for others (including family) stand in the way of appetite. This would, of course, unleash on the nation a particularly aimless generation that lacked any sort of moral grounding or contextual framework for viewing its world. Insecurity, arrogance, and gullibility would be the dominant features that distinguished the children fathered by the worst generation.

Thankfully, not all in my generation succumbed to its popular notions. Some (such as my wife) saw this for what it was from day one. The rest of us would have to muddle through and experience life in its real complexities for several years until we could see what an infantile set of premises this was predicated upon. Yes, all those things had sounded so noble and seemed so axiomatic but they simply (like it or not) had no relationship to reality. Worse than this, they turned out to be extremely destructive. But not all in my generation would allow reality to intrude upon cherished youthful assumptions. A sizeable number would stubbornly resist learning the lessons, no matter how many times these assumptions, put into practice, produced devastating results.

Today, this group of hardcore progressives from the worst generation and its offspring has found itself a home. It has entrenched itself in the power structure of the modern Democratic Party, where dissenting voices are no longer tolerated. It fills judgeships, doling out imperial decrees from on high, ignoring any constitutional restraints. It fills the ranks of the dominant media, blaring its irrational propaganda, ever ratcheting up the hysteria. Others sit in ivory towers as tenured professors—free to indoctrinate malleable young minds with hate-filled bilge; protected by speech codes that override the First Amendment, thus eliminating any possible challenge.

The Frankfurt School would be pleased with the soulless and mindless generation sitting in college classrooms today. Where universities were once institutions of higher learning where young minds were challenged to wrestle with competing ideas, to explore new horizons by looking deeper into their assumptions, discovering whether those ideas could be sustained by unyielding facts and sound argumentation, universities have now been reduced to cathedrals of totalitarianism, nurseries of a fragile species that abhors critical thinking and must be insulated from hurtful views. To that end, colleges have now created a new and most destructive reality—the absence of conflict. To be without conflict is to *deny* the soul those new horizons, unique challenges and opportunities to stand or flee. Without conflict, there can be no journey of self-discovery, no way to ever distinguish oneself from paramecium. But of course, that was always the intent—to extinguish human souls.

To further reduce the possibility reality might breach the illusion of these delicate daffodils, one more layer of political correctness has been divined—microaggressions. Microaggressions take the concept beyond mere conscious, deliberate racism into the realm of unconscious, subtle racism expressed in phrases such as "taking personal responsibility," "hard-work ethic," "playing by the rules," "honesty," "there is only one race, the human race," etc. Thus, any attempt to make *any* case against the orthodoxy of leftist ideology, no matter how thoughtful or well-reasoned, is deemed racism and out of bounds. This is a direct repudiation of the First Amendment which *invites* new ideas, open debate, and even protects the vilest speech. Substituted now for independent, rational, critical thought is groupthink, oblique non sequiturs that of course hang on the suspension of any empirical reality (who are you going to believe, Marx or your lying senses?).

Apart from the virtual reality the Left has imposed, it has also returned us to an ancient virtual freedom—that kind of freedom that brings human beings back into bondage to the lowest impulses, demanding immediate satiation. No longer is there any recognition of privileges, no sense of gratitude for grace, only an increasing preoccupation with self and an insistence that it must be preeminent. Such a reality, in contrast to the expanding horizons Christianity once ushered in, continually collapses in on itself (much like the old Soviet Union).

Because progressivism is a return to essential paganism, the state of nature is the only remaining standard. Since the only constant in nature is change, the concept of justice is reduced to an always-evolving utilitarianism. The result is the Left's shallow, squishy, rage-sustained, inverted counterpart to justice—"fairness." The greatest sin is, of course, intolerance. Where political correctness identifies intolerance, fairness is its *prescription*.

Where justice informs us as to set consequences we can expect when we choose to engage in certain activities (good or bad), fairness casts a perpetual pall because expectations under its dictates are not only unclear but consequences can widely diverge from one time to the next and often after the fact. Where justice establishes a rigid baseline with which all, great or small, are free to exploit their individual talents without undue interference, fairness at best rewards (ostensibly) the few by punishing the many. Where justice recognizes and upholds human dignity, fairness maintains a constant vigil for new groups to dehumanize. Justice is blind; fairness is sensitive to the most superficial distinctions, with an eye to institutionalizing those differences. Long-term negative effects are seldom within the purview of fairness;

the intent trumps the effect in any case. Fairness, rigidly moored in feelings, is contemptuous of the accumulated wisdom of the ages.

It was entirely upon the concept of justice that the US Constitution was founded. The Constitution is a covenant between all citizens of this nation, regardless of rank or economic status. We all pledge (tacitly) to live under those rules as set forth in our governing document and to abide by the decrees that flow from its lawful execution. It is established on the principle that every citizen (including the highest government official) is under the rule of law, and not under the rule of will of any man or elite ruling body.

Though fixity was and remains the intent behind the Constitution, there is provision for change, when necessary, through the amendment process. Of course the Left has very little patience with the amendment process, complaining it is far too cumbersome, but that is the very reason it is so important. The Founding Fathers, from their examination of all systems of government in history, understood that remedies hastily concocted out of kneejerk impulses were the most direct route to tyranny. *Resisting* impulse and taking the slow, deliberative process to arrive at the best possible answer was the truest model of Bible-centered wisdom.

The rights we all enjoy in this nation are the direct result of deliberate *limits* the Constitution places on governmental power. As reflected in the Declaration of Independence, the Founders recognized that rights came from God—thus, the imperative for restraining government so we may *exercise* God-given rights. In complete denial, progressives fervently believe rights are bestowed *by* government, thus the necessity for ever more ingenious ways to unshackle government so more "rights" may be granted. Of course, these are not rights at all but "entitlements." Rights come with a sacred responsibility to uphold the social contract we have all entered under our Constitution. Entitlements come with no recognition of responsibility to one's fellow man, but an expectation that one must be coddled and protected from absorbing any consequences for bad choices.

The contrast between the two approaches to balancing the scales by modern courts, justice and fairness, is most evident in the interpretive philosophy applied. For any court (or judge) to be truly committed to justice, a philosophy of strict constructionism must be applied. To be a strict constructionist (or constitutional originalist) is to first recognize that the Constitution (as higher law) is and *must* have the final say when trying to arrive at its fullest meaning. One is consciously aware that he or she does not occupy a legislative but a *judicial* office, that one is duty bound to keep faith with our social contract by consulting the Constitution and not a personal ever-evolving quest for elevating "human dignity"—no other quest has so effectively *destroyed* human dignity. It further means one is seeking to determine, as much as possible, the *intent* behind the laws our Founding Fathers built into the Constitution.

The other philosophical approach, judicial activism, flows directly from the inverted version of justice—fairness. Judicial activism of course, insists the Constitution must be a fluid document, always subservient to the passion of progressive judges who, evidently, are eminently qualified to eschew all accumulated wisdom in favor of their own "compassionate" feelings. Judicial activists are particularly scornful of "divining the intent of the Founders," insisting the Framers themselves seldom agreed on what the Constitution should mean and that to this effect our founding document is really nothing but a "bundle of compromises." And, so goes the complaint, even if we can arrive at some fundamental principle they held in common, whatever fundamentals may have been relevant to that day cannot possibly be relevant more than two hundred years later.

That above statement is especially telling, for it reveals that judicial activism (and fairness) rejects the concept of absolute truth (the basis for justice), and that fairness resides in moral relativism. As to the assertion that it is not possible to know original intent, the overwhelming evidence is to the contrary. The Framers wrote extensively and left no doubt they were united in their Judeo-Christian worldview and basic values. Though there were certainly heated disagreements, these were never over fundamentals but over how best to apply those shared principles in the differing circumstances.

It is also odd that progressives would object to trying to determine original intent with respect to the Constitution, since this is an approach widely used in every other field today. When dealing with any legal document (wills, contracts, etc.) every effort is made to first arrive at the plain meaning of the document. If this is obscure, then an effort is made to arrive at the intent of those who wrote the document. Shouldn't this apply even more to such an important document as the Constitution?[1]

Affluent countries (especially America) are blamed for the poverty of destitute countries. It was the quest for fairness that drove Obama to declare, five days before the 2012 election, his intent to fundamentally transform the USA. Yet there are distinct patterns that are almost always present when comparing affluent vs. poor nations, and these are almost always ignored. "Exploitation" is not one of them. Walter Williams observes, "In non-poor countries people tend to have greater personal liberty, their property rights are protected, contracts are enforced, there's rule of law and there's a market-oriented economic system rather than a socialistic."[2] Does anyone notice that these factors (which progressives tend to despise) are *missing* in the poorest countries?

Fairness and compassion are now defined by rewarding irresponsible financial ventures, thus ensuring that failed policies, strategies, and behaviors will continue to be pursued. Recurring economic crises, we are told, is the evidence of the failure of capitalism. This is an incredible avoidance of facts. Such downturns invariably result from death by a thousand cuts inflicted by numerous government *disruptions* of the free market. Mortgage facilitators Fannie Mae and Freddie Mac represent the deliberate distorting of market forces, artificially propping up practices the market would have weeded out. These institutions, sort of half-government-sponsored/half-shareholder-owned mutations, bought up risky mortgages until the housing meltdown of 2008. The crisis was directly due to drastically loosened underwriting standards, not, as progressives insisted, insufficient regulation.

Fairness demands that Christianity, because of its intolerance to all other views, must not be permitted a foundational role in society, especially in politics. Yet, when have progressives refrained from bringing *their* religious convictions to the political table? We often hear platitudes from the Left, "Personally, we are opposed to abortion. But it would be wrong to let personal convictions interfere with legislative duty." Are they opposed because it is morally repugnant and extinguishes a human life? If not, then why would they be opposed in any sense? If this *is* the case, then wouldn't the execution of their duty lie in opposing something that is fundamentally wrong?

If progressives could potentially command the loyalty of a constituency that lobbied for legal slavery, would they feel compelled to set aside a *personal* repugnancy toward slavery to perform their *legislative* duty? Since legislation of any kind is ultimately about what one deems moral, how might it ever be possible to divorce one's personal morality from the process of *codifying* morality? Though a politician might pay lip service to, say, Christianity, wouldn't we suspect his true and deepest religious convictions are most evident by those issues he consistently and tirelessly champions? Wouldn't we suspect his *true* religion is progressivism when it is the sacraments of *this* religion (abortion, gay rights, global warming, socialism, etc.) that he expends all his energy putting in place?

Of course, progressives always base their condemnation of American history on a comparison of their own imaginary version of Utopia as they longingly fantasize. No nation, no matter how demonstrably superior to all others, can compete with a fantasy. To say America was once a Christian nation is not to equate it to the imaginary Utopia of the Left. The proper question is not, "Has the ideal ever been upheld?" but: "Has there been a nation that laid its very *foundation* squarely on Christian principles?" Is there sufficient evidence that the norms, customs, mores, culture, and limits on government that flowed directly from those principles shaped the character of its people in ways that profoundly distinguish it from all other nations and periods of history? Is there evidence this has unleashed a freedom revolution unprecedented in history culminating in an explosion of discovery, innovation, human ingenuity, prosperity, charity, courage, and self-sacrifice that has been the exemplar to the world?

It is undeniable there are plenty of shameful episodes in the unfolding of this nation. Yet here again we see something profound that is distinct to this nation's Christian heritage—a national conscience that will not permit the offense to continue. Those powerless classes who are the victims of injustice are unshackled by the empowered class. Rather than, as has always been the case historically, some oppressed minority having to overthrow the ruling majority by violent upheaval, the injustice is debated and resolved internally, sometimes at great personal cost to the empowered. Try to imagine the brutal suppression machinery of any other government in history allowing the freedom of conscience that has been the hallmark of this nation. Try to imagine the accommodation of views that would consciously, deliberately, and continuously undermine the foundation of that government.

A disturbing measure of the success the Left has had in advancing its worldview is now evident in a significant number on the Right having accepted much of the progressive premise and even conceding the language. This is especially evident in attacks conservative commentators have directed at basic conservative positions and issues, using tactics that are almost identical to their Leftist counterparts. One such striking example was on display in a column by Cal Thomas, titled "America Has Never Been a 'Christian' Nation."[3]

Mr. Thomas took the occasion of his column to lecture evangelicals for getting too involved in the political process, with special criticism reserved for Kentucky clerk of court Kim Davis, for her decision to choose jail over violating her conscience by issuing marriage licenses to same-sex couples. While the US Supreme Court had issued an edict, there was no Kentucky legislative body that had given legal standing to same-sex marriage.

We recall there are three equal branches of government. The Court is merely one of the three; it is not the supreme *authority* of the land, free to function as an oligarchy. It has no authority to make law, nevertheless issued a decree (striking down the Defense of Marriage Act), using the most tortured logic informed by nothing but its *own* religious agenda, bypassing the legislative process. This should have been enough for any thinking person, including a non-Christian, to see it for what it was—an exercise in tyranny, and to refuse to recognize its legitimacy.

By Mr. Thomas's assessment, the proper thing would have been for Miss Davis to resign if she felt this violated her conscience. Yet to do so would have validated the state's position that its edicts are more authoritative than God's. This would mean, contrary to our own Declaration, rights are not derived from God but government.

Although most societies in history have recognized the marriage institution of one man/one woman as the cornerstone of civilization, in Mr. Thomas' estimation, Miss Davis' courageous stand resembled the actions of a religious fanatic.

Mr. Thomas then goes on to give a splendid impersonation of a progressive's argument: "If Davis wants to be consistent she would refuse a marriage license for anyone who has sinned." This is a breathtaking trivialization of an issue that is so far-reaching in its scope that we can't even calculate the negative effects this will have if permitted to stand. We already know that, based on the "reasoning" of the Court, there are no obvious categories of marriage arrangements (from numerous partners, to child/adult, to person/potted plant) that can be ruled out of bounds on any rational grounds.

Having been a fan of Mr. Thomas for many years and heard him speak on numerous occasions, I am certain he is fully capable of making a distinction between the sins we all routinely commit every day out of impatience, frustration, selfishness, or thoughtlessness, and a solemn *cause* that demands nothing less than sacrificing the time-tested institution of marriage to the pagan shrine of political correctness, so its *particular* sin may be elevated to a sacrament. Thus, it is puzzling why Mr. Thomas would have felt the need to imply Miss Davis was on a personal witch hunt. In his words, "Kim Davis chose the wrong issue."

Mr. Thomas did not choose to tell readers what he considered the right issue, but he did offer something of a solution: Christians should not entangle themselves in preserving the order and freedom God gave the world in the American experience. They should embrace their proper role of reaching out to nonbelievers with God's salvation message. Whereas we can agree with doing everything possible to fulfill this latter part, is there some reason to conclude the two are mutually exclusive? Should this have been the response of patriotic American families when faced with tyranny from king and Parliament? Should they have refrained from rising up against oppression for fear of imposing their religious views on the mother country?

In the run up to the 2016 presidential election, certain conservative pundits routinely scolded those pathetic rubes in flyover country over intolerance, imposing religious views, failure to maintain proper political decorum, and worst of all, choosing the wrong candidate. There has possibly never been such a disconnect between those presuming to represent cutting-edge conservatism and those actually having to live with leftist devastation, with the Republican leadership continuing to offer the same old platitudes and empty suits. These expert pundits seemed oblivious to the war that had been declared on law-abiding Americans and the sense of urgency and desperation ordinary Americans were feeling.

Status quo conservatives would self-identify as "Never-Trumpers." Donald Trump's lack of polish was contemptible to the beltway class, but not nearly as much as his outsider status. They were so filled with disdain that some even openly rooted for Democratic nominee Hillary Clinton. With Trump's presidential victory, beltway conservatives have left no doubt that their concern for their own battered egos trumps struggling Americans playing by the rules.

Because President Trump was swept into office by a deep, wide, populist frustration he had tapped into, the Left immediately seized upon the narrative that he was a white supremacist sympathetic to the Neo-Nazi movement. The left-wing media took the lead in deciphering every Trump act or word as part of the narrative, no matter how tortured the path. It was suddenly uncanny how everything about Trump was a parallel to Hitler. We often hear the Left justify illegal immigration on the grounds that "these folks are taking jobs Americans just won't do anymore." There is one field where they may have a point—journalism.

Okay, so both Hitler and Trump rode a populist wave of deep frustration into power. Apart from this wafer-thin similarity, what about the differences? Citizens in post-World War I Germany were experiencing severe economic conditions (such as hyperinflation, where a loaf of bread cost a wheelbarrow of money) largely because of punitive terms imposed by the Treaty of Versailles. The bitter loss of the war was already an unbearable affront to the proud German psyche. But with the humiliating conditions piled on, any leader emerging who promised a vision of getting even with those who had perpetrated this evil would understandably command a significant amount of support.

American frustration had nothing to do with any bitter defeat or punitive action by any opposing nations, or the need to finger some ethnic or religious scapegoat. Our frustration was with those in our own government who, instead of acting in our interest, passed up no opportunity to punish us for daring to hold with an opposing view. Our frustration was with an arrogant, narcissistic president (Obama) who was so blinded by his sense of moral superiority that he either could not or did not care to see the hardship he was visiting with his policies.

Hitler, before rising to power, led an insurrection against the German government with the intent of bringing fundamental transformation. I seem to remember "fundamental transformation" is what Mr. Obama was all about. Hitler was not democratically elected president of Germany; his position of Chancellor was bestowed upon him by his political opponent, President von Hindenburg, after Hitler had lost the presidential election but showed sizable support. Hitler would proceed to actively undermine the rule of law and assume all sorts of new authority that had no basis in the German Constitution. I also seem to recall this was a common feature of President Obama's reign. Hitler did not single out Jews because he was in search of a clever political rallying point and decided, "yes, these folks will do nicely." He was motivated by a deep, pathological, irrational hatred that predated his rise.

The Left is always quick to label Hitler's reign as a "conservative" movement to dissociate itself from what might otherwise appear obvious. Yes, apart from the Left's affinity for a totalitarian, top-down, centrally planned economy; worship of the state while waging war on a sovereign, transcendent God; and reducing human beings to soulless organisms, one would be hard-pressed to find any substantive similarity. Remember, Hitler had contempt for Christianity and was greatly influenced, not by any biblical values, but by Darwinian themes and Nietzsche's "superman" ideal. If a Hitler were to rise to power in America, the first thing he would have to do is dismantle the rule of law. Again, it is the *Left* that has consistently waged war on the Constitution, regarding it as an impediment to its socialist, utopian schemes.

There is nothing to indicate Donald Trump has ever been ideologically driven. All his life he has been immersed in the business world, and he is (generally) a free-market capitalist. Of course, that is enough for the Left to hold him in contempt by itself. But it is an economic position at the other end of the spectrum from Hitler's and one that *inhibits* dictatorial control. His lack of any political philosophy most of his life is probably why in the past he could vacillate from one political party to the other. Over time he has leaned more to the Right, no doubt because it has become obvious his economic views have no natural home in the political Left.

Nevertheless, the Left persists in the narrative. Trump appealed to the "lowest common denominator" by promising to end a reckless policy that put Muslim refugees and illegal aliens above the lives of American law-abiding citizens. Though Trump's approach was specific to certain countries that were on *Obama's* terrorist list, this act became a parallel to Hitler's singling out Jews. But the vicious assault by Muslims on the West was not something Trump imagined or conveniently conjured up as a rallying point for white racism. *Thousands* have already been murdered here and, during Obama's reign, scarcely a week passed that we did not see some horrific act committed somewhere in the world against innocent unsuspecting men, women, and children. These were not being committed by Christians, Jews, Hindus, Buddhists, or any other group in the name of their religion. These were *uniformly* Muslim.

If the parallel is real and not just one more political construct, the Left should be able to demonstrate it. We should be able to see evidence of a worldwide Jewish movement (during Hitler's reign) that was actively seeking to dominate the world, using the most brutal tactics to force all to acquiesce to its religious view or be exterminated. We should expect to see Jewish front groups (such as CAIR that has worked as a surrogate for the internationally recognized terrorist group Hamas) that worked to undermine German law and to impose a new Jewish Law (something the equivalent of Islam's Sharia) which *superseded* the law of the land. We should find evidence of terrorist Jews who murdered German citizens wholesale while shouting "Jehovah be praised!" In fact, though, Jews in Hitler's Germany were fully assimilated German citizens themselves, going about their everyday lives just as their fellow-countrymen.

*   *   *

As we look at the progressive agenda from top to bottom, where is the evidence it has given hope to those it has championed? Since it *requires* division, agitation, and perpetual victimhood to fuel its flames, such a prospect is doomed from the outset. Yes, there are examples of grievous injustice in America's unfolding, though these were, again, done in *violation* of founding principles. However, the anarchy, the intellectual shallowness, the hatred, the abandonment of the scientific method, inner cities turned into war zones, the theft of dignity, the celebration of mental disorders (transgenderism), the assault on the rule of law, the erasing of America's history and its borders, the criminalization of political differences, the erosion of societal pillars, the drive to abolish biological distinctions, and the shrinking horizons the progressive movement has left as its legacy is not the result of any violation but of faithful and deliberate implementation of core principles. Seen in its full effect, the true mission of progressivism is social *revenge*.

Let's briefly revisit the German Aktion T-4 experiment of World War II and try to give perspective to the above discussion. The concept of progressive fairness is, after all, but another way of saying "quality of life" in comparison to "sanctity of life" (the grounding for justice). The record of history leaves little ambiguity. When absolute authority is denied to a sovereign, transcendent being, it does not simply cease. At some point, it becomes asserted in earthly powers, transforming the reigning authority into an *authoritarian* rule.[4] Keeping in mind, of course, one lesson of the German experiment—quality's appetite only becomes more voracious as it gorges itself on human imperfections. The fewer obvious imperfections left to devour, the greater the contempt for *potential* imperfections. Indeed, its interventionist engine cannot function without some person or human group thrown into its threshing machine.

The idea that the absolute state would mold its policies based on quality-of-life assessments is not comforting. To whom do those judged "unfit" appeal when it no longer recognizes any fixed moral code or any substantive difference separating human beings and insects; where tentative "science" is ultimate and good is defined only by those things that advance state objectives; where state assumes *primary responsibility* for "health care" in a death culture already desensitized by *sanctioned* mass murder of utterly defenseless babies?

Built upon the sands of relativism, "quality of life" (fairness) is necessarily subject to redefinition at any moment through ever-evolving expediency. Thus, the specter of "unfitness" is always ready to rear its ugly head and single out some uncooperative group or someone's father, husband, wife, brother, neighbor, or child, for the greater "good" of the whole. To those who struggle to survive and maintain a sense of sanity under the nightmare of such a regime, "noble motives" on the part of the ruling elite are no consolation; the horrors no less real.

What if T-4 had taken place after several generations of aggressive government-sponsored indoctrination of the public into naturalistic thinking and its relativistic assumptions, paralleled by the marginalization and diminished authority of "religion" to offer any useful input into matters of social policy? What if most religious leaders simply sought ways to fit their "theology" into whatever little nooks progressivism left in its magnanimity? What if the relative few who continued to point out the fallacies, inconsistencies, and potential dangers of the ruling orthodoxy were banished to the outer fringes, to be ridiculed and effectively dismissed as fundamentalist extremists or fanatics? Had the T-4 program taken place under all the aforementioned conditions, from what source would or could pressure have effectively been brought to oppose it? This is where America stands today.

The (apparent) defeat of Christianity has not brought about the defeat of irrationality; it has resulted in the *return* to irrationality. There is a strange misconception that the current liberation from "traditional values" was accomplished through the overthrow of history's most notorious and intolerant edifice. This presumption is perhaps the supreme irony. Such freedom as has existed in the West could only arise in a particular culture—one that was specifically conducive to the free flow of ideas and held with the intrinsic value of each individual. Have progressives ever bothered to consider the consequences of a truly Christian-free culture? For all the ostentatious pageantry of its grand pretensions, has the Enlightenment/Progressive movement been about anything so much as a determined march by humanity back to that wilderness from which God had spared no expense to rescue? By what twisted logic does it presume to represent progress, when its essential nature and consistent fruit is *regression*?

As disconcerting as all these symptoms of progressive sickness may be, there is one that is especially troubling. While a tangible, well-defined, exceedingly dangerous crisis looms large, the Left is preoccupied with deciphering every little bit of anecdotal evidence in the employ of a global warming "crisis" that can only be sustained by demagoguery which resolutely seals itself from thoughtful debate. There is a very real Islamic-Fascist force that threatens to bring the whole world in subjection to an intolerant, repressive religion that holds the freedoms of the Western world in abject contempt.

Because progressivism can only comprehend evil as the effect of American exploitation—something to be cured through American guilt therapy or militant activism—it is unable to conceive of a force that has deliberately set itself against good specifically to destroy and to devour. Though this enemy has tied its specific mission numerous times in a multitude of ways to a specific *religion* where it is impossible to mistake either the source of aggression or the intent, the Left steadfastly presumes this must be code talk for some kind of desperate plea to people of good will to reign in American exploitation. Because progressivism can only view reality through the Marxist prism of class struggle, for all the surface rhetoric, terrorists' motivation must really be about economic injustice. Because of this institutionalized blindness, we now have a major political party and a disturbing portion of its constituency that can look perhaps the greatest evil of history in the eye and still not see it. As Christ came two thousand years ago to conquer death, this evil comes to conquer life. And this is the subject of the next and final section.

Section IV

KINGDOM OR EMPIRE?

CHAPTER 33

ISLAM: ITS HISTORY AND GOALS

On September 11, 2001, the nation was shocked by an unparalleled act of barbarism on American soil. Many groped for answers to this inexplicable violation of any standard of human decency. Surely this savage rape must have been the act of a marginalized group that had perverted the true teachings of its religion. After all, everyone knows that religion (even if its methods are somewhat archaic) is about promoting peace and goodwill. Some assumed America must have somehow brought this upon itself. Others, unable to cope with the possibility that a very real evil existed which every American would have to confront or be left with the choice between annihilation or total subjugation, preferred to pretend that the American government had staged the whole event. The World Trade Center buildings had been brought down with strategically planted bombs. A government plot was easier to stomach than the uncomfortable reality of having to stand against the greatest evil of our time.

Trying to make sense of the despicable acts of 9/11 is a hopeless quest without first confronting certain unpleasant realities about the religion animating those acts. It is necessary to understand, in particular, the historic roots of that religion and its specific mission as transmitted to the world and exemplified by its founder.

The story of Islam begins in the Arabian desert on the outskirts of Mecca. Here it is believed that in AD 610 the Prophet Muhammad, while meditating in a cave, received revelations from God (Allah) through the angel Gabriel. Muhammad was himself dubious of the source of these revelations. as these had come while he was in the throes of uncontrollable seizures. Apparently, it was his wife Khadija who convinced him his revelations were divinely given and not demonic.

The new religion that Muhammad would bring to the world had a great deal in common with Arab practices in which he was thoroughly immersed. Unlike Christianity, Islam's founding years did not see it sharply contrasting itself against the surrounding culture; it largely reflected it. In his book, *Islam and Terrorism*,

Mark Gabriel (former Muslim Egyptian imam and instructor at Al-Azar University in Cairo) describes the culture before the time of Muhammad. The developments within Islam, as he shows, owe a considerable debt to Arabian customs that well predate Muhammad's life.[1] Long before this, Arabs made pilgrimages to Mecca to worship in the Kaaba (the temple) which contained a sacred black stone. In fact, the Quraysh tribe from which Muhammad would descend was the official guardian of the sacred Black Stone of Mecca.[2] Though clearly the Kaaba had been the focal point of pagan worship, Muhammad nevertheless retained this important contact with the Arabian past, converting it into the temple of Allah. What this shrewd political concession revealed was Islam's accommodation of and continuity with essential paganism.

Each tribe featured its own set of deities with a chief deity at the top of the hierarchy. "But unlike the pagan civilizations of the Mediterranean and the Asian subcontinent, there was no developed mythology among the Arabs; their deities did not have a past or distinctive character."[3] The Quraysh tribe was heavily involved in the cult of the moon god, Allah. Before Muhammad's revelations, Allah was not thought of as the Supreme Being of the universe. Though highly revered in Arabia, he was still only one of a pantheon of pagan deities. In fact, Allah had three daughters who were worshiped as well. After Muhammad's revelations, Allah was raised up out of the pantheon of pagan deities and given a new special status. Muhammad simply declared that Allah and the God of the OT (YHWH) were one and the same. As we shall see, however, Allah was never to shed certain and distinct pagan characteristics. By contrast, YHWH consistently demonstrated that He was the antithesis of all pagan gods.

Perhaps Islam's most important carryover from its Arabian past was manifest in a peculiar unyielding spirit. Writes Gabriel: "One of the stronger characteristics of Arabs in Muhammad's time was that they were known for being extremist in everything—extreme love, extreme hate and no tolerance of others who were different from them. . . . Muhammad was born into a culture where conquest and bloodshed were the norm."[4]

Muhammad freely borrowed concepts from Judaism and Christianity that he incorporated into the new religion he was revealing to the world. It is widely believed he had gained a shadowy understanding of these religious beliefs on trade-route caravans with his uncle that took him through Syria and Palestine. Unfortunately, it was these sketched-out and rather distorted forms which would lead him to many false impressions about the substance of these religions.

Muhammad's message could be summed up in a few simple points: Jews and then Christians had distorted the true teachings they had been entrusted with. Because the time had come to clear up the error, Almighty God (Allah) had sent

His messenger to set matters right. Muhammad, as the final prophet of God, was that messenger. Salvation was attainable now through this recitation, "There is no God but Allah, and Muhammad is His Prophet" and the observance of prescribed good works. Of course, one never knew if his good works were sufficient to merit entrance into Paradise at the end of life. Only dying while fighting Islam's enemies guaranteed one entrance into the heavenly realm.

Muhammad's followers would eventually write (on various scraps) the revelations of their leader. Long after his death, these would be compiled into a single source, the Koran. Composed of 114 Surahs (chapters), this was the sacred book of Islam. Second only to the Koran in commanding Islamic authority would be the hadiths. A hadith was a collection of sayings and deeds of the Prophet Muhammad. Six hadiths are today almost universally recognized as authentic. The traditions in these six are rated by degrees as to their reliability, ranging from "highly reliable" to "weak" and even to "forged." The Bukhari Hadith is generally held to be most reliable of the six. Unfortunately, those traditions that portray Muhammad in the most barbaric light (such as the story of the nine-year-old bride) are found in the category of "reliable" and find multiple attestations in the Bukhari. *Sunnah* is the understanding derived from the six hadiths. The Koran and Sunnah form the source of the *Sharia*—the sum of Islamic law that all Muslim governments are mandated to execute, and all Muslims bound to observe.[5]

By all accounts, Muhammad's initial approach to reaching "unbelievers" was full of humble exhortation. Despite his entreaties to his fellow Arabs, his new religion was met with intense hostility, especially by his own Quraysh Tribe. Muhammad and his few followers were finally forced to flee Mecca for the city of Yathrib (soon changed to Medina, "the city of the Prophet," in honor of Muhammad). The character of Muhammad and his approach changed radically after his expulsion from Mecca. Mark Gabriel sums it up this way: "[In Mecca] he invited people to be a part of Islam by preaching. [In Medina] he persuaded people to convert by the sword."[6] Islam would now undergo a change from an essentially spiritual movement to an essential political and even military movement encased in religious trappings. The mosque (center of spiritual worship) would even become the headquarters from which Muhammad would plan and direct military campaigns. That he became a man of war and violence is indisputable, as he would direct his men into seventy-four battles, twenty-seven of which he would personally lead.[7]

Muhammad moved to Medina in AD 622. Important Islamic principles were established here. The foundational principle, according to Gabriel, upon which all others would follow, "Anyone who conflicts with, disagrees with or does not support Muhammad and his teachings should be killed."[8] To illustrate, Muhammad had initially made overtures to the Jews of Medina, trying to convince them that he was a prophet in the line of OT prophets and had been sent by God to correct the error that had crept into Jewish (and Christian) Scripture. After successfully holding off the Meccan army's siege against Medina, in a mood of triumph Muhammad extended an ultimatum to the last Jewish tribe in Medina—convert or face the sword. All the Jewish men were subsequently beheaded in front of their families. The women were duly raped, Muhammad taking one of the survivors, who had just witnessed the merciless murder of her husband and father, into his personal harem. This represented what would become the unyielding Islam pattern—accept the gracious invitation of Allah or face pitiless slaughter or enslavement. Other principles to follow included the sanctioning of deceit and even murder to achieve Islamic ends. Even professing *Muslim* government leaders were not safe if it was determined they were in violation of Allah's exacting dictates.

From Medina, Muhammad's revelations took on a peculiar pattern. Allah was always ready to rescind any previous pronouncement or to grant Muhammad the right to commit any atrocity if it furthered the cause of Islam. Here, he grew ever more fierce and vengeful with virtually any action so easily and automatically finding divine sanction. Muhammad would take at least fifteen wives, and perhaps as many as twenty-five. Among these was a seven-year-old, a marriage he "mercifully" waited till the child was nine to consummate. As one carefully observes the pattern of Medinan revelations, Muhammad's prophecies, as with his God, appear suspiciously self-serving.

The fundamental principle of deceit as an acceptable tactic was on display when Muhammad, unable to overcome the military strength of the Quraysh Tribe, signed a ten-year peace treaty with Mecca. Soon after, Muhammad and his army attacked and conquered the city without warning. This has been the model for all negotiations since, especially evident since the rebirth of Israel in 1948: promise anything, sign any agreement, say whatever is politically expedient, then proceed to violate all terms. In other words, treachery is a vital tool in the Muslim arsenal of conquest. Muhammad had himself proclaimed, "War is deception."

Muhammad would leave to his followers the concept that ever since has defined the mission of Islam and the duty of every Muslim: The world, according to the Prophet, was divided into two basic realms—Dar al-Islam (the Land of Peace) and Dar al-Harb (the Land of War). Every place in the world that has not come under Islamic conversion (which includes the entire Islamic political-legislative system) is the Land of War. Muslims have a mandate from Allah through Muhammad to use whatever means necessary to bring any such land under total submission. This has served since the time of Muhammad as the basis for Islamic *jihad*. Gabriel quotes Islamic *fiqh* for the definition of *jihad*: "[Jihad] is fighting anybody who stands in the way of spreading Islam. Or fighting anyone who refuses to enter into Islam (based on Surah 8:39)."[9]

Gabriel describes the three progressive stages of *jihad*: the weakened stage, the preparation, and the *jihad* state. In the weakened state, Muslims submit to the ruling authority, feigning cooperation with the dominant culture while steadily building up their numbers. In the preparation stage, believers are actively building up "in every possible area—financial, physical, military, mental and in any other area."[10] The final stage of *jihad* is to actively seek through whatever means (deceit, violence, etc.) to impose Sharia law and Islamic jurisdiction over the entire country or region. All three stages, as Gabriel points out, are perfectly encapsulated within Muhammad's life. This was evident in his early career in Mecca, followed by his military planning in Medina and eventual bloody and deceitful conquest of Mecca.

Perhaps no other subject is as certain to inflame Muslim passion as the mere mention of the medieval Crusades. Yet when visiting the matter, seldom is it taken into consideration (whether by Arab or Western minds) that the places called "Muslim lands" at the time had previously been, and for several centuries, *Christian* lands. Seldom is any consideration given to how those formally Christian territories *became* Muslim. Ignoring history, the usual treatment is to cast the Crusades as a massive imperialist assault on Islam by the church. Thus, the very term "Crusades" becomes synonymous with Christian barbarism and Muslim indignity.

But how did Egypt, Palestine, Syria, Lebanon, and Asia Minor (famous in the NT as that region where Paul established various churches), all *distinctly* Christian provinces, become overtaken by Islam? We recall, of course, from an earlier section that Antioch and Alexandria were the main theological schools of Christian thought during the time of the Church Fathers and that important doctrinal positions were hammered out from the confrontations that often occurred. We also recall that Augustine hailed from Hippo in North Africa. These places were not, as is often assumed, nebulously connected to Christianity; they were important thriving centers of Christian thought. So how did these vital Christian nerve centers suddenly come under Muslim authority? Was this a peaceful, welcomed takeover? Hardly. Egyptian historian Bat Ye'or, in her book *The Decline of Eastern Christianity under Islam*, records the brutal facts. The taking of Christian lands was by violent, pitiless conquest. Her account is deeply disturbing, displaying the same breathtaking depth of cruelty and inhumanity in conquest after conquest.[11]

As for the Crusades and the role of the medieval church, this campaign, as much as it has been employed as a bludgeon against Christianity, was a belated response to imperialistic *Muslim* expansion into Christian territory, begun at least four hundred years earlier. In 1095, Pope Gregory gave his blessing to a mission to retake the Holy Sepulcher from Muslim control and to rescue Christians from

Muslim extortion and persecution. Atrocities were undeniably committed by those carrying the Christian standard in this campaign, and this should be a source of shame to all who profess the name of Christ. But where is the expression of regret or shame from the Muslim side of the equation? Perhaps no such apology is forthcoming, due to the very important distinction Robert Spencer makes: "Crusaders who pillaged Jerusalem were transgressing the bounds of their religion in all sorts of ways. As for the Muslim armies who murdered, raped, pillaged and enslaved—what Islamic principles were they violating? After all, they were following the example of the Prophet."[12]

It is true that some rulers did, in the name of Christianity, spread Christianity at the point of the sword (such as Charlemagne). But Muslim conquest was never a case of some representative having badly distorted or perverted Islam. These ruthless campaigns were modeled after Muhammad himself who set the parameters for all campaigns to follow. In the end, the Crusades failed to free former Christian lands, and Crusaders suffered devastating losses. This did not, however, end Islam's aims of expansion. Not until 1683, with Muslim forces bearing down on Vienna, was Islam's campaign of imperialist aggression finally halted.

The "Golden Age of Islam" (approx. 700–1100) is frequently hailed for its important contributions to civilization. Even if we were to concede these contributions were because of and not *in spite of Islam*, it is evident they were quickly abandoned. According to speculation by bin Laden biographer Yosef Bodansky, the abandonment of intellectual, artistic pursuit was due to the inexplicable (and previously unthinkable) Muslim defeat in the First Crusade (1099). In line with this speculation, the blame was placed upon intellectual strains that had diminished the exclusive authority of the Koran. It was believed that the solution was a return to a high Koranic fidelity.[13] If Bodansky is right, it surely reveals that any intellectual leanings or advances in the arts were not organic developments of Islam; they reflected a considerably compromised form of the Muslim religion. This supports Trifkovic's contention that these civilizing interludes were accomplished by side-stepping Islam.[14]

As for the generous tolerance for non-Muslims that is supposedly legendary in Islamic history, this turns out to be mostly myth as well. *Dhimmis* (subjugated classes living in Muslim societies, mostly made up of Jews and Christians) were constantly reminded of their subject state, from the clothes they were forced to wear, to demeaning services to which they were conscripted. *Dhimmis* lived and breathed at the pleasure of their Muslim hosts with essentially no rights. They were denied the right to possess weapons, to practice their religion openly, to build churches or synagogues, or convert any to their religion. In general, the laws regarding *dhimmis* could be said to retain the intent to humiliate as much as possible. This does not even address the *jizya* (non-Muslim poll tax) they were expected to pay. Those unable to meet this fee were forced to surrender their own children to the slave market. There was also the matter of churches and synagogues that were vandalized or destroyed almost routinely on the flimsiest pretext of failing to properly display respect toward Muslims.[15]

Following its "golden age," the Islamic world was swallowed up in the Turkish-ruled Ottoman Empire. The Ottoman Empire was rather suspiciously viewed by orthodox Muslims throughout its history, especially its more secularized aspects. Rather than a true Islamic dynasty, the Ottoman Empire fashioned itself into something largely bearing this outward appearance. The atrocities of this empire may have even exceeded the usual celebration of orgies. As Trifkovic puts it, "[being] Christian in the Ottoman Empire meant living in daily fear of murder, rape, torture, kidnap of one's children, slavery, and genocide."[16] It may be that the most insidious and evil practice was the *devshrime*—the periodic and forced taking of non-Muslim boys (mostly Christian) and conscription into the army for the Ottoman Empire. Robert Spencer maintains this may have resulted in the enslavement of as many as 200,000 boys.[17] Trifkovic also points to the strange selective amnesia Western academia suffers. The Turkish genocide of Armenians in 1915 is a close parallel to Hitler's European genocide, yet mysteriously fails to rise to the same level of outrage.

The blame for the "extremist" elements of Islam today is usually laid at the feet of a movement called "Wahabism." This can be traced to one Muhammad ibn Abd al-Wahhab, born in 1703. Perhaps largely as a response to the soft Islam of the Ottoman Empire, this man led the movement to purge Islam of any practice that did not have a literal foundation in the Koran. This was a determined drive to get back to "true Islam" especially as practiced by its founder, Muhammad. Though this influence/thought is often portrayed today as out of the mainstream, Trifkovic reminds, "the Wahabis were no more extreme or violent than the models for Islam in all ages, the Prophet and his companions."[18]

In the estimation of Mark Gabriel, the decision by Turkish leader Mustafa Kemal Ataturk in the 1920s to secularize the state of Turkey created the backlash in the Middle East that would propel the emergence of new extremist Islamic groups bent on the eradication of "compromised" Muslim leaders. Egypt would be the hub of this growing influence. Some important leaders to emerge in this drama were Sayyid Qutb, portrayed as the "Martin Luther of the modern jihad movement," Dr. Salah Serea, Shokri Moustafa, and Sheik Abdel Rahman (once a professor of Gabriel's at Al-Azar University). What these and other leading men of the movement held in common was the conviction that the Koran was not simply an important authority but that it must be the *only* authority directing governments and that its dictates must be carried out verbatim. They also rejected the notion that *jihad* could be reduced to some personal spiritual battle with sin. These insisted that Muhammad had demonstrated by his own actions that this concept in practice must embrace the total subjugation of those regions not under Muslim control. Furthermore, Muhammad was the supreme model for proper Muslim conduct. And not only had he not prohibited the use of violence and deceit in waging *jihad*, he had openly and enthusiastically *sanctioned* it.

The groups spawned by these Muslim leaders were responsible for assassinating heads of state and murdering scores of Egyptian policemen. These leaders scoffed at religious piety; this interfered with the serious business of *jihad*. To these men, and in imitation of the Prophet, *jihad* was not held as merely an important part of the Islamic mission; it was the very heart of it.

What is possibly most conspicuous as we closely examine their lives: none of these visionaries ever appealed to social injustice or Western exploitation as the justification for their actions. They unanimously and exclusively appealed to the Koran and Muhammad's specific examples of right Muslim conduct. "Exploitation" would not enter the modern *jihad* playbook until many years later, after the concept had become well established in the world of Western academe. Moreover, in the Arab world, Western exploitation was more a matter of decadent influences that had infiltrated Arab culture, than the West siphoning wealth from the Middle East. A far more prominent grievance than this, radical leaders were incensed with secularized Muslim governments and watered-down, lukewarm Muslim practices.

Sheikh Abdel Rahman would become the leader of al-Jihad (the amalgamation of many militant groups) and issue a *fatwa* (legal ruling) for the death of Egyptian President Anwar Sadat.[19] Sheikh Rahman, later on trial for the murder of Sadat, would be reprimanded by the Egyptian attorney general for his perversion of the Koran's message: "Jihad is not killing. This is not Islam's teaching. Jihad is a spiritual fight against evil, poverty, sickness, and sin. Killing is only from the devil."

To which the Sheikh replied: "From where does the attorney general come up with this understanding? Are there verses in the Quran that I don't know about that say jihad is a spiritual fight against evil, poverty, sickness and sin? Perhaps there is new inspiration from Allah that our attorney general received recently, and the rest of the Muslims do not yet know."[20] The Sheikh would go on to show the court that he (*if* he had been responsible for this act) had acted in exact accord with the Koran and the actions of its prophet.

Because Egypt based its law ultimately on Sharia, and because the prosecution could not show where the Sheikh had acted contrary to the ultimate recognized authority, the jury found him not guilty. Sheikh Rahman would later move to New York, where he would mastermind the first bombing of the World Trade Center in 1993. In his book, *Willful Blindness*, Andy McCarthy (who prosecuted the case against the Sheikh and his associates) expresses shock at finding that nothing in the Koran or any authoritative Islamic teaching could be found which would have put this intent to murder "infidels" in violation of any basic tenets.[21]

After the assassination of Sadat, those leaders in the al-Jihad movement who were not taken into custody fled Egypt. Those who settled in Afghanistan would link up with Osama bin Laden to form yet a new group, al-Qaeda. This group, like al-Jihad before, had a vision to take *jihad* to the West. Rather than working to reform Muslim nations that had succumbed to non-Koranic prac- tices, why not take the fight to the source of the evil influences: Europe and America?

With the above in view, consider that today Hollywood and ivory-tower elites are obsessed with fingering some shadowy institutionalized Western pathology (linked inherently with Christian traditions) as the cause of 9/11. In fact, the deca- dence and debauchery against which Islamic radicalism rails is perfectly epitomized in the present Hollywood culture (pornography, drugs, materialism, the homo- sexual agenda, women's rights, the pagan elevation of nature to divine status, etc.) and the egalitarianism of academe. Were these elites ever to succeed in their mission to tear down America's defenses to the point that Sharia became *the* law of the land; their necks would be the first to feel the sword of *jihad*.

In 1979, Iran became the axis of Islamic extremism with the revolution that ousted the Shah of Iran and established the Ayatollah Khomeini as the head of a new fundamentalist Islamic government. The story behind the Shah's overthrow is quite revealing. Who can forget President Carter's decision to gain favor in the Islamic world by essentially standing down when the Shah was being overrun by radical Islamic forces? This in spite of the pro-Western government he oversaw, and the relative stabilizing influence the Shah's regime had represented in the Middle Eastern cauldron. Nevertheless, in Carter's estimation, this regime had been too brutal, and its dissolution would no doubt be enthusiastically welcomed by the citizens of Iran. Trifkovic, commenting on Mr. Carter's foresight: "In the name of Allah and Islam, more people were killed in one year of Khomeini than during the preceding quarter-century of the Shah. . . . Hitler's or Stalin's *forma mentis* was dif- ferent from that of Khomeini only in quantity, not in quality."[22]

President Carter, never missing an opportunity to be on the wrong side of history as well as to prove his utter lack of appreciation for history's bigger picture, decided to make a deal with the devil. His decision was to promote an international network whose aim was to spread Islam throughout Central Asia as a counterbal- ance to, and destabilizing force against, Soviet expansion. As the law of unintended consequences would have it, this would give birth to the Taliban as well as provide recruiting methods and training camps for volunteers who would one day comprise al-Qaeda.

The protracted conflict with the Soviet Union, which would finally see the Russians leaving in disgrace, would embolden the Islamic world and tantalize with visions of grandeur that had been absent perhaps since its progress had been halted outside the gates of Vienna. To be sure, many complexities led to the modern dynamic in the Muslim world, but perhaps no single factor was as important as this policy decision by President Carter, arming and financing worldwide *jihad*. This, coupled with President Clinton's folly in Mogadishu and his decision to cast the war between Serbia/Croatia and Muslim-controlled Bosnia as "ethnic cleansing" (rather than the war between religions it truly was) was perhaps most responsible for the renewed hope that world conquest was once again a realizable Muslim dream.

Republican administrations have also been reluctant to identify the religion of Islam as *the* source of unrest in Central Asia, the Middle East, and much of Europe. This has even included President Reagan. The same myopia (and political correctness) has persisted, preferring to imagine that Islam, despite a 1,400-year history to the contrary, is a religion of peace. Thus, Republican remedies have also skirted the problem, seeking to mollify symptoms, ensuring the problem will never be addressed. Though far less direct in facilitating Islamic aims than their unwitting Democratic counterparts, Republican policies (much too often) have ultimately contributed to neutralizing any resistance to worldwide *jihad*. Just consider the Bush administration's constant pressuring of Israel to negotiate with thugs rather than giving the green light to defeat. Moreover, Bush did not follow his own promise to fight all terrorism no matter where it was found, but sought to make his own deal with the devil—Saudi Arabia and Pakistan, in particular.

The Islamic world has learned to play the human-rights card very well when demanding "fair treatment" for its Muslim citizens in Western countries. It has adroitly turned the West's own obsession with "fairness" against any remaining Western institutions. Fairness for Muslims, of course, can only occur when Muslim communities are not required to submit to any authority other than Sharia. Less than the full implementation of Sharia and Muslims, by definition, are oppressed. As we have seen by now, progressives will rearrange continents to end the oppression of non-white, non-European, and especially, non-Christian immigrants. So, this has obligingly provided the winning strategy—move significant numbers into neighborhoods and demand equal rights; portray it as a struggle for justice. This fairness business works equally well to silence those who expose the deadly aims of Islam. Rather than addressing the substance of charges, Islam apologists merely label critics "Islamophobes." Any reportage of Muslim militancy is "hate speech" and "promoting irrational fear."

The above may seem a very harsh indictment to the Western mind which finds it inconceivable that 9/11 could be the *intended* fruit of a religion. So, let's have a look at a sampling of the "peace and tolerance" we are so often reminded makes up the thrust of this religion:

> Fight and slay the Pagans wherever you find them, and seize them, beleaguer them, and lie in wait for them in every stratagem (of war); but if they repent, and establish regular prayers and practice regular charity, then open the way for them: for Allah is oft-forgiving, Most Merciful. (Surah 9:5, Ali Translation)[23]

> So, when you meet (in fight—*Jihad* in Allah's Cause) those who disbelieve, smite (their) necks till when you have killed and wounded many of them, then bind a bond firmly (on them, i.e. take them as captive. (Surah 47:4; The Noble Quran)[24]

> And fight them until there is no more *Fitnah* (disbelief and polytheism, i.e., worshiping others besides Allah) and the religion (worship) will all be for Allah alone [in the whole of the world]. But if they cease (worshiping others besides Allah), then certainly, Allah is All-Seer of what they do. (Surah 8:39; Noble Quran)[25]

> Take not the Jews and the Christians as *Auliya* (friends, protectors, helpers), they are but *Auliya* of each other. And if any amongst you takes them (as *Auliya*), then surely he is one of them. (Surah 5:51)[26]

> Shall I inform you of him who is worse than this in the retribution from Allah? Worse is he (Jews) whom Allah has cursed and brought His wrath upon, and of whom He made apes and pigs, and he who served the Satan; these are worse in place and more erring from the straight path. (Surah 5:60)[27]

> O you have been given the Scripture (Jews and Christians)! Believe in what We have revealed (to Muhammad) confirming what is (already) with you, before we efface faces (by making them like the back of necks; without nose, mouth, eyes) and turn them hindwards, or curse them as We cursed the Sabbath-breakers. And the commandment of Allah is always executed. (Surah 4:47)[28]

> If any do fail to judge by (the light of) what Allah has revealed, they are (no better than) those who rebel. (Surah 5:44,47; Ali Translation)[29]

Muslim apologists will be quick to cry foul. Yes, there are certain verses that, if taken out of context, tend to cast Islam in a very bad light; but Christianity can also be made to look monstrous if the focus is placed only on certain verses without consideration for context. In feigned indignation, they will insist that within the Koran there are at least 114 verses that speak about love, peace, and forgiveness. What they fail to mention is that all these verses have been *abrogated.* To the Umma (the worldwide Islamic community) and the Ulama (the whole body of scholarship interpreting the Koran and the hadiths), it is as if these verses never existed. Mark Gabriel explains that the overriding of certain verses was accomplished through the principle of *naskh,* "based on the fact that the Quran was revealed to Muhammad at different times over a period of about twenty-two years. . . . [It was] decided [by scholars] that new revelation would override (*nasikh*) previous revelations."[30] Thus, those who cry foul know their argument is based upon a false premise. They know that the "love, peace, forgiveness" verses were all written in Muhammad's early Meccan days, and have been vacated by the latter Medinan verses for almost 1,400 years!

As for context, Muslim apologists are not even making an apples-to-apples comparison. The Bible does feature different unfolding dispensations and a specific context that not only limits the violence to a specific people, time, and/or location but explains why the event is happening. From the Medinan passages on, the Koran only features a single context—worldwide *jihad.* Moreover, the Koran's decrees are binding for *all* regions, in *all* circumstances, in *all* ages. Ill-will toward non-Muslims is in the very soul of Islam.

"The above assertion is grossly unfair. Most Muslims are not terrorists and do not wish ill on non-Muslims." The first part of this is undoubtedly true. The second part is debatable, when considering the almost-universal Muslim condemnation of Israel in particular and Jews in general. Though most Muslims would want nothing to do with acts of violence, especially against those of other beliefs who have become trusted friends, what are they to do when pressed on the authority of the Koran by charismatic or radical (usually one and the same) leaders who spell out the duties of a Muslim and remind of the harsh retaliation (possibly against their own family) to those who shirk their duty? To what or to whom can they appeal for some rational defense of their nonviolent stand? Not the Koran. Not the Sunnah. Not the Ulama. Not Muhammad.

The Koran simply does not concur with the Bible's implication that all are of equal value in God's eyes. The Koran does not agree that all humans are entitled to certain basic rights. Only Muslims have rights, and these are almost entirely held by men. Under Sharia law, a woman who is a *victim* of rape is subject to the death penalty (unless she can get four Muslim men to testify to the rape) because she is technically guilty of adultery or fornication. A man may divorce his wife by simply saying to her three times, "I divorce you." Because women are assumed to be the root of evil (indeed, practically a curse), husbands are encouraged to beat their wives. Women have no right to expect any sexual gratification and live only to fulfill the expectations of their husbands. The testimony of a woman is equal to only half that of a man. If a man is not satisfied with his wife, he may have up to three additional wives. With respect to children, the husband has all parental rights. Finally, Muhammad himself declared that hell would mostly be inhabited by women.[31]

CHAPTER 34

JEHOVAH AND ALLAH: A STUDY IN CONTRASTING CHARACTER AND REVELATION

There is a widely held belief in the West that the US is somehow responsible for the poverty and hopelessness of the Arab world. This is based on the zero-sum fallacy—that wealth is a fixed pie. Because we have such a disproportionate share of that pie, other countries, especially those more easily exploited, are left to divvy up measly crumbs. Though actually, wealth is expanded and contracted according to *production* (and never exists as some fixed entity), there are a few salient questions that never seem to be asked. Since Muslim countries command a disproportionate share of the world's oil wealth, why is a finger never pointed at the leaders of Arab nations? Why are they never branded ruthless exploiters? Why doesn't all that wealth ever seem to find its way to the poverty-stricken? And why is *America* to blame for the consistently corrupt actions of Muslim leaders? Finally, why don't Muslim institutions which are responsible for the poverty of material resources, as well as the poverty of *spirit,* ever come under criticism?

It is neither economics *nor* Western imperialism that fuel Islamic *jihad.* It is a desire to fulfill a mandate given through Muhammad to convert the world. The first attack on the World Trade Center was not just some random target for Sheik Rahman in 1993. This was the symbol of the freedom and prosperity of the West. *These* are the enemies of Islam. That September 11 was chosen by bin Laden to stage his vicious rape of the US seems hardly coincidental. September 11 just happens to be that day in 1683 when the Muslim push into Europe was turned back just outside Vienna. To those who take Muhammad's directives seriously, this, ever since, has been an ignominious date of unforgivable and unforgettable insult to the "holy" mission of worldwide *jihad.* This left a hatred that smoldered just beneath the surface for the following centuries, with Islam *appearing* to have lost all connection with its original mission. In truth, it was merely biding its time, waiting for Allah

315

to supply the "right opportunity" to reassemble its forces of destruction. Allah, as it turned out, would not need to. Enlightenment progressivism would.

If only the civilized world truly *were* (as bin Laden and others characterized Bush's response after 9/11) engaged in a "crusade against Islam" (its *values*). The whole world, including millions of Muslims trapped in a thoroughly dehumanizing worldview, would be so much the better for this honest acknowledgement and resolve to confront the real issue. Instead, we must apologize again and again for noticing how often Islam is at the center of repeated barbarism on civilization, pretending this is an uninteresting, incidental fact. But how do we defeat (or confront) an enemy we refuse to identify?

Robert Spencer analyzes the situation: "The problem the West faces is that unless and until Islamic orthodoxy is radically redefined (with the overwhelming agreement of the *umma*), it will not finally call off the struggle."[1] Since this, by every reasonable measure, seems to lack a single plausible element, does not Mr. Spencer perhaps have the situation topsy-turvy? Is it not the West that must redefine itself, rejecting the Enlightenment nihilism that threatens to strip America of everything that made it a beacon of freedom and the only remaining foil to enslaving forces?

*   *   *

"But isn't this entire case against Islam also an indictment of Christianity? After all, Islam is rather closely modeled on Christianity, proposing a transcendent monotheistic God who sets stringent standards that, if not obeyed, will place the unbeliever in a state of eternal damnation?" Yes, there are superficial similarities. But a peek beneath the surface reveals that Islam is not only a distorted imitation of Christianity but, in every important way, the opposite.

Consider Surah 57:3: "God is the First and the Last, the Outward and the Inward; God is the knower of everything." Sufis in particular (the mystic strand of Islam) take this as justification for stressing the pantheistic nature of Allah. Just as Allah cannot be confined to a personality, neither can he in any sense be separated from his creation. No atom may exist that is not fully permeated with his essence. Mainline Islam of course denies this ultimately causes Islamic cosmogony to descend into a form of pantheism (all is God, God is all). But this seems inescapable.

Because Islam rejects the concept of the triune nature of God (as well as misunderstanding the concept—supposing the three persons to be Jesus, Mary, and God), it runs headlong into the problem of the one and the many. If the concept of God as sovereign eternal absolute is true, then from His/its very nature must spring all reality. If God's nature is unity in singularity (as the Koran sets forth, and not unity in multiplicity as Christianity "declares") then reality can never transcend ultimate oneness. This means no true separation or differentiation could ever be possible. Without distinction, God cannot even be conscious of His own existence, for such must be set against something *other*. This can only and has always eventually led to a purely subjective view of reality which in turn leads to the *negation* of morality. Any sort of individualism (unique drives, desires, personality) is hopelessly at odds with a reality of undifferentiated oneness.

Nevertheless, Islam strives mightily to plug itself into Old Testament theology and to assume a type of monotheism in the tradition of Judaism and Christianity. But the Koran is not a sustained historical narrative telling the story of God progressively and painstakingly revealing His plan of redemption for mankind. It borrows important themes, but these are almost completely superficial. What, for instance, is the significance of resurrection in Islam? There is no apparent purpose; no reclaiming the physical universe back to God nor reconciliation with God; no *victory* over sin which held the physical hostage; no victory over death as the *ultimate* evil. Thus, there is no glorious triumph over evil.

Islam looks very much like a cut-and-paste religion which seeks to pretend that the insertion of key words—monotheism, judgment, sin, martyrdom, resurrection, heaven, hell—can magically transform it into something *other than* paganism. But all such insertions are obviously artificial when they fit into no rational framework. At rock bottom, Allah creates good and he creates evil. He creates human beings with whom he reveals his will, but very little of himself.[2] He predestines some for wrath and some for blessings. Yet whether one ends up ultimately in paradise or hell, Allah binds himself to no personal code prohibiting the reversal of this state many times at his pleasure. Since we are left with no rational center to the God Islam has constructed, it is a self-defeating proposition to try to reconcile meaning and purpose to this "path of enlightenment."

There is no joining or communing with Allah. There is only (at best) a state of reward completely *apart* from God (possibly with the exception of Muhammad, though this is unclear). It is blasphemous to strive to be like Allah, for it is to presume to know what he is like. Paradise is transformed into something that resembles nothing so much as a celestial whorehouse, where men are treated to their seventy-two virgins—and apparently many boys as well. What is the reward for women (allowing for the rare woman who gets there)? If most favored, they may get to be one of the seventy-two for their former husband.

Islam's reduction of God (as well as Allah's pagan roots) is evident in his capricious nature. Where the God of Christianity is of utmost holiness (separated from sin, of perfect integrity and imposing restrictions on His own actions—"cannot lie," "no shadow of turning," etc.), it is blasphemous to suggest that Allah must hold himself to *any* standard. Allah's nature cannot be revealed by studying the facts of his creation, because he can rescind or reverse the very laws of nature as many times as he desires. Thus, the seeking, searching, inquisitive hunger in man is left utterly unrequited.

Because Islam recognizes no original fall,[3] Allah is yet further reduced. If man has never existed in a sinless state from which he by his own transgression fell, then all evil in the world does not merely reflect the *effect* of separating from the source of all goodness (much as the absence of heat leaves cold or the removal of light results in darkness) but must reflect some aspect of God himself. Either he is incapable of producing a perfect state, or evil is intrinsic to his nature and he its original agent. In either case, God becomes seriously flawed. No fall also means that death is not an enemy of God but something he has intentionally imposed on his creation. Mankind is thus not an object of God's love but a toy.

No fall also means there no longer exists a rift between God and man—only an eternal unbridgeable gulf, because they never *were* in a communal relationship. Sin is no huge affront to God, merely a reflection of man's created nature. Allah does not love *first*. What remains of love (if such is even possible) is purely arbitrary and impersonal as it is not given or identified as part of his nature. His Word (the Koran) means little since he must be free to change his ordinances as he sees fit; justice thus is not intrinsic to his nature either. As with all pagan themes, *change* is the only constant.

Islam is critical of the concept of the cross. "Allah can forgive sin without recourse to all this elaborate atonement business." This is another demonstration of Muhammad's misunderstanding of Christianity and Islam's lack of depth. Theoretically, a God who is all-powerful can forgive sin without the cross. But to do so means he surrenders his perfect integrity and the concept of justice. It means he no longer (if he ever did) binds himself to a code of ethics. Hence, he is arbitrary and devoid of holiness. No holiness means humans have no remaining basis for trusting in God.

It is not too hard to see Islam combining all the classic elements of paganism. God is unknowable; God is capricious; God is inscrutable; communion/relationship with God (as with the gods) is impossible and absurd; God (at best) must be placated by endless human sacrifices (in this case, infidels who refuse to submit to the unyielding law of absolute capitulation); God (as with the gods) is indistinguishable from his/its creation. A disdain for the material world is as well evident. This side of paradise, there is nothing worth salvaging. At best, the world is a testing ground but still a prison of sorts to be escaped. The revered pagan practice of scapegoating is as well eagerly displayed (if Allah is displeased, it's because too many infidels still live). Finally, Islam leaves no doubt of its deep pagan roots with its celebration of all things sensual in their basest forms.

A comparison of the founders of these two major religions is perhaps even more revealing. Jesus set a standard so holy, so selfless, that His followers cannot possibly measure up (though they are expected to try); Jesus took no life but freely gave up His own to redeem mankind. Muhammad's standard was to *exempt* himself from the expectations placed on others. For him, fulfilling lusts, denying himself no pleasure or want was a proper reward for serving as Allah's Prophet. Lacking any self-sacrificial nature, Muhammad gleefully slaughtered thousands with no mercy and with no approach, no matter how deceitful, off limits. Jesus validated the sanctity of life. Muhammad validated the sanctity of death.

Jesus submitted willingly to the most brutal form of murder imaginable. Muhammad willingly *ordered* the most brutal forms of murder. Jesus was completely selfless. Muhammad was jealous and possessive, depriving himself of nothing his sensual appetites craved. Though He was the Son of God and sinless, Jesus exempted Himself from none of the Jewish law, keeping all of it perfectly. Muhammad was constantly changing the law, making it conform to his personal needs. In common with the usual pagan praxis, Muhammad made himself the law speaking. Jesus Christ, though impaled on a cross and in excruciating agony, took no revenge on His tormentors; though He had the power and authority to instantly incinerate them, He instead *forgave* them. Muhammad, subject to nothing worse than ridicule by a female poet (Asma bint Marwan) had her put to death.[4] In comparison to Muhammad's low opinion of women (hell would mostly be filled with them), Jesus put to shame the crowd that sought to stone the adulterous woman and then forgave her sins.

Jesus stepped into a two-thousand-year context minutely prepared specifically for Him. He proceeded to reveal Himself as the *fulfillment* of that context by His every word and deed (including specific miracles). Muhammad, though he sought to conscript that same context for his purposes, began his ministry in the context of pagan Arabia and proceeded to *magnify* an already violent and pitiless culture. Finally, the bones of Muhammad still lie in his grave. No one has ever found the bones of Jesus.

The Bible's test for an authentic prophet is presented in Deuteronomy 18:19–22. What exactly is the test for a Muslim prophet? How well do Muhammad's "prophecies" hold up against the record of history? These turn out to be few, lacking specifics, and always dealing with some very near future event. Perhaps the most frequently cited prophecy in Islam and proof of the Koran's infallibility is taken from Surah 30:2–3: "The Roman Empire has been defeated in a land close by; but they [even] after [this] defeat of theirs, will soon be victorious within a few years." Muslim scholars say this is a clear reference to the Persian victory over the Byzantine Romans in AD 615 in Syria. The "predicted" Roman victory materialized about

628, thus a powerful validation of the Koran. There is also a second part to this occurring in Surah 54:45, "Or do they [the Meccan disbelievers] say: 'We are a great multitude, and we shall be victorious?' Their multitude will be defeated, and they shall turn their backs [in flight]!"

Muslim scholars insist this latter Surah is a reference to a Muslim victory over a Meccan army at Badr which would occur roughly at the same time as the Roman victory above. The victory was prophesied, even though Muslim forces were outnumbered about 315 to 800[5] (Muslim scholars say 1,000). Thus, it is maintained, we have a remarkable "double prophecy" which leaves no doubt of the supernatural power of the Koran. Laying aside the fact that these were "fulfilled" within Muhammad's lifetime and so may have been "prophesied" after the fact, there is little that is compelling in these forecasts. They are either vague or fairly ordinary. Remember the point of prophecy is to validate the existence of divine agency (to establish omnipotence, omniscience, etc.). To be credible, prophecy must be complex, specific, multifaceted, involve vast time spans, and/or transcend physical capability. On various occasions throughout history, underdogs have vanquished enemies against imposing odds without supposing divine intervention.

The Koran ascribes no miracles to Muhammad but presents him as a warner of those who do not submit to Allah. Indeed, again and again, Muhammad is seen resisting calls to demonstrate feats in the miraculous. Compare this to the breathtakingly accurate predictions of coming empires in Daniel or the more than one hundred concerning Christ's first coming and the range of miracles He performed to validate His claims.

From its formulation of God to the life of the prophet to the Sharia, there is nothing in Islam that inspires one to reach for a higher, nobler calling. There is no challenge to transcend the base appetites to seek a sublime beauty that instills hope. To the contrary, it is these same base instincts, those most easily perturbed, that find consistent *sanctification*. Though the Bible is often indicted for endorsing the practice, slavery was not sanctioned by either the Old or New Testaments but recognized as a reality brought by sin. Remember, it was Christian influence that began the movement to *end* slavery in the West. The Koran *does* give this institution divine sanction, and slavery in fact still exists under Islamic rule in Mauritania and the Sudan.[6] Practically everything Christianity has introduced to the world, every candle it has lit to illuminate some formerly darkened corner, Islam has made its mission to snuff out. Where Christianity has unshackled the human spirit, Islam is a wasteland of the soul.

Islam and Enlightenment progressivism are both forces of destruction, helpless to restrain the impulse to eat away at any civilizing principles. They are partners in nihilism, leaving in their wake a scorched Earth and an impoverished human spirit. Enlightenment began as a subtle and insidious cancer that almost imperceptibly peeled away the layers of civilization while maintaining the highest pretensions. Though its evil core was revealed in the French Revolution, this was discounted as an aberration. Its full modern flower, progressivism is now barely distinguishable from Islam's full-frontal assault relentlessly and mercilessly mowing down everything in its path. They constitute the two sides of the same unmistakable imperialist pagan coin. Unless there is an American awakening, it is hard to say at this point which will be first to destroy America—the last Judeo-Christian refuge of hope.

CHAPTER 35

THE REBIRTH OF ISRAEL IN 1948

An enduring narrative of both progressives and Islamists is that the greatest source of Muslim terrorism is the existence of Israel. In line with this, if not for the unlawful occupation of Arab land by the Jews, and the West's (particularly the US's) continuing support of this "criminal regime," there would be no source of constant friction in the Middle East and thus no terrorist threat. The only problem with this view is that it bears no connection to any facts. Perhaps the greatest deception in the Middle East today is the myth of "the Palestinians."

When Israel became a state on May 14, 1948, the Muslim nations that surrounded her (Egypt, Iraq, Transjordan, and Syria) attacked the very next day. Lebanon would soon follow. This war, which had the intent of driving the newly recognized nation into the Mediterranean, would end with between 600,000 and 800,000 Palestinian Arabs either voluntarily leaving or being expelled from their homes.[1] Most of these were evacuated by order of Arab leaders. After the unthinkable happened, with Palestinian Jews prevailing against overwhelming odds, a strategic decision was made by the Arab world. Though one might have expected the humane thing would have been for these attacking nations to absorb these now-homeless into their own populations, since there was commonality of historic tribes among all these groups, the humane solution was not to be.

It was quickly realized what a valuable propaganda tool these displaced could be if, instead of being assimilated into local populations, they were placed in United Nations-sponsored refugee camps. Here they could be employed as a constant source of agitation against "Zionist aggression." History would soon give way to revision.

Historically, no such people as "the Palestinians" had ever existed. In fact, the only instances where the term appeared in history were in reference to the *Jews*. "Palastina" was the derisive term applied to the region by the Romans in the second century AD. The term was a bastardization of the historic bane to the Jews—the

Philistines. No matter—not only would refugees be supplied with this new name (to distinguish from other Arab tribes of the region), they would also be assigned a new history which maintained that their "Palestinian ancestors" had called this region home for hundreds of years. In fact, it was the Jews who had maintained a presence in the land for at least three thousand years.

There is an important context to the international war Palestinian Jews would fight against surrounding nations that is left out of modern condemnation of Israel. Palestinian Arabs were offered the opportunity to have their own independent state on separate occasions, beginning in 1937. Each time, the offer was refused; Arab independence always predicated its acceptance on the condition of Jewish expulsion. Never did Palestinian Jews predicate their quest for statehood on the absence of Arabs. The UN proposed and passed a partition on November 29, 1947 that would have recognized a Jewish state and an Arab state. The response by Palestinian Arabs was to attack Palestinian Jews.

As the date of the end of the British mandate (May 14, 1948) drew near, a Jewish policy of limiting the fight to only defending Jewish communities was becoming too costly to maintain. The Jews would have to take the fight to the enemy. Those houses that supplied support to the guilty were destroyed. But Arabs and villages that remained at peace were to be left alone. Eventually, Jewish leadership, faced with a blockade that threatened their very survival, would reluctantly choose an aggressive posture of destroying villages used as staging areas for assaults, and expelling their inhabitants.[2] And yes, atrocities were sometimes committed during these events, though in violation of strict Jewish policy and never rivaling the magnitude of atrocities committed against Jews, the sober fact to which David Brog alludes, "Had the Palestinian Arabs not rejected partition in 1947, there would not have been a war."[3] And of course, no refugee crisis.

There is a history that predates the birth of modern Israel and the "Palestinian question" which is also ignored. Under the Ottoman Empire, former states had seen boundaries fade away into one great expanse of Turkish-held territory. Regions of the empire came under the jurisdiction of appointed viziers who ruled (rather loosely) from the nearest major city of a given territory. In the mid to late nineteenth century, Ottoman authorities began an initiative, bringing European Muslims to Palestine to counter a growing Jewish immigration movement. Egyptian historian Bat Ye'or: "The Ottoman government settled these emigrants in troubled regions, thereby tightening its control through a policy of Muslim colonization. In 1878 after annexation of Bosnia-Herzegovina by Austria, Bosnian Muslim colonists arrived in Macedonia and on the coastal plain of Palestine."[4]

Hal Lindsey explains the concept of the *effendis*: These were essentially Ottoman landlords who "only cared about profit and seldom left the luxury of Istanbul [the Turkish capitol] to check on their real estate."[5] Under the usual arrangement, Muslim peasant farmers would pay extortionist fees to effendis for the right to work the land. Because the cost made it nearly impossible to eke out a profit, most peasants would eventually abandon the cause and the land to increasing desolation. For *effendis*, the resurgence of Jews in the land presented an opportunity for double exploitation: They could sell these otherwise worthless tracts of land at exorbitant rates *and* make the Jews the scapegoats for "the theft of Muslim land." Never mind that Muslims now flocking to the area for jobs were enjoying a much higher standard of living in comparison to the heartless exploitation suffered under the *effendis*.[6]

Returning Jews to Palestine, as Hal Lindsey puts it, "faced a harsh life in a barren Malaria-infested land."[7] Yet the Jews continued to come and to build up the wasteland, with the founding of Tel Aviv occurring in 1909. In the early 1900s, after a meeting with Chaim Weizmann, leader of the Zionist movement, former British prime minister Lord Balfour made public his intent to extend a gesture to the Jews. The intent was to try to make amends for the ill-treatment they had suffered from time immemorial, of "doing something material to wash out an ancient stain upon our own civilization."[8]

With the outbreak of World War I, the intricate network of treaties and agreements would eventually engulf the Middle East; with the Ottoman Empire siding with the German-led Central powers. In 1917, in fulfillment of the former prime minister's sentiment, the Balfour Declaration was issued. This promised the Jews that they would finally, after nearly two thousand years, have a recognized homeland in Palestine again. Many in England were caught up in the spirit of ancient prophecies suddenly unfolding. With the Allied victory that resulted and the fall of the Ottoman Empire, the land was carved up into new states. A tract of land was staked out for the Jews as a reward for their assistance to the Allies. Just years later, the League of Nations would make this official.

Lindsey lists the signatories to the formal agreement concerning the territory mandated to the Jews: "His Royal Highness and the Emir Feisal ibn-Hussein, representing and acting on behalf of the Arab Kingdom of Hedjaz, and Chaim Weitzman, representing and acting on behalf of the Zionist Organization."[9] The League of Nations unanimously approved the boundaries. "The territory to become the state of Israel—then variously referred to as 'Palestine,' 'Western Palestine,' 'South Syria,' or even as part of Turkey—extended east and west of the Jordan River from the Mediterranean to Lebanon and Syria."[10] The lands that would become Saudi Arabia, Syria, and Iraq were also recognized now as independent states.

In violation of every recognized standard of law, Britain would give away 75 percent of the promised land to appease Abdullah, brother of Feisal ibn Hussein (signatory to the formal agreement). Writes Lindsey: "When Britain gave Transjordan to Abdullah, it specifically violated Article 5 of the Mandate given unanimous approval by the League of Nations at the San Remo Conference on July 24, 1922."[11] As Lindsey points out, the Mandate given Britain by the League of Nations was to facilitate the immigration of Jews to Palestine, *not* Arabs. Britain did precisely the opposite. And as a little sidebar, Lindsey reminds observers of an inconvenient fact that is almost completely lost in the modern "Palestinian question": There does indeed already exist an *independent Palestinian state*—Jordan, carved out of the Palestinian land that was promised and legally mandated to the Jews.[12]

While turning a blind eye to Arab immigration to Palestine, British restrictions on Jewish immigration became increasingly stringent. Nor was much done to stem the tide of Arab violence against Jews. The British solution was to limit *Jewish* immigration and land purchases.

It is not even arguable from the record that Britain's restriction on Jewish immigration was responsible for the death of untold numbers of Jews. Many German Jews not only sought to flee to Palestine when the first ominous clouds manifest on the horizon, but would have been permitted to if not for unconscionable British obstacles. Adolf Hitler, in a 1938 speech, declared, "I can only hope and expect that the other world, which has such deep sympathy for these criminals [Jews], will at least be generous enough to convert this sympathy into practical aid. We on our part, are ready to put all those criminals at the disposal of these countries, for all I care, even on luxury ships."[13] In 1941, the Grand Mufti of Jerusalem, Amin al-Husseini, met with Hitler to convince him to expand his anti-Jewish program into the Middle East. The Mufti expressed his gratitude for Hitler's Muslim sympathies and the campaign he was waging against their common enemy.

Since Israel's formal recognition by the United Nations in 1948, this tiny nation's existence has been in constant peril. The day after the official ratification (as already noted) Israel would find herself engaged in a fifteen-month war against five Muslim nations that would cost more than six thousand Israeli lives. More than a thousand more Israeli civilians would be killed by Egyptian-sponsored terrorists between the years 1949–1956. In 1956 Israel would again find herself at war, after Egypt prohibited Israeli shipping through the Suez Canal; Israel would capture the Sinai Peninsula and the Gaza Strip. After Egypt ceased hostilities, these spoils of war were quickly returned, though Israel had not been the aggressor and was under no obligation to return the land. In 1964, the Palestine Liberation Organization (PLO) was formed, with Yasser Arafat soon to assume leadership. The PLO would be responsible for thousands of attacks on unsuspecting Israeli citizens.

In 1967, Egypt, Syria, Iraq, and Jordan massed more than 250,000 troops and Soviet supplied tanks on Israel's borders. In just six days, against any rational expectation, Israel not only defeated this imposing force but managed to capture the Gaza Strip and Sinai Peninsula from Egypt, the Golan Heights from Syria, and the West Bank from Jordan. The best explanation as to why this tiny nation was not annihilated by this Goliath: divine intervention. Palestinian Arabs would not self-identify as "Palestinians" until after this war. Even the Grand Mufti of Jerusalem had insisted, following World War I, that Arabs living in Palestine considered themselves historically part of Syria. Both the UN and the Arab League did not officially recognize a distinct "Palestinian people" until the 1970s.[14]

In 1973, while Israel was observing the holiest day of its year (Yom Kippur), Egypt and Syria attacked without warning. Completely caught off guard, Israel would pay her highest cost yet to finally turn back overwhelming numbers. Since this time, the Muslim world has put increasing pressure on the entire world, through terrorist campaigns and constant UN agitation, to withdraw any support for Israel.

Based on the usual portrayal by the media, one would think Israel is the big bully on the block that can't help throwing its weight around. In fact, Israel's land mass is about one-sixth of 1 percent of the land mass of the Arab world. In comparison to over 300 million Arabs and Muslims of the Middle East, there are 6.5 million Israeli Jews. No war that has taken place between Israel and the surrounding nations has ever been *initiated* by Israel. Though Israel has responded (to constant deliberate targeting of the most helpless unsuspecting portion of her civilian population) with precision strikes that target military sites such as ammunition depots and terrorist training bases, the media chooses to portray the actions of both sides as a moral equivalency. Israel is decried as an "occupier" of Arab land, though the Jews have had the largest presence in Jerusalem since the early 1870s.

In 1979, Israel agreed to return the Sinai Peninsula to Egypt as a gesture of goodwill. In 2000, Israel withdrew from Lebanon, and in 2005 relinquished Gaza and a portion of the West Bank. The result? The terrorist organization Hamas immediately took over Gaza to launch continuous attacks against Israel, and Hezbollah from Lebanon. Nevertheless, Israel is constantly pressured to surrender still more "land for peace."

In the closing days of his administration, President Obama abstained from voting on a UN Security Council resolution condemning Israeli settlements in contested territory as a flagrant violation of international law. Though America had veto power, Obama allowed a 14–0 passage that instantly rendered criminal status to those Israelis living outside of the pre-'67 borders. This openly invited a new escalation of anti-Semitism and justified any number of hostilities against Israel, from serious economic sanctions to violent attacks. Moreover, had Israel accepted this UN resolution, her national security would have been militarily indefensible.

How are we in any practical terms to explain the nation of Israel, no bigger than the state of New Jersey, becoming a world-class military power in a single generation? What are we to make of a desert wasteland that suddenly blossomed with the arrival of this people (as was prophesied)? How are we to account for an occurrence that is unprecedented in history? Just how do we explain the Jews retaining their unique identity, despite suffering numerous captivities and being scattered literally all over the earth? History tells us any such group would have long ago assimilated into these foreign populations, and any distinguishing characteristics long since disappeared. How do we explain a tiny sliver of land, surrounded by hostile nations committed to her destruction, not only repelling a series of attacks beginning at her inception, but actually expanding her borders in these unprovoked assaults, though hopelessly outnumbered? Why has this same little sliver along the eastern Mediterranean become the fulcrum for virtually all international political posturing?

Finally, why has the Muslim world, despite a never-ending campaign of terror, hatred, and propaganda, been unable to displace this tiny island of resistance? There is an answer. Regardless of Muslim rhetoric or how many politicians try to engineer an alternate reality, the land occupied by the Jews at present was originally promised to them not by man, but by God. "And the LORD said unto Abram, after that Lot was separated from him, Lift up now thine eyes, and look from the place where thou art northward, and southward, and eastward, and westward: For all the land which thou seest, to thee will I give it, and to thy seed *for ever*" (Gen. 13:14–15, emphasis mine). This promise is amplified in Genesis 15:18: "In the same day the LORD made a covenant with Abram, saying, Unto thy seed have I given this land, from the river Egypt unto the great river, the river Euphrates." The apostle Paul would remind the church at Rome that God's gifts are *irrevocable* (Rom. 11:29). Those who want concrete evidence of God's existence and that the Bible is trustworthy need look no further than the thoroughly modern miracle of Israel.

If America is to beat back the forces of progressivism and fascism, we must seek God's favor and forgiveness. Perhaps the most direct route to both is to stand in full solidarity with His chosen nation. Fortunately, President Trump has taken concrete steps to turn back the serious jeopardy into which his predecessor has placed Israel, as well as the serious damage to our relationship with the only democracy in the Middle East.

Today, the meltdown of civility, the fear of economic and environmental collapse, and the Islamic threat have produced a pervasive sense of insecurity. Many would be willing to surrender a great portion of their personal freedom just for the hope of universal stability. Progressivism, with its new partner in crime, Islamism (which will eventually turn on its patron), is now presuming to offer the solution to the very instability it deliberately cultivated.

Ever since the fall, human beings have sensed the disharmony in the universe. Virtually every form of human government has been geared toward restoring that balance. God intended that governments should be a terror to evil (Rom. 13:3). Because they have so often refused to acknowledge His sovereign authority and have, instead, fashioned themselves into the agents of salvation, governments have often been a terror to the people. This has been true from Babylon, to Greece, to Rome, to Nazi Germany, to the Soviet Union, and to the present progressive efforts to radically transform America. The Tower of Babel was perhaps the culmination of the first concerted effort to fuse the various strands of human ingenuity with human conceit. In imitation of the evil master it defaulted to (knowingly or otherwise), fallen humanity would exalt its throne above God's. God split this up, dispersing humanity.

The Roman Empire was the culmination of a great human effort to mend that rift. Jesus Christ came and broke this up. But He did something more: He gave the world something very tangible to compare against pagan empire. He gave the world a preview, though but the faintest shadow, of the kind of ultimate world transformation that will one day take place under the kingdom of God. Nevertheless, the Enlightenment has chosen to rebuild the Tower of Babel, brick by brick, content with nothing less than pulling God out of the heavens and casting Him under the garbage heap of obsolete ideas. The rallying cry of Enlightenment man: "We have no king but Caesar!"

For nearly two millennia, God has offered *the* solution to the world, the King of kings. One nation boldly took up that offer and, though it sometimes faltered, became a shimmering jewel of liberty, prosperity, human dignity, and hope unparalleled in history. Its greatest sin, the one for which it can never be forgiven, it once put the lie to Caesar's claims.

*   *   *

"I call heaven and earth to record this day against you, that I have set before you life and death, blessing and cursing: therefore choose life, that both thou and thy seed may live" (Deut. 30:19). "For what shall it profit a man, if he shall gain the whole world, and lose his own soul? Or what shall a man give in exchange for his soul? Whosoever therefore shall be ashamed of me and my words in this adulterous and sinful generation; of him also shall the Son of man be ashamed, when he cometh in the glory of his Father with the holy angels" (Mark 8:36–38). This book, the Bible, has been written that you might choose life. The invitation is extended to all, Jew, Muslim, atheist, agnostic, Republican, Democrat, black, brown, yellow, red, and white.

CHAPTER 36

A FEW FINAL THOUGHTS,
ESPECIALLY FOR CHRISTIANS

The Bible warns of a time of God's wrath coming upon the world that is usually referred to as the Great Tribulation. In Bible theology, this represents the culmination of human history and God's final response (in history) to rebellion. While I find no Scriptural grounds for refuting that coming wrath, there is an attitude sometimes manifest in my fellow Christians who hold this view that is troubling. For some, it seems that praying and working for American (and worldwide) Christian revival and seeking to turn back the evil that has overtaken this nation is, well, an intrusion. Some take it beyond this and suggest such activism is an outright denial of Scripture and an effort to circumvent God's plan.

To the latter it must be asked, can there ever be a time when it would be an affront to God to fulfill the Great Commission? Why would we ever assume we have entered a time when we no longer need to be "salt and light" to the world? It has been argued that the Bible is silent concerning any sort of great revival prior to the prophesied wrath, thus there is no reason to suppose this is even possible. While I do not necessarily agree, even if we accept this, would silence *preclude* such a revival? Would the Bible have to specifically mention it for it to be possible? Did the Bible mention either the first or the second American Great Awakenings? Even if we could all agree there are overwhelming signs indicating Christ's return and that God's wrath are near, how would that make it acceptable to stand down in the face of evil and let it have its way? Wouldn't we want His coming to find us actively engaged in pushing back the darkness, rather than spectating on the sidelines?

One caller to a radio show derided Christians for thinking we could somehow circumvent God's wrath by voting certain candidates into office. To be clear, the desire to restore America has nothing to do with thinking Christians can change God's plan. Yet, there is something very odd about equating working to bring multitudes of souls into the kingdom and opposing evil with "disrupting God's plan." For the first time in so many years, Christians have tangible hope that America can be brought back from the brink (even if only for a season) but there seem to be no shortage of Christians *offended* by this. This, of course, brings us to President Donald Trump.

To be sure, President Trump is not and cannot be a savior. But he can be God's instrument for finally taking on the most odious disease to ever inflict this nation—political correctness. Frankly, where have we ever seen any political figure willing to stand in the face of the whole range of leftist fury without backing down? Consider how unlikely Mr. Trump's ascendancy to the presidency has been. Having never run for *any* political office before, he had to overcome the inertia of many decades, with only the people standing behind him. The opposition included the dominant left-wing media, European global elitists and their vision of open borders, the Democratic Party, the ruthless Clinton machine, the Republican establishment, and many "conservative" commentators who attacked Trump with a vigor we have never seen directed at our supposed mutual opponents. All these viewed Trump as a grave existential threat to the status quo.

The odds of Mr. Trump overcoming all these are so overwhelming that, surely, we must at least entertain the notion of divine intervention—that there is a *possibility* this may represent God's answer to multitudes of prayers that so many have sent up for so long. Indeed, Trump is a flawed man, but how does that disqualify him? It's cliched, nevertheless true, that unless Christ is on the ballot even our most preferred candidate will be flawed, and that each election will always be a matter of choosing the lesser of the evils. If flawlessness was essential to God placing one in a crucial pivotal role, Martin Luther's obscene vilification of Jews would have disqualified him (and surely King David's acts of adultery and murder). Yet frustratingly, this is what seems so utterly lost on those Christians and conservatives who remain never-Trumpers on "principled grounds." With all due respect, which lofty principle would have abstained on an opportunity to stop Hillary Clinton?

One of the Left's most persistent strategies for erasing our borders has been the attempt to subsume American sovereignty under UN treaties. Had Mrs. Clinton won, she would have appointed at least one and possibly as many as three Supreme Court judges who could have ensured a full generation of rule by supreme edict instead of rule by law, possibly ending the American dream forever. What would have almost certainly happened, however, is something almost too evil to contemplate. Mrs. Clinton would have revisited and vigorously pushed for something she first championed during her husband's presidency—the UN Convention on the Rights of the Child.

Perhaps the fundamental and most cherished form of government in God's eyes is the family. It is within this structure that self-discipline and character develop. Here is where respect for authority and especially respect for God is fostered. Here values are painstakingly nurtured, human beings molded into the civic-minded citizens who will define the culture of tomorrow. For some, it is where they will learn the fundamentals of godly government over which they will preside.

No better example of rotten fruit exists than the shattered families (especially black families) left in the wake of progressivism. It is within this fundamental God-ordained institution the Left has waged its most intense and sustained war. Only recently, the Supreme Court has dealt a serious blow to this institution with its decree that homosexuals must be afforded the same constitutional marriage protections as heterosexuals though there is, actually, no *right* of marriage mentioned anywhere in the Constitution. It was also an activist court, informed by progressive dogma, that gave us Roe v. Wade, leaving a legacy of more than 50 *million* murdered babies.

Had Mrs. Clinton won the presidency, emboldened by the gains of the last eight years (and what would have appeared to be the silencing of the last whimper of resistance), she would have had the highest confidence that ratification of this treaty was now within reach. Let's consider just a few of this treaty's "rights."[1]

Article 12, para. 2: "For this purpose [freedom to express personal views], the child shall in particular be provided the opportunity to be heard in judicial and administrative proceedings affecting the child." Under this right, children would be entitled to take their parents to court and challenge parental decrees.

Article 13, para. 1: "The child shall have the right to freedom of expression; this right shall include freedom to seek, receive and impart information and ideas of all kind, regardless of frontiers, either orally, in writing or in print, in the form of art, or through any other media of the child's choice." In practice, this would mean any child could not be denied access to pornography in any form he desires. Any child would be entitled to seek any sort of information including from the vilest and most corrupting sources in direct contradiction to parents' wishes.

Article 14, para. 1: "States Parties shall respect the right of the child to freedom of thought, conscience, and religion." Translation: no parent can compel any child to receive the religious instruction of the parent's choice. The child must be free to make that choice, which includes no religion at all if he so chooses.

Article 15, para. 1: "States Parties recognize the rights of the child to freedom of association and to freedom of peaceful association." Children would thus be free to associate with whomsoever they choose with no parental oversight, including the right to associate with pedophiles or the worst criminal element.

Such a treaty, of course, would reduce parents to nothing more than physical providers and facilitators to whatever whims strike the fancy of their children. No more moral guidance, no imparting serious consequences to rebellious actions, or any significant role for parents in shaping the lives of their children. And while the UN Convention on Child's Rights does at various points qualify its assertions, these are in deference to local community or government and not to parental authority. Remember also, Christian religion is already considered a form of child abuse to those who would interpret these rights. Ignoring the Framers' own narrow interpretation, progressive courts could have easily twisted Article VI, paragraph 2 of the Constitution into justification for superseding Constitutional protections and restraints.

In President Trump, we have possibly the least likely person we could ever imagine God might use to affect major change in America; to pull her back from the brink of destruction and maybe even to turn this nation back to God. Whatever his flaws, Mr. Trump has identified the corrupt fruit of so many years of progressivism run amok ("the swamp") and courageously taken it on. We have learned, sadly, that the swamp is not limited to the Democratic Party and the "deep state" but runs through the Republican establishment. One can at least respect the Democratic Party for its willingness to fight for its values. But for a smattering of conservatives, Republicans have no apparent principles, showing only lukewarm support for the president.

What if "for just such a time as this" God has raised up this man to give us one last precious opportunity to restore His order? Do we (the church) dare walk away from this without at least making every good faith effort? Whether we care to own it, statism has been able to fill the void and flourish only to the extent to which the church has abandoned the field. It seems we Christians are sitting in our pews, intent on hearing the latest sermon on sound biblical parenting techniques, oblivious to the barbarians at the gate who are perilously close to taking our children away.

Fear and intimidation seem to have driven the church to a point of near-denial and rationalization. Pastors are so frightened of the labels that will attach if they speak from their pulpits on the cultural rot of our day—identifying the *source*—that they have convinced themselves they must avoid taking sides. It is as though pacifism and "acceptance" in the face of escalating evil is a virtue and the evidence one is fair-minded and loving. This shows the extent to which the church has (unknowingly) accepted the narrative of the Left and surrendered control of the language to progressivism.

Should there *ever* be a time when the church willingly, obligingly retreats in the face of evil? When we consider the unique gift God has given the world in this nation called America, will we who have reaped the fruit not be held accountable for allowing it to be trampled into the dust? Can it be good that something so precious paid for in the toil, sweat, tears, blood, and in a great many instances, the personal sacrifice of our forerunners, should be surrendered with scarcely any resistance?

Those who take exception to the above are quick to point out that the Romans 13 passage (which speaks on God's institution of human government) was written by the apostle Paul during intense persecution of the church. Yet, it is stated, Paul made no exceptions for Christians regarding the respect they were to give to the state. There are a few points worth considering. First, any government's God-given authority is based on an implied contract with the people it represents and is legitimate only to the extent it executes God's ordained role—to serve as a terror to evil. When any government abdicates this primary responsibility and *becomes* the instrument of evil and a terror to the people, it forfeits any allegiance from those it represents. It was precisely on these grounds the Founding Fathers declared their moral right to sever ties with England. The Christian clergy took the lead in asserting that only to the extent government operates *within* established rules of law and especially God's *higher law* are citizens duty-bound to obey.

Perhaps the most important point overlooked in citing the Romans passage is the *reason* Christians were suffering this intense persecution: They, including Paul, were engaging in *civil disobedience*. While they were willing to "render unto Caesar that which belonged to Caesar," they were not willing to render unto Caesar "that which belonged to God." They were not anti-government; they were anti-*statist*. They refused to accord allegiance or authority to any entity overstepping its rightful God-ordained authority, even though it meant surrendering their lives. This is an exact parallel with today's Christian conservative movement. We also are not anti-government but anti-statist. Nothing in our movement is about opposing government per se. We stand against exactly what the early church stood against.

We are not, as is often charged, trying to impose a theocracy upon this nation any more than our Founders were. This is not about trying to "Christianize" the country, nor to "beat people into purity." It is about voting for the best available candidates—and if possible, Christians, as there will be a greater likelihood they will uphold biblical principles. It is not about voting to *deny* anyone the freedom to sin or force any to perform acts of righteousness against their will. It is about voting for and supporting legislation that either returns us to or reinforces the *Constitution*. Our zealous support of the Constitution is not simply for selfish benefit but is the *only* guarantee that those with whom we profoundly disagree will be protected. That legislation which we oppose which eviscerates the Constitution and that *seems* to benefit, say, homosexuals or transsexuals creates only (and at best) an *illusion* of protection because these extra-Constitutional "rights" eventually erode fundamental rights and enslave the very people they presume to help.

"Conservatism" is simply a comprehensive Christian answer to the question, "How then shall we live?" which *must* engage the politics of the day that respect *no* personal boundaries. It is fundamentally about supporting and reestablishing the Christian principles and order that once undergirded this nation and are embodied in our Constitution. While this movement zealously preserves the freedoms and opportunities of all Americans, there is nothing about it that compels anyone to submit to Christianity. While we in this movement do oppose such things as abortion and same-sex marriage, it has nothing to do with forcing our views on others any more than, for instance, opposing *any* form of murder would mean that we expect potential murderers to "share our values."

So, the concern for the church encroaching on the role of the state is not only misplaced but puts it exactly backward. It is the state (under progressivism) that has aggressively sought to assume every intended role of the church and is now dangerously close to being there. Christian conservatism's efforts have largely been aimed at rolling back this dangerous intrusion and reasserting the church's rightful authority (in accordance with our founding), while attempting to reassert vital constitutional restraints on the state. Without these restraints, we (including atheists) are all on the road to tyranny.

My earnest prayer is that the church would finally wake up to take its rightful place in the spiritual battle raging for the soul of America. My hope is the church will assume once again its role as salt and light to the world and no longer limit itself to preaching to the choir. But that can only happen when preachers recognize that a cultural war is being waged against God's order. This war is not taking place in some arena outside the church's jurisdiction; it is being waged *against the church*. If we are to take this seriously, it must begin with a willingness to engage the culture, to speak out and take a principled stand *in the public square* where we are willing to take the persecution that will immediately come our way.

In our church meetings, we must be willing to take an honest look at how culturally irrelevant the church has become. We must realize that many of the methods we have used in the past have been wholly inadequate. Typically, our children have all their young lives attended Sunday School where they are given nice stories about Jesus or Daniel and the lion. They are given cartoon cutouts of Noah and his cute animals hanging out of a silly-looking boat. These are fun stories to be sure, but they are presented in almost fairy-tale settings that, far too often, do little to distinguish themselves from Aesop's fables or Santa Claus. There is almost no effort made (even in high school years) to ground beliefs in sound apologetics.

As a result, when young students go off to college, they are completely unprepared for the progressive barrage that will greet them. Because typically little was done to lay out the big picture for them, they do not understand they are encountering, head-on, Satan's alternative to God's order. Soon, they are overwhelmed by what they assume are the unrelenting facts of science and scholarship against their very feeble fairy tales. Had they been raised from early on to understand what they believe and why, taught the facts of America's founding, and trained to recognize the numerous holes in Satan's illusion and how to testify to others of its bankruptcy, not only would they have survived the barrage but could have thrived and used this opportunity to educate their peers.

To be clear, Christians' first responsibility is to confront personal sin. Yet there is no reason to suppose the Holy Spirit is incapable of empowering Christians to walk and chew gum at the same time. Not only can we be empowered to wage war on these two fronts, but I do not see from a biblical viewpoint how we can successfully confront either without confronting the other. If we content ourselves with being "good men" within an ever-shrinking sphere, we eventually become the Christian version of what C. S. Lewis referred to as "men without chests" ("We castrate and bid the gelding be fruitful"[2]).

Edmund Burke once said, "All that is necessary for the triumph of evil is that good men do nothing." This sums up the concern. Today, we have numerous good men, good *preachers*, who have for so long been standing on the sidelines trying mightily to convince themselves this is really not the church's fight. I once believed that, too. But how can we honestly think we have no role in standing against evil? In this last century, Dietrich Bonhoeffer put it this way: "Silence in the face of evil is itself evil: God will not hold us guiltless. Not to speak is to speak. Not to act is to act."

Mr. Bonhoeffer was a German Christian minister who, against the deafening silence of most of the German church, chose to speak out against Hitler's murderous campaign against Jews. This courageous act would cost him his life. Incidentally, Hitler's policy toward the German church was eerily similar to President Obama's Justice Department: Clergy and laity were free to worship according to their conscience within the four walls of their church buildings, but could expect the iron fist of a jealous state if those convictions challenged government policy.

*   *   *

A search through history will show that statism—government that refuses to bow to God as His tool for dispensing justice, but insists it must assume the role of God—is always animated by an agenda that not only shares no commonality with biblical principles but manifests in a concerted rebellion against a sovereign God who is not malleable to man's whims, rebellion only sustained by constantly and artificially propping-up an inverted reality. Recall some of these elements brought to light in the course of this book: an inverted creation story (evolution); an inverted form of justice (fairness—"leveling the playing field" through government deciding the winners and the losers); morality (the end justify the means, coupled with "raw power equals truth"); heaven (a manmade earthly utopia); an alternate savior (the state), and an alternate king (Caesar). Statism demands that man, not God, must be the ultimate interpretive principle. It also must reject the notion of original sin, so it may embrace the perfectibility of man. Finally, statism recognizes no limitations to its reach, placing the restraining emphasis entirely on the governed.

Where statism eventually results in a vacuum of meaning, Islam is only too willing to fill the void with its "promise of transcendence." But because it shares an essential pagan core with the former, it cannot offer a significant alternative. It too cannot present itself out in the open where it may be thoughtfully investigated, evaluated and weighed in the balance. It can only thrive if wrapped within an agenda.

Truth (personified by Jesus Christ) has no agenda. The test for any cause as to whether it is truth-driven or agenda-driven is always evident. Truth does not require whipping up a crowd into an emotional frenzy; it never requires pitting one group against another; it does not divide according to economic class or superficial characteristics; it does not need to conceal any of its intent; it does not require a scapegoat because it instead always demands one first look inwardly in serious sober self-examination before blaming others; it does not require hatred or marginalization of some group to justify its actions or legitimate its existence; it never objects to giving full consideration to *all* facts; it does not require masquerading as something else because its real nature would be rejected if known.

An agenda cannot be sustained without engaging in all these early and often. Unlike Marxism, Islamism, and all such statist schemes, truth never seeks a way to get even but demands forgiveness. When truth is forced to deal harshly, it does so only after long, careful, thoughtful deliberation and only because justice demands it. Have there been times when large segments calling themselves Christians and supposedly standing for truth displayed some or all of the deceptions above? Yes, unarguably. And to the extent they did, they showed they were actually *haters* of God.

Sadly, for much too long, we have allowed the false leftist narrative to divide us. The real demarcation has nothing to do with pigmentation, gender, economics, or any other convenient political demographic. The battle line is and always has been between those who love truth and humbly receive it, whatever the personal cost, versus those so fearful of relinquishing that most coveted throne of self that they would prefer the gall of strong delusion—the fleshpots of Egypt—to liberty in Christ. Notice, folks of every stripe are on either side.

To those Christians clinging to the idea there is something noble or compassionate in the socialist/progressive experiment (or that a bridge to Islam is possible), please understand that you are trying to exist simultaneously in two separate and irreconcilable worlds. Now that a clear distinction has been drawn, please accept this invitation to walk away from the suicide spiral of the "social gospel" into the radiant, liberating light of *Christ's* gospel. Your treasure is far too valuable to surrender even a tiny portion to Satan's clever though deadly counterfeit, when the *eternal* life-affirming promises of God's kingdom are calling you to service.

ENDNOTES

Chapter 1 Closing the Gap

1. Quoted in M. Stanton Evans, *The Theme Is Freedom* (Washington, DC: Regnery Publishing, Inc, 1994), 133.

Chapter 2 Separated to Reveal a Holy God

1. K. A. Kitchen, *On the Reliability of the Old Testament* (Grand Rapids, MI: Wm. B. Eerdmans Publishing Co., 2003), 425.

Chapter 3 The Jews Enter Canaan: A Genocidal Campaign?

1. Timothy Freke and Peter Gandy, *The Laughing Jesus: Religious Lies and Gnostic Wisdom* (New York: Three Rivers Press, 2005), 5.

2. Ibid., 7.

3. Ibid.

4. Ibid., 17.

5. Ibid., 15.

6. Lou Michel and Dan Herbeck, *American Terrorist* (New York: Harper Collins, 2001), 142–143.

7. Freke and Gandy, *The Laughing Jesus*, 14.

8. Ibid., 21.

9. Ibid.

10. Ibid., 47.

11. Ibid.

12. Ibid., 22.

13. Ibid., 49.

14. For a fuller treatment of this subject see Glenn Miller, "How Could a God of Love Order the Massacre and Annihilation of the Canaanites?" The Christian Think Tank, http://christianthinktank.com/qamorite.html.

15. Freke and Gandy, *The Laughing Jesus*, 50.

Chapter 5 Power-Hungry Misogynists or Courageous Christian Soldiers?

1. Freke and Gandy, *The Laughing Jesus,* 77.

2. Ignatius, *Epistle to the Magnesians*, in The Ante-Nicene Fathers, Vol. 1, eds. Alexander Roberts and James Donaldson (Peabody, MA: Hendrickson Publishers, 1995).

3. Justin Martyr, *The First Apology of Justin*, The Ante-Nicene Fathers.

4. Irenaeus, *Against Heresies*, The Ante-Nicene Fathers.

5. Bryan M. Litfin, *Getting to Know the Church Fathers* (Ada, MI: Brazos Press, 2007), 112.

6. Ibid., 176–183.

7. Ibid., 194–205.

8. Ibid., 217–230.

Chapter 6 The God-Man Who Revolutionized the World

1. Evans, *The Theme Is Freedom*, 150.

2. Tom Bethel, *The Noblest Triumph* (New York: St. Martin's Press, 1998), 79.

3. Ibid.

4. D. James Kennedy and Jerry Newcombe, *What If Jesus Had Never Been Born?* (Nashville: Thomas Nelson, 1994), 183.

Chapter 7 Racism and Slavery

1. Dinesh D'Souza, *The End of Racism* (New York: The Free Press, 1995), 22.

2. Ibid., 350.

3. Ibid., 351–352.

4. Ibid., 352.

5. Ibid., 353.

6. Ibid., 105–106.

Chapter 8 The US Constitution and the Philosophy That Inspired Our Founding

1. John Eidsmoe, *Christianity and the Constitution* (Grand Rapids, MI: Baker, 1995), 356–358.

2. Evans, *The Theme Is Freedom*, 206.

3. Ibid., 237–238.

4. Ibid., 201.

Chapter 9 The Renaissance and the Enlightenment

1. Josh McDowell, *The New Evidence That Demands a Verdict* (Nashville: Thomas Nelson, 1999), 628.

2. Friedrich Nietzsche, *Beyond Good and Evil* (New York: Barnes & Noble Books, 1996), 11–12.

Chapter 10 Providence and Liberty

1. Eidsmoe, *Christianity and the Constitution*, 51–53.

2. Evans, *The Theme Is Freedom*, 245–246.

3. Quoted in Evans, *The Theme Is Freedom*, 285.

4. Quoted in Daniel L. Dreisbach, *Thomas Jefferson and the Wall of Separation between Church and State* (New York: New York University Press, 2002), 55.

5. Ibid., 58.

6. Ibid., 59.

Chapter 11 Four White Men and the Most Brutal Century of Human Destruction

1. *The New Encyclopedia Britannica*, 15th Ed., Vol. 20 (Chicago: The University of Chicago, 1991), 489.

Chapter 12 The Darwinian Triumph

1. Quoted by Gertrude Himmelfarb, *Darwin and the Darwinian Revolution* (Chicago: Elephant Paperback, 1996), 12.

2. Charles Darwin, *The Origin of Species*, Online Literature Library, https://pdfs.semanticscholar.org/d109/120334dc0d0a33f698e411c8af903c59bc5d.pdf.

3. David Stove, *On Enlightenment* (New Brunswick, NJ: Transaction Publishers, 2003), 87.

4. Himmelfarb, *Darwin and the Darwinian Revolution*, 341.

5. Stove, *On Enlightenment*, 68.

6. Himmelfarb, *Darwin and the Darwinian Revolution*, 406.

Chapter 13 Marxism

1. *The New Encyclopedia Britannica*, Vol. 23, 579.

2. Ibid., Vol. 28, 1000.

3. Tom Bethell, *The Noblest Triumph* (New York: St. Martin's Press, 1998), 144.

Chapter 14 Higher Criticism, and the Wellhausen Documentary Hypothesis

1. McDowell, *Evidence*, 409.

2. Ibid., 392–394.

3. Ibid., 419–436.

4. Cyrus H. Gordon, "Higher Critics and Forbidden Fruit," *Christianity Today* 4 (Nov. 23, 1959), 133–134.

5. McDowell, *Evidence*, 476.

6. Ibid., 426–427.

7. W. J. Martin, *Stylistic Criteria and the Analysis of the Pentateuch* (London: Tyndale Press, 1995), 22.

8. McDowell, *Evidence*, 414.

9. A. T. Chapman, *An Introduction to the Pentateuch* (Cambridge: The University Press, 1911), 39.

10. K. A. Kitchen, *The Ancient Orient and the Old Testament* (Chicago: InterVarsity Press, 1966), 125.

11. For a thorough refutation of the documentary hypothesis, see McDowell's *The New Evidence That Demands a Verdict*.

Chapter 15 Daniel: History or Prophecy?

1. Freke and Gandy, *The Laughing Jesus*, 39–40.

2. Ibid., 41.

3. Ibid., 38.

4. Barry J. Beitzel, *Biblica: The Bible Atlas* (Sydney: Global Book Publishing, 2006), 382.

5. Ibid., 386.

6. Freke and Gandy, *The Laughing Jesus*, 64.

7. J. P. Holding, "The Book of Daniel Defended," Tekton Apologetics, http://www.tektonics.org/af/danieldefense.php.

8. Ibid.

9. Gleason Archer, *A Survey of the Old Testament Introduction* (Chicago: Moody Press, 1974), 374.

10. John C. Whitcomb, *Daniel* (Chicago: Moody Press, 1985), 56.

11. Archer, *Survey of Old Testament*, 397.

Chapter 16 Higher Criticism and the New Testament

1. McDowell, *Evidence*, 547.

2. Ibid., 544–546.

3. Quoted by F. F. Bruce, *The New Testament Documents: Are They Reliable?* (Grand Rapids, MI: Eerdmans, 1997), 91.

4. Michael Grant, *Jesus: An Historian's Review of the Gospels* (New York: Scribner, 1995), 199.

Chapter 17 Was Jesus Truly Resurrected?

1. Lee Strobel, *The Case for Easter* (Grand Rapids, MI: Zondervan, 2003), 21.

2. McDowell, *Evidence*, 274.

3. J. N. D. Anderson, *Christianity: The Witness of History* (London: Tyndale Press, 1969), 97.

4. Gary R. Habermas, *The Historical Jesus* (Joplin, MO: College Press Publishing, 1996), 154.

5. Ibid., 155–156.

6. Quoted in Bruce, *New Testament Documents*, 117.

7. Habermas, *The Historical Jesus*, 203.

8. *Baker Encyclopedia of Christian Apologetics* (Grand Rapids, MI: Baker, 1998), 384–385.

Chapter 18 Jesus: Just Another "Dying/Rising God-Man" Myth?

1. Charles Penglase, *Greek Myths and Mesopotamia: Parallels and Influence in the Homeric Hymns and Hesiod* (New York: Routledge, 1994), 6.

2. Glenn Miller, "Good Question . . . Was Jesus Christ Just a CopyCat Savior Myth?" A Christian Thinktank, http://christianthinktank.com/copycat.html.

3. Jonathan Z. Smith, "Dying and Rising Gods," *The Encyclopedia of Religion*, Vol. 4 (New York: Macmillan, 1987), 522.

4. J. P. Holding, "Zoroaster vs. Jesus?" Tekton Apologetics, www.tektonics.org/copycat/zoroaster.html.

5. Ibid.

6. N.T. Wright, *The Resurrection of the Son of God* (Fortress Press, 2003), 124–125.

7. Ibid., 125. See this same page for a listing of anti-Zoroastrian-hypothesis scholars.

8. Ibid., 123.

9. Ibid., 124.

10. R. C. Zaehner, *The Dawn and Twilight of Zoroastrianism* (New York: G.P. Putnam's Sons, 1961), 57.

11. For a definitive repudiation of the notion that Judeo-Christian resurrection could be derived from any other culture, see Wright's massive work *The Resurrection of the Son of God*. This work addresses at length the various takes on life-after-death in the ancient world, cultural influences and considerations, the complexities that attached to the term "resurrection" within the Jewish milieu, the unbridgeable gap between Jewish views on afterlife, and all other pagan views.

12. Miller, "Was Jesus Christ Just a CopyCat Savior Myth?" See this for all conceivable "forerunners" of the Christ story.

Chapter 19 The New Testament: The Teachings of Jesus, or Political Reaction to Gnosticism?

1. Bruce, *The New Testament Documents*, 16–17.

2. Josh D. McDowell, *The New Evidence that Demands a Verdict* (Thomas Nelson Publishers, Inc., 1999), 34.

3. Ibid., 52.

4. Irenaeus, *Against Heresies*, 415.

5. Darrell L. Bock, *The Missing Gospels* (Nashville: Thomas Nelson, 2006), 213.

6. Irenaeus, *Against Heresies*, 326.

7. Bruce, *New Testament Documents*, 25.

Chapter 20 Symbolism vs. Literalism

1. Freke and Gandy, *The Laughing Jesus*, 61.

2. Ibid.

3. Ibid., 62.

Chapter 21 *The DaVinci Code*

1. Dan Brown, *The Da Vinci Code*, Special Illustrated Edition (New York: Doubleday, 2004), 1.

2. Richard Abanes, *The Truth behind the Da Vinci Code* (Eugene, OR: Harvest House Publishers, 2004), 49–52.

3. Laura Miller, "The Last Word: The Da Vinci Con," in Secrets of the Da Vinci Code (special edition), *U.S. News and World Report* (2004), 76–77.

4. Amy D. Bernstein, "Decoding the Da Vinci Phenomenon," in Secrets of the Da Vinci Code, 7.

5. Ibid.

6. Miller, "The Da Vinci Con," 77.

7. Dan Burstein, "The Hoax behind It All," in Secrets of the Da Vinci Code, 75.

8. Brown, *The Da Vinci Code*, 241.

9. Ibid., 131.

10. Irenaeus, *Against Heresies*, 317–323.

11. Brown, *The Da Vinci Code*, 318.

12. Timothy Freke and Peter Gandy, "The Origins of the Coverup," in Secrets of the Da Vinci Code, 44.

13. Ibid., 45.

Chapter 22 Misquoting Jesus

1. Bart D. Ehrman, *Misquoting Jesus* (New York: Harper One, 2005), 259–260.

2. Ibid., 260.

3. Ibid., 11.

4. Timothy Paul Jones, *Misquoting Truth* (Downers Grove, IL: InterVarsity Press, 2007), 32–33.

5. Ehrman, *Misquoting Jesus*, 89–90.

6. Jones, *Misquoting Truth*, 44.

7. Ehrman, *Misquoting Jesus*, 10.

8. Ibid., 177.

9. Ibid., 62.

10. Ibid., 67.

11. Ibid., 69.

12. Ibid., 132.

13. Ibid., 136.

14. Ibid., 139.

15. Ibid., 143.

16. Ibid., 152.

17. Ibid., 153.

18. Ibid., 155.

19. Ibid., 166.

20. Ibid., 166–167.

21. Ibid., 168.

22. Ibid., 171.

23. Ibid., 174.

24. Ibid.

25. Ibid., 175.

26. Ibid.

27. Ibid.

28. Jones, *Misquoting Truth*, 85.

29. Ibid., 100.

30. Ehrman, *Misquoting Jesus*, 204.

31. Ibid., 207–208.

32. Jones, *Misquoting Truth*, 77.

33. Ehrman, *Misquoting Jesus*, 214.

34. Ibid., 149.

35. Ibid., 214–215.

36. Ibid., 187.

37. Ibid., 217.

38. Ibid., 248.

Chapter 23 The Early Strands of Conservatism

1. Russell Kirk, *The Conservative Mind*, seventh revised edition (Washington, DC: Regnery Publishing, 1995), 40.

2. Ibid., 41.

3. Stove, *On Enlightenment*, 151.

4. Thomas Jefferson, letter to Doctor Benjamin Rush, Washington, April 21, 1803.

Chapter 24 Twentieth-Century Currents, and Hitler's *Aktion* T-4

1. Nietzsche, *Beyond Good and Evil*, 197–203.

2. Clarence B. Carson, *Basic American Government* (Phenix City, AL: American Textbook Committee, 1994), 370.

3. Thomas Sowell, "An Economic 'Plan'?" Townhall, Sept. 11, 2012, https://townhall.com/columnists/thomassowell/2012/09/11/an-economic-plan-n1374163.

4. Carson, *Basic American Government*, 352.

5. Charles Darwin, *The Descent of Man, and Selection in Relation to Sex* (Princeton, NJ: Princeton University Press, 1981), 168; quoted in Benjamin Wiker, *10 Books That Screwed Up the World* (Washington, DC: Regnery Publishing, Inc., 2008), 88–89.

6. Wiker, *10 Books That Screwed Up the World*, 156.

7. Klaus Dorner, Nationalsozialismus und Lebensvernichtung: *Vierteljahrshefte fur Zeitgeschichte*, 5:2 (April 1967), 151; quoted in Hugh Gregory Gallagher, *By Trust Betrayed* (Arlington, VA: Vandamere Press, 1995), 85.

8. Gallagher, *By Trust Betrayed*, 287.

Chapter 25 The Frankfurt School

1. Evans, *The Theme Is Freedom*, 56.

Chapter 26 Modern American Enlightenment Fruit

1. Thomas Sowell, *The Vision of the Anointed: Self-Congratulation as a Basis for Social Policy* (New York: BasicBooks, 1995), 8.

2. Ibid., 27.

3. Ibid., 11.

4. Ibid., 30.

5. Carson, *Basic American Government*, 436.

6. Thomas Sowell, *Economic Facts and Fallacies* (New York: BasicBooks, 2008), 129.

Chapter 27 Three Twenty-first Century Presidents

1. Norman Podhoretz, "Who Is Lying about Iraq?" *The Wall Street Journal*, Nov. 14, 2005, https://www.wsj.com/articles/SB122538428507184645.

2. Dinesh D'Souza, "Why Barack Obama Is an Anti-Colonialist," *The Washington Post*, Oct. 8. 2010, http://www.washingtonpost.com/wp-dyn/content/article/2010/10/07/AR2010100705485.html.

3. Barack Obama, *Dreams from My Father* (New York: Three Rivers Press, 2004), 220.

Chapter 28 Global Warming

1. Dixy Lee Ray and Lou Guzzo, *Environmental Overkill* (Washington, DC: Regnery Gateway, 1993), 37.

2. Lawrence Solomon, *The Deniers* (Minneapolis: Richard Vigilante Books, 2008), 8.

3. Al Gore, *Earth in the Balance* (New York: Houghton Mifflin, 1992), 260.

4. Ibid., 246–247.

5. Ibid., 119.

6. Ibid., 297.

7. Ibid., 273.

8. Solomon, *Deniers*, 12–14.

9. Ibid., 16.

10. Ibid., 19.

11. Ibid., 76.

12. Ibid., 86–91.

13. Ibid., 98.

14. Bjorn Lomborg, *Cool It* (New York: Alfred A. Knopf, 2007), 115.

15. Ibid., 115.

16. Ibid., 121–122.

Chapter 29 *The God Delusion*

1. Richard Dawkins, *The God Delusion* (New York: Houghton Mifflin, 2008), 58.

2. Ibid., 58–59.

3. Ibid., 259.

4. Ibid., 366–367.

5. Ibid., 309.

6. David Berlinski, *The Devil's Delusion* (New York: Crown Forum, 2008), 26.

7. Dawkins, *God Delusion*, 83.

8. Ibid., 99.

9. Jonathan Sarfati, *Refuting Evolution 2* (Green Forest, AR: Master Books, 2002), 106.

10. Jonathan Sarfati, *Refuting Evolution* (Green Forest, AR: Master Books, 1999), 84.

11. Ibid., 138.

12. J. Madeleine Nash, "When Life Exploded," *Time*, Dec. 4, 1995, 67.

13. Ibid.

14. Ibid., 69.

15. Dawkins, *God Delusion*, 118.

16. Ibid., 122.

17. Ibid., 120.

18. Ibid., 123.

19. Ibid., 137.

20. Ibid., 146.

21. Ibid., 149.

22. Ibid., 154.

23. Berlinski, *Devil's Delusion*, 108.

Chapter 30 *The God Delusion*, Part II

1. Dawkins, *God Delusion*, 159.

2. Alister McGrath and Joanna Collicut McGrath, *The Dawkins Delusion?* (Downers Grove, IL: InterVarsity Press, 2007), 27–28.

3. Dawkins, *God Delusion*, 160–161.

4. Ibid., 185.

5. Ibid., 190.

6. Sarfati, *Refuting Evolution 2*, 155.

7. Dawkins, *God Delusion*, 219.

8. Ibid., 232.

9. Ibid., 238.

10. Ibid., 284.

11. Ibid., 285.

12. Ibid., 285.

13. Ibid., 117.

14. Ibid., 320.

15. Ibid., 342.

16. Berlinski, *Devil's Delusion*, 177.

17. Dawkins, *God Delusion*, 346.

18. Ibid., 349.

19. Ibid., 403.

20. Ibid., 410.

21. Ibid., 419.

22. Ibid.

23. Ibid., 143.

24. Ibid., 411.

Chapter 31   The Implications of Darwinist-Materialist Thought

1. McDowell, *Evidence*, 193–194.

2. Ibid., 194.

3. Quoted in Henry M. Morris and John D. Morris, *The Modern Creation Trilogy*, Vol. 2 (Green Forest, AR: Master Books, Inc., 1996), 168–169.

4. Kennedy and Newcombe, *What If Jesus Had Never Been Born?*, 236.

Chapter 32 The Worst Generation

1. Eidsmoe, *Christianity and the Constitution*, 401.

2. Walter E. Williams, *Liberty versus the Tyranny of Socialism* (Stanford, CA: Hoover Institution Press, 2008), 212.

3. Cal Thomas, "America Has Never Been a 'Christian' Nation. Kim Davis Picked the Wrong Issue," Fox News, https://www.foxnews.com/opinion/america-has-never-been-a-christian-nation-kim-davis-picked-the-wrong-issue.

4. Evans, *The Theme is Freedom*, 121.

Chapter 33 Islam: Its History and Goals

1. Mark A. Gabriel, *Islam and Terrorism* (Lake Mary, FL: Charisma House, 2002), 66–67.

2. Serge Trifkovic, *The Sword of the Prophet* (Salisbury, MA: Regina Orthodox Press, 2002), 21.

3. Ibid., 22.

4. Gabriel, *Islam and Terrorism*, 66–67.

5. Trifkovic, *Sword*, 57–58.

6. Gabriel, *Islam and Terrorism*, 69.

7. Ibid., 78.

8. Ibid., 105.

9. Ibid., 28.

10. Ibid., 86.

11. Quoted in Robert Spencer, *Islam Unveiled* (New York: Encounter Books, 2002), 134–135.

12. Ibid., 137.

13. Ibid., 124.

14. Trifkovic, *Sword*, 196.

15. Spencer, *Islam Unveiled*, 149.

16. Trifkovic, *Sword*, 117.

17. Spencer, *Islam Unveiled*, 153.

18. Trifkovic, *Sword*, 138.

19. Gabriel, *Islam and Terrorism*, 145.

20. Quoted by Ibid., 160.

21. Andrew C. McCarthy, *Willful Blindness* (New York: Encounter Books, 2008), 315–316.

22. Trifkovic, *Sword*, 206.

23. Quoted in Gabriel, *Islam and Terrorism*, 30.

24. Quoted in Ibid., 33.

25. Quoted in Ibid., 35.

26. Quoted in Ibid., 35.

27. Quoted in Hal Lindsey, *The Everlasting Hatred: The Roots of Jihad* (Murrieta, CA: Oracle House Publishing, 2002), 144–145.

28. Quoted in Gabriel, *Islam and Terrorism*, 35–36.

29. Quoted in Ibid., 37.

30. Ibid., 30.

31. Spencer, *Islam Unveiled*, 75–90.

Chapter 34 Jehovah and Allah: A Study in Contrasting Character and Revelation

1. Spencer, *Islam Unveiled*, 129.

2. Trifkovic, *Sword*, 67.

3. Ibid., 60.

4. Ibid., 39.

5. *The New Encyclopedia Britannica*, Vol. 22, 3.

6. Spencer, *Islam Unveiled*, 63–66.

Chapter 35 The Rebirth of Israel in 1948

1. David Brog, *Reclaiming Israel's History* (Regnery Publishing, 2017), 147.

2. Ibid., 130–135.

3. Ibid., 146.

4. Bat Ye'or, *The Dhimmi* (Rutherford, NJ: Fairleigh Dickinson University Press, 1985), 108.

5. Lindsey, *Everlasting Hatred*, 168.

6. Ibid., 170.

7. Ibid., 168.

8. Ibid., 184.

9. Ibid., 191.

10. Ibid., 194.

11. Ibid., 198.

12. Ibid.

13. Quoted in David B. Green, "This Day in Jewish History, 1938: Nations Discuss Jewish Refugees, Get Nowhere, but Then They Hadn't Planned To," Haaretz, July 6, 2015, https://www.haaretz.com/jewish/.premium-1938-nations-feebly-discuss-jewish-refugees-1.5375335.

14. Brog, *Reclaiming*, 154–155.

Chapter 36 Final Thoughts: Especially for Christians

1. Office of the High Commissioner, United Nations Human Rights, "Convention on the Rights of the Child," https://www.ohchr.org/en/professionalinterest/pages/crc.aspx.

2. C. S. Lewis, *The Abolition of Man* (New York: HarperCollins, 2001), 26.

CPSIA information can be obtained
at www.ICGtesting.com
Printed in the USA
LVHW081145191222
735461LV00008BB/551